INSIGHT GUIDES
COSTA RICA

APA PUBLICATIONS
L

Part of the Langenscheidt Publishing Group

INSIGHT GUIDE
COSTA RICA

Editorial

Project Editor
Alyse Dar
Art Director
Steven Lawrence
Picture Manager
Tom Smyth
Series Manager
Rachel Lawrence

Distribution

UK & Ireland
GeoCenter International Ltd
Meridian House, Churchill Way West,
Basingstoke, Hampshire RG21 6YR
sales@geocenter.co.uk

United States
Ingram Publisher Services
One Ingram Boulevard
PO Box 3006
La Vergne, TN 37086-1986
customer.service@
ingrampublisherservices.com

Australia
Universal Publisher
PO Box 307
St Leonards NSW 1590
sales@universalpublishers.com.au

New Zealand
Hema Maps New Zealand Ltd (HNZ)
Unit 2, 10 Cryers Road
East Tamaki, Auckland 2013
sales.hema@clear.net.nz

Worldwide
**Apa Publications GmbH & Co.
Verlag KG (Singapore branch)**
7030 Ang Mo Kio Avenue 5,
08-65 Northstar @ AMK
Singapore 569880
apasin@singnet.com.sg

Printing

CTPS-China

First Edition 1995
Fourth Edition 2011

CONTACTING THE EDITORS
We would appreciate it if readers would alert us to errors or outdated information by writing to:
**Insight Guides, PO Box 7910, London SE1 1WE, England.
insight@apaguide.co.uk**

www.insightguides.com

About This Book

The first Insight Guide pioneered the use of creative full-color photography in travel guides in 1970. Since then, we have expanded our range to cater for our readers' need not only for reliable information about their chosen destination but also for a real understanding of the culture and workings of that destination. Now, when the internet can supply inexhaustible (but not always reliable) facts, our books marry text and pictures to provide those much more elusive qualities: knowledge and discernment. To achieve this, they rely heavily on the authority of locally based writers and photographers.

Insight Guide: Costa Rica is structured to convey an understanding of the region and its people as well as to guide readers through its attractions:

◆ The **Best Of Costa Rica** section at the front of the book helps you to prioritise what you want to do.

◆ The **Features** section, indicated by a pink bar at the top of each page, is a series of illuminating essays that cover the natural and cultural history of the region, as well as daily life, architecture, and the arts.

◆ The main **Places** section, indicated by a blue bar, is a complete guide to all the sights and areas worth visiting. Places of special interest are coordinated by number with the maps.

◆ The **Travel Tips** listings section, with a yellow bar, provides full information on transportation, hotels, activities from culture to shopping to sports, an A–Z section of essential practical information, and a handy phrasebook with Spanish words and expressions. An easy-to-find

biologist and long-time Central America expert **Henry Genthe** wrote the Sports article and several of the Places chapters. **Cindy Hilbrink** wrote on rural aspects of Costa Rica. **David Burnie**, a biologist and natural history writer, wrote features on the flora and fauna.

Other writers whose expert text has been adapted and updated from earlier editions include **Carol Weir**, **Moisés Leon**, **John McPhaul**, **Juan Bernal Ponce**, **Tony Avirgan**, **Martha Honey**, **Marjorie Ross-Cerdas**, **Mary Sheldon**, and **Alexander Skutch**.

Most of the stunning photographs in this edition were taken by experienced travel photographer **Corrie Wingate** who also contributed to *Insight Guide: Ecuador & the Galápagos* and *Insight Guide: Guatemala, Belize & the Yucatán*.

Thanks go to **Janet McCann** for proofreading the guide and also to **Helen Peters** for compiling the index.

Map Legend

—— - -	International Boundary
——————	Province Boundary
— • —	National Park/Reserve
— — — —	Ferry Route
⊖	Border Crossing
✈	Airport: International/Regional
🚌	Bus Station
✉	Post Office
❶	Tourist Information
∴	Archaeological Site
✝ ✝	Church/Ruins
✝	Monastery
☾	Mosque
✡	Synagogue
∩	Cave
🏛	Statue/Monument
★	Place of Interest
⚑	Beach
⌖	Lighthouse
🏰	Castle (ruins)
☀	Viewpoint

The main places of interest in the Places section are coordinated by number with a full-color map (eg ❶), and a symbol at the top of every right-hand page tells you where to find the map.

contents list for Travel Tips is printed on the back flap, which also serves as a bookmark.

The contributors

This new edition, was commissioned by **Alyse Dar** at Insight Guides' London office and copy-edited by **Pam Barrett**. The book was updated by **Dorothy MacKinnon,** a freelance writer and editor in Costa Rica and a regular contributor to the *Tico Times*. Like many of the migrant birds MacKinnon takes pleasure in observing, she migrated south from Canada. MacKinnon also wrote the new adventure sports photo feature, "Going to Extremes."

This version builds on the invaluable work of earlier editors and writers including **Paul Murphy**, **Huw Hennessy**, and **Harvey** and **Dona Haber** who contributed most of the book's historical pieces, Marine

Contents

LEFT: view of the Arenal Volcano from Tabacón hot springs.

Maps

THE BEST OF COSTA RICA: TOP ATTRACTIONS

From paradise beaches, serene waterways, and magical rainforests to volcanoes and amazing wildlife, this is our guide to the best that Costa Rica has to offer

△ **Tarrazú Coffee** Nothing says Costa Rica like high-altitude coffee from Tarrazú, ranked among the best in the world. Taste a cup in Santa María de Dota in the mountains south of San José. *See page 257*

▷ **Punta Uva** Crystal-clear, warm, shallow waters for swimming and an active coral reef close enough to swim to make this beach idyllic. *See page 236*

▽ **Tortuguero Canals** Drifting silently in a canoe along Tortuguero's narrow waterways overhung with vine-draped trees, you can spot caimans along the shore, iguanas sunning, and monkeys in the trees. *See page 229*

△ **Manuel Antonio National Park** Small but exquisite, this park packs a wealth of monkeys and birds into a compact jungle edged by three long arcs of white-sand beach. No wonder it's the most popular national park. *See page 171*

▷ **Canopy Tour** Get a bird's-eye view of life at the top, as well as a thrilling ride, as you zip through the forest, suspended from a cable strung along platforms set high in the tree canopy. *See page 157*

△ **Osa Peninsula** Wilderness, wildlife, and adventure: everything the eco-minded traveler comes to Costa Rica to find is here, in the remotest part of the southern Pacific area with its legendary biodiversity. *See page 247*

▽ **Arenal Volcano** Cone-shaped Arenal puffs plumes of smoke and ash during the day and, on clear nights, puts on a spectacular sound-and-light show, spewing fiery rocks and molten lava. *See page 215*

▷ **San José Museums** The Museo del Oro Precolombino is Central America's largest treasury of ancient gold artifacts; Museo del Jade contains the most extensive collection of New World jade objects. *See pages 135–6*

▽ **Las Pailas Trail** Experience some volcanic action up close, along this self-guided loop trail in Rincón de la Vieja National Park. The forest path skirts boiling mud fumaroles and sulfurous hot rocks. *See page 189*

△ **Resplendent Quetzal** Even for visitors who aren't bird-watchers, catching a glimpse of the shimmering, crimson, and green resplendent quetzal, one of the most magnificent birds in the western hemisphere, is a thrill. *See page 204*

THE BEST OF COSTA RICA EDITOR'S CHOICE

National parks that offer opportunities to see glorious wildlife and hike amid beautiful scenery; beaches for swimmers, surfers, and divers; drives along dramatic mountain roads; plus museums, churches, and markets. Here are our recommendations for a visit to Costa Rica

BEST WILDLIFE VIEWING

● **Corcovado National Park** The last frontier for many endangered animals, including Baird's tapir, white-lipped peccary, and jaguar, along with a host of endemic birds. See page 248.

● **San Gerardo de Dota** One of the most reliable places for spotting the resplendent quetzal, along with other highland bird species, on Cerro de la Muerte. See page 256.

● **Monteverde Cloud Forest** A misty cloud-forest preserve protects an astonishing range of butterfly, mammal, and bird species. See page 203.

● **La Selva Biological Station** This wet lowland forest is home to thousands of insect species, plus mammals, snakes, and more than 400 birds, including the endangered great green macaw. See page 220.

● **Ostional Wildlife Refuge** Nothing beats the nocturnal *arribadas* (mass arrivals) of Olive Ridley sea turtles at this protected beach north of Nosara. See page 201.

● **Tortuguero National Park** With a sharp-eyed guide, you'll see myriad birds, mammals, and reptiles in this labyrinth of natural jungle canals. See page 229.

● **Wilson Botanical Garden** Brimming with bromeliads and heliconias, the garden attracts birds and small mammals, while monkeys and snakes inhabit the adjoining primary forest. See page 254.

BEST BEACHES

● **Nosara** Two beaches side by side: Playas Pelada and Guiones offer surfing, swimming, spectacular Pacific sunsets and yoga-on-the-beach. See page 200.

● **Punta Uva** The only beach on the Caribbean with a sunset view also has excellent snorkeling, along with warm, shallow water for swimming. See page 236.

● **Playa Montezuma** Funky, off-the-beaten-path retreat with dramatic crashing surf on rocks, plus wide stretches of sand and horseback beach rides to refreshing waterfalls. See page 184.

● **Manuel Antonio** Three long arcs of powdery white sand, backed by a jungle park bursting with birds and monkeys. See page 171.

● **Manzanillo** Swim, surf, dive; watch the local fishermen bring in their catch or follow the beach into the Gandoca-Manzanillo Wildlife Refuge. See page 236.

● **Playa Tamarindo** A surfer's dream, with eight prime spots to catch a wave, plus a raft of trendy restaurants and a lively night scene. See page 196.

● **Playa Hermosa** A family-friendly beach on the North Pacific coast, with warm, safe water for swimming, affordable accommodations, and sunset cruises. See page 194.

ABOVE LEFT: riding on the beach at Montezuma.

BEST HIKES

● **The Pacific Coastal Path** Heading south out of Drake Bay, this wildly scenic footpath cuts a swath between dense, green jungle and blue Pacific surf. *See page 248.*

● **Chirripó National Park** The ultimate hike to Costa Rica's highest peak, climbing through oak forests and alpine moors; for the fittest walkers only. *See page 257.*

● **Rincón de la Vieja National Park** A two-hour hike through forests and meadows to La Cangreja Waterfall with thermal springs and a cool swimming hole. *See page 188.*

● **Volcán Barva** An uphill hike through magical, mist-enshrouded primary forest above Barva de Heredia leads to a pristine green crater lake. *See page 150.*

● **Corcovado National Park** The trail between La Leona and La Sirena stations alternates between beach and forest, with refreshing river dips and scarlet macaws squawking overhead. *See page 248.*

● **Carara National Park** Just off the highway, this is one of the most accessible jungle trails, through majestic primary forest to an oxbow lake. *See page 167.*

LEFT: owl butterfly. **ABOVE:** Carara National Park. **BELOW:** ox-cart wheel; artifact, Museo del Oro Precolombino.

MOST SCENIC DRIVES

● **Ruta de Los Santos** Charming coffee towns named after saints are strung along a winding paved road in a high mountain valley lined with steeply terraced coffee *fincas. See page 256.*

● **Braulio Carrillo Highway** The twisting highway to the Caribbean cuts through mountains of pristine primary forest, with dramatic waterfalls and misty green vistas. *See page 156.*

● **Orosí Valley** Wend your leisurely way past coffee fields, stopping at colonial-era churches and scenic overlooks for panoramas of this pretty river valley. *See page 153.*

● **Costanera Sur** The wide, paved road from

Dominical, south to Coronado, combines sparkling Pacific views with dramatic vistas of mountains hugging the coastline. *See page 243.*

● **Puerto Jiménez to Carate** Only off-road vehicles should attempt this rough but ruggedly beautiful road, with exciting river crossings and few signs of modern civilization. *See page 251.*

● **Paso Real to San Vito** Following a high ridge, the road offers panoramic views of bucolic valleys on both sides and the towering Talamanca mountains to the northeast. *See page 255.*

CULTURAL BESTS

● **National Theater** Ornate, neoclassical theater modeled after the Paris Opera House, built in 1897, and now the home of the National Symphony and touring performers. *See page 133.*

● **Museo del Oro Precolombino** Central America's largest collection of pre-Columbian gold artifacts, arranged to show how gold was woven into indigenous cultures. *See page 135.*

● **Basílica de Nuestra Señora de los Angeles** Impressive, multi-domed church in Cartago, dedicated to the

country's patron saint whom thousands of pilgrims come to honor in August. *See page 150.*

● **Guayabo National Monument** The country's only excavated pre-Columbian settlement has an imposing stone road and ruins of stone aqueducts and buildings. *See page 155.*

● **Ujarrás** Romantic ruins of Costa Rica's oldest church; a paradise for picnickers and photographers. *See page 152.*

● **Sarchí** You may not need an ox-cart, but watching artisans paint the whirling, kaleidoscopic patterns is worth a visit to this traditional crafts center. *See page 160.*

THE HAPPY MEDIUM

Amid the turmoil that often characterizes Central America, Costa Rica is a land more at peace with itself and nature

Nestled between Nicaragua and Panamá on the Central American isthmus, Costa Rica is a small, democratic country, famous for its natural environment and a peaceful political climate that is unusual in a troubled region.

Since the armed forces were abolished in 1949, the government has been able to devote a large percentage of its resources to education, health, and conservation. About a quarter of the country is protected in national parks, biological reserves, wildlife refuges, and private reserves. With more than 850 species of birds, 250 mammals, and some 6 percent of the world's total identified species, Costa Rica is a paradise for anyone who delights in the unspoiled natural world.

A land of dense jungles, active volcanoes, and pristine beaches, this tiny country is full of geophysical contrasts that make it seem much bigger. More than half the population (total 4.6 million) live in the temperate Central Valley that houses the modern capital of San José. But as any *Tico* (Costa Rican) will tell you, the "real" Costa Rica will only be found in the *campo*, or rural areas.

An official at the World Bank first called Costa Rica the Land of the Happy Medium. And while its economy is far from perfect, the high standard of living and social development belie its "Third World" status.

Since 1994, tourism has been one of the country's leading industries. More than 2 million visitors now arrive every year, the vast majority of them coming from North America and Europe. Eco- and adventure tourism are the buzz words that distinguish tourism here, encompassing such diverse activities as birdwatching and whitewater rafting. Costa Rica has come a long way from the sleepy, agricultural land it once was, but it retains a laid-back charm, especially in the more remote areas. ❑

PRECEDING PAGES: Manzanillo on the Caribbean coast; birdwatching from an eco-lodge in Carate, Osa Peninsula; three-toed sloth in Manuel Antonio National Park. **LEFT:** pink torch ginger flower in the Orosi Valley. **TOP:** children in Montezuma. **RIGHT:** hanging bract of a heliconia. **BOTTOM LEFT:** Tarzan swing in Selvatura Park.

COAST TO COAST

Costa Rica may be small in area but it is a land of great diversity, with two oceans, rushing rivers, fiery volcanoes, and chilly peaks touching nearly 4,000 meters

Costa Rica lies at the heart of the Central American isthmus and these days few people mistake it for an island in the Caribbean. Traveling around the countryside gives you the sense of being in a large country; geophysically there are so many things going on. In reality, though, it is quite small. From northwest to southwest it measures only 460km (285 miles) and at its narrowest point it is only 120km (74 miles). In total, Costa Rica's land area is just 51,000 sq km (20,000 sq miles), one-third smaller than Scotland.

Stretching between 8 and 11 degrees latitude above the equator, Costa Rica is bounded on the north by Nicaragua, and on the south by Panamá. To the east is the tranquil Caribbean Sea cheek by jowl with the stormier Atlantic. To the west is the tumultuous Pacific Ocean, with many kilometers of surf crashing onto beaches.

A fertile land

First and foremost, Costa Rica is a rich agricultural land. *Tico* culture is steeped in *campesino* (farmer) traditions, many of which still dominate national life. The soil of the Central Valley is exceptionally fertile, owing primarily to the volcanic ash that has fallen through the centuries. This rich, drainable soil, especially on mountain slopes, is ideal for producing Costa Rica's famous coffee. The tropical climate also guarantees a year-round growing season for plantations of pineapples and bananas.

The fertile central plateau, which lies in the temperate zone at 975–1,980 meters (3,200–6,500ft), also supports misty cloud forests at high altitudes and, lower down, steaming tropical jungles teeming with tropical flora and fauna. This wealth of biodiversity has attracted a large international community of conservationists, biologists, birdwatchers, environmentalists, naturalists, and the ecologically attuned.

The coast

Never far away is the coastline. In fact, there are many accessible points from where you can simultaneously view both the Caribbean Sea and the Pacific Ocean. The Caribbean coast measures only 220km (135 miles) in length, while the Pacific coast of Costa Rica, with its deep gulfs and indentations, is several times that length. On

LEFT: sarongs in Puerto Viejo, Caribbean coast.
RIGHT: shy but curious *Tica* welcome.

the Pacific there are two major peninsulas: the developed Peninsula de Nicoya to the north, and the more remote Peninsula de Osa to the south. And, remote and mysterious, many kilometers off the Pacific Coast, is the exceptionally beautiful, still pristine Isla de Coco.

Peaks of delight

Although most of Costa Rica's volcanoes are extinct, some are still active. In the Central Valley, Poás Volcano, at 2,700 meters (8,900ft), has one of the world's largest craters, measuring nearly 2km (1½ miles) in diameter; and Irazú Volcano, at 3,440 meters (11,320ft), is occasion-

ally active. Both these rumbling volcanoes can be viewed at relatively close range.

At 1,630 meters (5,350ft) high, Volcán Arenal to the northwest is the most picturesque of Costa Rica's volcanoes, with a perfect cone shape. It is also the most consistently active. The rumbling, explosive spectacle of Arenal Volcano at night is the single most impressive pyrotechnic display in the whole country. Recently, Turrialba Volcano, on the east coast, suddenly came to life after decades of dormancy and is still fuming away. Its plumes of vapor and ash can be viewed from as far away as the hills of Heredia, above the capital, San José.

Three spine-like ranges of highland mountains traverse Costa Rica from the northwest to the southeast, rising to more than 3,800 meters (12,500ft). These are the magnificent Guanacaste, Central, and Talamanca ranges. Chirripó Grande, at 3,820 meters (12,500ft), is the highest elevation point in the country. Between the peaks, cool highland valleys with gently rolling, wooded pasture land remind visitors more of Switzerland than of a tropical country.

Climate and ecosystems

Although Costa Rica is geographically situated in the tropics, the great majority of the population live in "perennial springtime" on the Central Plateau, at elevations between 450 meters (1,500ft) and 1,400 meters (4,500ft), with average temperatures ranging from 20–26°C (68–78°F), day and night.

Near the coasts, though, temperatures are indeed tropical, with distinct alternating wet and

VIEWING WILDLIFE

For many visitors, the iconic image that draws them to Costa Rica is a dense rainforest full of wildlife. But actually seeing wild animals is not as easy as it sounds, or as it looks in nature films. With the exception of monkeys, agoutis, and coatis, most forest mammals are nocturnal. And forest creatures are very adept at staying hidden. Even Costa Rica's largest mammal – the 272kg (600lb) Baird's tapir – is capable of tiptoeing through the jungle without being spotted. Some birds do feed on or near the forest floor, making them easier to see, and others travel in noisy, visible mixed flocks, specializing in following columns of army ants and snapping up small insects fleeing the ants' advancing front.

Sudden fluctuations in water level – brought on by tropical downpours – are common events, and freshwater animals are experts at taking cover when flow levels abruptly increase. Along lowland rivers, where water flow is more sluggish, wildlife is more easily spotted, especially on muddy banks, which are home to caimans and alligators.

But the full richness of rainforest wildlife actually takes place in the canopy high overhead, where a complex community of species lives, with only minimal contact with the ground. So if you want to see wildlife, your best bet is to get up into the canopy on one of the raised suspension bridges or on a tree-top platform.

dry seasons, at different times of year for both the Atlantic and Pacific. Tropical downpours arrive with great predictability in the afternoons during the rainy seasons along the coasts and are undeniably awesome. If you are caught out in one, you will never forget the experience.

Much of Costa Rica's biodiversity is due to mountains, which create a range of "life zones" at different altitudes. Costa Rica also forms part of a natural "land bridge" that allows wildlife to migrate between North and South America.

Away from the humid tropical coasts, the climate is greatly determined by the altitude above sea level. At each level, daytime temperatures remain fairly constant regardless of the time of year. At night, however, the heat of the coastal plains cools only slightly, while high up on the mountains and volcanic slopes, pleasant sun-warmed temperatures plunge dramatically at night, sometimes to just above the freezing mark.

For its size, Costa Rica contains a remarkable variety of natural ecosystems. A journey of just a few kilometers is often enough to take you

LEFT: Arenal volcano in the northeast of the country.
ABOVE: aerial view showing the rainforest's density.

from one to another, each home to quite different plants and animals.

Dry tropical forest

In the drier parts of Costa Rica where little rain falls for four or five months of the year, the natural vegetation is dry tropical forest, with most trees shedding their leaves soon after the dry season begins. The trees are rarely more than 30 meters (100ft) high, and there is usually a tangled understory of spiny and thorny shrubs. Although the trees are leafless during the dry season, few of them are fully dormant, and many burst into flower soon after their leaves have been shed.

Rainforest

Across most of the Costa Rican lowlands, the climate is wet and warm enough for trees to keep growing for much of the year. The result of this nonstop growth is generally called rainforest. Strictly speaking, though, botanists restrict use of this term to the wettest forests of all. Unlike the trees in tropical dry forests, rainforest trees are evergreen, and their dense crowns form a continuous canopy that casts a deep and almost unbroken shade. These rainforests – both on low ground and also at higher altitudes – harbor an immense variety of life.

Páramo

On Costa Rica's highest peaks, the forest gives way to a treeless landscape known as *páramo*. Cold and frequently swathed in cloud, *páramo* seems a world away from the warmth and lushness of lower altitudes. This ecosystem is dominated by tough, low-growing shrubs that can withstand strong winds. *Páramo* is also found in the Andes, and Costa Rica's scattered patches of it – for example, atop Cerro de la Muerte in the Southern Zone – are the northernmost in the Americas.

Freshwater wetlands

Running as veins of precious ore through the body of the country is an intricate network of waterways, rising and falling through the mountains, then flowing quickly to the sea and providing a steady source of fresh water and hydraulic power.

Smaller forest streams usually flow beneath a continuous overhead canopy, but most rivers are broad enough to allow light to reach the forest floor. The result is a linear "light gap," and a profusion of plant growth of the kind rarely seen inside forests themselves.

Costa Rica's largest body of fresh water – man-made Lake Arenal – has a distinctly highland feel. In contrast, the shallow lakes and marshes of Palo Verde National Park and Caño Negro in the Northern Zone are seasonal wetlands, attracting numerous wading birds and reptiles.

Coastal waters

Mangroves are the natural vegetation of muddy, low-lying coasts throughout the tropics. In Costa Rica, there are five species of mangrove, and they form extensive forests on both the Caribbean and Pacific shores.

Apart from these mangrove swamps, Costa Rica's coastline consists largely of extensive beaches – often of dark volcanic sand – punctuated by low-lying rocks and a small number of offshore islands.

Costa Rica also has some small coral reefs on its Pacific coast, and one significant reef on the Caribbean side, at Cahuita. Reef-building corals need sunlight to grow, and they can only survive in clear water. This limits them to areas well away from the mouths of silt-laden rivers, but it also makes them vulnerable to any

MANGROVE SWAMPS

Beating a path through rainforests, tourists often miss the equally interesting mangrove swamps. Although often inaccessible, smelly, and hot, they abound with life. Mangrove trees have evolved to survive in seawater and saline silt, using mechanisms for getting rid of excess salt, and elaborate roots that anchor them in the shifting mud. Mangrove mud also makes an important contribution to the marine food chain with nutrient-rich algae. Paddling through a mangrove in a kayak, you will spot crabs picking over tree roots and scrabbling in the mud for food, plus huge iguanas draped in branches, and occasional troops of howler monkeys.

increase in silt run-off. Unfortunately, in recent years, almost all of Costa Rica's reefs are threatened by deforestation, which has increased silt levels in the surrounding water.

Despite increasing pressures from development, especially along the coasts, Costa Rica is the greenest country in the world, according to the 2009 *Happy Planet Index*. From the edge of the almost tideless Caribbean to the pounding Pacific coast, up and across the slopes of the volcanic cordilleras, and finally to the highest peak of cold, brittle Chirripó, the landscape is endlessly variable and gloriously invigorating.   ❏

ABOVE: palm tree-lined beach in Manzanillo.
RIGHT: Jesus Christ lizard, Tortuguero National Park.

Decisive Dates

12,000–4000 BC
First signs of human habitation in Central America.

4000–1000 BC
Earliest settlements, based on crop cultivation.

1000 BC–AD 1500
Expansion of organized farming communities, with trade and communication links.

1502
Christopher Columbus drops anchor for two weeks off the island of Uvita (near Puerto Limón) where he encounters the Cariari tribe.

1510–70
The Spanish conquest.

1572
Colonial period begins. Costa Rica remains poor for 250 years, largely ignored because of lack of mineral resources.

1823
Civil war between conservative imperialists and republicans *(liberalistas)* who finally win. San José replaces Cartago as the capital.

1824
Juan Mora Fernández becomes first head of state.

1825
The first constitution of the free state of Costa Rica is promulgated.

1832
First coffee exports to Europe, via Chile.

1838–42
Dictatorship of President Braulio Carrillo.

1848
Declaration of the Republic of Costa Rica.

1858
Costa Rica defeats William Walker, who tried to turn Central America into a colony of the southern American states.

1870
Tomás Guardia Gutiérrez takes over power after a military coup and introduces a new liberal constitution.

1871
Railroad construction begins.

1880
First banana exports.

1882
Death penalty abolished.

1886
Introduction of compulsory education.

1890
First free and honest democratic elections in Central America bring José Joaquin Rodriguez to presidency. The Atlantic Railroad, from Cartago to Limón, is completed.

1914–18
Costa Rica loses export markets because of World War I.

1919
A popular uprising ends two-year dictatorship supported by coffee barons.

1934
A strike among banana workers at United Fruit Company leads to establishment of right to strike and minimum wage.

1939–45
Coffee exports stagnate. Costa Rica declares war on Germany, Japan, and Italy.

1998
New President Miguel Angel Rodríguez (PUSC) encourages foreign investment and privatizes state companies.

2000
Nationwide protests against proposed privatization of ICE, the government-run electricity and telecommunications monopoly.

2002
Abel Pacheco (PUSC) wins the first-ever presidential run-off vote. Costa Rican astronaut Franklin Chang, aboard US space shuttle, goes for a walk in space.

1940–44
President Rafael Calderón successfully implements social reforms.

1945
The Social Democratic Party (PSD) is founded, later to become Partido Liberación Nacional (PLN), under José Figueres.

1948
Calderón Guardia declares election results to be annulled and reassumes the presidency. Civil war ensues. Junta led by Figueres takes power.

1949
Under the new constitution, the army is disbanded and replaced by a Civil Guard. Figueres hands over power, but governs again from 1953–8 and 1970–4. Blacks and women enfranchized (1949).

1979
The Sandinistas in Nicaragua topple the Somoza dictator-

ship. During ensuing civil war, Costa Rica becomes a fallback area for guerrilla groups and anti-Sandinistas. Hundreds of thousands of Nicaraguans seek refuge in Costa Rica.

1986
Oscar Arias Sánchez elected president and helps restore peace to the region. For his efforts, he is awarded the Nobel Peace Prize in 1987.

1990
The Social Christian Unity Party (PUSC) wins the elections. Rafael Angel Calderón Fournier becomes president. Costa Rica sends a national team to the soccer World Cup for the first time.

1991
An earthquake strikes Limón province, killing more than 60 and causing extensive damage, destroying the Atlantic railroad.

1994
José M. Figueres becomes Costa Rica's youngest-ever president, but his term is dogged by scandals.

1996
Hurricane César strikes, killing dozens of Costa Ricans and causing massive damage.

2006
In close-run election, Oscar Arias Sánchez (PLN) is elected to unprecedented second term as president.

2007
Central American Free Trade Agreement (CAFTA) is ratified following close referendum.

2010
Laura Chinchilla (PLN) is elected the first woman president of Costa Rica.

PRECEDING PAGES: United Fruit Company banana train, 1916. FAR LEFT TOP: pre-Columbian artifact, Museo del Jade. LEFT MIDDLE: gold exhibit in Museo del Oro, San José. LEFT: portrait of idyllic early Amerindian life by the chronologer Figueroa. ABOVE: ceiling mural in San José's Teatro Nacional. RIGHT: President Chinchilla.

BEFORE COLUMBUS

The Amerindians' early culture was largely agrarian. Influenced by their Mesoamerican neighbors, they learned to fashion goods from stone, jade, and gold

O n September 8, 1502, Cristóbal Colón (Christopher Columbus) arrived on the Atlantic coast of Costa Rica and took refuge in the calm waters just off the coast, between tiny Uvita Island and what is now the Port of Limón.

The native population greeted the Spaniards with interest and brought out goods to trade with them. They swam out to the ship carrying cotton cloth, shirts, *tumbaga* pendants (an alloy made of copper and gold), and weapons such as clubs, bows, and arrows.

Golden dreams

Dreaming of gold, Columbus had charted the coastal area from Honduras to Panamá and named it Veragua. He was so enamored by the golden mirrors that the Amerindians of Costa Rica wore about their necks, and by their many stories of gold and gold mines along the coast to the south, that he named the area the Rich Coast of Veragua.

Rich though it seemed to Columbus at the time, the newly discovered area was not to be a great, rich jewel in Spain's crown. In fact, the "Rich Coast" turned out to be one of the poorest of Spain's American colonies. Impassable mountains, impenetrable forests, raging rivers, unbearable heat, floods, disease, swamps, shortages of food and of labor, internal rivalries, lack of natural resources or a way to generate wealth all oppressed the settlers. They were often reduced to living like the "savages" they had come to conquer: wearing goat-hair

garments or clothing made of bark; using cacao (chocolate) beans for currency; eking out a bare subsistence in the fields, using native methods to cultivate native crops.

This bleak reality was yet to come. Columbus naively returned to Spain brimming with dreams of great riches and grandeur, to the point of asking the king to confer on him the title of duke of Veragua.

Natural riches

Unrealistic visions of gold aside, what was life in the newly discovered territory really like? It was a rich land, if not in gold, then in natural resources, with forests, mountains, rivers,

---

PRECEDING PAGES: monument to Costa Rican workers, San José. **LEFT:** gold artifacts on display in Museo del Oro. **RIGHT:** pre-Columbian exhibits, Museo del Jade.

grasslands, and abundant animal and plant life. In the Atlantic watershed area, where much of the land is flat, navigable rivers and their tributaries were swelled in some areas by more than 400cm (160ins) of rain a year. In the heavy tropical vegetation grew wild rubber trees, orchids, and ferns. Fish, alligators, and an occasional shark lived in the rivers. Waterfowl, turkeys, iguanas, spider monkeys, howler monkeys, peccaries (wild pigs), and jaguars inhabited the forests.

To the northwest, in the Nicoya region, were tropical dry forests, also abundant in plant and animal life: on the broad, seasonally dry plains

Highlands, where broadleaf evergreen forests, palms, and white oaks grew on the luxuriant hillsides, harboring innumerable species of birds, animals, and plants.

Native settlers

Groups of indigenous peoples with diverse languages and cultures lived throughout these areas in small chiefdoms called *cacicazgos*. They were agricultural people, cultivating crops of yucca, corn, *pejibaye* (the bright orange fruit of the peach palm), and numerous other plants. They supplemented their diets with wild fruits and game from the forests, fish and shrimp

grew the beautiful wide, green *guanacaste* tree; the *javillo* with its poisonous sap and thorny trunk; the *cenicero* with its flesh-colored flowers; the *guapinol* with its characteristic seed pods, referred to as "stinky toes;" and many varieties of cacti and spiny shrubs. White-faced monkeys, howler monkeys, red squirrels with grey tails, tapirs, coatis, deer, jaguars, mountain lions, coyotes, and other small animals lived in the forests. In the trees, scarlet macaws and colorful parrots squawked and roosted. Avocados, papayas, guavas, and countless other fruits grew wild.

And the grasslands and swamps of the southern Pacific region, also known as the Diquis region, were lush with life, as were the often misty green hills and valleys of the Central

WHAT'S IN A NAME?

The Spanish colonists gave the Amerindians the names by which we know them today (which was often the name of the chief at the time of the Spanish Conquest): the Chorotega, Bribri, Cacebar, Coctu, Corobicí, to name a few. We do not know the names the people called themselves. Since some groups were completely wiped out before the Spanish arrived, we do not have names for them, or know what languages they spoke. Because of this, archeologists usually refer to Amerindian groups by the areas in which they lived: Guanacaste/Nicoya region, the Atlantic Watershed/Central Highlands region, and the Diquis, or Southern Pacific, region.

from the rivers, and crustacea and small oysters from the ocean.

At the time of Columbus's arrival, the people of the Guanacaste/Nicoya region lived in well-developed settlements, some with populations as large as 20,000. These settlements, supported by the cultivation of corn, were constructed around central plazas, marketplaces, and religious centers.

Guayabo city

In the Atlantic Watershed/Central Highlands area, high up in the mountains near the present-day city of Turrialba, was a city with wide, cobble-stoned walkways, freshwater springs bubbling out of stone-lined pools, and a stone aqueduct system carrying fresh water to some of the stone mounds on which houses were built. This ancient ceremonial or administrative center, Guayabo, flourished and disappeared (approximately 1000 BC to AD 1400) before the arrival of the Spaniards. From Guayabo, ancient roads of stone led to towns and may have even reached the ocean.

Other groups within the Atlantic Watershed/ Central Highlands region were less settled. They cultivated root crops, and hunted what small game was available, and then moved on to new lands when the soil or supply of game became depleted.

In the Diquis region, people also hunted, cultivated root crops, and lived in well-fortified villages that were strategically laid out to protect villagers from enemy attack.

Crossroads of the Americas

Influenced by some of the other great indigenous cultures of the Americas, the native peoples of Costa Rica had become skilled in the arts of ceramics, of gold-work and metal-work, fine weaving, and stone carving. Costa Rica, it appears, was a kind of mercantile and cultural crossroads of the Americas. Linguistic and cultural influences, not to mention a wealth of artifacts and materials, were being exchanged both within the country and without, from as far north as Mexico and as far south as Ecuador.

The native Costa Ricans were enthusiastic traders and prized jade pieces and ceramic ware,

as well as gold and stone carvings from Mesoamerica and South America.

The Nicoya area, with its quiet Pacific bays and safe anchorages, provided pre-Columbian commercial ports. Merchant marines from ancient Ecuador, making ports of call all along the Pacific coast of Mexico, Central and South America, frequently stopped at sites in Nicoya, bringing with them the crafts and arts of places they had visited. Perhaps it was they who introduced Olmec influences to the area – or perhaps the Olmecs (and others) came themselves. Regardless, the influence of the Olmecs was evident in the Pacific North-

west in the impressive range of pottery styles; utilitarian articles such as grinding stones; and the practice of certain customs, such as filing human teeth into points.

Over the years, the pottery of Nicoya developed into a vigorous hybrid style that for centuries would be traded around Central America and southern Mexico. A collection of such work is now on view at the National Museum. It is lively, bold, colorful work: large globular jars and vessels; figures of men and women, some with oversized genitals and physical deformities; animals of all kinds; mysterious effigies of man-birds; haunting funerary masks; and some quieter pieces that are almost luminously beautiful.

LEFT: a model display depicts pre-Columbian life in Museo del Jade, San José.
RIGHT: figurine at the Museo del Oro, San José.

Mystery of the spheres

The Diquis region is the site of one of the great pre-Columbian riddles. Spheres made of granite, andesite, and sedimentary stone have been found in their thousands along river beds and arranged in cemetery sites. Some are as small as oranges while others weigh up to 14 metric tons, and measure up to 2 meters (7ft) in diameter. They are perfectly spherical to within a centimeter or two and are perhaps the finest example of precision stone carving in the ancient world.

The stone spheres are unique – none has been discovered anywhere else in the world. How were they made? How were they shaped to be so perfectly spherical? How were they transported more than 30km (20 miles) from the source of the stone to the ceremonial sites where they were arranged? And what do they mean? Today, they stand mute in their new locations, at the National Museum and in the gardens of expensive homes throughout the Central Valley. You can also see them in their original habitat, Isla del Caño, near Corcovado National Park.

Gold and cotton

The Diquis region also abounded with gold, which the Amerindians washed out of rivers, or obtained from shallow digs in the

THE RIDDLE OF JADE

In addition to the enigma of the country's lithic spheres *(see above)*, there is another pre-Columbian riddle in Costa Rica that continues to perplex historians and archeologists: it is the source of jade for the many pieces found throughout the country, as no jade quarries have ever been found in Costa Rica. Guatemala is believed to be the principal source, although some jade may have come from Mexico.

Many of the objects appear to have been treasured for years, passed down as heirlooms; others seem to have arrived in one form, and to have been re-sculpted to the tastes of their new owners.

One interesting theory holds that some of the jade was brought to Costa Rica by pre-Columbian looters of Mayan burial sites, and this would help to explain the presence of Mayan hieroglyphs inscribed on the stone – which apparently had no value or significance to the Costa Ricans.

The Jade Museum in San José *(see page 136)* has the largest display of jade in the Americas, with more than 6,000 pieces. Many of the pieces are *colgantes* (amulets or pendants), generally in the form of birds, animals, or humans, but there is a great variety of other exhibits, including notable oddities such as a tooth with a jade inset, and jade breast supports, thought to have been worn by high-ranking women.

savannahs, under groves of trees on hilltops or on the plains. They became experts in the art of gold-working and employed different techniques, including the "lost wax" method, to craft all manner of items: gold headbands, arm and leg bands, collars, bracelets, beads, bells; golden ornaments sewn on clothes; gold tweezers for plucking away unwanted facial hair; gold awls, fish-hooks, and needles; gold sheathing for teeth; gold to use on decorative masks.

The Gold Museum in San José (*see Museo del Oro, page 135*) – has more than 1,000 of these gold artifacts on display, newly rearranged to demonstrate how gold was an integral part of early indigenous cultures.

The people of the Diquis region also wove fine, white cotton cloth, which was used to wrap the dead. Although no archeological evidence has been uncovered, since cotton clothing does not survive for millennia, the cloth may also have been made into shirts to be worn by both men and women for ceremonial occasions.

Wars, rituals, and religion

Taken in isolation, archeological evidence on village life, diet, and the arts and commerce of the early Costa Rican people might suggest that life in those times was plentiful, complete, and quite idyllic. In fact it was anything but – war was almost continuous.

In the Guanacaste/Nicoya region, wars were unceasingly fought between rival groups to obtain captives, who were perhaps for human sacrifice (and maybe even consumption). Throughout Costa Rica there were wars to capture women and youths for slaves; to obtain the heads of enemies, which were carried as trophies; and to obtain access to new land. Sometimes, as in the Diquis region, men and women warred together.

Artifacts and skeletons found in unearthed graves suggest that the dead were honored. Funerals and the burials of high-ranking people were elaborate affairs: people of rank were buried with riches – and their slaves were sacrificed in order to serve their masters once again in the other world.

LEFT: pre-Columbian artifacts in Museo del Jade, San José. **RIGHT:** one of the many exquisite gold ornaments displayed in the capital's Museo del Oro.

Spiritual life

Of their spiritual beliefs little is actually known, although much has been speculated. Phallic images and figures in pottery and stone, emphasizing male and female genitalia, suggest a religion focused on fertility. Fertility rites probably included the music of pottery drums, bone and clay flutes, trumpets, ocarinas, and rattles made of clay or gourds. Large vessels for the fermentation of corn, yucca, or palm fruit suggest ritual inebriation. And there were medicine men – shamans – with vast knowledge of the flora of the forests, who cured illness, forecast the future and dealt with supernatural matters.

The pre-Columbian lineages disintegrated with the arrival of the Europeans, who captured their leaders, disrupted their communities, enslaved their people and destroyed their ceremonial and religious articles. Spirited artistry gave way to a lackluster mediocrity, and dynamic spiritual beliefs were replaced by a half-hearted hybrid religion. Little by little, Costa Rica's rich pre-Columbian traditions were all but extinguished.

Most of Costa Rica's 70,000 or so indigenous people today live on 22 remote reserves. And instead of Columbus Day, which used to be celebrated on October 12, the country now celebrates "Meeting of the Cultures Day" on the same date. ❑

CONQUEST

The conquest of Costa Rica followed the sad pattern
of much of Central America, bringing disease, death,
and slavery in the largely fruitless quest for gold

When Christopher Columbus set sail from Spain in 1492 on his first voyage to the New World, he was hoping to find a group of islands near Japan, which he conceived to be about 2,400 nautical miles to the west of Spain. There, he determined, he would build a great city and trade gold, gems, and spices from the Indies with the cities of Europe. He imagined himself as a rich governor, lord of it all.

His ambitions coincided with the interests of the Spanish Crown. The wars to oust the Moors from Spain had depleted the royal treasury and the promise of the wealth of the Indies was very attractive indeed.

On his return to Spain, Columbus was given a grand reception. He was named Admiral of the Ocean Sea and was ordered to organize a second voyage to further explore Hispaniola.

The voyages of Columbus

The first of his four voyages took Columbus to the Bahamas, where he established the first Spanish settlement in the New World, at Hispaniola, where present-day Haiti and the Dominican Republic are situated. He built a fort and left 40 men behind to search for gold. He returned to Spain in triumph, with several captive local people.

The second expedition reached Hispaniola only to discover that the 40 settlers had been killed after mistreating the local people. Undeterred, Columbus sailed to the north coast of Hispaniola, where he attempted to establish another settlement.

Leaving his brother Diego in charge, he went off to explore for gold. But the settlers fought among themselves and with the Amerindians. Frustrated gold hunters returned to Spain angry; they grumbled about the disappointingly small amounts of gold and the cruelties of Columbus, who, according to historic accounts, was indeed an arrogant commander.

Nevertheless, a third voyage saw Columbus exploring the Atlantic coast of South America and claiming it for Spain. Meanwhile, Hispaniola was seething with discontent. "Not enough gold!" was the cry. Columbus tried to placate the rebels, as would his successors throughout Central America, by permitting them to enslave the indigenous population.

But even that measure failed to satisfy many. Large numbers of men returned to Spain demanding back pay and Columbus's head. Columbus was sent back to Spain in chains. Through the intercession of Isabella and Ferdinand, he managed to secure his release and set out on his fourth voyage.

The "discovery" of Costa Rica

It was on this voyage, in 1502, sailing up and down the Atlantic Coast looking for a passage to what would later be called the Pacific, that Columbus discovered in Central America the Rich Coast of Veragua.

While in Cariari, Columbus made repairs to his damaged ships as the near tideless ocean lapped on beautiful beaches and coconut trees swayed in the breeze. The respite was sorely needed: a violent storm off the coast of Honduras had caused considerable damage to his ships, and his men, one-third of whom were only boys, aged between 13 and 18, were sick and exhausted. Columbus himself, at 51 years of age, was almost crippled with the pains of arthritis.

A difficult passage home

The return voyage was difficult. Columbus's ships had been attacked by worms and were

He spent 18 days in what was later to be called Costa Rica, near the present-day port of Limón, in a place he called Cariari. There, the local people sent out two girls to welcome the party. In a letter to King Ferdinand, Columbus wrote: "As soon as I got there they sent right out two girls, all dressed up; the elder was hardly eleven, the other seven, both behaving with such lack of modesty as to be no better than whores. As soon as they arrived, I gave orders that they be presented with some of our trading truck and sent them directly ashore."

LEFT: *conquistador* statue, San José. **ABOVE:** "The Spanish Governor Captures the Kings," Theodor de Bry.

battered by foul weather: they were leaking badly. He made it only as far as Santa Gloria, Jamaica, and spent a year there, marooned, unable to get help from the governor of Hispaniola, who was worried that Columbus might usurp his position. There were food shortages and an attempted mutiny, but eventually Columbus and 100 of the original 135 men did return to Spain in 1504, shortly after the death of Queen Isabel.

Columbus spent his final years in increasingly failing health, attempting to secure for himself the governorship, trade and other benefits that had been promised to him by the queen. But the king refused even to see him, and the struggle to attain title, territory, and wealth fell to his sons and in turn their sons (Columbus' grandson was finally named Duke of Veragua in 1546), and to the *conquistadores* who followed him to the Americas. As for his spiritual and material heirs, they too were to encounter hardships.

The *conquistadores*

It is tempting to characterize the conquest of South America as a brutal cartoon: greedy, ruthless *conquistadores* bungling explorations, slitting each other's throats for gold, territory, or titles; murdering, stealing from, and enslaving the peoples of the land.

It took 60 years from the time of Columbus's arrival at Limón until the first European settlement in Costa Rica was actually established. The rough terrain, the unfriendly oceans, the extreme weather, and a feisty local population all played a large part in the delay. But the continuous, jealous feuding among the *conquistadores* themselves was also a major factor in the failure of the many colonization attempts and should not be overlooked.

Gold was consistently the big theme. When the *conquistadores* asked the Amerindians about the location of gold mines, they simply pointed south to the fabled mines of Veragua. It gave the

GOLD FEVER

The Amerindians of Costa Rica, wearing gold necklaces, guided the Spaniards around the area, and spoke of great mines of gold, pointing south.

"I have seen more signs of gold in the first two days than I saw in Hispaniola during four years," Columbus wrote to the Spanish king and queen.

Columbus thought he had struck it rich. But the riches he fantasized about never materialized. Costa Rica's gold supply was limited to small surface and river deposits. The Gold Museum in San José is the country's best, with thousands of examples of pre-Columbian gold artifacts *(see page 135)* securely housed in an underground, vault-like space.

Spaniards gold fever. But if the indigenous population really knew where the mines were, they never revealed their location, and to this day the great, legendary mines remain undiscovered. The *conquistadores*, spurning the gold to be found in rivers, had to content themselves with taking the locals' gold, which they did – until there was no more. Then they had to determine how to survive, let alone get rich.

More expeditions

In 1506, two years after Columbus returned to Spain, King Ferdinand sent Governor Diego de Nicuesa and a group of settlers to establish a colony at Veragua. It was the first of many ill-fated attempts to establish settlements.

Nicuesa's ship ran aground in Panamá and he and his group set about walking up the coast to their destination. Food shortages and tropical diseases were acute; the terrain was devastating. Indigenous peoples along the way burned their own crops rather than yield their food. By the time the settlers finally arrived, their numbers had been halved.

Around this time, expeditions from Spain were landing throughout the Atlantic coast of Central America. They were capturing Amerindian slaves and sending them to work in the mines of Hispaniola, stealing their gold and desperately searching for a passage across the

continent to the other ocean. Finally, in 1513, Vasco Nuñez de Balboa, a young stowaway escaping debts on Hispaniola, led an expedition across the isthmus and discovered the Pacific Ocean. It wasn't long before rudimentary shipyards appeared on the Pacific coast to accommodate would-be explorers who had sailed into Atlantic ports then walked across the isthmus, ready to set sail on the Pacific and continue their explorations. The unexplored Pacific had better anchorages, and was thought to have more gold.

Left: Columbus and *conquistadores*.
Above: the Virgin of the Navigators.
Above Right: the *Pinta* founders in a storm.

The adventures of Gil González

The second inland expedition to Costa Rica was led by Captain Gil González in 1522, and it, too, ended without establishing a settlement. Faulty ships hastily constructed on the Pacific coast of Panamá took on water and forced González and his men to abandon the sea and move forward on foot.

The expeditions of González, which included a walk of 224 leagues (over 1,000km/600 miles) from the south Pacific coast of Costa Rica to the north, and into Nicaragua, have a mythic quality. At the age of 65 – and suffering from arthritis aggravated by the unceasing rain –

González sometimes had to be carried on a litter, but he insisted on completing the arduous trip. González rested for 15 days in the home of the Térraba chief near Boruca. According to his accounts, he baptized some 32,000 of the indigenous people here, and collected golden items of vast value.

He also encountered Chief Diríagen, who appeared out of the blue one day along with 500 Amerindians, each carrying one or two turkeys; 17 women covered from head to foot in gold disks; 10 men carrying standards; five trumpeters and other attendants bringing 200 golden hatchets. The party stopped in front of the house where González was staying, the trumpeters played and then the chiefs, women, and lords entered. When González asked their business, Chief Diríagen replied that they had come to see the men with beards who rode upon strange beasts. Probably Diríagen had come to ascertain the strength of the Spaniards, because three days after his visit, he

> In 1546, Luis, the grandson of Christopher Columbus, was named Duke of Veragua. He set out with 130 men to claim his legacy, but he was attacked by Amerindians, lost most of his men, and retreated in failure.

his life and his treasure. His expedition had brought smallpox, influenza, and plague to the area, and tens of thousands of Amerindians died. Survivors of the epidemics faced another danger: enslavement. Indigenous peoples from the Nicoya region, who then lived in large population centers, and were vulnerable to such attacks, were captured, branded with hot irons, and shipped off to Panamá and Peru to be sold as slaves.

The second attempted Costa Rican settlement was at Villa Bruselas, near present-day Orotina, not far from the large port city of Puntarenas. It lasted only three years and succumbed to feud-

returned and attacked them. It was an attack that González, with fewer than 20 men, at least according to the legend, easily repelled.

González ran into trouble later on with Pedrarias, governor of Panamá, who was responsible for the deaths of many Spanish *conquistadores*, including Balboa, his own son-in-law, whom he had beheaded. Pedrarias's ire was aroused by the enormous amounts of gold González had collected and by González's refusal to give up his claim on Nicaragua. The affair ended with González fleeing Panamá with his treasure.

Pestilence and slavery

The people of Nicoya and Nicaragua were not so fortunate as González, who got away with

ing among the settlers and Amerindian attacks.

During this period, the *conquistadores* who arrived in Central America were free to exploit the indigenous population in virtually any way they wished. The Spanish policy of *requerimiento*, which went into effect in 1510, permitted settlers to wage war on those who refused to be baptized, a convenient justification for killing Amerindians and plundering their gold.

Later, *encomienda*, a royal grant from the Crown, gave settlers in Central America the right to force indigenous peoples to labor without compensation – or to demand goods as tribute. It was, in effect, slavery. The Amerindians were relocated to live on the land where they worked, and were considered the property of the grant holder. Without the system of *encomienda*, the *conquistadores* could not realize their aspirations of becoming landed aristocracy. All of the rights and assumed privileges of title had no real value without Amerindians to work the land.

Encomienda was not as widely practiced in Costa Rica as it was in other Central American colonies for a variety of reasons: the Amerindian labor force in Costa Rica was smaller; the Costa Rican Amerindians, outside of the Nicoya area, were not living in as large population centers as were, for example, the Maya of Guatemala. Instead, they lived in smaller, autonomous groups spread throughout the country. Thus the Spaniards were not able simply to move in and conquer large numbers in a single effort as they had in Mexico.

Moreover, the Costa Rican Amerindians did not adapt well to slavery and fiercely resisted its imposition. Many fought and died avoiding enslavement, and many others fled to the mountains where they could not be followed. Finally, the practice of *encomienda* was abolished well before large numbers of Spanish settlers arrived in Costa Rica.

Church intervention

The Church proved to have an uneasy time with the *encomienda* system. After forceful campaigning by many churchmen, including the Dominican friar Bartolomé de las Casas *(see next page)*, who was himself a former *conquistador*, *encomienda* was abolished in 1542.

This set off violent protests among the settlers, who believed they could not survive without slave labor. In Nicaragua, feelings ran so high that an armed uprising of colonists murdered the bishop who had supported the repeal of the *encomienda* system. Settlers petitioned the king, arguing that they had invested their lives and possessions, and the Crown had derived much benefit from their sacrifices. To his credit, the king refused.

Repartimiento

Still, the Crown had to support the colonists' need for labor. *Encomienda* was replaced by a system called *repartimiento* (meaning to divide

LEFT: depiction of the harbour entrance at Punta Arenas, *c.*1870. **RIGHT:** Catholic missionaries among the local people.

up) which required all Amerindian men between the ages of 16 and 60 to labor for one week of each month for private individuals, religious institutions, municipalities, and/or government offices.

On paper, the system was supposed to provide indigenous peoples with compensation for their labor and leave them free to work their own fields for the remaining three or so weeks of the month. But, in practice, things were very different, and abuses became commonplace.

Local people were required to devote considerably more than a week's labor to the Span-

iards, since they had to walk very long distances, sometimes for days on end, from their villages to their places of work. And they were charged for the food and any other goods they consumed – thus using up their miserably small amount of pay.

Years passed and the search continued for the fabled great gold mines of Veragua. But the mines were never found. Spanish *conquistadores* plundered the coastlines, laying claim to whatever booty they could find, capturing local people and enslaving them, and fighting all the while among themselves for claims to the new lands. English pirates appeared on the scene, also competing for gold and slaves.

Spain's Central American colonies were

developing, with administrative centers springing up in Panamá, Nicaragua, and Guatemala. In 1539, officials in Panamá used the name Costa Rica for the first time to distinguish the territory between Panamá and Nicaragua. But still there were no permanent settlements.

In 1559, Phillip II of Spain insisted that Costa Rica be populated, this time well inland. In 1561, Juan de Cavallón arrived with a group of 90 Spaniards recruited from Guatemala and Nicaragua, along with a team of black slaves and auxiliary Amerindians from Nicaragua.

Bringing indigenous peoples from one area to another was a common practice among the

> *Bartolomé de las Casas was to chronicle the methods of Spanish colonization in Latin America in his* History of the Indies. *He later became bishop of Chiapas, in Mexico.*

and thence to El Guarco, and it was there, for the first time, that a permanent community took root. Coronado's tactics with the Amerindians of Costa Rica were different from those of his predecessors. While he fully intended to settle their lands and take what gold he could lay his hands on, he was friendly toward them,

conquistadores, since these displaced people scarcely ever attempted to escape and return to their homes.

Cavallón also brought along livestock, including horses, cows, goats, pigs, chickens, and ducks, to improve the community's chances of success. It was a well-planned and well-financed expedition. Finally, 60 years after Columbus had arrived in Veragua, the first inland settlement in Costa Rica was established. It was christened Garcimuñoz, after Cavallón's place of birth.

Juan Vásquez de Coronado

Hailed by some historians as the true conqueror of Costa Rica, Coronado moved the Garcimunõz settlement to the Cartago Valley

he treated them with respect, and he requested, rather than demanded, labor and tribute.

Coronado was pressured by his soldiers and the settlers, who weren't particularly interested in peace, to be more aggressive with the indigenous population. The settlers wanted food, gold, and labor, or at least the promise of wealth and an easier life. During this time, they were continually threatening to desert Costa Rica, claiming life was too difficult. Coronado's peaceful strategies were effective, however, and the colony flourished.

Pacification and punishment

Among Coronado's successes was the surrender (pacification, it was called) of a local chief named

Quitao. At a meeting of all the chiefs in the area, Quitao announced that he was tired of hiding in the jungles and was ready to submit to the Spaniards. He told the other chiefs they were free to decide for themselves what they would do. The chiefs asked Quitao to decide for them and he replied that they would have to serve the king and his representative. Those who did not go along with this would be severely punished. As a token of his submission, he sent 150 local people to serve the Spanish, an act that was "cause for great admiration among the Spaniards."

Coronado's chronicles of his explorations throughout Costa Rica include keen, almost affectionate, observations of the Amerindians. In the Diquis region, visiting the Coctu, he wrote of the well-organized and well-developed villages, unlike any he had previously seen. He noted that the people had a lot of gold, which they acquired from tribes on the Atlantic coast and scooped from the rivers, and wore fine cotton clothing as well. He described them as a very good-looking people, bellicose, skillful in their manners, and very honest, "a thing rarely seen in indians."

It was among the Coctu that Coronado met the "most good-looking indian" he had ever seen, Chief Corrohore, who asked his assistance in recovering his sister, Dulcehe, who had been kidnapped by a neighboring chief. Coronado succeeded and Dulcehe was returned.

The situation was not always peaceful, however. Coronado, known for making peace among some of the warring tribes of Costa Rica, joined them in their wars against one another. There were also Amerindian uprisings in the colony. Returning after an exploration, Coronado found that all the Amerindians of the area, including Quitao, were at war with the Spanish. (The Spanish had been stealing the indigenous people's corn.) Amerindians in Orosi had killed eight Spaniards and their horses. His old friends, the chiefs Aserrí, Currirabá, Yurustí, Quircó, and Purirsí, had been made prisoners. In an attempt to calm the situation, Coronado went to speak to the Amerindians and, in a fit of temper, ordered two of them to be dismembered.

The lack of gold, food shortages, and indig-

enous revolts imposed continuous hardships on the settlers. Supplies and new settlers were brought in from Nicaragua, but life was almost unendurable for the Spaniards. In 1569, settlers demanded indigenous slaves, threatening to abandon the colony if their demands weren't met. Perafán de Ribera, Coronado's successor, a frail man of 74 years, defied Spanish law and permitted the settlers to enslave the local people.

The late 1560s marked the end of the conquest of Costa Rica. By then the majority of the indigenous population of the new colony had been killed, had died of diseases, had submitted to the Spaniards, or had fled to the forested

mountains of Talamanca. The land was now available to the settlers from Spain to come and make a new life.

Some traces of indigenous roots, however, survive to this day, particularly in place names honoring ancient chiefs – Aserrí, for example, is a town south of San José. Columbus's original name for Costa Rica – Veragua – has recently been resurrected and now graces a 1,620-hectare (4,000-acre) nature reserve and rainforest research center on the Caribbean Coast with a view of the spot where the Spanish ships first dropped anchor. Less gloriously, the indigenous word for chief – *cacique* – is now best known as a major brand name for *guaro*, a cheap but potent alcohol made from sugar cane. ❑

LEFT: portrait of Phillip II by Alonso Sánchez Coello.
RIGHT: French map dating from 1764, showing the provinces of Nicaragua and Costa Rica.

COLONIALISM AND INDEPENDENCE

After years as a forgotten penurious colony that received news of its independence by mail, Costa Rica discovered coffee and launched a fledgling democracy

The Costa Rican colony grew slowly. In 1573, there was a total of 50 families in Cartago, and a fledgling community farther west that would later become San José. Spanish immigrants arrived from Extremadura, in the west of Spain; from Andalucia, in the south, with its strong Moorish influences; and from Castile, the heart of old Spain. The Spanish had also founded colonies on the Pacific coast, at Espiritú Santo de Esparza and Nicoya. Although the population of Costa Rica was slowly growing, life was anything but easy.

During the conquest, *conquistadores* had loaded their ships and lined their pockets with gold, and had sent their obligatory percentages off to the royal treasury, which had swelled with their contributions. But by the end of the 16th century, what little gold there was in Costa Rica was gone. There was little Spanish currency available and it appeared as though there was no way to generate wealth. Cacao beans were used as money and barter became common. Even the few goods the colonists "bought" from Spain were traded for wheat flour, pigs, lard, chickens, tobacco, and liquor produced on their farms. Most families lived on isolated farms in the Central Valley, using primitive methods of agriculture. Social and even church life was nonexistent, and the populace lived in a state of grim impoverishment.

The forgotten colony

By now Spain was paying scant attention to its far-off colony and even the colonial governor in Guatemala made very little effort to

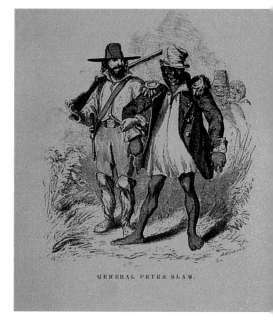

GENERAL PETER SLAM.

acquaint himself with the colony's concerns. It was, after all, a three-month trip from Guatemala by horse, and there was little reason to travel to Costa Rica.

Official neglect did have a positive side effect, however. Without large landholdings or plentiful peon labor to work plantations, even Costa Rica's governor and the aristocratic Spanish settlers were forced to work their own fields. Despite the grueling labor, the land at least was fertile, enriched by volcanic ash and irrigated by rivers. Colonists grew wheat, vegetables, and sugar, and raised livestock and poultry. Slowly but surely, the seeds of an economy began to take root.

LEFT: Henry Morgan, the Welsh pirate.
RIGHT: *Miskito* bandits, scourge of the colonists.

The birth of commerce

The first export of the Costa Rican colony was mules. They were walked along the Mule Road to Panamá, where they were sold to hardy souls who needed beasts to bear goods from the Atlantic to the Pacific coast. Later came cacao production on the Atlantic coast, and then tobacco,

Traces of Miskito influence remain in the Atlantic coast area, where many of the place names come from their language, including Talamanca (Talamalka), Sixaola, and Cahuita.

The *Miskitos*

In 1641 a slave ship was wrecked off the coast of Nicaragua/Honduras, and the black slaves on board escaped onto the Atlantic coast. Well liked by the Amerindians, they intermarried and, over the years, developed an identity and language of their own, called *Miskito*. British pirates joined forces with the *Miskitos*, and together they wreaked havoc along the Atlantic coast of Costa Rica and in the cacao plantations. For the *Miskitos*, the undefended plantations offered little resistance. They sailed in for their biannual raids, took the cacao, captured the black slaves, and set off again.

in the Central Plateau. In an attempt to give Costa Rica a product to export and a dependable income that could be taxed, the Crown set up tobacco-processing plants and granted Costa Rica sole rights within the colonies to grow tobacco. But Costa Rican tobacco was of poor quality, and there was not a large market for it.

On the Atlantic coast, piracy and slave-trading were the business of the day. The Atlantic waters were continually plundered by English pirates, including Drake, Mansfield, Morgan, and Owens; and by French, Dutch, and Portuguese buccaneers. They were all attempting to control the territory so they could cross the isthmus, from the Atlantic to the Pacific, and thus avoid the Spaniards in Panamá.

In 1742, after many years of such devastation, the government built Fort San Fernando in Matina, north of present-day Limón. Only five years later, however, the fort was destroyed by the pirate Owens and the *Miskitos*, under orders of the British-controlled Jamaican governor (the British and the Spanish were by then at war).

Protection money

By 1779 the pirate situation was so out of hand that the government started paying tribute to the *Miskitos* and leaving them "gifts" of coats made of fine fabric, shiny buttons, or three-cornered French hats, to collect at Matina.

Many years later, in 1841, President Braulio Carrillo refused to continue paying tribute to, or bestow gifts upon, the *Miskitos* and threatened to bring the resources of the country to war against them. Probably because cacao production had dwindled greatly by then, the *Miskitos* stopped raiding Matina.

Amerindian resettlement

Owing to mountainous terrain and inaccessibility, the Talamanca region of Costa Rica escaped the conquest. Groups of indigenous people, some of them refugees fleeing oppression elsewhere in the country, lived there, undisturbed by the invading Spaniards. However, as more colonists arrived in Costa Rica to clear land, build

Monte, now San José, was born; and in 1782, Villa Hermosa, now Alajuela, was settled.

Costa Ricans, living at subsistence levels, were too busy trying to survive to be much affected by the currents of thought and the conflicts that led to Central America's struggle for independence from Spain. The discord that was brewing elsewhere in Central America, fueled by class distinctions and onerous trade restrictions, largely passed them by.

Independence – by mail

Costa Ricans like to tell the story of how they received independence by mail. In fact, a cou-

roads, and farm, the paltry size of the available Amerindian labor force became a serious problem. The solution was to begin raids on the Talamanca region. After numerous forays, attempts to conquer Talamanca proved unsuccessful. There were counterattacks and cruel revenges on both sides. Ultimately, hundreds of Amerindians were "relocated" to the Central Valley by the Indian Resettlement Policies of 1747.

Meanwhile, in the Central Valley, communities were being established. In 1706, the village of Cubujugui, which later became Heredia, was founded; in 1737, Villa Nueva de la Boca del

LEFT: English pirates sack a village near the Pacific.
ABOVE: a public beheading in Talamanca.

rier aboard a mule arrived in the Central Valley of Costa Rica with the news on October 13, 1821, nearly a month after colonial officials in Guatemala City had declared independence for Costa Rica from the Spanish Empire.

The news aroused ambivalence, confusion, and conflict over what independence meant for the backwater region of Costa Rica. Being the province farthest removed from the colonial capital, Costa Rica came under the least influence of the Spanish Crown, the Catholic Church, the colonial bureaucracy, and the monopolistic Guatemalan traders who dominated colonial life in the rest of Central America. Tucked away in the recesses of the country's central highlands, leaders of the four small communities of San José,

Cartago, Heredia, and Alajuela began a lengthy debate over what they should do next.

Which way now?

Taking their cues from the 1812 Spanish Constitution, written with the participation of a distinguished Costa Rican liberal named Florencio de Castillo, local leaders drafted their first Constitution, the *Pacto de Concordia*, on December 1, 1821. A split quickly developed over whether or not to follow the lead of other Central American countries in joining Mexican nationalist and emperor Agustín de Itúrbide's empire, or to opt for total independence.

Leaders of the towns of San José and Alajuela, inspired by the revolutionary ideas that were then sweeping the world, argued for independence, while those of Cartago and Heredia leaned toward the Mexican Empire. There were even those who argued passionately that Costa Rica should become a part of Colombia, at the time ruled by Simón Bolívar.

The disagreements reflected the basic disparity in the respective characters of the cities. Cartago and Heredia had been founded to create Catholic congregations out of the early settlers: these towns evolved into centers of conservative thought and were more closely

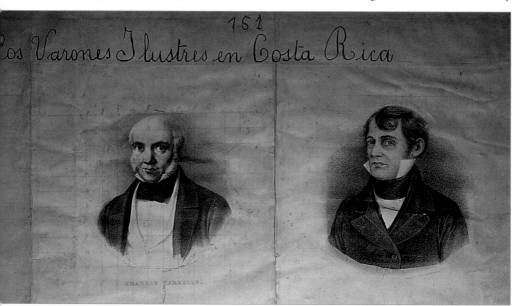

Los Varones Ilustres en Costa Rica

THE OLD CAPITAL

The country's first capital of Cartago was founded in 1561 by Juan de Cavallón as Castillo de Garcimuñoz. The site and name were abandoned when Coronado moved all the inhabitants to El Guarco in the Cartago Valley. Then Perafán de Ribera moved it again, to Mata Redonda, near present-day Sabana. Later, the peripatetic city returned to the Cartago Valley, to its present location.

In 1723, Irazú Volcano erupted, covering Cartago in layers of ash. At that time, Costa Rica's capital comprised just 70 houses, a parish church, and two shrines. It had no shops, no drug store, not even a resident doctor.

linked to the Church and the old colonial bureaucracy. By contrast, San José was founded by settlers who had been banished from Cartago for defying the strict colonial trading laws on smuggling. Alajuela, too, developed into a fringe agricultural center where the smuggling of tobacco flourished. Both towns developed more freewheeling, commercially based liberal attitudes than those of their strait-laced neighbors.

The issue of whether or not Costa Rica would join the Mexican Empire was settled on April 5, 1823. Two armies from the rival cities met in battle on the Continental Divide between San José and Cartago in a skirmish that left 20 men dead. The victorious independence forces, led by a former merchant seaman named Gregorio José Ramírez, took the town of Cartago.

Independence from the Mexican Empire was assured. As it turned out, they need not have bothered: the Costa Ricans belatedly learned that Itúrbide had been declared a traitor several days before the battle, and had been captured and executed. And with him had gone the Mexican Empire.

Farmers and teachers

Gregorio Ramírez set a precedent by relinquishing power in order to return to his farm, an example that would be followed by other victorious Costa Rican leaders. He later returned to put down an army coup, establishing civilian dominance over the military at a very early stage in the country's development.

Statehood was conferred upon a rather ambivalent Costa Rica by the Federal Republic of Central America. This confederation was a noble effort to create a "United States of Central America" out of the five former Spanish provinces, with a capital in Guatemala City. But it was doomed to failure because of class disparities and the tenacity with which the elite class clung to the local colonial social order in other parts of Central America. Costa Rica, on the other hand, was largely a nation of family farmers. It lacked both an elite class and a well-defined social order, so it offered neither great resistance to, nor enthusiasm for, the confederation. As a sovereign federal state, the country elected its first head of state, Juan Mora Fernández, in 1824. An elementary school teacher, Fernández distinguished himself by conducting the affairs of state with prudence and humility.

The first printing presses arrived in Costa Rica under Mora Fernández's tenure. By the time his successor, another elementary school teacher named José Rafael Gallegas, was elected, (against his will) in 1833, several newspapers were in print. One of them, *La Tertulia*, published humiliating attacks on Gallegas. Not much interested in the office to begin with, Gallegas resigned as head of state. One of *La Tertulia*'s major complaints was the social disintegration that had befallen the community as a result of the first modest signs of prosperity brought on by the planting of coffee, near San José. That limited prosperity brought with it prostitution, gambling, and property theft at levels unknown during the more austere colonial era. A strong, no-nonsense authoritarian hand seemed called for, and a San José lawyer, named Braulio Carrillo, was the right man in the right place at the right time.

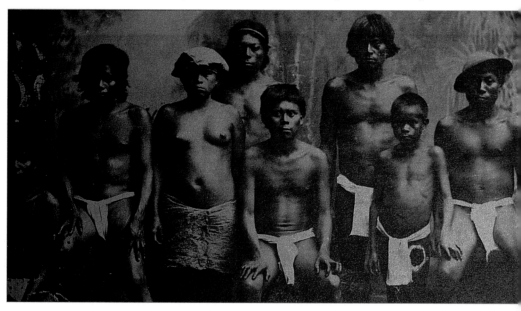

LEFT: 19th-century heads of state.
ABOVE: early 20th-century Nicoya group.

Braulio Carrillo

Carrillo imposed vagrancy laws, withdrew Costa Rica from the faltering Central American Federal Republic, and enacted liberal reforms such as a civil and penal code. He also outlawed the Church's right to tithes and earned the enmity of Central Valley townships by imposing a tax on

> To minimize the rivalries between the four main population centers during these turbulent times, the honor of being capital was rotated among them every four years.

his way back home with a cargo of pelts, put in to Puntarenas, a Costa Rican port on the Pacific coast, in search of ballast for his ship, which had been battered by storms off the Mexican coast. He loaded some 230,000kg (500,000lbs) of coffee into his hold and the Costa Rica–Liverpool connection was established. Thus were the British Isles and, ultimately, the European continent, opened up as an important new market for Costa Rican coffee.

The economic power that coffee gave to the citizens of San José further encouraged Carrillo's reorganization of the country's institutions around the new source of wealth, but caused

rural land, using the revenues to build roads and ports. Carrillo also settled Costa Rica's share of a debt to British bankers that had been incurred by the founders of the Central American Federation. Other Central American countries would have that debt hanging over them until well into the 20th century. The payback of the "English debt" eventually paid dividends in the form of good credit with which to invest in the country's new-found source of wealth: coffee.

Coffee power

Carrillo had, with unabashed autocracy, reorganized public administration to support the demands of the coffee economy. Serendipitously, in 1843 William Le Lacheur, an Englishman on

resentment from the other townships. In 1837, Cartago, Alajuela, and Heredia challenged Carrillo and San José in the *Guerra de la Liga*. Emerging victorious from the battle, Carrillo moved the capital permanently to San José.

When his term was up in 1837, Carrillo left office, only to return in a military coup the following year, after his successor tried to roll back some of his reforms. Continuing to force the country down the road to a coffee-fueled progress, he proclaimed himself president-in-perpetuity.

General Morazán

By 1842, the new social order created by Carrillo rose up to overwhelm him. Members of the budding coffee oligarchy called on General

Francisco Morazán, a hero of the Central American Federal Republic, to free them from what they perceived as Carrillo's despotism. Morazán was welcomed as a liberator when he arrived in Costa Rica, in April of 1842, with an army of 500 mostly Salvadoran volunteers. The head of Carrillo's army, Vicente Villaseñor, met up with Morazán just as the general and his men neared Alajuela on their march from the Pacific port of Caldera, and offered to join forces with him. The *Pacto de Jocote* sealed, Carrillo fell and was forced into exile in El Salvador.

A special assembly named Morazán provisional head of the state of Costa Rica. The general received a hero's welcome in Heredia and Alajuela, but received a somewhat restrained and cooler reception in San José.

Morazán wore out his welcome when he attempted to use Costa Rica as a base to revive his moribund confederation. The general sent missives to the other Central American countries calling for a National Constituent Assembly to revive his dream of a unified Central American nation. He threatened to impose compliance by force of arms. When Morazán tried to conscript Costa Ricans to enforce his ultimatum, the people of San José revolted. After three days of fierce fighting, Morazán was captured and, on September 15, 1842, he was executed in San José's Central Park.

Less than three years later, Braulio Carrillo, too, was to meet a violent end, assassinated in El Salvador. Today, Costa Ricans have mixed feelings about Braulio Carrillo. He is remembered as both a despot and as a strong, sometimes benevolent, leader who, perhaps, was the right man at the right time. He forced Costa Rica to break with its colonial past, placing the country firmly on the path to nationhood.

William Walker

In 1855, a Tennessee adventurer named William Walker took control of Nicaragua. One of his aims was to institutionalize slavery there and in neighboring countries so that he could sell slaves to the United States. Certain US industrialists liked the plan and gave support to Walker. The following year, with an army of 300 mercenaries, called *filibusteros*, he invaded Costa Rica, advancing as far as the site of the present

Santa Rosa National Park. Walker and his men entrenched themselves in the fortified Santa Rosa mansion. Costa Rican President Juan Rafael Mora, a member of the coffee oligarchy, had been monitoring the threat and had already mustered a force of *campesinos* (farm workers) to repel Walker. The Costa Ricans were numerically superior, though many were poorly armed with little more than farming implements and rusty rifles. On May 20, 1856, they engaged Walker in a 14-minute-long battle and forced him to retreat toward the Nicaraguan border.

The Costa Rican army pursued them and, at Rivas in Nicaragua, trapped Walker in a

wooden fort. A young drummer boy named Juan Santamaría volunteered to torch the fort, but was shot dead in the process. With the fort in flames, Walker's men were routed and his Costa Rican adventure was over. Three years later, he met his end in front of a firing squad in Honduras. The name of Juan Santamaría lives on in Costa Rican folklore as a youthful hero and symbol of national freedom, and in the country's main international airport, which is named after him.

President Mora was not such a hero. Despite his victory, his domestic policies were unpopular. He rigged the 1859 elections to win another term in office, was deposed, attempted an unsuccessful coup d'état, and was executed. ❑

LEFT: coffee berries being spread in a plantation yard, 1800s. **RIGHT:** statue of Juan Santamaría in Alajuela.

MODERN TIMES

Economic difficulties and the rising tide of reform came to a
head in civil war, but 21st-century Costa Rica became
Central America's peace broker

In 1889, with the drafting of the country's liberal constitution and the institution of a reliable, quadrennial electoral process, Costa Rica entered an era of bucolic prosperity and political stability. Affairs of state were left in the hands of so-called "Olympian" political plutocrats who administered public affairs with a laissez-faire assurance.

The coffee coup

It was not all plain sailing, however. The presumed downward trickle of profits in the coffee economy failed to reach enough people, especially in the neglected urban centers. Faced with the closing of European coffee markets during World War I, Costa Rica's first reformist president, Alfredo Gonzáles Flores, instituted a tax on coffee, incurring the wrath of the coffee establishment, which backed the president's own army chief, Federico Tinoco, in a successful coup on January 27, 1917. Tinoco assumed the presidency and named his brother, Joaquín, to head the army.

The warrior priest

Popular reaction to the repressive Tinoco dictatorship brought Jorge Volio Jiménez onto the country's political stage with a dramatic flourish. The pious scion of a Cartago coffee family, Volio began studying for the priesthood at Belgium's Leuven University in 1903. Heavily influenced by Belgian social Christian thinking, he returned to Costa Rica in 1910 to become pastor of a Heredia parish. No simple parish

priest, in 1912 Volio denounced the silence of the Costa Rican government over the intervention of US marines in Nicaragua and backed up his words by leading a group of Nicaraguan revolutionaries into battle. He was seriously wounded in the battle of Paz Centro in southern Nicaragua.

For his military adventure Volio was suspended from the Church, but was later reinstated. His passion for social justice led him to more clashes with the conservative local hierarchy, and, in 1915, he left the priesthood to devote himself to working for social change.

As the Tinoco dictatorship gradually became increasingly more repressive, Volio and a

---

PRECEDING PAGES: volunteer militiamen.
LEFT: young soldiers in a border dispute with Panamá.
RIGHT: saddling a mule, *c.*1960.

handful of other Costa Ricans left the country and formed an armed resistance, but the revolutionary forces were defeated by government troops led by army chief Joaquín Tinoco in battles near the Nicaraguan border in early 1919.

The Tinoco dictatorship was brought down not by this armed resistance nor by a military coup, but rather by outraged school teachers and students who rioted after soldiers marched on them during a demonstration in July of 1919. On August 9, 1919, Federico Tinoco resigned the presidency. The next day, Joaquín Tinoco was gunned down. The gunman was never identified.

He agreed to join forces with Jiménez, accepting the vice-presidency and a seat in Congress. But, rather than compromising, Volio used his seat to bewilder his fellow congressmen with forceful attacks on the country's upper classes.

When the government once again showed indifference to strife in neighboring Nicaragua, Volio commanded a force across the border to intervene. Concerned as to what an increasingly belligerent Volio might do with his force upon his return, Jiménez ordered the general to be intercepted when he arrived in Liberia. After a gunfight that left two government soldiers and Volio himself wounded, he was apprehended

¡Viva Volio!

His military defeat notwithstanding, Volio received a hero's welcome on his arrival in San José, and the ready cry "¡Viva Volio!" expressed the hope for change in the country's stodgy political status quo. The title of general was conferred on Volio by Congress. But much to Volio's consternation, the fall of Tinoco meant a return to business as usual in Costa Rica. Volio established the Reformist Party in 1923, which set an agenda for agrarian reform, decent housing, job security, and social protections. During the same year he ran for president on the Reformist ticket against Ricardo Jiménez and Alberto Echandi. Volio came in a close third in a vote that gave none of the candidates a majority.

and taken back to San José where doctors diagnosed him as suffering from "nervous hypersensitivity." Rather than imprisoning the patriot, Jiménez allowed him to be taken to Belgium for psychiatric care. Volio's promising political career came to an ignominious end.

The growth of reform

Volio's brand of reformism collapsed with his party, but the reformist movement was important in giving voice to the aspirations of sectors of society on the margins of the agro-export economy. It also inspired young intellectuals to action, including Manuel Mora, who, in his own words, "used to follow Volio around like a puppy dog." Disillusioned with Volio's political flirtation with Jiménez, Mora split with the Reformist Party to eventually form the Communist Party in 1931. The Communists immediately made their presence felt in the lowland banana zones. During a strike in 1934, the Communists won wage guarantees and the right to unionize, but only after a heated battle with both government troops and the United Fruit

> Labor organizer Carlos Luis Fallas immortalized the 1934 strike in the lowland banana zones in his novel Mamita Yunai.

Company. Meanwhile, plummeting coffee prices during the Great Depression had created additional hardship for a great many Costa Ricans.

Calderón Guardia

The rising tide of reform finally found its champion when, as the economic crisis reached its breaking point, Costa Ricans elected Dr Rafael Angel Calderón Guardia to the presidency in 1939. Inheritor of his father's humanitarian legacy and backed by the coffee establishment, he seemed the perfect choice.

Calderón Guardia, also steeped in social Christian doctrine at medical school in Belgium, carried out reforms beyond the hopes of even the most fervent reformers and the fears of the most entrenched liberal, creating a social-security system, a labor code, and various other social guarantees.

Costa Rica declared war on Germany and Japan following the attack on Pearl Harbor – a day before the United States. But Calderón Guardia added insult to injury for the coffee barons by using his wartime emergency powers to confiscate the lands of German families, some of whom had been in Costa Rica for generations and who had intermarried with the oligarchy.

Having alienated himself from the traditional source of political power, Calderón Guardia made common cause with Manual Mora and his Communist Party, and with the Catholic Church, led by the socially minded Archbishop Victor Sanabria. Together they

defied the coffee barons and the economic liberals who had dominated Costa Rica since the end of the 19th century and set about expanding the role of the state in providing for people's needs. The nascent bureaucracies would invariably be headed by a member of the Communist Party. Manuel Mora was named head of the country's army.

When the worldwide anti-Nazi alliances – which made this peculiar church-state-party pact feasible – vanished, so too did the wide-based, popular support for Calderón's leadership. As the government clung to power, a disillusioned Mora was paid a visit by an old

friend who offered his support. It was the elderly and ailing General Jorge Volio Jiménez.

History has shown that the winners of the ensuing 1948 civil war, led by José (Don Pepe) Figueres, had no intention of rolling back the social guarantees. Instead, they further institutionalized the legacy of nearly 30 years of reformist struggle. It was a legacy summed up by the immortal cry: "¡Viva Volio!"

The grandfather of Costa Rica

José Figueres is best known abroad for abolishing the army, but Costa Ricans remember him for the way in which he lived his life, and for the heritage of democracy that he created and solidified. Don Pepe was born of Catalán parents,

---

LEFT: an early attempt to lure tourists. **RIGHT:** José Figueres surrounded by his supporters after his political party won the civil war in 1948.

and for many, that somehow explained his ego, his opinionated, self-righteous, impossibly principled, obstinate, courageous, unyielding, unpredictable self. He was self-educated, and as a young man he virtually lived in the Boston Public Library, where he became infected with the new and exciting spirit of North American liberalism. He returned to Costa Rica from Boston and New York City in the 1920s with a romantic vision and deeply held belief in the nobility of the human spirit, and hope for social justice for the people of his country.

Until 1942, Don Pepe had no real political experience. Then, on July 2, the *San Pablo*, a

United Fruit Company vessel, was sunk by a German submarine in the Port of Limón. All the Costa Ricans aboard were killed. President Calderón responded by imprisoning German and Italian citizens of the Atlantic region. Two days later, 20,000 people rioted after a German-educated medical doctor's window was smashed. Looting followed, and the government not only did nothing to control the mob, but also allegedly encouraged it.

In the aftermath of the riots a climate of fear and suspicion grew. Don Pepe blamed Calderón for failing to maintain public order and safety. He decided to express "what everyone felt but was afraid to say," and purchased radio air time on "America Latina." In strident mocking tones

he accused the administration of an inability to govern. His denunciation of the government was interrupted mid-sentence as the director-general of the police arrived and hauled him away. The result was, perhaps all too predictably, the making of a martyr and national hero out of the imprisoned Don Pepe Figueres.

The seeds of revolution

Figueres spent the next two years in exile in Mexico. Force, he was convinced, was the only way to overthrow the government of Rafael Angel Calderón. Figueres forged agreements with exiles, intellectuals, and revolutionaries from other countries, and began stockpiling arms. In 1944, after a particularly violent and discreditable election, Teodoro Picado, Calderón's political successor, was elected president. The fraudulent election, the faltering economy, the Communist presence and widespread official corruption were too much for Figueres. He returned to Costa Rica in May 1944. Determined to do something about Calderón, he jumped into opposition politics, but felt that only a violent revolution would bring about real change.

In the fateful 1948 presidential elections, Otilio Ulate, publisher of the San José newspaper, *Diario de Costa Rica*, ran against Calderón. Ulate won by a substantial margin, but the *calderonistas* maintained control of congress. There were charges and countercharges of fraud, and, in the midst of the violent confrontations, a large number of ballots were set ablaze. The electoral tribunal, which had been entrusted to oversee fair elections, and to which the nation was looking for a verdict, failed to issue one.

LA LUCHA SIN FIN

Don Pepe founded a farm high in the mountains, to the south of San José, and called it *La Lucha Sin Fin* (The Endless Struggle). It was a success, and he used the profits to open schools, libraries, stores, movie houses, soccer fields, and medical clinics for local people.

At *La Lucha*, Don Pepe worked at liberating the *campesino* (farm laborer) from ignorance and poverty and attempting to turn some of the Utopian theories he had studied into a workable reality.

The day-to-day way of life on the farm provided lessons that in many ways Don Pepe Figueres was later to apply to all of Costa Rica.

With no action forthcoming from the tribunal and no compromise possible between the candidates, the *calderonista*-controlled Congress, in an unprecedented act, annulled the presidential election. Ulate was arrested by Picado's police colonel, and his closest advisor, Dr Carlos Luis Valverde, was shot and died the following day. In San José, businesses were closed and storefronts were boarded up. It felt as though a bomb were ready to go off. Meanwhile, Figueres was in the mountains near his ranch, *La Lucha Sin Fin* (the Endless Struggle), planning for the coming war.

Civil war

The War of National Liberation began on March 11, 1948. It consisted of a well-planned offensive carried out by men with no formal military background, trained by guerrilla fighters from the Dominican Republic and Honduras, and armed with guns flown in from Guatemala. Forty-four days later, 2,000 men, one in every 300 Costa Ricans, had been killed during the violent, sad war of liberation. Figueres' forces were victorious, despite the efforts of the Nicaraguan dictator Anastasio Somoza, and his invasion of the north of Costa Rica. President Picado, who had never really believed an armed insurrection would occur, and who had no heart for conflict, saw that a swiftly negotiated peace was essential; he announced his surrender.

The Second Republic

Don Pepe Figueres, as both the acknowledged winner of the battle and head of the victorious junta, entered San José five days after the ceasefire and led a triumphant parade. His National Liberation Army marched up Avenida Central to the airport at La Sabana. Figueres addressed the people, outlining his goals and fundamental concepts, which he referred to as "the greatest good for the greatest number." More precisely, he described the four main objectives of what he called his Second Republic: the re-establishment of civic ethics, elimination of the spoils system in public administration, social progress without Communism, and a greater sense of solidarity with other nations.

One of Figueres' first acts was to place a 10 percent tax on wealth, a law that was resented,

LEFT: Don Pepe, the country's grandfather *(left)*, and Oscar Arias, Costa Rica's president and the Nobel Laureate *(right)*. **RIGHT:** a pensive Don Pepe.

badly administered, and, in most cases, evaded by the affluent. He expanded the social-security system, enacted full voting rights for all women, created a minimum wage, established low-cost national health care services for all, passed legislation on child support, and proposed nationalizing the banks. The firing of large numbers of bureaucrats and schoolteachers, in an attempt to reorganize government agencies, exacerbated his declining popularity. And then the assets of individuals connected with the Calderón-Picado governments were frozen. Don Pepe's extreme and, to some, arbitrary politics alienated many. Even the press became hostile to him.

The constitution of 1949 did reflect many of the goals of the Second Republic. It included political and individual freedoms, and added new social guarantees. It established the principle of public regulation of private property and enterprise, and empowered the state to take actions assuring the widest distribution of wealth possible. But arguably its finest social guarantee was to extend citizenship to everyone born in Costa Rica. This was an important issue for Afro-Caribbean residents, who until that time had been treated as second-class people.

The end of the military

The new constitution also abolished the military. This was perhaps Figueres' most celebrated and memorable achievement, one that he would point to over and over again. In a public ceremony, he delivered the keys of the Bella Vista military fortress to the minister of public education, and told him to convert it into a national museum. Don Pepe knew how to exploit the moment: with photographers standing by, he raised a sledgehammer and symbolically smashed at the wall of the fortress. His supporters considered it a final blow to militarism. His enemies regarded the abolition of the military as a clever move: lacking the full backing of the military, he simply decided to get rid of it.

dent, Oscar Arias, who was trying to mediate a peace settlement in the escalating regional conflicts. By now El Salvador, Honduras, and Guatemala were also embroiled in various types of war or disputes. Costa Rica, for all its economic problems, was at least an oasis of peace. In 1987, Arias was awarded the Nobel Prize for his efforts to bring peace to Central America. He also accepted millions of dollars of aid from the US, compromising Costa Rica's neutral position.

A family affair

Despite the success of Oscar Arias abroad, his party was voted out in 1990 in favor of Rafael

Calm before storm

The 1960s and 1970s were essentially peaceful and prosperous decades. The development of a welfare state and bills protecting indigenous peoples were just two highlights of a progressive regime. But in 1979, the anti-government Sandinista forces in neighboring Nicaragua toppled the Somoza dictatorship. Costa Rica became a fallback area for guerrilla groups and anti-Sandinistas, largely at the behest of the US, to whom Costa Rica was financially indebted.

Equally bad news, if not worse, was the collapse of both the banana and coffee markets, reaching a peak in the early 1980s. Throughout the decade, debt continued to mount. The silver lining on the cloud was provided by its presi-

Calderón Fournier, the son of post-war president Dr Rafael Calderón Guardia. Following a lackluster term, he was succeeded by José Maria Figueres, son of Don Pepe, who was, of course, Calderón Guardia senior's arch rival. Sadly, the young Figueres was unable to repeat his father's success or even improve much on the previous miserable administration, and proved to be one of Costa Rica's most unpopular presidents. In 1998 the Social Christian Unity Party (PUSC) won the election under conservative economist Miguel Angel Rodríguez, who pledged to liberalize certain key economic sectors and slash government spending. Despite attracting foreign investment such as the Intel silicon-chip plant, and signing free-trade deals with Canada and Mexico, many Costa Ricans suspected that his privatization plans for the state-run telecommunication and energy monopolies pointed to corruption. Critics accused his government of lack of transparency, triggering the largest street demonstrations since the 1948 revolution.

In April 2002, PUSC retained power with the election of Abel Pacheco, who placed much emphasis on tourism as the country's greatest economic priority. His tenure was plagued by incompetence, lack of leadership, an intransigent, uncooperative Congress, and a plethora of political, financial, and environmental scandals. In 2004 two ex-presidents were arrested on corruption charges, including Rodríguez, who had to step down from his post as the first-ever Central American Secretary General of the Organization of American States. More arrests followed, and, in the end, five former presidents were under investigation for corruption.

Financial scandals included the collapse of half a dozen unregulated tax shelters and mutual funds, in which the expat community was heavily invested and hard hit. Pacheco's environmental reforms were never passed and the country's national park system deteriorated, with uncontrolled poaching and logging, thanks to lack of funding for park guards.

A political phoenix

The 2006 election was a prolonged showdown between Citizen Action Party (PAC) leader Ottón Solís and the National Liberation Party's Oscar Arias, who had managed constitutionally to overturn the country's ban on presidential re-election. After a recount, Arias won with the slimmest of margins. Some 20 years after his first term started in 1986, Arias returned to the Casa Presidencial to preside over the passing, in 2008, of CAFTA, the US-Central American Free Trade Agreement, which had violently polarized the nation. Arias also resumed his role as regional peacemaker, giving refuge to deposed Honduran President Manuel Zelaya in 2009.

The 2010 election made history when Laura Chinchilla, former vice-president in the Arias administration, became the first female president of Costa Rica. History was also made in October 2010 when former President Rafael Angel Calderon Fournier was found guilty on

corruption charges, and became the first president to be sentenced to a prison term.

Country wide, an increase in violent crime and a growing gap between rich and poor today threaten Costa Rica's image as a peaceful, safe country. The child-sex industry has also cast a pall over tourism. On the bright side, Costa Rica has set an admirable goal to become the first carbon-neutral country by 2021. And, despite its social and economic problems, in 2009 the UK-based New Economics Foundation, which ranks countries on the basis of life expectancy and ecological footprint, named Costa Rica the happiest place on earth. ❏

FICKLE FRIENDS

During his second term of office (2006–10), President Oscar Arias unceremoniously dumped Costa Rica's long-standing trading partner and benefactor Taiwan in favor of China. So much for gratitude for the Costa Rica-Taiwan Friendship Bridge, built with Taiwanese funds in 2003 to link the Nicoya Peninsula with the mainland. Local pundits have dubbed the bridge *Puente de la Apuñalada* (Back Stab Bridge). The country is now reaping the benefits of association with China. Apart from wide-open new markets for both countries, Costa Rica's change of heart is being rewarded with a huge new national soccer stadium in San José, built by Chinese workers.

LEFT: a Sandinista helicopter delivering weapons.
RIGHT: Oscar Arias, winner of the Nobel Peace prize.

THE PEOPLE OF COSTA RICA

Costa Ricans, or *Ticos*, come in all shapes, sizes, and colors.
"We are all *Ticos*," is the proud claim, though some *Ticos*
fare better than others

Racially and ethnically, Costa Rica is not a simple place. Along with the overwhelming majority of Spanish-heritage *Ticos*, there are four other distinct ethnic groups. The people of Guanacaste have dark skin, and resemble their Nicaraguan neighbors in manner and accent. In the southern, mountainous regions of the country, the Amerindians of Costa Rica, who were here long before the Spanish, belong to six discrete linguistic groups. Though they increasingly speak Spanish, they still debate whether it is more important to retain their indigenous cultural identity or to assimilate more into mainstream Costa Rican culture.

The blacks of the Atlantic Coast are the country's largest immigrant minority; they speak Caribbean-accented English and talk with pride of their Jamaican heritage. Sino-Costa Ricans are called *Chinos*. Descendants of indentured laborers, they own many of the bars, restaurants, and stores, especially in small towns.

And all these different races are *Costarricenses*.

Indigenous people

Archeologists, using very different methods of calculating populations, estimate that anywhere from 30,000 to 400,000 native people lived in Costa Rica when Columbus arrived. Today, about 70,000 native people remain, although it is hard to establish an accurate figure since many indigenous people have had mixed marriages.

The history of the Amerindians of Costa Rica is much like that of other indigenous peoples

PRECEDING PAGES: one man and his horse, Montezuma; *Tico* baton twirlers in San Isidro. **LEFT:** riding in the northeast. **RIGHT:** babysitting in Tortuguero.

of the American continent. The Europeans brought diseases to which the native populations had no immunity. Entire tribes were obliterated before they had even seen a white man.

In pre-Columbian times, the Chorotegas, cousins of the Nicaro, inhabited Guanacaste and the Nicoya Peninsula. They lived in patrimonial groups, grew corn, and were culturally similar to groups from southern Mexico. These peoples were devastated during the Spanish Conquest by disease and by slave traders who shipped them off to Panamá and Peru. Their surviving descendants are today mostly integrated into contemporary Costa Rican life.

Other native groups spoke dialects originating in Colombia. They were divided into clans, to which the Spanish gave names, and their original names are mostly lost to history: the Guaymí, for example, call themselves Ngabe, pronounced Nobe. The other clans were named the Terraba, the Boruca, and, in the Talamanca mountains, the Bribri and Cabecar. These people lived in matrilineal societies in clearings in the jungles. With the coming of the Europeans, many of them fled to the almost inaccessible jungle regions of the southern mountains. Much of their culture has been preserved by their descendants, who still speak their original languages and live in the remote regions of the Talamanca mountains.

who live for the most part without electricity and running water. Alcohol is another problem, with some migrant workers spending a week's wages at the local bar while wives and children wait anxiously outside. The cultural imperialism of the airwaves is persistently penetrating the world of people who have resisted the *conquistadores* for some 500 years. Among the young, the temptations of this high-tech world are enticing and the desire to assimilate is strong.

Today, indigenous peoples live on reserves designated for their use in 1971. By law, non-native people cannot own land inside these areas, but this has been difficult to enforce

Despite the influence of Christian missionaries, many native people have not forsaken their animistic religious traditions. The Bribri call their deity Sibu and trust in shamans, with their vast knowledge of the rainforest's medicinal herbs, to cure a range of illnesses. Farther south, along the Panamá border, the Guaymí continue to live in their traditional areas, which span political boundaries.

Modern temptations

No matter how remote their jungle reserves, the Amerindians are still not insulated from contemporary culture. Battery-powered televisions bring pressure to consume soft drinks and junk food, as well as images of the First World to these people

THE TICO SPIRIT

Costa Ricans call themselves *Ticos* in a reference to their use of the diminutive ending "*ico*": "*Un momentico, por favor*" (Just a little minute, please) or "chiquitica" (nice little girl). You'll also hear a lot of "*cito*," as in "*cafecito*," (a nice little coffee). There is a sweetness to the way they speak Spanish. For instance, they will use the gentle verb "*regalar*" (give me, as in a present) rather than the direct *dar* (give me) when ordering in a restaurant. *Ticos* are politically temperate, too, and, for the most part, shy and unaggressive. Demonstrations, protests, strikes, and rallies are common events, yet people behave respectfully and election day has a distinctive party atmosphere.

and non-Amerindians have gradually moved into these territories, which just happen to contain a significant proportion of the country's mineral wealth.

Black settlers

As early as 1825, Afro-Caribbeans came to Costa Rica to fish, hunt turtles, and to market coconuts. These immigrants were part of a migration from the West Indies to the Central American Caribbean coast. From Panamá to Honduras, they came looking for ways to support themselves. Many were transient. One man might harvest cacao in Limón, then find employment on the barges in Nicaragua and next labor on the construction of the Panamá Canal; they went where there was work.

In 1872, under contract from Minor C. Keith, who later became the founder of the

Encroaching contemporary society threatens the indigenous peoples' language, their cultural identity, and their way of life. Caught in time between two worlds, slowly relinquishing the old, but not yet embracing the new, native peoples are extremely vulnerable. Many NGOs and humanitarian groups are involved today in building schools and providing medical services in remote reserves to support them. But in the five centuries since the European conquest, little has changed for the aboriginal Costa Rican people.

LEFT: inhabitant of Santa Elena, Monteverde.
ABOVE: an Afro-Caribbean descendant paddles a boat along one of Tortuguero's waterways for a tour group.

United Fruit Company, blacks from the West Indies came to work on building the Atlantic railroad. They proved more successful than previous laborers imported by Keith in their ability to tolerate the hazardous working conditions, which included exposure to yellow fever, malaria, and venomous snakes, as well as severe physical labor and oppressive management. The maltreatment of workers in the banana fields of the Caribbean United Fruit Company is well documented. However, the blacks were certainly not invulnerable and they, too, died in their thousands while building the tracks, the endless numbers of bridges, the docks, and the wide, rectangular streets of the port city of Limón.

Other Afro-Caribbeans came to the Caribbean coast on their own, looking for any kind of work to escape the poverty of their native islands. Some ultimately were given land along the railroad right of way, and others, thanks to their command of English, rose from the ranks of laborers to become managers in the banana business and on the railways. Most originally planned to earn whatever they could and then return to their islands.

When United Fruit left the Caribbean region and moved to the Pacific coast, the blacks were left behind, unemployed. Many emigrated for the same reason that had motivated their par-

ents to immigrate to the country in the first place: they were again seeking work. Those who stayed behind lived for the most part at subsistence level, producing what they could from small plots of land. They retained their English language and their Protestant religion, remaining proudly separate from the Hispanic Costa Ricans and enriching these coastal communities with a distinct Afro-Caribbean flavor. At the same time, they endured racist immigration and residency laws that restricted their movement until the middle of the 20th century.

When the Constitution of 1949 declared that anyone born in Costa Rica had automatic citizenship, doors finally opened for blacks. For the first time they were allowed to travel outside

Limón province and they began to attend public schools and enter politics. When, in the 1950s, the value of cacao soared on the international market, many of the squatter-farmers were able to achieve a certain level of prosperity. And, in an ironic reversal of historical patterns, they then hired Hispanics to work their fields. Many members of the subsequent generation of blacks were well educated and, preferring professions to farming, left the Limón area. Indeed, many left Costa Rica entirely to find jobs elsewhere.

Some middle-class, educated blacks who remained in Costa Rica married Hispanics, but their assimilation into Costa Rican society is not total, owing to the curious, two-sided racism that exists. Blacks usually consider themselves more civilized and superior to Hispanic Costa Ricans, while Hispanic Costa Ricans sometimes insist that blacks are racially inferior.

Today, just under 3 percent of the total Costa Rican population is black, and less than 25 percent of the population of the Caribbean coast is of black ancestry. Increasingly, young Afro-Caribbeans attend Spanish-speaking schools and Caribbean-accented English is more often heard among the older generation.

The construction of the railroad to the Caribbean coast brought other waves of immigrants during the late 19th century. Among the builders, managers, and technicians of the Northern Railway Company were English, Irish, and North Americans. But the largest group of immigrants, apart from the Afro-Caribbean workers, were laborers from southern China, who joined the blacks on the railroad, essen-

> After 4,000 West Indians died during the laying of the first 32km (20 miles) of the Atlantic Railroad, businessman Minor C. Keith simply imported another 10,000 laborers.

tially as slaves, but euphemistically referred to as "indentured workers."

Chinese immigrants

The first Chinese to set foot in Costa Rica were 77 indentured servants, in 1855. Almost two decades later, despite the existence of a law against the permanent settlement in Costa Rica of African and Asian races, contractors for the Atlantic railroad imported "one thousand healthy, robust Chinese of good customs and addicted to work." These two ethnic groups were to become the founding fathers of the Chinese colony of Costa Rica.

Those contracted by the railroad left as quickly as they could escape, to work as cooks and domestic servants. As their fortunes improved, Chinese immigrants set up small eateries, groceries, and liquor stores. The steady trickle of Chinese immigrant laborers that followed the first railroad workers benefitted from those who were already established. Through work contracts and credit assistance from other Chinese, they set up commercial ventures along the railroad, in the port cities, and in growing rural communities throughout the country. Their small-scale businesses required little capital investment, only a minimal acquaintance with the language, and allowed all members of the growing family network to become involved in tending the business. Chinese family traditions upheld the authority of elders and reinforced an already strong generational hierarchy. Well-defined divisions of labor, plus a strong work ethic, ensured that their businesses flourished.

Chinese colonies, headed by businessmen's associations, evolved into strong business groups in the cities and towns of Costa Rica. By the beginning of the 20th century, a number of Chinese immigrants had become wealthy, and were then able to sponsor the immigration of other family members and acquaintances.

Among the first generations of Chinese to settle in Costa Rica, many men lived with local Costa Rican white women, while retaining marriages established in China with childhood brides. The money they sent to China was often used to finance family enterprises back home.

In the last century, successful Sino-Costa Rican businessmen traveled to China to oversee their holdings, raise a family and invest toward retirement in the home of their ancestors. During their absence from Costa Rica, their businesses were managed by close younger kin.

With the Communist takeover of mainland China in 1949, return to their ancestral homeland became less attractive, and most Sino-Costa Ricans forsook any hopes of a permanent return to China.

More recent events also reinforced this influx from the East. The prospect of the British colony of Hong Kong being transferred to Chinese hands caused a steady flow of Asian immigrants from Hong Kong as long ago as the 1970s. Today, 1 percent of the total population in Costa Rica is Chinese, and there are more than 250 Chinese restaurants in the San José area alone.

Those Chinese born of mixed Costa Rican-Chinese families consider themselves full members of Costa Rican society, identifying heartily with its ways and traditions, while, at the same time, expressing a strong sense of devotion to their immigrant forefathers.

ORIGIN OF THE SPECIES

The national myth holds that most Costa Ricans are descended from Spanish farmers who came from egalitarian stock. In reality, most Costa Ricans are descended from Spanish settlers who intermarried with the local population. Among colonial immigrants from the Iberian peninsula there were also Jews and Arabs, Catalans and Basques, as well as many people from the Middle East. In the 19th century, lured by the hope of coffee prosperity, German and English settlers set up import-export trades, while Lebanese, Turks, and Polish Jews became powerful merchants. All these newcomers contributed to the demographic mix and, clearly, were no simple agrarian folk.

LEFT: a Cahuita resident on the verandah of his wooden house in the traditional architectural style.
RIGHT: Cahuita girls on the town's black-sand beach.

Many among them have married Hispanics, and faced opposition from their parents and ostracism by the Chinese community. Nevertheless, they have retained venerable family traditions that express Chinese values of ancestral wisdom and family solidarity.

Many young Sino-Costa Ricans have now joined the ranks of the professionally educated; although they are doctors, lawyers, engineers, business administrators, and university professors, many also still continue to oversee the family businesses that allowed their ancestors to achieve economic success in Costa Rica.

The most illustrious Sino-Costa Rican is

engineer/physicist/astronaut Franklin Chang, a veteran of seven US Space Shuttle missions. Since his NASA years, Chang has spearheaded and encouraged high-tech scientific education and brought new space-age enterprises to Costa Rica.

The Italians

The Atlantic railroad had serious difficulties retaining Chinese laborers. In an attempt to find an alternative working force, in 1888 the railway managers imported 1,500 "good, humble, thrifty Italians of a superior race." The disagreeable working conditions soon led the Italians to leave the railroad project. Many remained in Costa Rica, and in the 1950s they were joined by an influx of Italian farmers who settled in a government-sponsored colony, San Vito, in the southern Pacific region of Costa Rica (*see page 255*).

Today, San Vito still has a distinctive Italian flavor: there is a Dante Alighieri Society; there are a dozen shoe stores in town, as well as *pasticcerias* serving Italian *gelato* and enticing pastries. More recently, entrepreneurial Italians have come to Costa Rica to open restaurants and hotels all over the country, bringing a dash of style and culinary gusto that is appreciated by Costa Ricans and visitors.

The gringo

They are unmistakable in San José, their heads sticking out above the throng of people crowding the chaotic city sidewalks. *Gringos*, fairer and usually taller than local people, easily catch the eye. A pejorative word in much of Latin America, *gringo* is a much milder term here, applied not only to US citizens but also to Canadians and Europeans. They have been coming to Costa Rica for a long time. Early in the 19th century, attracted by the promise of wealth from coffee, French, German, and British entrepreneurs, along with teachers, scientists, and professionals, came to Costa

> *Chinese participation in the social life of the towns they settled is nowhere more in evidence than at the Limón Carnival, when the traditional Chinese dragon snakes its way alongside flamboyant Caribbean dancers.*

Rica. Many married Costa Rican women, and most became thoroughly assimilated into the aggregate of *Tico* culture. Today, many powerful families in the arts and politics bear British or German surnames.

In the 1950s, Quakers from the US came to Costa Rica looking for peace. They found it in the cloud forest of Monteverde, where they formed a community dedicated to a life of harmony with the land. They created a successful dairy and cheese industry, which today supplies much of Costa Rica's specialty cheese market.

Since the 1960s, Costa Rican laws favoring North American and European retirees led to the establishment of a large number of comparatively wealthy *gringos* in the Central Valley area. These retirees, recently estimated at more than 35,000, are officially called *pensionados* or *residentes*, non-nationals living in Costa Rica with a guaranteed monthly income. They come to Costa Rica for the warm climate and for the higher standard of living their dollars afford them.

In recent years, though, the welcome mat has been pulled back a bit. In 2009, after much debate, legislators passed a new law that requires non-nationals to pay into the national social-security system, as well as pay higher application fees and maintain a greater monthly income in a Costa Rican bank.

For them the country is a laboratory, a place where the viability of living in harmony with the environment can be demonstrated to the world at large. Their arrival has stimulated major changes in the environmental awareness of the country.

A large cadre of biologists, botanists, and scientific researchers has also had a huge impact on both the academic world in Costa Rica, and on research efforts into conservation.

While Costa Ricans are proud to show off their beautiful land, tourism often has a downside: the small landowner may lose his land for a biological reserve; dairy farmers can't afford

With the growing disparity in the country between haves and have-nots, foreigners are sometimes viewed less favourably these days, especially those who come to Costa Rica in order to make a quick buck in sometimes shady or environmentally insensitive property developments.

Effects of tourism

The most dramatic influx of people today is the result of the country's flourishing tourism industry. Environmentally concerned people of all ages come to carry out ecological work.

to buy fresh pasture because property speculation has driven prices sky high; cattle ranchers without enough water for their livestock in the dry season watch as huge resorts build water-hungry golf courses. Profits often flow abroad to large hotel groups, and promised local benefits often amount to little more than the modest wages of waiters, hotel maids, gardeners, and pool attendants.

Sustainable tourism, which benefits the local community, has become the watchword of both international conservation organizations active in Costa Rica and the Ministry of Tourism, although in recent years, government policies have vacillated between paying lip service to conservation, and actually putting some teeth

LEFT: portrait of a Costa Rican woman from Santa Elena.
ABOVE: local gentlemen passing a Sunday in San Isidro.

into environmental protection. A program that awards "green-leaf" status, according to the eco-friendliness of hotels, has been successful, along with the Bandera Azul (Blue Flag) program that promotes clean beaches around the country.

Latin American newcomers

More recently, Costa Rica has become a haven for those fleeing violence, wars, and economic problems: during the past couple of decades, onerous political conditions and deteriorating economic circumstances in their home countries have brought significant numbers of South Americans to settle in Costa Rica, including educated Chileans, economically stressed Argentinians, opportunity-seeking Uruguayans, and Colombians escaping drug-war violence. On the whole, these different groups of people have greatly enhanced Costa Rica's cultural sensibilities over the past two decades or so.

Absorbing poorer, more desperate illegal immigrants, especially from Nicaragua, has also undeniably caused difficulties. With the arrival of many Colombians in the late 1990s, most of them respectable people, but some criminals as well, drug trafficking, armed robberies, and kidnappings have also increased,

HEALTH AND EDUCATION

The standards of health and education in Costa Rica are impressive. In 1920, infant mortality was nearly 26 percent; today it is less than 10 percent. Costa Ricans are healthier and living longer, too. They are ranked higher on the overall health index than Americans, and life expectancy has increased to 78.8 years. The only cloud on the horizon is the persistence of teenage pregnancies – with ever-younger mothers. The number of mothers under the age of 15 has nearly doubled since 1984.

The general good health of the nation is not due to sheer luck, or the quality of the air. Without the burden of supporting expensive armed forces, Costa Rica is able to invest around 10 percent of its GNP in health care. The public system, accessible to all, is showing lots of wear and tear. But the quality of care is high enough, especially in the private sector, that medical tourism is a booming industry, especially cosmetic surgery and dental work. Many tourists build a vacation around having "work" done.

Costa Rica is also an exceptionally literate nation, with 95.8 percent literacy across the population aged 10 and over. Again, this is a figure that compares favorably with the United States and many European nations.

The country has always been progressive in electing teachers to high political posts. In fact, in 1869, Costa Rica became the first country in the world to make education both mandatory and free of charge.

on the part of both newcomers and *Ticos*. In general, the country has officially accepted newcomers with a mix of grace and tolerance (*see box on Ticos page 68*).

Ticos today

A Latin American writer once observed: "The problem is that the Costa Rican looks too much to the North. He should be looking to the South." But even if he did, the *Tico* would insist that he is different from most Latinos because of what he sees as his "whiteness," (fair skin, light hair, and light-colored eyes) or his European heritage.

it. They know that almost endless problems beyond easy resolution abound. But despite some skeptical complaining, they express confidence that their government is still the most honest in Latin America.

Travelers to Costa Rica find it difficult to identify just how different Costa Ricans are from people in other Central and South American countries, yet they notice it in subtle ways. There is a certain civility to life here, even in busy San José. People on the streets of the towns and cities are, more often than not, well dressed, polite, and quick to help a stranger. Cardboard shanty towns that dominate the cityscape of

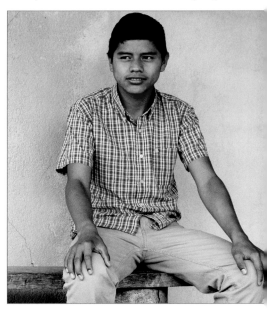

Just go to Guatemala, Panamá, or El Salvador, and observe the differences. These countries are only short distances away, but the Costa Rican is as different from these other Latin people as, say, the Swiss is to the Italian, or the German to the Dane. Costa Ricans revel in the difference and are unabashedly proud of it.

Grace under pressure

Costa Ricans have a graceful sense of the universal corruption that surrounds them. They shake their heads, lamentably acknowledging

LEFT AND ABOVE: young and old citizens of Tortuguero.
ABOVE RIGHT: young man from an inland town in the north of the country.

other developing countries are less evident here. Homeless people are not as omnipresent as they are in other Latin and Asian countries, or indeed, in many large US cities.

Small-town family life

To fly to Costa Rica, leaving behind the numbing babble of Los Angeles or the crowded bustle of Western European cities, and to head for a small town here is like leaping backwards to an earlier time. But it is not an earlier time by North American or even European standards; it is somewhere more idealized and far more precious.

In the villages and small towns of Costa Rica there is a connectedness, a familial unity.

On the street, people will nod and say "*Buenos Días*" or "*Adiós*" even to complete strangers passing by. The family is still the main focus in this country Young people usually live at home until they are well into their twenties and thirties, and some even stay at home after getting married.

The pressure of life in the cities is essentially at odds with this national character. But even for busy city people, the extended family is the focus of their social life, and many city families retain close links with their rural past, spending most weekends and holidays at family *fincas* (farms).

branches of foreign companies and in large customer-care call centers.

Costa Rica welcomes foreign investors. There are duty-free zones, tax-free incentives to foreigners setting up industry, and other incentives to build tourist facilities. Several government institutions exist to encourage people to come and view the country's marvels and to invest here.

A fragile world

Costa Rica is a fragile country, sandwiched between politically volatile Nicaragua and Americanized Panamá. Foreign investors are able to buy whatever appears profitable; politi-

US influence

Because the United States is by far the richest neighbor in the hemisphere, and the most powerful broadcaster of image and ideology, Costa Rica knows a great deal more about the United States than the United States knows about Costa Rica. *Ticos* know the names of sports figures, actors and actresses, television personalities, musicians, and politicians from the US. And they are aware of the strange collection of fact and fallacy that viewers derive from watching satellite-relayed North American television shows and subtitled Hollywood movies.

Increasingly, a bilingual education is the key to success for the young generation of *Ticos*, many of whom will have careers working for

cal and economic refugees come in from other parts of Central America; and drug dealers infiltrate the shores and ports of this relatively violence-free country.

Yet somehow you feel that Costa Rica will endure. Though Costa Ricans may not be perfect, they are essentially a democratic, benevolent, and peaceful nation. There is a kind of strength in their fragility. After coming to visit, many people from all over the world are inspired to do whatever they can to ensure the survival and intelligent growth of this vulnerable country and its peaceable people.   ❏

ABOVE: *Ticos* celebrate an elderly lady's birthday on a beach at Playa Carillo.

The Great Immigration Debate

Since the 1980s, Nicaraguans, Costa Rica's major immigrant group, have been blamed for the country's social ills. But that may be changing

An estimated 500,000 Nicaraguans (although some action groups suggest up to a million) work and live in Costa Rica, many of them illegally. Back in the 1980s, most Nicaraguan émigrés were fleeing the poverty, violence, and upheaval of their own war-torn country. In 1998 two natural disasters – a devastating drought and Hurricane Mitch – prompted a new wave of illegal immigration into Costa Rica.

Most of today's newcomers are economic refugees, swelling the numbers of illegals that make up the majority of the country's growing informal sector, with low wages, under-the-table payments, and no access to the country's socialized health service. Many work as maids, nannies, gardeners, or construction workers, or sell snacks or trinkets in the streets. The sugar cane and coffee industries depend on Nicaraguan workers for their harvests.

Not all Nicaraguan refugees are poor, however. Middle- and upper-class supporters of the Somoza regime also came in the 1980s, seeking refuge from Nicaragua's civil war. Many run successful businesses today.

Always a troubling issue in Central America, the immigration debate has become more polemic as the country's economic resources shrink. Shanty towns of Nicaraguan immigrants ring the capital, and many squat, rent, or own farms in the Northern Zone. *Ticos* are often prejudiced against their northern neighbors, who are stereotyped as "dirty," or "violent," and are unjustly accused of committing an inordinate number of crimes. "*Nicas*," as they are known, are often blamed for the perceived social decline of the country and for putting a burden on the health service, schools, and the workplace. Coming from poverty and an unstable society, *Nica* couples tend not to marry, instead finding temporary *compañeros sentimentales* (live-in lovers). Despite their own high divorce and teenage pregnancy rates, *Ticos* are offended by these social arrangements.

ABOVE: Nicaraguan woman and child.

There is also a racial aspect to the low opinion *Ticos* hold of *Nicas*, with their darker skin and their thick accents. The irony that the province of Guanacaste was once part of Nicaragua is lost on most Costa Ricans.

Nicas are generally quieter and less educated than *Ticos*. Most are hard workers and many people prefer to hire Nicaraguans as domestic help, especially since they will work for lower wages. In reality, the immigrants are doing the work many *Ticos* refuse to do, and without them coffee, banana, and sugar production would grind to a halt. On the plus side, Nicaraguans bring with them a love of poetry and music, and a tradition of camaraderie.

In a strange twist of events, *Nicas* are beginning to move up in the estimation of *Ticos*, as more recent immigrants become the new scapegoats for whatever ails the country. *Ticos* now tend to blame newly arrived Colombians, Ecuadoreans, Salvadorans, and Mexicans for the country's startling increase in violent crime, much of it drug-related. Colombians are the largest new immigrant group, many of them arriving in large family groups that pool resources to invest in legitimate businesses. But money launderers and criminal elements have also arrived, along with the legitimate immigrants, and the daily newspapers are full of reports of Colombian drug-gang busts. The sad reality is that more and more Costa Ricans are involved in the drug trade and the violence it brings with it. ❑

THE RISE AND FALL OF SAN JOSÉ

Thanks to the coffee boom, San José enjoyed an architectural golden age in the early 1900s. Remnants of those glory days survive, despite modern urban ills

In 1737, the authorities ordered the construction of a thatch-covered hermitage on the flatlands of the Boca del Monte. It was to be the centerpoint of a new village to bring together the residents of the area, whose small homes were scattered over the valley. From this humble beginning sprang the city of San José.

For its first 39 years, it was still just a village, with mud-covered streets and miserable little houses. Then an official ordered the construction of a tobacco factory, and it was from here that the country's tobacco industry monopoly was administered. It proved to be an activity that brought a certain degree of prosperity.

The coffee boom

Tobacco was a short-lived success, as was cacao. But then came experimentation with a new crop: coffee. It grew with such ease and bore fruit with such abundance that this small Central American colony soon had the wherewithal to leave behind the squalor it had known.

England was interested not only in buying coffee, but also loaning funds, on account, against the next harvest. The surrounding areas filled quickly with orderly rows of coffee plantations, and the people, with their new wealth, sought the city life, transforming San José into a prosperous coffee-growing center.

Beside the town square there was at first only the Church of Mercy and the Town Council building. But other conveniences, created to serve the foreigners who were beginning to arrive, were soon set up. At the end of the 18th century, the Education Building was erected, as was a cathedral, at the front of which stood a beautiful central park, where both Amerindians and farmers of Spanish extraction held

their weekly fairs. Money was minted at the Currency House, and, to support the nascent militia, military quarters were erected.

Social and cultural life

In 1821, Costa Rica gained its independence from the Spanish Empire and became a republic. The small town of San José soon grew into a commercial city, then a capital city, and the newly installed authorities struggled to improve the streets, build bridges, and open roads to the ports. Guards, armed with rusty muskets, patrolled brick-layered streets that were illuminated at night by kerosene lamps.

In the dance parlors of the bourgeoisie, the quadrille was in vogue. An actor would recite poetry and a young lady would play Chopin sonatas amid conversations concerning the price of coffee in London.

Social and economic life was rigidly defined, limited to the descendants of the Spanish who lived in the central part of town where they built large adobe houses with corridors opening onto enclosed vegetable gardens.

Cultural life centered around the Mora Theater, where fourth-rate companies would perform, along with jugglers and an occasional virtuoso musician. The ladies would sit and listen, dressed in their regal dresses, while the gentlemen stood around, robed in their Spanish capes, smoking and engaging in small-talk concerning politics.

Foreign visitors would stay in a rooming house and venture forth to see the town's sights. Some considered the possibility of entering the coffee-export business and others idly took notes for their travel diaries.

The European influence

Earnings from the export of coffee engendered an illustrious bourgeoisie, who traveled to Europe so that their children could be educated in France. When they returned home in San José, the children missed the theaters, the boulevards, the cafés, and the fine architecture of Europe, and as they grew up, they insisted on improving the appearance of their native capital city. As coffee production led to greater prosperity, the leading planter families increased their investments, which inevitably led to rivalries among them, and ever grander plantations were created in an effort to stay ahead of competitors.

Costa Rican architects visited the Universal Exposition of Paris in 1900 and, along with other new and imported ideas, brought back the concept of metal buildings for schools. They imported finely wrought metal plates for walls, steel columns, building crests, and Italian mosaics. The homes of the coffee growers soon began to look like the mansions of the wealthy in New Orleans and Jamaica: French adobe walls; wide, inclined roofs; ornate verandahs with white balustrades, and woodwork cut in the style of gingerbread. Jalousies (louvre shut-

ters) and shades protected the windows made of colored glass through which shone the brilliant tropical sun.

The city's golden age

Toward the end of the 19th century, Monsieur Amon Faiseleau Duplantier, who received the concession to establish the streetcar system, divided his farm on the sunny slopes of the Torres River and there began the business of real-estate sales. The best of San José society fought for the urban lots, building mansions, a few of which still survive in Barrio Amón. Soon the coffee plantations were replaced with

A German scientist, visiting San José during the mid-19th century, wrote: "There is not a building that calls attention for its beauty. The government buildings, the garrison and its gallery, the university and the theater are insignificant structures. The cathedral has an air of negligence and economy. There aren't even any chairs. The president of the republic has to sit with his followers on a wooden bench." By contrast, a French journalist noted: "The presidential palace is an enchanting square building with an internal half-Spanish, half-Arab patio. A circular stair led to the congressional room where a ball was staged for me."

LEFT: detail on San José's Correos, the Post Office Building completed in 1917. **RIGHT:** the National Palace in 1894, San José.

tree-shaded streets and stately residences with large gardens. At the same time, Mother Superior Barthelemy Rich was opening her prestigious girls' high school, the Colegio de Sión, where the daughters of the bourgeoisie received their refined education.

On October 19, 1897, the president and a select audience entered the wide doors of the National Theater to inaugurate the building. That opening night featured a magnificent presentation of Gounod's opera *Faust*. The sumptuous building with its four levels and a floor plan in the shape of a horseshoe was financed from the national budget and by a tax

society, artists, and diplomats; a little beyond, the windows of the Golden Eagle were filled with French wine and liquors and Spanish preserves and fine oils. The *Talabarteria Inglesa* and *La Tiendita* satisfied the most demanding tastes in matters of decoration and leatherwork.

The Ford agency exhibited its 1912 model, which was priced at US$975. It competed with a number of other import agencies, along with booming real-estate businesses that offered farms, lots, beaches, and Victorian residences. The streetcar ran to the limits of the city carrying great numbers of merchants, their employees, and office workers.

In 1863, San José officials tripped a switch and turned on electric lights throughout the city. It was the first city in Latin America, and the third in the world, to be electrified.

paid by the rich coffee growers.

By the early 1900s, the former village had given way to a glowing city, which, even if it did not attain the elegant, urbane layout to which it aspired, had developed a comfortable lifestyle permitted by its growing prosperity.

In front of the National Theater was the elegant Hotel Français. Nearby, the Petite Trianon was a fashionable coffee house favored by high

The other side of the tracks

Not all members of San José society enjoyed a privileged, rose-colored lifestyle. The city had expanded far too rapidly, with vast, obscure, and sad suburbs encircling older areas. The outbreak of World War I and the accompanying fall in coffee demand and prices brought wide-scale unemployment to those who had previously been able to live relatively well, and those who still had jobs worked for salaries that fell well below the poverty level. The Society of Casas Baratas (cheap houses) began the construction of workers' housing units of the type known as *puerta ventana*, where several families would cram into narrow and poorly ventilated rooms.

To the south and near the railroad station from where trains ran to the Pacific coast, there soon appeared barracks, warehouses, and factories, where soap and candles were manufactured. An industrial zone with beer factories, ice-making factories, printing presses, mechanics' shops, and lumber mills slowly began to surround and envelop the elegant urban center. With the advent of cement-built structures, the arrival of the new rich, and the industrialization of the city, there also came the desire to modernize, to create new statements, based largely on North American models, and to destroy vestiges of the past.

San José spilled over and outward in a random fashion. Car ownership permitted the wealthy classes to move their residences from what had now become the depressed inner city to the more desirable, close-in suburbs of Escalante, Los Yoses, Curridabat, Paseo Colón, Sabana, and Rohrmoser. By the 1960s, several satellite town centers evolved, in the style of the suburban United States.

Certainly San José would no longer win any beauty prizes. Although traffic pollution and congestion are constant irritants, there are some conservation efforts under way, including restoring notable buildings and turning down-

End of an era

In the mid-20th century, the city fathers set about "modernizing" San José. Under the pick and sledgehammer, the magnificent National Palace, the Garrison, the National Library, the Union Club, and many lovely residences disappeared. The inner city lost its sense of identity and was invaded by mediocre commercial constructions. Fast highways opened up, breaking up neighborhoods, and no-nonsense North American architectural influences began to replace elegant European ideals.

Left: San José, around 1928.
Above: a street scene in San José today. Despite modernization, some *barrios* remain distinctive.

town streets into pleasant pedestrian zones. Some *barrios* still possess a certain charm: Barrio Amón has some grand mansions, many of them now converted into attractive boutique hotels; Barrio Mexico retains an Art Deco ambiance; and Parque d'España is like a tiny, urban rainforest.

You won't find in San José the monumental scale of Guatemala City nor the cosmopolitan quality of Panamá City; yet there is a vital quality to the hustle and sheer movement of the place, along with tangible remains of the coffee-growing bourgeoisie who, in their heyday, enriched the city with neoclassical architecture, European elegance, and whimsical Caribbean-colonial style. ❏

NATIONAL PARKS

With so much of its land under protected status, Costa Rica is the flag bearer for the forces of conservation. But, while many battles have been won, the war goes on

An astonishing 26 percent of Costa Rica is designated as national park, biological reserve, wildlife refuge, or some other category of protected area, either private or public. Increasingly, individuals and groups are purchasing tracts of Costa Rican wilderness in order to preserve it. And so, more than a quarter of the country has been set aside in some form or another by human beings to protect it from the potential exploitation and ravages of other human beings.

Heroes and villains

The story of the creation of Costa Rica's parks and protected areas is one of drama, ideals, and sacrifice. One of the first in a long lineage of international protectors was Nils Olaf Wessberg, who, with his wife, came to Costa Rica from Sweden in 1955 and bought a farm in Nicoya near Montezuma. Fervent naturalists, they built a home of palm leaves, determined to live in harmony with the land.

Yet even in this remote corner of the world they did not escape what many call progress, and they watched, dismayed, as the destruction of virgin forest took place at Cabo Blanco, on the Nicoya Peninsula. Nils became an activist, working ardently to raise money to purchase the land and thereby preserve it.

After three years and 1,000 pages of letters, he raised the US$30,000 he needed to buy the 1,200 hectares (3,000 acres) that constitute the Cabo Blanco Strict Nature Reserve. Today, a plaque inside the park is a memorial to Nils, who, while trying to establish another park in the Osa Peninsula, was murdered by those who had vested interests in preventing his work. In 2004, a new reserve near Montezuma was

NATURAL WONDERLAND

Costa Rica's natural abundance translates into many astounding statistics. In a space that occupies less than 0.03 percent of the earth's surface are 4 percent of all of the scientifically identified plant and animal species on the planet. In total this numbers somewhere around 500,000 species of flora and fauna including: more than 300,000 species of insects (some the size of small mammals!) including thousands of species of moths and butterflies; over 1,200 species of orchids; 800 ferns (more than in all North America and Mexico); 212 species of mammals; more than 850 species of birds; 200 species of reptiles (half of which are snakes).

established and named after his wife, Karen Mogensen Fischer.

Another committed individual, Mario Boza, a student of Costa Rican forestry, was able to put his conservation ideas to work in the creation of Santa Rosa, the country's first national park. In 1969, the Forestry Law trumpeted the creation of the Santa Rosa National Monument and established the National Parks Department. But with little funding and few personnel to enforce it, the new law went unrecognized, and the land continued to be used as it had been in the past, as grazing pasture for cattle and as the homesteads of slash-and-burn squatters.

also to children, young people, and adults who should not be denied the joy of direct contact with nature in its pristine state. All of this represents the contribution of the Costa Rican people to peace among men and goodwill among nations."

The economy versus the ecology

As admirable as Costa Rica's conservation initiatives may be, the environmental efforts of this Developing World country are counter to its economic development. Parks are, after all, expensive. Urban sprawl – resulting from the concentration of more than 60 percent of

Unable to halt the destruction through bureaucratic channels, Boza went to the press. "Santa Rosa in Flames; National Park Being Ruined" read the headlines. The public was outraged and park authorities were duly authorized to move out the squatters and protect the land from the encroachment of livestock and agriculture.

Rodrigo Carazo, president of Costa Rica from 1978 to 1982, described the national parks as "splendid natural laboratories, which we offer to the international scientific community and

the country's population in the most fertile area of the country, the Central Valley – covers the land with concrete and asphalt, and it continues at a frenzied pace. Extensive soil erosion, an effect of the rapid deforestation of the country by the destructive use of land for cattle grazing, causes a phenomenal loss of topsoil.

Threats to the watershed, as well as the nation's extensive hydroelectric system, are another unwelcome result. Uncontrolled dumping of toxic waste from the banana, coffee, and fertilizer industries has contaminated coastal and inland waters. Agricultural chemicals used in pesticides, once employed only on the traditional export crops of bananas and sugar,

PRECEDING PAGES: Tortuguero Park's canals and forest. **LEFT:** white-faced capuchin monkey, Manuel Antonio National Park. **ABOVE:** crocodile in the Tarcoles River.

are now being used by vegetable and flower growers; pesticide poisoning has resulted in, among other things, the virtual elimination of large species such as armadillos and crocodiles along the Tempisque River. And the crazed rush to feed the demands from North America and Europe for exotic plywood is resulting in the deforestation of the land surrounding the magnificent Tortuguero canals. And so it goes on.

In its understandable attempts to imitate much of North America and the rest of the developed world, the country is experiencing the inevitable conflict between consumption

Scraping tons of stones out of rivers to build a new highway in the remote Osa Peninsula is killing the goose that laid the golden egg. As river habitats are devastated, the road to bring tourists closer to nature is destroying nature.

and conservation. Trying to balance these opposing forces are armies of international naturalists. Environmentalists and ecologists from all over the world come to Costa Rica to join the side of "the good guys." Today, Costa Rica has environmental experts in abundance, and dozens of international conservation organizations working on behalf of the country's ecological efforts.

Conservation by education

Believing that true conservation can only be accomplished by the will of the people, the national parks system has made a great effort to educate the *Ticos* who are most affected by the transfer of land into protected parks. The cooperation of these people is necessary for the parks' survival. For example, the traditional custom of hunting species for whom the parks are a refuge needs to be changed. Large animals, such as pumas and jaguars, require an extensive amount of free territory in order to survive. Convincing people not to kill them, or the wild pigs that large cats depend on for food, is an enormous and often thankless task.

Ecotourists and traditional travelers to Costa Rica support the national parks system by coming to visit, paying park fees, and staying at the private reserves, as well as through their work and contributions to the many conservation foundations working in Costa Rica.

Some eco-projects even cross Costa Rica's borders. La Amistad Biosphere is a Unesco-designated reserve that spans the Panamanian border. A new biosphere to the north, called *Agua y Paz* (Water and Peace), includes vast tracts of Costa Rica's northern wetlands and Nicaragua's San Juan River. These are just two examples of the potential that national parks have to engender cooperative international relations.

Future perfect?

Yet is this good news good enough? The fact that Costa Rica is thought of as a safe, quiet democratic place is perhaps both the nation's greatest blessing and greatest problem. Ironically the wealthier nations of the world may not be sufficiently moved to donate aid, attention, and media coverage to such a gentle democratic place, when there are so many other, highly visible, demands from places that seem more needy.

It is not clear as yet which side will prevail: the conservationists or the forces demanding economic development at all costs; it is still up in the air whether Costa Rica will become a successful environmental model or just another failed experiment in ecological idealism. ❏

LEFT: walking trail in Monteverde Cloud Forest Reserve, in the country's northwest.

A Tropical Forest Watcher's Guide

To spot wildlife in Costa Rica's dense forests and impenetrable jungles you'll need to walk softly and learn to see in a new way

Don't be disappointed if, on your first few visits to the tropical rainforest, you fail to see any of the hundreds of bird species, monkeys, and sloths that live there. In fact, your first impression of the forest will probably be of a great green wall of vegetation, not the spectacular variety of colorful animals you had hoped to see. However, be assured that a great diversity of organisms does inhabit the tropical forest, and their very survival depends not least on how successful they are at hiding from predators, which include humans.

Before setting off into the forest, do your homework. Study specialist guidebooks that describe animals living in the area and familiarize yourself with such identifying characteristics as color, shape, and behavior.

Determine the time of day or night when animals are most active. A good pair of binoculars is essential; they can also be used backwards as a powerful magnifying glass. Take every opportunity to charter a boat for lake or river trips; they are always worth the investment.

Observe safety tips before proceeding. Remember that even though it may look like Disneyland, it isn't. Here snakes slither, insects bite, and animals may (in very rare cases) become aggressive. Notify someone of your intentions: where you are going, when you plan to arrive, when to expect you back. Take water, insect repellent, flashlight, sunscreen, umbrella or rain poncho, and a hat.

Look before you touch, step, sit, or lean. Scan the trail for slippery rocks, mud, downed trees, ants, and snakes. Then move ahead while you search the canopy for animals. Continually shift your gaze. Don't wander off into the woods following a bird without looking carefully where you step. Snakes are rare but potentially lethal. Antivenin serum is available throughout the country. Try not to panic, and try to remember the snake's colors.

A general guideline: forest wildlife-viewing is easiest in the early morning and late afternoon, and

---

RIGHT: birdwatchers in Monteverde Cloud Forest.

most productive along habitat "edges" next to rivers, beaches, open fields, roads, and trail heads. Look for shapes, colors, and behaviors that stand out and do not appear to "fit" the design of the forest vegetation. In the dry season deciduous forests lose their leaves, opening the canopy for viewing; and shrinking water sources are frequented by thirsty animals.

Seasoned forest-watchers, like legendary animal trackers, are alert to easily overlooked clues that indicate the presence of animals or birds present in the forest. Things rustling or dropping from the forest canopy (especially on a windless day) and unexplained noises are often a sign that an animal is

nearby. Seeds or leaves dropping from above are probably caused by parrots, monkeys, or sloths in the canopy. Fruits, nuts, seed husks, or leaf fragments on the trail mean a food tree is nearby and perhaps sustaining feeding animals or birds.

Large, dark shapes in tree crevices might be sleeping sloths, anteaters, or monkeys. Logs on river banks could be crocodiles. Rotten tree sections are often home to amphibians, insects, fungi, and mosses. Holes in trees might contain precious birds' nests.

When you've developed skills in seeing and identifying some of the plants and animals, think about what they eat and why they live where they do. Soon you will begin to understand the complexity that makes the forest so mesmerizing. ❏

A PASSION FOR PLANTS

From the beautiful to the bizarre, Costa Rica's many species of flora offer a vibrant introduction to the kaleidoscopic plant wealth of the tropics

Many visitors' first contact with Costa Rica's spectacular plant life comes at the hotel reception desk, which is often adorned by a vase of heliconias – strikingly angular red or orange flowers, also known as lobster claws, which grow in the country's forests.

Heliconias are typical of the outsize blooms that flourish in Costa Rica's warm and humid climate. As a rule of thumb, the biggest and most robust flowers – including heliconias – are pollinated by birds or bats, while more delicate flowers are pollinated by insects. This second category includes most of the country's orchids – another group of plants for which Costa Rica is justly famous.

Costa Rica has a prodigious number of native plants, including approximately 1,000 different species of trees. To add to this botanical richness, many other species have been introduced from different parts of the tropics, for food or for ornament. Food plants include bananas, which arrived in the early 1500s; coffee, mangoes, and sugar cane; and also the African oil palm, first cultivated on a large scale in the 1960s. Many of the showiest garden and road-side plants are from distant parts of the world. Among the most eye-catching are jacarandas, South American trees that produce a mass of purplish-blue flowers.

ABOVE: colorful berries nestle inside the elongated bracts of a *Heliconia stricta*, one of 30 or so native helonica species. Some hummingbirds have bills long enough to reach the nectar deep inside.

BELOW: the white *costus* bloom can last up to a month. The plant is also known as "spiral ginger" for the way the stem swirls to follow sunlight – it is, however, a separate species from true ginger.

LEFT: the scepter-like flower of the waxy torch ginger is also called emperor's rod.

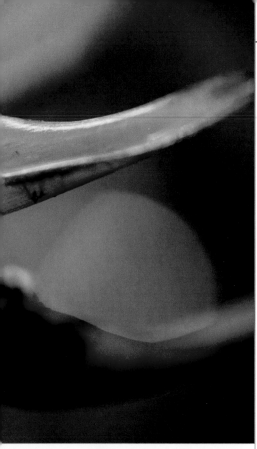

THE PLANTS THAT GROW ON PLANTS

Costa Rica's forests are home to an immense variety of epiphytes, or plants that grow on the shoulders of other plants, often far above the ground. Epiphytes manage this remarkable feat by collecting rainwater and by scavenging nutrients from any organic debris that is washed or blown their way.

Of all the country's epiphytes, bromeliads are the most conspicuous. Tank bromeliads collect water by funneling it into a central reservoir formed by their leaves. These plants can measure more than 1 meter (3ft) across, and their tanks can hold several liters of water. Other epiphytes, including most orchids, have specialized roots that absorb water and nutrients before they have a chance to evaporate or drain away.

In forests, a different collection of plants – including philodendrons and the *Monstera deliciosa*, also called the Swiss-cheese plant for its huge leaves pitted with a pattern of holes – start life rooted in the ground, but soon head for the sunlit treetops. In the wild, the Swiss-cheese plant and its relatives have a bizarre growth pattern. If the plant climbs up a tree that turns out to be too short, it simply drops back to the forest floor and searches for another likely, taller, host.

ABOVE: humid, dense forests harbor more than 800 species of wild ferns, ranging from low-lying plants blanketing the rainforest understory, to tree ferns that can soar as high as 25 meters (82ft). Costa Rica also exports a huge number of cultivated ferns, used to adorn flower bouquets worldwide.

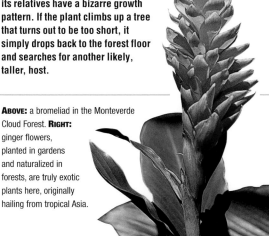

ABOVE: a bromeliad in the Monteverde Cloud Forest. **RIGHT:** ginger flowers, planted in gardens and naturalized in forests, are truly exotic plants here, originally hailing from tropical Asia.

THE SPORTS SCENE

Activity holidays are booming in Costa Rica. Getting wet – whether by spilling out of a raft or falling off a board – is usually part of the game

Sport is a much-loved pastime in Costa Rica, especially the national sport of *fútbol* (soccer). *Ticos* are always happy to have visiting foreigners join them in watching an important game of soccer. Personal fitness is also popular and you will see joggers and cyclists puffing up impossibly challenging hills in the Central Valley in the early morning. On weekends, enormous La Sabana Park, on the west side of San José, is filled with thousands of athletes: soccer teams, basketball players, swimmers, volleyball players, rollerblade teams, and baseball enthusiasts. On the Central Valley plateau, private golf and tennis clubs with complete health spas cater for wealthy suburbanites.

The country's tidal wave of water sports, however, is the main attraction for an increasing number of visitors who come to Costa Rica to surf isolated beaches, to windsurf on magnificent Lake Arenal, and to experience some of the best whitewater rafting in the world.

Whitewater rafting

The brightly colored inflatable raft rushes down a chute of cascading white water, then plunges over and through waves that are nearly 2 meters (6ft) high. Those in the raft gleefully dig their paddles into the frothing water, and then shriek with delight as they maneuver the raft between boulders the size of small cars. After a pulse-racing few minutes, the rafters reach a calm spot on the river, an eddy, from which they can pause and look up from the roaring river course to inhale and appreciate

PRECEDING PAGES: kayaking at Puerto Jimenez. **LEFT:** surf's up at Playa Tamarindo. **RIGHT:** beach football.

MAKING A SPLASH

Sadly, every year whitewater accidents do happen and even the most experienced rafters, caught in a powerful river eddy, can drown. So choose your trip according to your level of expertise and find an outfitter that sticks to all the safety precautions: life vest, helmets, and accompanying safety/rescue kayaks. Before you enter the water in the raft you should have a practice drill to ensure everyone understands the instructions (often shouted over the thundering water). You should also check your travel insurance policy to ensure that you are covered for rafting. River water is unsafe to drink, so if you do tumble in, keep your mouth closed!

the beauty of the Reventazón Gorge. The scenery along the wide river includes the colossally broad panorama of the canyon, rolling fields of coffee, sugar cane, wild grasses, and radiant flowers blooming unexpectedly in the canopy of trees overhanging the river.

Costa Rica has more accessible whitewater rivers and rapids than any other place in the world. It is, of course, the unique geography of the country that makes it one of the world's great destinations for whitewater rafting. To have the right kind of rapids, you need a river that descends in a fairly steep gradient. The four mountain chains that wind down the axis of Costa Rica provide the perfect conditions. The Talamanca range and the Cordillera Central have many steep, wide, perennial rivers that are regularly supplied with bounteous rainfall.

The variety of these rivers provides an enormous range of wilderness experiences. Some offer idyllic float trips through luscious landscapes with abundant wildlife, while others contain explosive whitewater and raging rapids that challenge the most experienced rafter.

The Sarapiquí River flows through the lowlands of Heredia, providing stunning scenery and exceptional whitewater. About a two-hour

WHITEWATER RAFTING – THE MAJOR PLAYERS

Whitewater rafting, also known as river running, offers anyone in moderately good health an exhilarating way to observe the scenery and wildlife of the country. Several professional outfitters in Costa Rica will provide all of the necessities: life preservers, helmets, and rafts.

You can be assured that you are in good hands: guides have been through training in the classroom and on the rivers. Most Costa Rican head guides have been trained at whitewater schools in the US, and many have worked with the world's best.

The first whitewater exploration of Costa Rican rivers was made by a company called Costa Rica Expeditions on the Reventazón River in 1978.

The following year the same company pioneered commercial whitewater rafting in Central America. Ríos Tropicales, founded in 1985, started rafting on the Sarapiquí and Sucio rivers, and local graduates of their kayaking school have represented Costa Rica at the World Championships of Whitewater Racing. Aventuras Naturales is the third major company in this field. Others of varying expertise have also sprung up more recently in San José, Turrialba, and elsewhere.

Many of these organizations offer day-trip packages from San José, including transportation, breakfast and lunch, and all the necessary gear, at very reasonable rates. *(For details of rafting companies see page 287.)*

drive from San José, the upper portion of the Sarapiquí contains moderate rapids that are suitable for novice paddlers. On the calm, lower section of the river, the jungle closes in and gives rafters the opportunity to relax for a while and view the monkeys, otters, and abundant waterfowl of the area.

The head of the Reventazón River is a 90-minute drive from San José and offers some of Costa Rica's most turbulent whitewater and spectacular scenery. Rafting companies run four sections of the river. The first, which is just below the hydroelectric power plant of Cachí, is steep and contains continuous rapids of moderate to high difficulty. The second section, from Tucurrique to Angostura, is suited to novice paddlers and provides splendid views of the surrounding volcanoes.

The final two sections of the Reventazón, from Angostura to Siquirres, have some of the most challenging whitewater in the world.

Many consider Costa Rica's most famous whitewater river to be the Pacuare. Accessible from the Central Valley via Turrialba, it passes through a deep gorge in dense jungle that contains rich flora and wildlife. Most groups spend two or more days descending this river from Tres Equis to Siquirres, and camping in riverside sites within view of thundering waterfalls and great flocks of birds.

This is the gentlest of all Costa Rica's rafting rivers and is ideal for rafters who are also keen birdwatchers. In the adjacent Palo Verde National Park, more than 300 species of birds have been observed, and many can be seen from rafts on the Corobicí. Because the river's perennial flow is controlled by a dam on Lake Arenal, it becomes an oasis that attracts birds, monkeys, and lizards during the dry season in Guanacaste.

Surfing

Costa Rica's unending beaches are a fixture on the international surfing circuit, and attract hordes of surfers from North America, Australia, and Europe. These aficionados generally concur that the quality of Costa Rica's surf is firmly in the top four – along with California, Hawaii, and Australia. Moreover, they find that the surf

---

LEFT: almost anyone can experience the adrenaline rush of whitewater rafting. **RIGHT:** surfers on Playa Grande, one of the beaches on the Nicoya Peninsula.

here is plentiful and relatively uncrowded, the water temperature is a comfortable 27°C (80°F) throughout the year, and there is still the chance of experiencing the rare thrill of having a wave all to yourself, just offshore from a pristine and empty beach.

Costa Rica is blessed with masses of beaches: there are some 200km (120 miles) of Caribbean coast and 1,000km (630 miles) of Pacific shore, sculpted with sandy beaches, rocky headlands, offshore reefs, and river mouths close to coastal jungles.

There is also a large number of open beaches that are exposed to ocean swells coming from

many directions. However, much of the coastline is removed from civilization, so there may be no facilities, food, or emergency services of any kind within many kilometers. A four-wheel-drive vehicle is often essential, especially during the rainy season.

Popular surf spots

With hundreds of kilometers of coastline, there are, of course, many undiscovered, nameless surfing beaches. But among the favorites are the following:

Jacó, bordering a Central Pacific town southeast of the Gulf of Nicoya, is less than two hours by car or bus from San José. It is a long, silty beach trapped between two rocky points, with waves that are particularly good for body surfing or boogie boarding. The surf is easily accessible, just beyond the patios of many of the high-rise hotels and *cabinas* that line the beach. For non-surfers, however, the beach is overdeveloped, unattractive, and the currents and rip tides are strong.

Just under 3km (2 miles) to the south of Jacó is Playa Hermosa, site of many a surfing competition. It is possible to hitchhike, rent a bike, or take a bus around the point south of Jacó to this beach. South from Jacó to Playa Panamá are many superb unexploited surfing spots. North of Jacó, near Puntarenas, the sandspit at the mouth of the Barranca River produces what is reputed to be one of the world's longest left-breaking waves.

Like Jacó, Dominical is another major surfing beach town, farther down the South Pacific coast. It is much less built up, with a laid-back, funky atmosphere, and a long break with waves to suit all levels.

Far to the north, the beaches of Guanacaste province have some of the best surf anywhere, particularly during the dry season when steady offshore winds help to create the waves. The break near Roca de la Bruja *(see page 193)* at Playa Naranjo is one of the most spectacular

SWELLS AND BREAKS

Wave-making conditions are complex in Costa Rica. On the Pacific coast, swells originating from storms in the north and central Pacific Ocean occur frequently from November through March. South swells from distant storms prevail for the remainder of the year.

The beaches of the Pacific are shaped by sediment that is carried to the sea by major rivers. The silt migrates up and down the coast on strong onshore currents. Sandbars produce beach breaks with long and fast right and left rides along much of the coast. Sandspits form at the river mouths, and create long, and often clean, point breaks. But because the sand floor is unstable, bars and sandspits change according to the season. Tides and

winds are other factors that will have a strong influence on wave shape.

From December to April, large swells caused by winds and storms originating in the Caribbean arrive at Costa Rica's east-coast beaches. The steep, fast-moving waves break over shallow coral reefs, often in shapes and sizes that rival those of the north shore of Oahu in Hawaii. Smaller west swells from trade winds originating in the West Indies prevail from June through August. The only time when there is generally little or no surf on the east coast is September through November.

To check on prevailing conditions before you set out, visit www.surfingcr.net.

waves; the number of surfers is officially limited because it is in Santa Rosa National Park. Surfers need to book ahead with one of the many local surf shops and travel by boat to this surfing spot.

The Nicoya Peninsula to the south of Guanacaste is scalloped with beaches, notably Playa Avellanas and Playa Negra; many of them have rideable waves. Some of the best surfing in the country is found in remote Pavones on the Golfo Dulce coast.

Near Limón, 2½ hours east of San José, Playa Bonita is a good, popular surfing beach. About one hour south of Limón, Puerto Viejo, a tranquil Caribbean village, is the site of the sometimes awesome Salsa Brava, a surf break that has acquired an international reputation. From December through March, consistent, large north swells hit the coral reef with tremendous force.

Windsurfing

Since Costa Rica held its first windsurfing contest on Lake Arenal in the early 1990s, the country has been recognized as an outstanding destination for international windsurfers. With strong trade winds whipping the picturesque lake into a sea of whitewater and waves, it compares favorably with the world's best windsurfing locations, such as the Columbia River Gorge in Oregon and Maui in the Hawaiian Islands (with the only caveat that the waves are sometimes rather choppy).

Almost every other day between January and April, consistent winds of around 20 knots whip the waves to a meter-high swell along the length of Arenal, creating excellent short-board sailing conditions. For the rest of the season, lighter winds predominate and are ideal for longboard sailing.

Lake Arenal is not a suitable place for beginners. Sideshore winds are consistent and blow across the full width of the lake. During high winds, steep swells provide the right conditions to practice acrobatic speed runs, jumps, and loops. The water is a comfortable 18–21°C (64–70°F) all year round. Hotel Tilawa and River Rock Lodge are good places to hire equipment.

LEFT: surf school on Jacó Beach, which is famous for its waves. RIGHT: strong winds at Bahia Salinas bay, close to Nicaragua's border, attract kite-boarders.

If you are looking for the "funnel effect," try windswept Bahía Salinas, near La Cruz, in the far northwest of the country.

Golf

Golf is a popular game in Costa Rica and new golf courses are popping up all over the country. The Hotel Cariari and Country Club, northwest of San José, was the country's first championship course and hosts many tournaments. A less pricey option in the Central Valley is the scenic Valle del Sol public course, designed by golf architect Tracy May, in Santa Ana, a western suburb of San José. Since the 1990s, other

famous golf architects have designed courses in Costa Rica. There are excellent courses on the Nicoya Peninsula, including the par-72 Garra de León, designed by Robert Trent Jones Jr in the Paradisus Meliá Playa Conchal Hotel, and the par-72 courses at Hacienda Pinilla, designed by Mike Young. The newest, and most expensive, course is at the Four Seasons Papagayo Resort at the north end of the peninsula. There is also a Ted Robinson-designed course at the Marriott Los Sueños Hotel in the Central Pacific zone.

There are some fairly good 9-hole courses, too: at Tango Mar, which overlooks the Gulf of Nicoya; the private Costa Rica Country Club in Escazú; and the Los Reyes Country Club in La Guácima, which welcomes guests.   ❏

BIG FINS AND FRESH FISH

Costa Rica is a paradise for both fresh and saltwater fishing. It's quiet, too: you will run into other fishing folk only if you really want to

The king of game fish swims calmly toward Costa Rica's Caribbean coast. At around 70kg (150lbs), he fears no predators, except sharks, as he cruises toward the mouth of the Colorado River. Where the tarpon has come from is a mystery. He could have been off the coasts of Florida, South America, or West Africa. Or he may have been in local waters the entire time.

But now he is with an ocean school of 100 fish of the same size. Suddenly they spot a school of *titi*, a small, sardine-like fish, and chase them to the surface. The tarpon cause an acre of the Caribbean to explode as they churn the water and devour the *titi*. If you are lucky enough to witness this scene, it is simply a matter of casting into the chaos to get into contact with what many consider the most exciting aquatic quarry on earth.

Tarpon enter the river mouths all along the Caribbean coast of Costa Rica, from the Colorado River in the north to the Sixaola River, which forms the border with Panamá. In most rivers, they swim a few hundred meters upstream in search of food, and then return to the sea. Only in the Río Colorado do they keep going upriver, following the *titi*, in an incredible journey of more than 200km (124 miles) to Lake Nicaragua, close to the Pacific Ocean.

Freshwater "lakes"

As the tarpon begin their long swim, they pass a series of thin fingers of water stretching northward almost to the border with Nicaragua. These freshwater "lakes" are full of a variety of exotic fish that make great sport on light tackle. One of the most fascinating is the alligator gar, known in Costa Rica as *gaspar*. Looking like a throwback to prehistoric times, this fish has

RULES OF ENGAGEMENT

In tarpon fishing, the rules of angling must be suspended or reversed, or there's no chance of success. The first trick that goes against all that you've learned is to retrieve the lure with the rod tip low – at water level or, better yet, in the water. That way, when it's time to set the hook, the rod tip can be brought up and backwards in a long arc. The maneuver must be repeated rapidly at least three times with a force that would tear the hook out of the mouth of almost any other fish. The success rate of experts is to land about one out of every 10 hooked, though try telling that to your friends when you go back empty-handed after a day's tarpon fishing.

a long, narrow snout as full of sharp teeth as an alligator's. Its coffee-colored body is covered with tough skin and large scales. Its tail is broad and powerful. The meat of the *gaspar* is firm and sweet, not unlike shrimp. But the eggs should never be eaten as they are highly toxic.

The tarpon is not alone in his upriver swims. Snook also make the long journey following the *titi*. And following them all are bull sharks.

The sharks, like the tarpon, continue all the way to Lake Nicaragua. Their presence has led many people to believe there are "freshwater sharks" in the lake. Actually, they are just visitors from the faraway Caribbean.

The Río Frío

An exception to this rule of relative inaccessibility is the Río Frío, which passes right through "downtown" Los Chiles – an approximate three-hour drive, on paved roads, from San José.

The Río Frío is full of tarpon, snook, white drum, gar, and other exotic species. Some people fish right from the municipal landing in Los Chiles; others with boats launch them there and venture north or south. For those who don't have a boat, it is possible to rent a *panga* (barge), driven by a knowledgeable local person who also acts as a guide. These *pangas* can be found at the municipal landing.

Snook are the mainstay of sport fishing in Costa Rica. Large snook are plentiful along all parts of the Caribbean and Pacific coasts, as well as in rivers throughout the country.

All along Río San Juan are lesser rivers flowing into it. At the confluence of the San Juan with the Colorado, Sarapiquí, San Carlos, Infernito, Pocosol, Medio Queso, and Frío rivers there is some excellent angling for tarpon and snook. None of these rivers is heavily fished and all require a bit of enterprise to reach. But those who make the effort are usually well rewarded.

LEFT: a shoal of tarpon. **ABOVE:** a fisherman shows off his catch: a dolphin fish, also known as "dorado" and "mahi-mahi."

ROLLING FOR AIR

Tarpon are one of the few fish that are capable of taking in air directly through the mouth rather than by filtering water through their gills. This ability is necessary for survival because these big, active fish need more oxygen than they can get from the waters that they sometimes inhabit.

This method of direct breathing accounts for the phenomenon known as "rolling," when the tarpon come to the surface and flop onto their sides while gulping air. This unusual adaptation also makes it possible for tarpon to swim freely between saltwater and freshwater, and even in oxygen-depleted waters.

Some tarpon, as they swim up the Río San Juan, apparently take diversions far into the side rivers. This is the case with the Río Frío. Thirty minutes by boat south of Los Chiles is the convergence of the Río Frío and the Río Sabogal. Here tarpon up to 45kg (100lbs) seem to be present at all times.

Every morning and every evening the giant fish, too big to be in a narrow river, leap high into the air, re-entering the water with a thundering splash. It is a sight every fishing enthusiast would love to see. It can also be one of the most frustrating experiences imaginable, because there are days when these fish just

won't take a lure. However, just the sight is well worth the trip – and there is always a good chance of hooking into one of them.

More river fish

The Río Frío, as well as most of the other rivers of Costa Rica, is full of a fish often overlooked by anglers. The *machacha*, a silvery speedster, is an unusual fish in that it is primarily a vegetarian. *Machacha* can often be found under the overhang of *chilemate* trees waiting for ripe fruit to fall into the water. Costa Ricans fish for them using pieces of banana or tomato, but *machacha* will also take small lures or flies, running, changing directions, diving and leaping into the air. They can grow up to 9kg (20lbs)

and 1–2kg (2–5lb) fish are common and offer great sport. Their flesh is bony but tasty.

Up a few of the rivers that feed into the San Juan, particularly the Sarapiquí, you can find the *bobo*, a difficult but rewarding quarry. These fish, which weigh up to 14kg (30lbs), feed in shallow, fast-moving water. They are relatives of the salt-water mullet and are pure vegetarians. They can be taken on small spinners and they offer great sport as they fight hard through the rapids.

In these Atlantic-slope rivers you can also find other exotic species including the *mojarra*, a strong, sharp-toothed, brightly colored pan fish resembling a perch on steroids, and related to the sun fish.

For land-lubbers who prefer to eat fish rather than catch them, the mountains south of San José abound in stocked trout *lagos* (artificial ponds), where you can sink a line baited with *masa* (dough), land your trout in minutes and have it cleaned, scaled, and cooked on the spot.

> You can buy your fishing license, required by law, at most fishing-boat docks. Most sport fishing operators will include it in the cost of a charter trip. The license costs $24 and is good for a year.

Sea angling

For most people, fishing off the Pacific coast of Costa Rica means angling for sailfish, marlin, and tuna. All along the Pacific coast there are boatloads of sport fishing operations.

Operators in the Gulf of Papagayo enjoy the most productive sailfishing in the world. Sails here are not the scrawny Atlantic variety. They are hefty, healthy Pacific sailfish averaging over 45kg (100lbs). Fought on a 7kg (15lb) line or less, they offer fantastic sport and a spectacular show full of graceful jumps. Laws require that all sails (except record catches) are released, and fishermen generally respect these rules.

In recent years, marlin have been discovered along most of the Pacific coast. Offshore, *mahi-mahi*, tuna, and rainbow runner are plentiful. Offshore reefs also offer great fishing for snapper, including the prized *cubbera*.

Often overlooked are the fishing possibilities straight from the Pacific beaches. Every beach on the Pacific coast offers the chance to take various types of jack and drum, as well as trophy-sized snook from the surf. Mouths of rivers and streams often attract congregations of snook. Casting from rocks often locates snapper and roosterfish.

Roosterfish abound on Costa Rica's Pacific coast. The colorful, wide-bodied, and powerful fish with the long, spiky dorsal fin that gives it its name, is particularly plentiful in the water surrounding the rocks in Puntarenas or the nearby Pacific port of Caldera. Once hooked, the roosterfish raises its "comb" and speeds away across the surface, offering a unique show and fight.

Neither ocean nor lake, the Golfo Dulce is a deep, tropical fjord in Costa Rica's South-

guapote is to a bass what a diesel is to a model train; it is not a light tackle fish. Once hooked, it heads for cover with the force of a rhinoceros and if it gets there it will almost certainly cut the line on underbrush.

The *guapote* is a spectacular fish. A breeding male has large bulbous protrusions above the eyes that "light up", displaying many colors on its flank. *Guapote* in Lake Arenal, the main place where they are fished, weigh up to 9kg (20lbs) or more, although a 7kg (15lb) fish is about as much as most can handle. The *guapote pinto*, or painted *guapote*, can be found in rivers that flow into the San Juan. ❑

ern Zone. Sport fishers here chase marlin and swordfish offshore, and find plenty of snapper, snook, and yellowfin tuna inshore.

The *guapote*

The star inhabitant of Costa Rica's few lakes is the *guapote*. Some people call this fish the "rainbow bass," although taxonomically it has nothing at all to do with bass. The only real similarity to bass is in the way it is fished: casting or flipping plugs or spinner baits. Once hooked, the resemblance is soon forgotten. The

LEFT: a small tarpon.
ABOVE: a sailfish caught off the Osa Peninsula, southwest Costa Rica.

TROUT AND MACHÍN

Wild trout have never done well in Costa Rica (although farmed trout do very well indeed). Despite numerous attempts to stock them in high mountain streams, they have never really thrived. Trout fishing is possible in the breathtaking mountains between San José and San Isidro del General, such as the Río Savegre in the San Gerardo de Dota valley area. Even if the fish are somewhat small, the scenery alone makes a day spent here worthwhile.

If you cannot find any trout then a good substitute is the *machín*, a fish that is found in rivers where trout would be expected. It puts up a vigorous fight, very similar to that of a trout.

GOING TO EXTREMES

More and more sensation-seeking visitors are challenging themselves by taking the plunge and trying out thrilling, new adventure sports

If even whitewater rafting seems too tame for you, Costa Rica serves up other out-of-the-ordinary exciting activities that will get your adrenaline going.

The most popular and the most readily accessible adventure sport is zip-lining, also known as a canopy tour. The original canopy tour was built in Monteverde and involved donning a waist harness, climbing inside a huge, hollowed-out *matapalo* (strangler fig) tree up to a wooden platform, hooking your harness onto a wire cable, then stepping off the platform, perhaps 30 meters (100ft) off the ground, into thin air and whizzing along, suspended from the cable, to the next platform in the tree tops. The idea is a refinement of the method used by biologists to get up into the canopy to perform research. Some tours retain that focus on natural history and the chance to get close-up looks at life in the canopy. But most zip lines today are focused on fun and thrills. Sky Trek, the highest and longest zip line, also operates in Monteverde, but with the screams of people zipping through the air at up to 48km (30 miles) per hour, there isn't much wildlife sticking around to be observed.

ABOVE: a serene zip-liner shows perfect form as she glides through the forest, suspended from a cable. After the initial ride, it doesn't take long before many zip-liners start upping the thrill factor by zipping backwards or performing aerial aerobatics.

Taking that first step into thin air is quite a thrill. Cables, harnesses, and safety equipment have to meet high government standards, but you are still at the mercy of human error, so choose a canopy tour operator who talks a lot about safety measures and gives careful, complete instructions to neophytes.

RIGHT: ready to fly through the air on a Tarzan swing.

WETTER, WILDER, AND HIGHER

For a wet and wild adventure, try waterfall rappeling (*see above*). Instead of zipping along a cable, you step off the top of a waterfall and rappel your way down, attached to ropes secured by guides at both the top and bottom of the waterfall. It takes a fair bit of courage to take that first step backward, but the thrill is worth it, and you stay cool thanks to waterfall spray.

Other tree-top adventures include climbing 30-meter (100ft) trees, using ropes, or spending a night in a tree-top platform. Hacienda Barú on the South Pacific coast offers both in its 330-hectare (815-acre) nature reserve (www.haciendabaru.com).

If you are looking to go higher than the tree tops, take a parasailing tour with Aguas Azules (www.costaricaparasailing.com), sailing over the ocean and Manuel Antonio National Park, suspended from a parachute kept aloft by a fast motorboat. Or if you would rather leave the flying to someone else, step into a two-person ultralight, fixed-wing plane and let the pilot take you on a thrilling bird's-eye view of ocean and jungle. Skyline de Costa Rica (www.flyultralight.com) offers ultralight tours in Uvita on the South Pacific coast and near Samara on the Nicoya Peninsula.

ABOVE: adventurers with no fear of flying can take to the skies in a piloted ultra-light (microlight) for breathtaking views.
LEFT: a tree-climber dons a safety harness for a different kind of canopy adventure. With the help of ascenders, she will scale a rope 35 meters (113ft) up into a tree at Hacienda Barú Lodge.

ABOVE: waterfall rappelling on the Osa Peninsula. **RIGHT:** paragliding gives an exciting bird's-eye view.

TICO COOKING

When you can find Painted Rooster and Married Man on the menu in Costa Rica's *sodas*, why spend time at fast-food or international restaurants?

While it is perfectly possible in Costa Rica to order anything from sushi to tandoori chicken, part of the joy of traveling is sampling local cuisine. The *Ticos'* traditional diet is a simple, healthy one, low in fat, and rich in protein and carbohydrate. Health is increasingly becoming an issue here, and organic markets are springing up around the country. Fruit, fresh vegetables, rice and beans, naturally lean beef from Brahman cattle, and cabbage salads are the trademarks of Costa Rican cooking.

Picadillos are served in every *Ticos* home: diced potatoes, *chayotes* (water squash or vegetable pears) or string beans are mixed with finely chopped meat, tomatoes, onions, *culantro* (fresh coriander), bell peppers, and whatever the cook feels may add flavor to the pot. Leftover *picadillos*, fried with rice, are served for breakfast, usually with hot *tortillas* (a kind of pancake), and are called *amanecido*.

Costa Ricans season their food with a mixture of dry spices called *condimentos mixtos*, which are readily available at the markets. There are many different brands of liquid sauces as well, the most famous being *Salsa Lizano*. Most often these sauces contain cornflour, salt, garlic, black pepper, onion, cilantro, paprika, and a small amount of hot chili.

So-called "English sauce," the native version of Worcestershire sauce, is also used, albeit sparingly, by most cooks. Jalapeño peppers, from the mountain towns of Zarcero and Cervantes, are very good, and not as hot as the Mexican varieties. Most Costa Ricans do not like very spicy food, although tabasco and chili sauce are always on the table in inexpensive restaurants.

Gallo pinto and casado

The classic Costa Rican dish of *gallo pinto* (literally, painted rooster) is rice and black or red beans mixed with seasonings including onion, cilantro (coriander), garlic, and finely chopped bell peppers. Guanacaste, the northwestern province that once was part of Nicaragua, claims to have originated this dish. While predominantly a breakfast dish in the city, rural Costa Ricans eat *gallo pinto* three times daily, accompanied by home-made corn *tortillas*. For breakfast they order it with scrambled or fried eggs and sour cream, or *natilla*.

For lunch, businesspeople, students, and farmers alike usually have a *casado* (meaning husband) – a hearty combination including rice, beans, cabbage salad, fried sweet plantains, and sauced chicken, fish, or beef. An example of *Ticos'* sardonic humor, the name *casado* derives from the ordinary daily fare a man supposedly receives after he is married.

More Tico favorites

Another typical dish is the hearty *olla de carne* (literally, meat pot), which includes a small amount of stewing beef cooked with many vegetables common to the region: often *ñampi* and *camote* (both relatives of the sweet potato), *chayote* (water squash), carrots, and potatoes. It is usually served with white rice – something *Ticos* feel no meal is complete without, along with a side dish of black beans. This dish can be traced back to Cervantes' novel *Don Quixote*.

The *olla podrida* is the great-grandparent of the soup the people in Costa Rica love the most. What gives the distinct flavor to the Costa Rican version is the mixture of vegetables cooked in it: yucca, green plantain, sweet potato, *tannia*, *tacacos*, taro, pumpkin, carrot, *cho-cho*, onion, cabbage, and whatever else comes to hand.

Another interesting soup available at neighborhood restaurants throughout the country is *sopa negra*, made with black beans, onions, and cilantro, with hard-boiled eggs floating on top.

For lunch or dinner, *arroz con pollo* (fried rice with chicken) or *arroz con mariscos* (rice with seafood) are filling, inexpensive meals served in *sodas* (small family-run diners) and hotel restaurants.

Other local favorites include *lengua* (cow's tongue) and *mondongo* (cow's stomach lining). While tongue is tender and often deliciously prepared, *mondongo* has a strong taste and odd texture (think tripe), and is not appreciated by most foreigners.

The ubiquitous accompaniment to most meals is plantains – a relative of the banana. They can be sweet *(maduro)* or green, but they must be cooked before eating and are usually cut into strips and fried in oil or lard (called *manteca*).

Bocas and bebidas

Some bars still serve *bocas* (mouthfuls) with drinks in the same tradition as Spanish tapas. Traditionally they were complimentary, but these days they are increasingly sold separately.

Favorite *bocas* include *ceviche* (raw fish marinated in lemon juice), *carne en salsa* (meat stewed in a tomato sauce), fried cassava, and fried chicken. Beer, rum, and *guaro* (a sugar cane alcoholic drink) are favorite local tipples.

Special occasions

On weekends, Costa Ricans love to eat two versions of *chicharrones* – either deep-fried pig skin (including the layer of fat just below the skin) or tender chunks of lean pork that have been simmered slowly. *Chicharrones* are served with *tortillas* and wedges of lemon.

COSTA RICAN NOUVELLE CUISINE

Costa Rican nouvelle cuisine may sound like a contradiction in terms, but new markets for food exports have stirred interest in the country's vegetables and fruits. New recipes are being created, traditional ones rewritten, and local flavours added to international recipes to create a tropical fusion cuisine. One of the stars of the new cuisine is *pejibaye* soup, a delicate orange creamy broth, made from peach palm fruits. Mashed black beans *(frijoles molidos)*, seasoned with onions, sweet peppers and cilantro, are now served at formal dinners as hors d'oeuvres. Posh hotel restaurants offer Costa Rica Nights, with such delicacies as plantain soufflé and pork-filled cassava pastries.

PRECEDING PAGES: palm peaches at a road-side fruit stall, Dominical. **LEFT:** *gallo pinto* for breakfast. **RIGHT:** *casado* for lunch.

At Christmas, everyone eats *tamales*, which are made with *masa*, a corn dough, stuffed with different fillings, then wrapped in banana leaves and steamed. The dish is of Aztec origin and is eaten throughout Central America. It is very rarely the same in any two countries. In Costa Rica, *tamales* are traditionally filled with tender bits of pork, rice, carrots, olives, and sometimes dried plums.

Easter fare

Since colonial times, the Easter meal has been an important and traditional celebration. The Catholic Church's prohibition on eating meat

and generally sticking to a frugal diet during Lent explains why fish, pastries, and sweets are popular for the Easter celebration. Since the 19th century, *bacalao con papas* (salt cod and potatoes) has been traditionally prepared for Easter. Huge quantities of salt cod are imported from Europe especially for this occasion. Sardines are also popular.

Just before Easter week, particularly in and around the Cartago area, you will see *chiverre*, a type of pumpkin, but oval in shape and quite large, sold in the streets. With the pumpkin flesh local cooks make a sweet preserve called *cabellito de angel* (angel's hair), which is eaten during Easter on its own, or as a filling for sweet pastries.

Costa Rican *ceviche* is an Easter speciality, but is also available all year round at any neighborhood *cevichería*. It is prepared by marinating small cubes of fresh white fish or shellfish in a sauce made with lime juice, olive oil, fresh cilantro, onions, and bell peppers, for at least 12 hours. Most Costa Rican cooks believe in keeping the lime juice to a minimum and using cilantro freely to perfume the fish. It is similar to the Peruvian dish of the same name. Salty soda crackers or *patacones* – slices of green plantain mashed, then crisply fried – often accompany *ceviche*.

Fresh *palmito* (palm hearts) are also traditionally eaten during Lent, but can be bought any time, pickled in vinegar. *Palmitos* and rice is an elegant, festive dish served with grated cheese on top. *Flor de itabo* is the flower of a plant often used in the fences of the coffee farms. The plants have large bunches of lily-like, white flowers, which are also eaten for Easter, stewed in butter with eggs and tomato.

Regional cooking

Costa Rica is only a small country, but it still has several clearly differentiated regional cuisines.

The foods of Limón Province on the Caribbean coast are exotically tropical and flavorsome. The area offers a wide diversity of dishes influenced by African and West Indian cooking. The names of the ingredients (*baki, yokotaw, bami, calaloo*) echo the beat of Calypso and reggae, as do the names of the dishes themselves (*tie-a-leave, dokunu, johnny cake*).

The trademark of Limón cooking is coconut. Coconut oil and milk are used generously in most recipes, including the traditional rice and beans: rice is cooked in a pot filled with red beans, coconut milk, and aromatic herbs. It is the regional variation of the traditional *gallo pinto*, but in Limón it is usually served on Sundays and on festive occasions. Another local dish is *rondón*, a slow-cooked spicey fish and root-vegetable stew, which is, sadly, getting hard to find amongst all the fast-food pizza and fried chicken now on offer.

From their African background the *Limonenses* have kept the original names of many ingredients and the traditions of using a lot of tubers, such as yams, and adding green leaves to soups and stews. Their African heritage also shows in their use of herbal teas made with an infinite variety of plants. From their ancestors' hard lives in the sugar plantations of the West Indies, the *Limonenses* have inherited many products that were included in the daily slave rations: breadfruit, salt cod, mangoes, cassava, plantains, and a great variety of tropical fruits. And from the demands and preferences of their former British masters, they have retained several recipes for cakes, pastries, and breads, including *pan bon*, rum-flavored fruit cake.

In Guanacaste, pre-Columbian traditions in cooking are very much alive. A larger variety of corn dishes are cooked there than in the rest of the country, including delicious pastries. *Tamales*, *chorreadas* (cheese-flavored tortillas), *tamal*

the ones eaten in the rest of the country. African slave women were brought to the region during colonial times to work in the kitchens of the *haciendas*. They also left their mark in the form of the many exotic recipes still cooked in that province. *Ajiaco* and *bajo*, stews made with a mixture of meats and vegetables, maintain their African origins.

On the Pacific coast, Puntarenas specializes in recipes using ingredients from the sea, including *guiso de cambute* (conch stew) and various shellfish dishes featuring different combinations of fresh shrimp, lobster, and *chuchecas* (black clams). ❏

de elote (sweet corn pudding), and many other regional delicacies can still be found throughout Guanacaste. Some beach hotels there are starting to include them on their menus.

Since cattle farming is one of Guanacaste's main resources, milk products are often very good. *Bagaces* (a hard, salted cheese, used grated and added to other recipes) has been, since the 19th century, an important part of the salary of the *peones* (farm hands). *Cuajadas* (fresh cheese balls) are usually served at breakfast, eaten with hot *tortillas guanacastecas*, which are larger than

LEFT: making *arepas* (maize snacks) at San Raphael de Heredia's Sunday market. **ABOVE:** *ceviche* – raw fish marinated in lemon juice.

THE CHOROTEGA LEGACY

Long before the white man arrived in Costa Rica, the indigenous Chorotega tribe prepared a very thin unleavened cornmeal pancake called a *tortilla*. It is the main ingredient of Costa Rican *gallitos*, an hors d'oeuvre made by wrapping *tortillas* around mashed black beans, spicey meat, vegetable stew, pork chunks, or whatever else takes the chef's fancy.

The Chorotega also prepared *tamales*, rectangular pieces of corn dough stuffed with deer or turkey meat and a sauce made from tomatoes, pumpkin seeds, and sweet peppers. The sauce, called *pipian*, is still prepared today in a very similar way.

FRUITS OF COSTA RICA

Whether piled high in the market, served up on a plate, or whipped into a milkshake, Costa Rica's rainbow of fruits is a delightful feast for the senses

Fernández de Oviedo, a Spanish writer who came to Costa Rica in the 16th century, was probably the first European to chronicle the country's astounding variety of tropical fruits. Enthusiastic at every new discovery, he pronounced the pineapple the "best-looking, most wonderful lady in the vegetable world."

De Oviedo probably didn't get to taste all of Costa Rica's different fruits. There are simply too many, and they are available for every possible taste preference throughout the year. Get up early in the morning in San José and visit the Mercado Borbón, or the dozens of fruit stalls near the Mercado Central. Or go to the open-air produce and fruit markets held on weekend mornings, in almost every town on the Central Plateau, to see and taste the season's harvest. Along the highways and main roads will be vendors of all kinds of fruit and fruit drinks. Herewith, a look at Costa Rica's A–Z of fruits – from *anona* to *zapote*.

Anona

A strange-looking heart-shaped fruit, also called "the bullock's heart," the *anona* changes from green to a dark reddish-brown as it ripens. The sweet pulp is milk white and contains several large black seeds. After cutting it in half, eat it with a spoon, using the skin as a bowl. The *anona* is related to the custard apple (*anona chirimoya*) found in the northern part of the country. It has a delicate sweetness and a delightful fragrance like rose-water. Mark Twain described it as "deliciousness itself."

Breadfruit

Breadfruit, like bananas, are grown in the Atlantic region of Costa Rica. This fruit of Polynesian origin was introduced to the West Indies by Captain Bligh, and the Jamaicans planted it in Limón. An attractive, ornamental tree with large leaves, the breadfruit is an ingredient in many savory Caribbean dishes.

Caimitos and other stars

The *caimito* or Costa Rican star apple looks just like a star when cut, similar in taste to the mangosteen (an exotic fruit found in Malaysia and Thailand). This glossy fruit varies in shade from purple to light green. The sweet flesh is usually eaten fresh, but in Limón you can still find it made into a mixture called "matrimony," prepared by scooping out the pulp and adding it to a glass of sour orange juice.

Carambolas (star fruit) are often cut in thin

slices crosswise and used as garnishes for desserts. This shiny, five-sided pinkish-yellow fruit also makes a refreshing juice.

Cashew fruit

An exotic cousin of the mango, the cashew fruit is best known for the kidney-shaped nut attached to its lower end. The fleshy portion, or apple, varying in color from brilliant yellow to flame-scarlet, is eaten fresh. Its superb color and penetrating, almost pungent, aroma make this one of the most delectable of all tropical fruits. The flesh is soft, very juicy, and zesty. It is also used to make jam, wine, and a refreshing

There was a wonderful side effect, too: parakeets and parrots adore the fruit, and many species that were almost extinct are now increasing their numbers while feeding on abundant cashew apples. Beware, if the nuts are not roasted before being eaten, they are poisonous.

Granadilla

The sweet *granadilla* (passion fruit) is a favorite all over Central America. It is oval and orange to orange-brown. Within the hard, crisp skin, a bundle of seeds is surrounded by an almost liquid, translucent, and wonderfully tasty pulp. Use a spoon to eat it, or try passion fruit juice.

Fruit drinks (naturales) *accompany every Costa Rican meal. A bottled fruit drink called Tropical is also sold everywhere, but try to hold out for the real thing made with fresh fruit or fruit pulp.*

beverage similar to lemonade, which retains the special aroma and flavor of the fruit. In the late 1970s, the government decided to plant many areas with cashews, for export. The venture was a failure, but the trees are still there.

LEFT: pineapples for sale at San Raphael de Heredia's market. **ABOVE:** the majority of Costa Rica's watermelons are exported to Holland.

Guanábana

Related to the *anona*, the *guanábana* is unrivaled for its use in sherbets and refreshing beverages. Foreigners find the flavor somewhat suggestive of a combination of pineapple and kiwi, but *Ticos* consider that to be heresy.

Guava

A bestselling book by the acclaimed Colombian writer Gabriel García Márquez has the provocative title *The Fragrance of Guava*. You will better understand how the title elicits the Latin American experience if you visit a home when guava jelly is being cooked, and the entire house fills with the aroma. But cooking is not obligatory; you can simply eat the guava raw.

Another fruit, called in English "Costa Rican guava" *(cas)*, is round, yellow, and has soft white flesh. It is acidic, but highly valued for jelly-making and for drinks. If you see it on a menu, try a freshly squeezed *jugo de cas* (cas juice).

Loquat

The loquat *(níspero)* is a small, oval-shaped fruit with a large stone, pale-yellow to orange in color. It is also called the Japanese medlar. The flesh, firm and meaty in some varieties, melting in others, is juicy, with a sprightly acid flavor. Although commonly eaten fresh, it can also be used in cooking.

Mombín

The Spaniards said the *mombín* (or *jocote*) was a type of plum when they first saw it, but it has nothing in common with the plum. This fruit is juicy and spicy, unlike any other. The *tronador* is the best variety. Street vendors sell brown paper

> North Americans and Europeans are starting to appreciate the health benefits of tropical fruits. One US health food chain sells tiny papaya pills and touts juice made from noni fruits, common on the Caribbean coast, as a health tonic.

Mango

Alajuela's Central Park is full of mango trees with their tempting fragrance, which is why the town, second in size only to San José, is called Mango City. Alajuela's mangoes are sweet, firm, and delicate. The ripe ones are sweeter and spicier, but smaller and softer than the unripe ones. The aroma is spicy and alluring. Few other fruits have a background as developed as the mango, and few others are so inextricably connected with religious beliefs. Buddha is said to have been presented with a mango grove, so that he might find rest beneath its graceful shade.

Besides eating them as dessert fruits, Costa Ricans make mangoes into chutney, as well as preserves, sauces, pies, and juice.

bags full of *mombínes* from August through October, the color varying from dark green to bright red, depending on ripeness. The *mombín* is usually eaten fresh, as is its yellow-version cousin. Some refer to the yellow variety as the hogplum because hogs are very fond of them and fatten on the fruit that falls to the ground from wild trees in the forest.

The coco-plum *(icaco)*, on the other hand, is never eaten fresh, but its white flesh is made into a sweet preserve, called *miel de icaco*. Another cousin, the *ambarella (yuplón)*, was brought to Jamaica by Captain Bligh of *Bounty* fame. It came to Costa Rica in the hands of Jamaican immigrants to Limón. It is eaten uncooked, with a little salt, or made into a preserve.

Nanzi

You'll recognize a nanzi *(nance)* by its fragrance. This small, round yellow fruit has been popular among Costa Ricans since pre-Columbian times, but foreigners tend to find its smell too strong. It is used for preserves, wines, and jellies. *Nances en guaro* (nanzis in liqueur) are very good. Left to ferment in liqueur for nine months, they take on an amber-brown color. Nanzi sherbets are also very popular.

Papaya

Papaya (or paw-paw) grows almost everywhere in the country, and most tourists are particularly enamored of a drink called *papaya en leche*, a sort of papaya milkshake. There are two varieties: the huge local papaya and the smaller, sweeter Hawaiian version. Papaya is also excellent as a meat tenderizer.

Pejibaye

More a vegetable than a fruit, this was a treasured food of the aboriginal peoples. You will surely see it on the fruit stands, with its glossy orange skin and black stripes, resembling a large acorn. Cooked and peeled, its yellow pulp tastes very good when a little mayonnaise is added to it to soften the rather dry texture. It cannot be eaten fresh. Cream of *pejibaye* soup is one of the most exceptional dishes of Costa Rican cuisine.

Rambutan

The most exotic sight in a fruit market in Costa Rica has to be the rambutan *(mamon chino)*. The bunches of red and orange fruits, sometimes called "hairy lychees," look like gooseberries covered in fleshy spines. To eat them, simply cut the leathery rind with a sharp knife and pull it back from the pulp.

Rose-apple and mountain-apple

The fragrance of the guava is rivaled only by that of the rose-apple *(manzana rosa)*, a beautiful round fruit, whitish green to apricot-yellow in color, and perfumed with the scent of the rose. The flesh is crisp, juicy, and sweet. As a preserve or crystallized, it is delicious. If you eat it fresh, don't overdo it because the seeds are poisonous when eaten in large quantities.

LEFT: bananas, coconuts, mangoes, star fruit, and yucca at a Sunday market. **RIGHT:** a roadside fruit stall.

A relative of the rose-apple, the *ohia* or water-apple *(manzana de agua)* is a beautiful oval fruit, white to crimson in color. Its flesh is apple-like: crisp, white, and juicy but not very flavorful. *Ohia* jam is exquisite.

Sapodilla

One of the best fruits of tropical America, from the province of Guanacaste, is the *sapodilla* or naseberry, here called *chicozapote* or *níspero*. It is a dessert fruit, rarely cooked or preserved in any way. The French botanist Descourtilz described it as having the "sweet perfumes of honey, jasmine, and lily of the valley."

Zapote

A relative of the *sapodilla*, the *mammee-sapota* or marmalade-plum *(zapote)* kept Cortés and his army alive on their famous march from Mexico City to Honduras. The bright salmon-red color of the pulp catches the eyes of tourists walking along the Avenida Central in San José. Street vendors, knowing the sales appeal of the beautiful color, cut the marmalade-plums in halves.

Beware, however, that if you are not used to the very sweet fruits of the tropics you may find the flavor of the tempting *zapote* rather cloying. Very ripe *zapotes* are used to make the most wonderful ice creams and sherbets – try one if you get the chance. ❑

COFFEE

When white coffee blossoms blanket the fields of the Central Valley, filling the air with a sweet jasmine-like fragrance, the *Ticos* call it "Costa Rican snow"

You might well surmise that coffee is indigenous to Costa Rica, but it is not. The Spanish, French, and Portuguese brought coffee beans to the New World from Ethiopia and Arabia. In the early 1800s, when seeds were first planted in Costa Rica, coffee plants were merely ornamental, grown to decorate patios and courtyards with their glossy green leaves, seasonal white flowers, and red berries. Costa Ricans had to be persuaded, even coerced, into growing them so the country might have a national export crop. Every *Tico* family was required by law to have at least a couple of bushes in the yard. The government awarded free plants to the poor and grants of land to anyone who was willing to plant coffee on it.

The Central Valley has the ideal conditions for producing coffee: altitude above 1,200 meters (4,000ft); temperatures averaging between 15°C and 28°C (59°F–82°F); and the right soil conditions. Coffee estates quickly occupied much of the land, except for that needed to graze the oxen that lugged the coffee-laden carts. As the only Costa Rican export, the country's financial resources were organized to support it. By 1840, coffee had become big business, carried by ox-cart through mountains to the Pacific port at Puntarenas, then by ship to Chile and on to Europe. By the mid-1800s an oligarchy of coffee barons had risen to positions of power and wealth, for the most part through processing and exporting the bean, rather than by actually growing it.

A mixed blessing

Despite its early successes, Costa Rica's coffee industry has been a mixed blessing at times. The country incurred a heavy debt borrowing US$3 million from England to finance the

Atlantic railroad so coffee could be exported from the Caribbean port of Limón. And when coffee hit bottom on the international market in 1900, the result was a severe shortage of basic foods in Costa Rica that year.

This dependency on an overseas market has left Costa Ricans vulnerable on many occasions. Throughout the 20th century, coffee prices fluctuated wildly and the health of the nation's economy varied accordingly.

Traditionally, banana, citrus, and poro trees were planted in the coffee fields to provide nutrients and shade for coffee plants. Later coffee hybrids did not need shade, and treeless fields produced more yield per hectare. These varieties, however, depleted the soil more rapidly and required fertilizer to enrich it, adding to the cost of production. Today, many coffee-growers have returned to the traditional shade-loving plants, pleasing environmentalists who advocate shade-grown coffee.

The coffee plant itself is grown in nurseries until it's a year old, at which time it is transplanted to the field. Two years later it bears harvestable berries and, with care, will continue to bear fruit for the next 30 to 40 years.

Since coffee grows best in a mountainous climate, many of the hillsides in the Central Valley are covered with rows of the bright green bushes, reflecting the sun with their shiny, luxu-

today, most coffee is picked by migrant workers from Panamá and Nicaragua.

Costa Rican coffee had been traditionally mixed with other coffees destined for worldwide export. But when low-quality coffee from Vietnam flooded the world market in 2000, a lot of low-quality producers in Costa Rica were put out of business. Thousands of hectares of *cafetal* were uprooted. Today, coffee growers are concentrating on only the best high-altitude, top-quality specialty coffees from the highland regions around Poás, Barva de Heredia, Tres Ríos, and Tarrazú, rated by many aficionados among the best in the world. ❏

riant leaves. Some fields seem almost vertical and it is difficult to see how pickers keep from tumbling down the slopes as they collect the berries. The answer lies in the ingenious solution of planting the trees directly behind one another so that the trunk of the downhill tree serves as a foothold for the pickers. Coffee is harvested from November to January, during school vacation and Christmas holidays. Traditionally entire families in rural areas picked coffee together, some of the money earned going for Christmas presents and new outfits. But

LEFT: Cooperative Santa Elena grows beans for fair-trade Cafe Monteverde coffee. **ABOVE:** coffee pickers *c*.1920, when every Costa Rican joined in the harvest.

CAFE BRITT

An entertaining way to get a taste of Costa Rica's coffee culture is to take Cafe Britt's Coffee Tour, in Barva, the heart of traditional coffee country, 1km (½ mile) north of Heredia (signposted from Heredia center). This theatrical tour de force takes visitors through the entire process, from growing the coffee cherry to correctly tasting the final product. Combining elements of professional theater, a multimedia show, a farm visit, a processing-plant tour, and tasting session, Cafe Britt whirls the visitor through the world of coffee in about two hours. You must reserve your tour in advance on tel: 2260 2748 or visit www.coffeetour.com.

PLACES

A detailed guide to the entire country,
with principal sites cross-referenced
by number to the maps

osta Rica may be a small country, but it's packed with things to see and do. Some of its beaches rival the Caribbean; inland, lush forests and towering volcanoes attract walkers and nature-lovers. With 28 national parks, eight biological reserves, and 73-plus wildlife refuges, Costa Rica deserves its reputation as the home of ecotourism.

We begin the places section in the small but bustling capital, San José. It is worth staying a day or so to visit some fascinating museums, from the underground Gold Museum to the Jade Museum atop a skyscraper. It is also a good base for exploring the nearby mountains, where lodges offer activities from horseback riding to whitewater rafting.

Next we focus on the Central Valley, the country's green and fertile heartland, with traditional market towns and coffee farms. From here it's a short hop to the beaches of the Central Pacific, including famous Manuel Antonio, whose perfect white sands are the stuff of tropical dreams.

Many visitors regard the north as the true Costa Rica, with the uncrowded beaches of the Nicoya Peninsula, the vast cattle lands of Guanacaste, and the natural riches of Monteverde and the Sarapiquí region. By night, Arenal Volcano belches sulfurous smoke and oozes red lava. By contrast, the Caribbean coast presents Costa Rica's laid-back face: its tall palms, radiant sunshine, and aquamarine waters beckoning visitors to share in its indolent lifestyle.

Our tour ends in the south, off the beaten track, amid a wild and won-

derful region of vast tropical forests, and Central America's highest peak. The Osa Peninsula and the Golfo Dulce are truly a world apart, often accessible only by boat, small plane, or on foot. And in special picture features we will tell you more about Costa Rica's volcanoes, traditional handicrafts, abundant flora, and spectacular birdlife including the aptly named resplendent quetzal.

The sites of interest are numbered on maps to help you find your way around. Don't worry about getting lost – everyone does. But then, just getting there is half the fun of enjoying this remarkable country.   ❏

PRECEDING PAGES: tree-top walkway in Selvatura Park, Monteverde; there is great surfing on both the Pacific and Caribbean coasts; squirrel monkey in the Osa Peninsula. **LEFT:** a *campesino* ponders the significance of a giant stone sphere. **TOP:** active Arenal Volcano. **ABOVE LEFT:** taking a break from surfing at Playa Tamarindo.

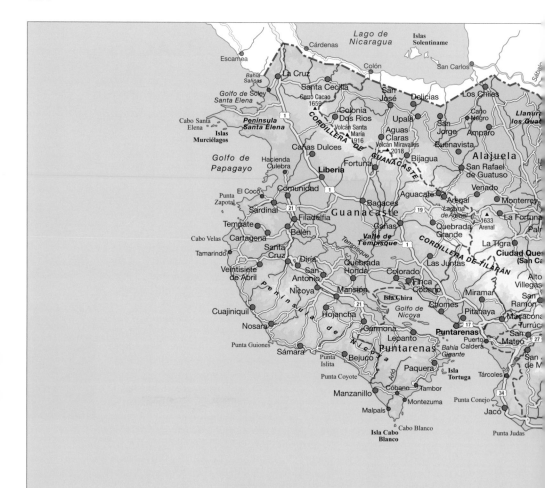

PACIFIC OCEAN

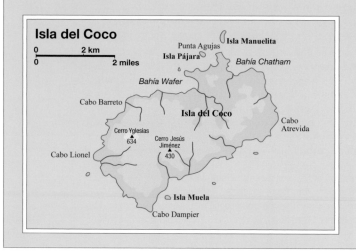

Isla del Coco

0   2 km
0   2 miles

Punta Agujas
Isla Pájara

Isla Manuelita

Bahía Chatham

Bahía Wafer

Cabo Barreto

Isla del Coco

Cabo Barreto

Cerro Yglesias
634

Cerro Jesús
Jiménez
430

Cabo
Atrevida

Cabo Lionel

Isla Muela

Cabo Dampier

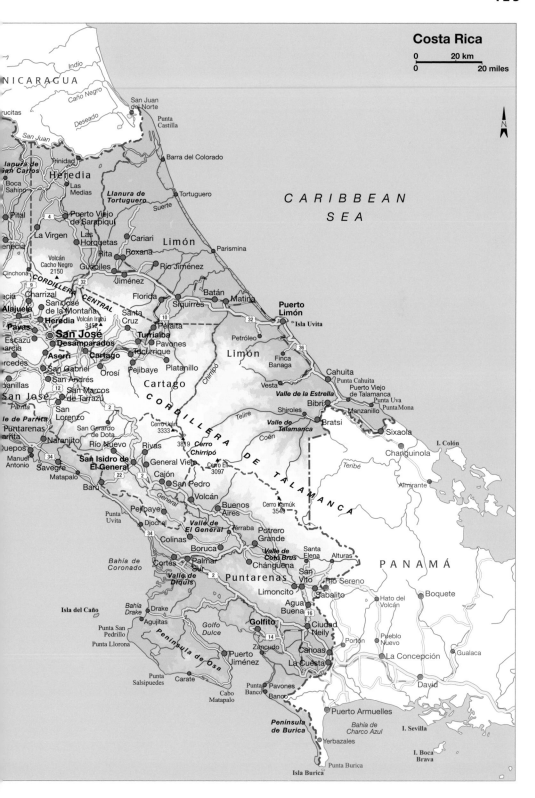

Costa Rica

0   20 km
0   20 miles

N

NICARAGUA

CARIBBEAN
SEA

Indio
Caño Negro
San Juan
del Norte
Deseado
Punta
Castilla
rucitas
San Juan
Barra del Colorado
Trinidad
llanura de
an Carlos
Boca
Sahino
Las
Medias
Heredia
Llanura de
Tortuguero
Pital
4
Puerto Viejo
de Sarapiquí
Tortuguero
Suerte
Parismina
La Virgen
Las
Horquetas
Cariari
Limón
nencia
Volcán
Cacho Negro
2150
Rita
Roxana
Río Jiménez
Cinchona
Guapiles
9
Jiménez
CORDILLERA CENTRAL
32
Batán
Matina
ecía
Charrizal
Florida
Siquirres
32
Puerto
Limón
Alajuela
San José
de la Montaña
Santa
Cruz
10
Peralta
Isla Uvita
Pavas
Heredia
Volcán Irazú
3452
San José
Turrialba
Pavones
Petróleo
36
Escazú
Desamparados
Tucurrique
Limón
arcia
Aserrí
Cartago
Pejibaye
Platanillo
Finca
Banaga
Cahuita
rcedes
San Gabriel
Orosí
Punta Cahuita
Puerto Viejo
de Talamanca
banillas
San Andrés
Cartago
Vesta
Valle de la Estrella
Punta Uva
San José
12
San Marcos
de Tarrazú
Shiroles
Bibrí
Manzanillo
Punta Mona
Parrita
San
Lorenzo
CORDILLERA
Telire
Valle de
Talamanca
Bratsi
Sixaola
le de Parrita
San Gerardo
de Dota
Cerro Urán
3333
Coén
Puntarenas
Río Nuevo
Rivas
3819
Cerro
Chirripó
Changuinola
uepos
Naranjito
San Isidro de
El General
General Viejo
Cerro Ení
3097
I. Colón
Manuel
Antonio
34
Savegre
Cajón
DE
Teribé
Almirante
Matapalo
22
San Pedro
Barú
Volcán
TALAMANCA
Cerro Kamúk
3549
Punta
Uvita
Pejibaye
Buenos
Aires
PANAMÁ
Djochal
Valle de
El General
Térraba
Potrero
Grande
Bahía de
Coronado
Colinas
34
Santa
Elena
Alturas
Boruca
Valle de
Coto Brus
Cortés
Palmar
Sur
Chánguena
San
Vito
Isla del Caño
Bahía
Drake
Valle de
Diquís
2
Puntarenas
Río Sereno
Sabalito
Hato del
Volcán
Boquete
Drake
Limoncito
Agua
Buena
Agujitas
Golfo
Dulce
Golfito
16
Ciudad
Neily
Pueblo
Nuevo
La Concepción
Gualaca
Punta San
Pedrillo
Peninsula de Osa
14
Zancudo
Portón
Punta Llorona
Puerto
Jiménez
Canoas
La Cuesta
David
Punta
Salsipuedes
Carate
Cabo
Matapalo
Punta
Banco
Pavones
Banco
Puerto Armuelles
I. Sevilla
Península
de Burica
Bahía de
Charco Azul
I. Boca
Brava
Yerbazales
Punta Burica
Isla Burica

San José

SAN JOSÉ

With modern high-rises ranked alongside faded 19th-century buildings, Costa Rica's capital may seem a jumble at first. Yet visitors soon discover that it possesses a certain *Tico* charm

The growth, some might say the flowering, of San José, began on that day, sometime during the first half of the 19th century, when Europe decided to have its daily cup of coffee.

By the 1850s, San José had been transformed from a humble little village to a boom town. As the city became wealthy, so its inhabitants, who called themselves *josefinos*, became more refined, more sophisticated, and more worldly.

The golden age

By the end of the 19th century, San José was living high on the profits of coffee exports. The city was third in the world to have public electric lighting and one of the first to have public telephones. It was also the first to allow girls to attend high school. Admittedly, the roads were still unpaved, but most upper-class homes had pianos.

Throughout much of the first part of the 20th century, San José continued to prosper and to build: a national library, schools, banks, parks and plazas, ministries, numerous hotels, theaters, a sumptuous post office, bookstores, hospitals, churches, a magnificent Palace of Justice, and an international airport all spoke of a city with money to spend.

PRECEDING PAGES: mural in San José. **LEFT:** Parque Morazán. **RIGHT:** the Correos (Central Post Office) contains a museum.

In 1956, Costa Rica's population passed the one million mark. By then, the international focus of influence had shifted. People ceased coveting things European, and became heavily influenced by North American standards and sensibilities.

The modern city

Cars and trucks began to appear where there had only been the gentle horse and buggy, ox-carts, pedestrians, and bicycles. The population doubled over the following two decades.

Main attractions

TEATRO NACIONAL
MUSEO DEL ORO PRECOLOMBINO
PARQUE CENTRAL
MERCADO CENTRAL
MUSEO DE LOS NIÑOS
MUSEO DE JADE
SPYROGYRA JARDÍN DE MARIPOSAS
MUSEO DE ARTE Y DISEÑO
  CONTEMPORÁNEO
PARQUE NACIONAL
MUSEO NACIONAL
MUSEO DE ARTE COSTARRICENSE
PARQUE LA SABANA

By the mid-1970s, the air in San José had become noticeably dirty, and the once civilized, narrow streets had become overwhelmed with a relentless rush of cars and people. Graceful, ornate old buildings were torn down and replaced with harsh, ugly copies of North American contemporary architecture. San José, the civilized 19th-century city, could not adapt its physical limitations to meet the demands of its consumerist 20th-century inhabitants. And today, in the early 21st century, this conflict has engendered a city that, by most standards, is traffic-clogged and unattractive.

Oases of calm

Fortunately, amid the miasma of diesel fumes, and the hordes of people, there are still some islands of repose. The National Theater is probably the most beautiful building in the country, and its elegant coffee shop is a favorite place to meet. Across the plaza, you can sip a *refresco natural* on the terrace of the Grand Hotel, while listening to *marimba* bands and the burble of 20 different languages.

Two downtown city parks also offer benches to sit on and a calm port in the city storm. The **Parque Morazán**, across from the Aurola Holiday Inn, has lovely jacaranda trees and a classically columned, open-air Temple of Music where public concerts are held. A couple of blocks to the east, the **Parque d'España** resembles a mini-rainforest in the middle of the city. Under the dense canopy of tropical trees draped with vines, you will share this cool space with statuary commemorating Spanish heroes, including *conquistadores* and Queen Isabel.

The National Museum and the Gold Museum are worth seeking out, along with the world-class Jade Museum. Among the souvenir shops, theaters, restaurants, and a few interesting art galleries, there are also some extraordinary remnants of old San José, hints of what a handsome, delightful place this city used to be.

Getting your bearings

Before you embark on the following tour of the city, or indeed go looking for any address within San José, sit

Cutting Down on Congestion

After a 2007 study showed untenably high levels of pollution from car exhausts on busy city streets, the government finally took action and instituted traffic restrictions. Car owners are forbidden to drive into the city on one day of the week – the day depends on the last number of their car's license plate. Some drivers were so incensed at having limits placed on their freedom to join city traffic jams that they filed a suit with the high court. Happily, they did not prevail and the restrictions remain.

There is a move afoot, as well, to rationalize bus routes in the city so that there aren't as many buses from the suburbs duplicating services. A bright spot on the horizon is the revival of train service. A train now runs from west to east through the city, and another runs between San José and Heredia, north of the city. The services are still fledgling, with two-car trains traveling mostly during rush hours, but they are the best hope for getting people out of their cars and onto public transport.

To further cut down on congestion and make San José a more people-friendly city, some major avenues are being closed to vehicles and turned into pedestrian zones. To cut down on the visual clutter in the city, unsightly overhead electrical wires are also being buried. San José may never be a beautiful city, but at least it is working toward improving the quality of life for residents and visitors alike.

down with our map *(see pages 128–9)* and familiarize yourself with the city's grid system of numbered streets *(calles)*, which run north to south, and avenues *(avenidas)*, which run east to west. The northern avenues and eastern streets have odd numbers; the southern avenues and western streets have even numbers. Confusingly, however, buildings are not numbered and, for the most part, only in downtown San José do any streets have names. Addresses are often given in the following format: Metropolitan Cathedral, Calle Central, Avenida 2–4, meaning that it is on the Calle Central between Avenida 2 and Avenida 4. Alternatively, and more commonly, addresses are given in terms of distance in meters *(metros)*, north, south, east, or west from known landmarks. It is as well to know, however, that *Ticos* often equate a city block with 100 meters (no matter how long or short it is). The end result is that *Ticos* and visitors alike can be seen wandering the city streets perpetually stopping one another to ask for directions. The good news is that people are generally happy to help.

The heart of the city

The Plaza de la Cultura marks the heart of the city. The area around this large square is a popular meeting point for peddlers, artisans, street musicians, in fact just about anybody and everybody. The pride of the square is the **Teatro Nacional** Ⓐ, without doubt the finest building in San José, if not all Costa Rica. Its construction was financed by 19th-century coffee barons, who, embarrassed that there was no appropriate venue here for the world-renowned opera star, Adelina Patti, to perform (she had snubbed San José on her 1890 tour of Central America), offered to raise money by paying a tax on every bag of coffee exported.

Modeled after the Paris Opera House and neoclassical in style, the theater was opened in 1897 with a production of *Faust*. The four-level floor plan is in the form of a horseshoe, with ornate detailing by Spanish and Italian artisans, and the acoustics are excellent. Ironically, Adelina Patti never did come to Costa Rica, but the country's top-quality National Symphony Orchestra performs here with illustrious

BELOW:
ceiling mural in Teatro Nacional.

City Buses

When in San José, do as the *josefinos* do: Hop aboard a public bus to see the city and get some insights into *Tico* culture

Buses are ubiquitous in San José. They go everywhere throughout the city and its surrounding areas. Many downtown streets are clogged with buses of all kinds. There are shiny new Mercedes models, personalized with their owners' names garishly painted on the rear window; some rusty wrecks emitting thick black smoke – although these are slowly being replaced by cleaner, hybrid buses; and recycled school buses from the United States, scrupulously cared for and graced with fanciful names.

Whether new and slick or decrepit and smoky, the buses have a common trait. They are wonderful windows into everyday Costa Rican life. Almost everyone uses them: students on their way to classes; women in high heels, dressy clothes, and impeccable make-up on their way to work; country folk coming into town to do business of one kind or another; young mothers taking children to doctors' appointments at the social security hospital; men with briefcases and neat pants and shirts. They are all on the bus, heading this way or that.

And for a fistful of *colones*, you can climb aboard and join in the great comings and goings of life in the Central Valley. A bus ride in San José is not particularly comfortable, especially during peak hours, but there is no better or more enjoyable way to make quick and often delightful observations on *Tico* life and characteristics.

For one thing, chivalry is still alive. Or is it just a simple sense of decency, of caring for others? Young men will assist older men, or women with children in tow up the steps; a seated passenger will offer to hold your packages while you stand; someone will always offer his or her seat to an older person or a pregnant woman. The driver will wait for someone making a last-minute dash to catch the bus. A young boy, known to the bus driver by name, boards on Paseo Colón and, for a few stops, takes on the role of the bus's official door-opener.

A wizened old *campesino* (peasant), returning from a trip to the city, takes a long time to board. He carries with him a heavy burlap bag, redolent of coffee beans and *pejibaye*.

A small girl in a rumpled pink dress enters the parked bus, waiting for its scheduled departure at the Coca-Cola bus stop. She speaks briefly to the driver, then stands at the front of the bus, singing a mournful song about love. When she has finished, she moves down the aisle with an open hand, into which the passengers all drop their small change.

Every visitor should take at least one bus ride in San José. Board near the beginning of the line, when you can still get a seat, and watch the rush of humanity come aboard, pausing to place their fare in the driver's hand, pushing past the turnstile, greeting friends and neighbors as they make their way down the aisle, more passengers boarding stop after stop, until it isn't possible to squeeze another body on.

Buses marked Sabana–Cementerio will take you on a loop around downtown, past the Central Post Office, the Central Market, Sabana Park, and the vast city cemetery. It's a good idea to take a ride outside the city too. The bus journey to Heredia, via Santo Domingo, will give you a glimpse of San José's prosperous suburbs as well as some of the shabbier parts of town. ❑

LEFT: a perfect example of the brightly colored buses used in San José.

international guest artists; their season begins in March. There are also daily tours where you can admire the marble, gold, bronze, tropical woods, crystal chandeliers, velvet drapes, and statuary. The ceiling fresco is famous and features an idyllic, if improbable, scene of coffee and banana pickers.

The **Cafe del Teatro Nacional** features changing art exhibits and is very popular, serving excellent salads, snacks, desserts, and specialty coffees. Across from the National Theater is the **Gran Hotel Costa Rica** 🅱, recently restored to its 1930s glory and renowned as a meeting place for tourists who gather in its outdoor café where musicians often entertain with marimbas *(see page 267)*.

Beneath the Plaza de la Cultura is the **Museo del Oro Precolombino** 🅲 (Gold Museum; www.museosdelbanco central.org; daily 9.30am–5pm; charge). On the east side of the square in cool, darkened, cavernous rooms, the collection features more than 2,000 brilliant pre-Columbian artifacts made by the indigenous peoples from the southwestern part of the country. Highlights include tiny half-man, half-bird figures, and erotic statuettes. The museum also contains the national coin collection and occasional temporary exhibitions of modern art. Before leaving the Plaza de la Cultura, pay a visit to the **Costa Rica Tourist Office** (ICT) at the entrance to the Gold Museum for news of what's on in town, and to pick up a free bus schedule.

More museums

A short walk west of the Plaza de la Cultura along Avenida 2 is the **Parque Central** 🅳 (Central Park), another great place for people-watching. The Gaudí-like kiosk in the center of the park was donated by the Somoza family of Nicaragua and sometimes hosts open-air concerts on weekends.

Directly in front of the park is the huge **Catedral Metropolitana** 🅴 (Metropolitan Cathedral). Notice the finely carved wood ceiling of the Chapel of the Holy Sacrament and its

walls, so carefully adorned with flower motifs that it almost looks as if they have been tiled. A monumental white statue of Pope John Paul II sits in the cathedral garden. The cathedral provides a refuge of peace from the hot bustling city, and the microphone-amplified midday Masses are always well attended.

Due north of Parque Central, along Calle 2, is the **Correos** 🅵 (Central Post Office), in a grand old, ornate building that also houses the **Museo Filatélico** (Post Office Museum; Mon–Fri 8am–5pm) and a pleasant café. Three blocks west of the post office, walking along pedestrianized Avenida 1, you will find the **Mercado Central** 🅶 (Central Market; Mon–Sat 6.30am–6.30pm), the city's best market, which has been here since 1881.

There are more than 200 stalls selling everything from old kitchen utensils to saddle bags, fresh fish, coffee and spices by the kilo, to religious icons. The prices are some of the cheapest in the city. At the center of the hall are the snack stands, a good place to find real *Tico* food at real *Tico* prices. Keep

A gold figurine in the Museo del Oro.

BELOW: fish stall in Mercado Central, one of the most dynamic places in the city.

TIP

At the northern end of the Parque Central, look out for the recently restored neoclassical facade of the Teatro Popular Melico Salazar.

your hand on your wallet as pickpockets operate here (and just love tourists), but don't be deterred from diving into this den to witness gritty *Tico* life at first hand.

If you have children in tow, you might like to make a diversion a few blocks north to the former Penitenciaria Central (City Jail), now the **Museo de los Niños** Ⓗ (Children's Museum; tel: 2258 4929; Tue–Fri 8am–4.30pm, Sat–Sun 9.30am–5pm; charge), which has interactive exhibits that are entertaining for adults, too. There is a good summary of the country's historical developments, with models of Amerindian huts, Caribbean wooden shacks, and modern housing.

The old prison also houses the modest **National Gallery** (hours as above), which exhibits work by local artists. The museum complex is in a rough part of town, however, so take a cab, rather than walking there.

On Avenida 7, on the north side of the lush **Parque España**, is the not-to-be-missed **Museo de Jade** Ⓘ (Jade Museum; Mon–Fri 8.30am–3.30pm, Sat 9am–1pm; charge). It can be found on the first floor of the National Insurance Institute, better known as the **INS Building**, a useful landmark that towers over the city. Alongside the museum's carefully crafted jade pieces *(see page 34)*, most of which are *colgantes* (amulets or pendants), are masterpieces of pre-Hispanic sculpture from all regions of the country. There is a nice shop on site, open the same hours as the museum. (There are plans to move the museum to its own building in 2012.)

Opposite the Jade Museum is one of the capital's most interesting old buildings, the **Edificio Metálico** (Metal Building School), which was shipped here in 1892 from Belgium to house 1,000 students.

Next door to the museum, under the shade of a magnificent ceibo tree, is the **Casa Amarilla** (Yellow House). Currently the home of the Foreign Ministry, it was constructed in 1816 as the Court of Justice. You can take a look inside the foyer and also take a peek into the back garden where a piece of the Berlin Wall has been made into a fountain.

BELOW: Edificio Metálico.

An Old-Fashioned Walk

To get a feeling for the San José of old, take a walk in Barrio Amón, where some vestiges of elegance survive. Start at the Casa Amarilla (Yellow House), the ornate, Spanish-colonial-style home of the foreign ministry, shaded by an enormous ceibo tree. Walk a block north to Avenida 9 and head west (left). You will pass by some elegant Victorian mansions, complete with gingerbread trim and stone lions guarding walled gardens.

Some of the grander houses have now been converted into boutique hotels, such as the Hotel Don Carlos *(see page 267)* which retains a classically Spanish inner courtyard, now used as the lobby bar. Along the Avenida 9 wall of the hotel, look for the charming series of tiled murals that depict *campesino* village life in a folksy, amusing style.

Nature in the city

A block north of the Jade Museum is the **Parque Zoológico Simón Bolívar**  (Simón Bolívar Zoo; Mon–Fri 8am–4.30pm, Sat–Sun 9am–4.30pm; charge), with a small, sad collection of ill-housed African and Costa Rican animals. In its heyday, the zoo was state of the art, but today it is constantly being criticized for bad management. The hope is that all the animals will soon be moved to a larger facility in the countryside west of the city.

For a cheerier view of Costa Rican wildlife, visit the enchanting **Spyrogyra Jardín de Mariposas**  (Spyrogyra Butterfly Garden; daily 8am–4pm; charge) across the river from the zoo. It's not far, as the butterfly flies, but the entrance is a long way off on foot, so you will need to take a cab from the zoo to get to this secret city garden. One of the main aims of Spyrogyra is to help rural women find alternative sources of income from field labor, by exporting butterfly cocoons to Europe and the US instead. In addition to the many colorful butterflies, there are gardens to wander through and hummingbirds to enjoy. Go on a sunny day when the butterflies are most active.

Arts, history, and culture

Across the street from the INS building is the former **Fábrica Nacional de Licores**  (National Liquor Factory), which now houses an arts and cultural center, as well as the Ministry of Culture. Pop into the pretty courtyard and amphitheater, a venue for plays and concerts, which lead to another part of the complex, the **Museo de Arte y Diseño Contemporáneo** (Museum of Contemporary Art and Design; Mon–Sat 10.30am–5.30pm; charge, free on Mon), which mounts changing exhibitions with the latest in avant-garde art, sculpture, and photography. Check the *Tico Times* for what's on.

One block southeast is the **Parque Nacional**  (National Park), the largest of San José's parks, where lovers drape themselves over park benches and bureaucrats eat their lunches under the shade of the 50 or so species of native trees. It's a very pleasant place by day, and well lit by night, but it is probably not advisable to stroll there

Jade model at the Museo de Jade.

BELOW: Casa Amarilla in Barrio Amón.

In an effort to reduce congestion and make the city more people-friendly, some of the streets are being pedestrianized.

RIGHT: skateboarding in Parque Morazán.
BELOW: Plaza de la Democracia.

alone after dark. In the center of the park a monument depicts victory in the war against the hated *filibustero*, William Walker *(see page 51)*.

Two blocks south of here, on Calle 17, is the **Museo Nacional** Ⓝ (Tue– Sat 8.30am–4.30pm, Sun 9am–4.30pm; charge), housed in the old Bellavista fortress, which still bears the bullet marks from the 1948 Civil War. Constructed in 1870, the building served as a barracks until the abolition of the army in 1949. The collections provide an overview of Costa Rica's history and culture, and include displays on burial ceremonies, a treasury of gold pieces, and rustic furniture from the colonial period. In the courtyard are cannons and some of the mysterious stone spheres found in the south of the country *(see pages 34 and 250)*. From the terrace of the building there are fine views down over the city and the amphitheater-like Plaza de la Democracia, where open-air concerts are held.

Sabana Park

The large grassy area of **Parque La Sabana** occupies what was Costa

Rica's first international airport. The Spanish-style building that once was the airport terminal has been converted into the **Museo de Arte Costarricense** Ⓞ (Museum of Costa Rican Art; Tue–Fri 10am–6pm, Sat– Sun 10am–4pm when there is an exhibition mounted; charge, free on Sun). The renovated museum reopened in 2010 with exhibitions of works by the country's finest 19th- and 20th-century painters and sculptors, as well as works by international artists and exhibits of the work of some exciting new artists.

In the *Salón Dorado* (Golden Room, upper story), French artist Luis Ferrón has immortalized Costa Rican history in a striking-looking stucco and bronze mural. Don't miss the museum's sculpture garden, which has some intriguing, monumental modern works.

Sabana Park is a popular weekend retreat for families who come to picnic, ride their bikes, skate, play, and feed the ducks on the artificial lake. Kite vendors also do a brisk trade on breezy days and it is often the venue for art and music festivals. In a large section of the park there are regimented rows of eucalyptus trees, planted where airport runways used to be. Slowly, these trees are being replaced with a more natural and pleasing variety of native species. Sporting facilities include soccer fields, tennis courts, and jogging trails. During the day, this is a relatively safe place as long as you stick to the paths. The park should be avoided after dark, however.

Pueblo Antiguo

A short bus ride northwest of Sabana Park in the district of La Uruca is the **Pueblo Antiguo** Ⓟ (Old Village; Wed–Thur 9am–5pm, Fri–Sat 9am–9pm, Sun 9am–6pm; charge), an idealized re-creation of old Costa Rica set in the Parque de Diversiones, a children's amusement park, where actors re-create 19th-century life in Costa Rica. Weekend dinner shows feature folklore and folk dancing. ❏

THE CENTRAL VALLEY

The heartland of Costa Rica is home to more than 60 percent of the nation's people. It is the center of government, agriculture, and commerce, and has the oldest cities and many cultural treasures

The Central Valley (Valle Central), or Central Plateau (Meseta Central), as it is often called, is strictly speaking neither a valley nor a plateau since it contains both kinds of landscape. The Central Highlands might be a more apt name for this area, only 24km by 64km (15 miles by 40 miles), where two mountain ranges meet. You will find rich, volcanic hills and river-filled valleys, with altitudes reaching up to 1,500 meters (4,500ft).

The good life

The countryside is beautiful and variable. The climate is salubrious. The air is sweet and soft. The people are generally friendly, dignified, and independent. Volcanoes, some still active, others dormant or extinct, rise up above the hills around the valley. Above them, a big sky is constantly changing – dark, charcoal rain clouds; intense, searing patches of blue; fluffy white cumulus; and rainbows galore. All come and go in quick succession.

There are misty, almost enchanted places such as the Orosí Valley; adobe villages such as Barva that sing of old Costa Rica; and crowded, noisy, relentlessly vital cities, such as Heredia or Cartago. And they are all easily accessible. Day trips by bus or car, or with tour groups, can easily be arranged.

PRECEDING PAGES: detail of an ox-cart wheel in Sarchí. **LEFT:** coffee plantation.
RIGHT: riding in a traditional ox-cart.

Passing through the small highland towns and villages, you see what in Central America is the unusual and impressive sight of people living in houses on plots of land that they themselves own and farm. Neighborhoods are often a hodgepodge of larger, fancy homes and smaller, humble ones. Housewives in aprons chat in front yards as they watch their babies. Children in school uniforms walk up the road for lunch at home. Produce from backyard fruit trees is for sale on little tables or stands in front of houses:

Main attractions
PARQUE NACIONAL VOLCÁN POÁS
ALAJUELA
BIOPARK/INBIOPARQUE
BARVA DE HEREDIA
CARTAGO
UJARRÁS
OROSÍ
PARQUE NACIONAL TAPANTÍ
MONUMENTO NACIONAL GUAYABO
PARQUE NACIONAL VOLCÁN IRAZÚ
PARQUE NACIONAL BRAULIO
  CARRILLO
SARCHÍ

Puerto Limón

32

Jiménez

Zona Protectora
Acuíferos Guácimo Y Pococí

Z. P. Acuíferos
Guácimo y Pococí

San Valentín

Parque Nacional
Volcán Turrialba

L i m ó n

Lajas

Bailla Arriba

Guayabo
Arriba

Santa
Rosa

CATIE (Centro
Agronómico
Tropical de
Investigación
y Enseñanza)

Estabobo

Atirro

18

Monumento
Nacional Guayabo

19

Turrialba

17

Bajos de Bonilla

Volcán Turrialba
3329

Santa Cruz

Guayabo

Juan Viñas

Pejibaye

Central Valley

5 km

5 miles

0

Capellades

Santiago

1865

Tucurrique

Selva

Pavones

Cervantes

Cot

Cipreses

San Rafael

Juárez

14

Paraíso

Jardines Lankester

13

Cachí

Tapantí

16

Parque
Nacional
Tapantí

Orosí

Río Macho

Orosí

15

Purisil

2205

C e n t r a l

T o r o A m a r i l l o

Sucio

Carrillo

32

Parque
Nacional
Braulio
Carrillo

21

Bajo Hondura

Alto Palma

Cascajal

Rancho
Redondo

Llano
Grande

Parque
Nacional
Volcán
Irazú

20

Volcán
Irazú
3432

San Juan
de Chicuá

Tierra Blanca

Tres Ríos

Cartago

12

Aguacaliente

San Isidro

Tejar

Tobosí

Muñeco

San Cristóbal
Norte

Z. P. Río Navarro
y Río Sombrero

San Isidro
de El General

C a r t a g o

Cangreja

Corralito

Fraijanes

Santa
Cruz

Empalme

Vara de
Roble

2506

Jardín

C O R D I L L E R A

Rainforest
Aerial Tram

22

Zurquí
Tunnel

Monte de la Cruz

8

Concepción

San Josecito

San Isidro

Bló Park/INBioparque

6

San Juan

San Vicente

Guadalupe

San Pedro

Curridabat

Desamparados

Z. P. Cerros
La Carpintera

San Miguel

San Rafael

2

Volcán Barva
2906

11

Sacramento

San José de
la Montaña

Charrizal

Museo
de Cultura
Popular

9

San Rafael

Santo Domingo

Heredia

Barva de
Heredia

10

Café Britt

7

San Juan

Rohrmoser

San José

Pavas

San Rafael

Alajuelita

Aserrí

4

Tabarcia

H e r e d i a

Poasito

Varablanca

Cartagos

La Paz
Waterfall
Gardens

9

Santa
Bárbara

San
Pedro

San
Antonio

Aeropuerto Internacional
Juan Santamaría

San
Rafael

Guácima

Alajuela

2

Santa Ana

25

Escazú

23

24

Jorco

Tarbaca

Monterrey

Vuelta
de Jorco

Rosario

San Gabriel

San Ignacio
de Acosta

San
Andrés

Z. P. Cerros
Caraigres

2506

Volcán
Cacho Negro
2150

General

A l a j u e l a

Reserva
Forestal Grecia

San Juan
Norte

San Pedro
de Poás

Tambor

Zoo-Ave

3

Bosque Encantado

Butterfly
Farm

5

Ventanas

Ciudad
Colón

R. I.
Quitirrisí

Z. P.
El Rodeo

Guayabo

San
Antonio

Floralia

Palmichal

Llano
Bonito

San José

Parque Nacional
Volcán Poás

1

Volcán Poás
2704

Sarapiquí

Jícaras

Puente
de Piedra

26

Grecia

Guácima

La Garita

Turrúcares

Atenas

Piedras
Negras

Desamparaditos

Guaitil

Cangrejal

Cangrejal

Teruel

Candelarita

Parque Nacional
Juan Castro
Blanco

Llano Bonito

Cirrí

Puebla

Sarchí

27

San Pedro

Rosario

Concepción

27

Virilla

Santiago de Puriscal

Barbacoas

Mercedes
Sur

Santa
Marta

Túfares

Sabanillas

Grande de Candelaria

R. I. Zapatón

Parque Nacional
La Cangreja

Zarcero

28

San
Juanillo

Naranjo

Z. P. Río
Grande

Z. P. Cerro
Atenas

San Ramón

1

soft-fruit preserves, home-made cheese and sour cream, oranges, candy-stuffed grapefruit, mangoes, tomatoes. Visitors are accepted with a mild, easy curiosity; no one seems especially surprised to have a *gringo* walk into the local *soda* (neighborhood restaurant) and order *arroz con pollo* (chicken and rice).

San José, Alajuela, Cartago, and Heredia are the largest and most important cities of the Central Valley. Radiating out from San José are towns and suburbs, each with its own flavor and identity: Americanized Escazú; residential, upscale Rohrmoser; exclusive Los Yoses with its lovely old residences; San Pedro, home to many good restaurants, the University of Costa Rica, and one of the largest shopping malls in Central America. There are also four national parks to explore, several volcanoes to climb, and Guayabo National Monument, the country's most important archeological site.

Though most travelers visit the Central Valley between December and March to escape the winter chill of North America and Europe, these months are Costa Rica's dry season,

its "summer." Frequent travelers to the area know that it is the rainy season in Costa Rica, with its afternoon downpours and dramatic displays of lightning, when the Central Valley is at its magnificent best, lush and colorful. Best of all, the air and San José itself are cleansed by a daily bath.

Poás Volcano National Park

The most developed of all the parks is **Parque Nacional Volcán Poás ❶**, a popular stop on the tourist trail. It is only 37km (25 miles) from San José on good roads leading through the city of Alajuela. Poás can become crowded and cloudy, so it is best to visit early in the day when views are better and before the throngs arrive. The cool freshness of the air as you ascend the mountain is invigorating, but it can get chilly and rainy, so bring a sweater or a rain jacket.

A map of the nature trails is available at the Visitors' Center, where there are nature exhibits, a gift shop, a cafeteria, and restrooms. If the weather closes in, as it often does up here, at almost 2,740 meters (9,000ft) above sea level,

Mangoes growing in Alajuela.

BELOW LEFT: fruit stall at San Raphael de Heredia's Sunday market.

The Day the Earth Moved

On January 8, 2009, an earthquake registering 6.1 on the Richter scale shook Costa Rica from top to bottom. It was the country's strongest earthquake in 150 years. The epicenter of the earthquake was Cinchona, a dairy village just west of Poás Volcano. Entire houses disappeared in minutes, swallowed in a giant landslide that also destroyed the highway from Varablanca heading northeast to Sarapiquí. Almost 100 people were killed or listed missing, and more than 1,200 people were displaced, with many of them still living in shelters more than a year after the disaster.

As devastating as the quake was for residents, it was also a disaster for the area's tourism, and therefore for local people's jobs. Poás National Park was closed until damage could be repaired. More than 400 people had to be evacuated from the area near the La Paz Waterfall, where the largest landslide occurred. Some were airlifted by helicopter and some hardy tourists hiked out on foot.

The winding, scenic road to Puerto Viejo de Sarapiquí was closed indefinitely, and all traffic re-routed through Braulio Carrillo to the east or San Carlos (Ciudad Quesada) to the west. Part of the road has since reopened, from Varablanca as far as the La Paz Waterfall Gardens *(see page 146)*. But one of the most scenic drives in the country has been lost forever.

the Visitors' Center is a good place to hunker down and warm up. From a lookout point above the crater, there is an overview of the volcano, which in 1989 shot ash well over a kilometer into the air. The main crater, which is 1.5km (1 mile) wide and 300 meters (1,000ft) deep, is one of the largest in the world. Poás rarely has violent eruptions and is one of the more accessible active volcanoes on the continent (although it was close to the epicenter of a 6.1 earthquake in January 2009; *see box on previous page*). It is active in 40-year cycles and is currently producing acid-like rain and sulfurous gases. It is therefore not advisable to stay for more than 20 minutes near the active crater.

Just a 20-minute hike away, along well-maintained trails through a landscape rich with wild flowers and a multitude of mosses, bromeliads, and ferns, is another crater filled with a jewel-colored lake, Laguna Botos. Keep an eye out for large-footed finches foraging along the trail, and volcano juncos, sparrow-like birds with yellow eyes and a pink beak.

Descend from the park to one of the nearby restaurants and enjoy the local specialty of *fresas en leche*, strawberry milkshake, or stop at one of the roadside stands to buy strawberry preserves and cookies made by local women. Alternatively, continue to the nearby **La Paz Waterfall Gardens** (daily 8am–5pm; charge) and set off on 3.5 km (1½ miles) of trails past hummingbird and orchid gardens, a huge butterfly observatory, aviaries and animal exhibits, en route to five impressive waterfalls. To spend more time in the mountain air, consider an overnight stay at **Poás Volcano Lodge**, and enjoy verdant views from your bathtub (*see page 273*).

Alajuela and environs

As you descend by some 200 meters (660ft) into the city of **Alajuela ❷** (pop 51,000) it becomes noticeably warmer. To relax, you can join the old-timers in the central park, amid an orchard of mango trees. Each April work crews use high-pressure hoses to fell the ripe mangos so they don't fall on people's heads.

BELOW: Laguna Botos, a crater lake near Volcán Poás.

Alajuela is the birthplace of Juan Santamaría, the young Costa Rican whose courage in helping to rout William Walker and his *filibusteros* from Costa Rica in 1856 is enshrined in national legend *(see page 51)*. The recently expanded **Museo Juan Santamaría** (Tue–Sun 10.30am–5.30pm; free), which occupies a restored former military barracks, one block from the central park, tells his story. A week-long festival of parades, concerts and dances centers around his birthday on April 11.

From Alajuela take the old highway toward the Pacific, via La Garita. En route is **Zoo Ave ❸** (pronounced zoh-avay; daily 9am–5pm; charge), which is primarily an animal rescue and research center, and takes care of more than 100 species of Costa Rican birds, as well as monkeys, deer, crocodiles, giant tortoises, and the occasional puma or ocelot.

La Garita ❹ is expansive and green, mostly a residential area filled with lovely gardens, fields of shiny green coffee bushes and plant nurseries *(viveros)*. On the road between Zoo Ave and La Garita, La Fiesta del Máiz restaurant is open from Friday to Sunday all day from 6am to 9pm. It features the near-endless variety of tasty dishes that *Ticos* make from corn.

A few kilometers southeast near Guacima is **The Butterfly Farm ❺** (daily 9am–5pm; charge), a breeding farm for more than 40 species of exotic butterflies, which are exported by the tens of thousands to Europe. The Butterfly Farm has waterfalls and extensive tropical plantings.

Coffee country

A day trip to the province of Heredia, the center of Costa Rica's coffee production, quickly takes you away from the heat and clatter of San José. Just 24km (15 miles) from the city, you can walk in an evergreen forest or cloud forest reserve rivaling those of much more remote and inaccessible areas.

En route to Heredia from San José is Santo Domingo, which still retains an historical charm with its low, white stucco houses trimmed in traditional royal-blue paint. Just to the southwest of the center of town is **BioPark/**

Fragant coffee beans from Costa Rica, roasted to perfection and ready for grinding.

BELOW LEFT: house plant nurseries.
BELOW: an owl butterfly, part of the country's incredible biodiversity.

INBioparque ❻ (tel: 2507 8107; Tue–Fri 8.30am–4pm, last admission 2pm, Sat–Sun 9am–4.30pm, last admission 3.30pm; charge), a 5.5-hectare (13-acre) coffee estate turned naturalist center that provides an entertaining introduction to Costa Rica's biodiversity. Trails lead through three representative ecosystems, passing a serpentarium, an ant farm, and tarantula and frog exhibits. There are guided tours by naturalists, excellent videos on biodiversity, exhibition halls that give an overview of the national parks' system, a pleasant restaurant, a lakeside café, and an excellent shop with unusual gifts for naturalists aged nine to 90.

Heredia ❼ (pop. 133,000) lies 11km (9 miles) north of San José, and is known as *La Ciudad de las Flores* (The City of Flowers). The city was first settled in 1706 by the Spanish, long before San José was even thought of. Historically a bastion of coffee wealth, the city today is even more prosperous, fueled by affluent suburbs housing professionals and Costa Rica's burgeoning middle class. Lots of trendy new stores are popping up, reflecting the global spread of North American brands and the gentrification of the town. **The National University** is located in Heredia; it turns out the nation's teachers and has one of the best veterinarian schools in Latin America.

The old town center, with its colonial Casa de Cultura, pitted fort tower, and lovely church, all facing the Parque Central, is a pleasant place to stroll. The **Inmaculada Concepción**, constructed in 1796, is adorned with bells brought from Cuzco, Peru, and its "seismic Baroque" construction has enabled it to survive many earth tremors.

Alpine scenery

Take the road to **San Rafael**, known for its impressive, cream-colored Gothic church, a landmark for many kilometers around, and begin the ascent into the mountains. Driving up the road to Los Angeles, you may get the feeling of having suddenly entered into an Austrian watercolor landscape. Wealthy *Ticos* of earlier generations were educated in Europe and returned to their country with a great apprecia-

tion for the architecture of Northern Europe, which is highly evident in this cool, mountain area.

Above San Rafael the temperature drops dramatically. About 8km (5 miles) above the town, in wonderfully fresh mountain air at mile-high altitude, **Hotel and Villas La Condesa** (tel: 2267 6000) offers horseback riding in the surrounding hills, hiking, an indoor swimming pool, luxury rooms, and a conference center *(see page 268)*. Along the way you will pass a sign to the private El Castillo Country Club, playground to the established old families that live here. The road beyond El Castillo continues to **Monte de la Cruz** ❽ where a huge, illuminated cross sits in a cloud forest reserve. This is a favorite destination for Sunday hikers.

Costa Ricans like to stroll these mountain roads, especially on Sunday, the traditional day for visiting with family; bus services are reduced on Sunday, further necessitating walking. *Tico* drivers are used to sharing the shoulder-less roads with pedestrians, but some foreigners in rental cars can find such driving conditions unnerv-

ing. There are quieter dirt roads with little traffic and country paths that are perfect for hiking, but you will need a guide to find them. Rich Tandlich (tel: 2267 6325), a long-time local resident and guide, knows them all.

Follow the signs along the road to **Hotel Chalet Tirol** (tel: 2267 6222), driving through a residential area of weekend cottages and retirement homes set in alpine fields. The road leads through a cypress forest where sun filters warmly through branches and dapples meadows of wild flowers. Chalet Tirol sits in the middle of a cloud forest reserve bordering Braulio Carrillo National Park. A fern-choked trail winding under orchid and bromeliad-laden old trees allows visitors to hike for several hours through the cloud reserve to the border of the national park. The hotel's A-frame wooden cottages are set around a miniature Swiss village *(see page 268)*.

Descending into the warmth of the valley below, the road to San José de la Montaña passes farms growing flowers for export in the wonderfully fresh, cool mountain air.

The Spanish fort in Heredia.

BELOW: Basílica de Nuestra Señora de los Angeles.

Vásquez de Coronado wrote to the Spanish king of Cartago: "I have never seen a more beautiful valley, and I have laid out a city between [its] two rivers."

BELOW RIGHT: the majority of Costa Rica's agricultural land is used for cattle farming.

Barva and environs

In **Barva de Heredia** , founded in 1561, colonial-era adobe houses surround the central park, giving the entire area the atmosphere of a colonial town. If you stand on the steps in front of the adobe **Basílica de Barva**, which dates back to 1767, and look out over the red tile-roofed adobe houses to the mountains beyond, you will get a sense of what the Central Valley probably looked like in the 18th century. The Basílica de Barva was built on an ancient Amerindian burial ground. Close by is the small grotto of the **Virgen de Lourdes** (1913).

In the hills just outside Barva is the lively and entertaining **Aventura de Café** tour at **Cafe Britt** ⑩ (tel: 2277 1600; www.cafebritt.com; tours 9.30am and 11am, year-round; charge). Guides at this coffee farm take you through every step of the process, from raw bean to hot, steaming final product, using a multimedia, theatrical approach. If you need it, transport to and from San José is available. Ask to taste the ripe, red fruit that surrounds the coffee bean. It is surprisingly sweet and good, though

beware of eating too many at once as they act as a mild laxative.

In **Santa Lucía de Barva**, 4km (2½ miles) north of Heredia, the **Museo de Cultura Popular** (tel: 2260-1619; Mon–Fri 8am–4pm, Sun 10am–5pm; charge) has renovated the charming and graceful González house, a 19th-century home, built just around the time that coffee cultivation was beginning to change Costa Rican life forever.

Barva Volcano

There is a steep road to the **Volcán Barva** ⑪ that runs just above the town of Barva de Heredia, through San José de la Montaña and on toward Sacramento. The volcano is on the western side of Parque Nacional Braulio Carrillo; the approach road is in terrible condition and cars without four-wheel-drive must be left 4km (2½ miles) from the park entrance. From the ranger station it's an enjoyable hike through cloud forest dripping with moss and epiphytes to the crater lake. An alternative one-hour hike will take you to **Laguna Barva**

La Negrita

The origins of Cartago's Basílica de Nuestra Señora de los Angeles are rooted in the miraculous. In 1635, a young girl walking through the forest that once grew on the site of the basilica discovered a dark-skinned statue of the Virgin Mary. A priest carried the statue, called La Negrita, to the parish church, but it mysteriously returned, twice, to its location in the forest.

In 1926, the Catholic Church built a basilica on the spot to house the statue. Today, in the shrine room, cases full of abandoned crutches, plaster casts, and votive offerings (some made of gold) representing various parts of the body testify to the cures effected by La Negrita, who is Costa Rica's patron saint. Water from the spring behind the church is also said to have healing powers and the faithful fill their bottles from there.

On the patron saint's feast day, August 2, thousands of pilgrims gather at the basilica. Many walk the 22km (14 miles) from San José, the most devoted penitents making the last part of the journey on their knees. So revered is the saint that some of the faithful walk from as far afield as Panamá and Nicaragua. The image of the black Virgin is carried in a solemn procession, through the city and back to its shrine in the basilica.

(2,900 meters/9,514ft), a green lake in an extinct crater rimmed with trees.

If you are still feeling energetic, there is the smaller Laguna Copey to explore, another 40-minute walk away. You may be rewarded by sighting a quetzal there – but don't bank on it. Wherever you hike on Volcán Barva, bring rain gear, a compass, and waterproof shoes or boots – even in the dry season – and be sure to keep to the designated paths. The roads in this area crisscross one another and are not at all well marked. Even *Josefinos* taking Sunday drives have to stop passers-by and ask for directions.

Cartago

Cartago ⓬ (pop. 155,400) is 22km (14 miles) south of San José. It was the capital of Costa Rica until 1823, when it lost its status to San José. Most of its illustrious colonial past is lost, however, since repeated earthquakes and eruptions of Volcán Irazú have destroyed most of the colonial-era buildings. Throughout their history, Cartagans have attempted to build a temple to Santiago (St James the Apostle), patron saint of Spain.

The first church, begun in 1562, was finished in 1570, and was one of only two in the entire country. When it was destroyed, a stronger building was erected in 1580 on the same site. This, too, was leveled by the trembling earth. Subsequent churches met the same fate, and when Cartago's massive cathedral, begun early in the 20th century, was toppled by the 1910 earthquake, all efforts to rebuild were abandoned. The roofless cathedral walls with their empty Gothic windows still stand. The site, called **Las Ruinas** (The Ruins), is now a popular and romantic spot with a lovely garden in the center of town.

Cartago, once the center of Costa Rican culture, is still her religious center. The enormous **Basílica de Nuestra Señora de los Angeles** (Basilica of Our Lady of the Angels), a domed, Byzantine structure that dominates the landscape for many kilometers, was built in honor of Costa Rica's patron saint, *La Negrita*, the Black Virgin *(see box opposite)*. It is worth a look inside to see the lovely stained-glass windows and the wood columns painted to look like marble.

The attractive central courtyard of Las Ruinas, Cartago.

BELOW: luxuriant Lankester Gardens.

EAT

Near Orosí is La Casona del Cafetal, a restaurant set in the *hacienda* of a large coffee plantation overlooking Lake Cachí. The weekend buffets are extremely popular and lavish, with a whole table of coffee-flavored desserts.

BELOW: the ruins of Nuestra Señora de la Limpia, Ujarrás.

Orchids in paradise

From Cartago it is a short trip to the **Jardines Lankester** ⑬ (daily 8.30am–4.30pm; charge) in Paraíso de Cartago, named, so legend has it, by weary Spaniards moving inland from the Atlantic coast who found its cooler weather and lack of malarial mosquitoes paradisiacal. English botanist Charles Lankester, sent to Costa Rica by a British company to work on coffee planting, arrived in 1900 at the age of 21. The coffee venture failed, but he decided to stay and bought 15 hectares (37 acres) of land to preserve local flora, especially orchids and bromeliads, and to regenerate a natural forest. Today, Lankester Gardens is run by the University of Costa Rica. Hundreds of species of orchids attract orchid fanciers from all over the world, particularly in the peak flowering months of January through April. The garden is also a great birdwatching spot.

The Sanchiri Mirador, 2km (1 mile) south of Paraíso, not far from Lankester Gardens, is a good place to stop for a light snack where there are stunning views across the Orosí valley.

Ujarrás

South of Cartago the landscape becomes green, misty, and magical, especially during the verdant rainy season. At **Ujarrás** ⑭, on a beautiful site in a sea of *chayote* vines, stand the ruins of Costa Rica's oldest church, Nuestra Señora de la Limpia, dating from the 17th century.

The first place of worship constructed in this region was not the church, but a shrine in honor of La Virgen del Rescate de Ujarrás, who, in 1565, it is said, appeared to an Amerindian fishing on the banks of the Reventazón River. The apparition came from inside a small tree. The man carried the trunk to the center of Ujarrás, but by the time he got there, it had become so heavy that even a dozen men could not lift it. The phenomenon was interpreted by the Franciscan fathers as a sign that the Virgin wanted them to construct a shrine on that spot to be used by both the indigenous population and the Spanish, and so it was constructed.

A hundred years later, in 1666, so the story goes, a band of pirates led

by the notorious Edward Mansfield and Henry Morgan landed on the Atlantic coast of Costa Rica with the intention of sacking the country. The Spanish governor, Juan López de la Flor, assembled all available fighting men and sent everyone else to the mission to pray. The pirates came inland as far as Turrialba and then, mysteriously, abruptly turned back.

Some say the pirates were tricked by de la Flor: other accounts attribute their retreat to a miracle worked by the Virgin. The grateful townspeople built the church of Ujarrás to commemorate the miraculous event, though it was destroyed 100 years later by an earthquake. Its picturesque remains stand among gardens and trees draped with Spanish moss. There is a pleasant picnic area beside the church, and restrooms nearby.

The Orosí River Valley

A few kilometers beyond Orosí, the **Cachí Hydroelectric Dam** channels waters from a reservoir on the Reventazón and Orosí rivers into an immense spillway. The concrete-dam

structure contrasts sharply with the lush natural terrain surrounding it, as does the power of the rushing water with the peace of the river.

Just west of the dam is **La Casa del Soñador** (The House of the Dreamer), a simple two-story cane structure embellished with primitive wood sculptures. Here Macedonio Quesada, a famous Costa Rican primitivist artist, lived and worked until his death in 1995. His two sons work here now, producing melancholy *campesino* (peasant) and religious figures from coffee wood. Visitors are welcome and the pieces can be bought for very small sums.

The town of **Orosí** ⓯ is untouched by the earthquakes that have leveled the colonial structures of Cartago, and it retains the look of an earlier Costa Rica, with wide streets and wooden houses with painted verandahs. Make your first stop the colonial church of San José de Orosí (the oldest church still in use in Costa Rica) and the former Franciscan monastery, now the small but fascinating **Museo de Arte Religioso** (Museum of Religious Art;

A tropical hibiscus in bloom.

BELOW: pink ginger flowers frame the Cachí Hydroelectric Dam's reservoir.

Turrialba is a popular rafting center.

BELOW: Cachí Hydroelectric Dam reservoir in the Orosí Valley.

Tue–Fri 1–5pm, Sat–Sun 9am–5pm; charge), just north of the church, which features artifacts from the colonial era. Take a walk around town and have a snack at one of the *sodas* or take a dip in the spacious heated *balneario* (pool). Just above the valley there is a lookout site *(mirador)* and park, maintained by the ICT (Costa Rican Institute of Tourism). The large area of sloping, well-trimmed lawns provides spectacular views over the Reventazón River with Cachí to the left and Orosí to the right. It makes a perfect spot for a picnic and a pleasant walk.

Tapantí National Park

The upper part of the **Orosí Valley** is one of the rainiest areas in the country, which renders it unsuitable for agriculture and means that it still has magnificent virgin rainforest. **Parque Nacional Tapantí ⑯** protects the rivers that supply San José with water and electricity. It also offers excellent birdwatching and hiking. Birdwatchers will want to get an early start to arrive in Tapantí when the park opens at 7am. The drive from San José is particularly beautiful at dawn, passing misty valleys and lush coffee farms, but the last 10km (6 miles) is over a rough road.

Trails are well marked in the lower part of the refuge. Oropendolas – black, raven-sized birds with golden tail feathers and stout ivory-colored bills – nest in noisy colonies within the park. Clusters of 30 or more pendulous nests hang from branches high in the trees. Visitors will usually hear oropendolas before seeing them, as the males let out a gurgling, liquid-like song, then bow and flap their wings to the females in unusual courtship displays.

The Orosí River runs parallel to the Oropendola Trail, inviting hikers to cool their feet in the water and lie back on the smooth, warm boulders for a mid-morning snooze in the sun. If you are a strong swimmer, you can also jump in, but beware of the fast-running current. Given its reputation as the wettest national park, though, it is always advisable to bring rain gear and a change of warm clothes.

Turrialba

Turrialba ⓱ (pop. 70,630) is a busy town bustling with people talking, yelling, buying, selling. The open fruit and vegetable market that lines the sidewalk along the river features some of the freshest and best-looking produce available in Costa Rica, most of it grown in the hills above town. Turrialba's reputation as a whitewater river-rafting center is growing, and rafters and kayakers from all over the world are discovering the Reventazón and Pacuare rivers *(see pages 94–5)*. Looming above the town is Volcán Turrialba, spectacularly active since January 2010, letting off plumes, mostly of steam.

Just a few kilometers beyond the town of Turrialba on the highway is **CATIE**, the **Centro Agronómico Tropical de Investigación y Enseñanza** ⓲ (Center for Tropical Agronomy Research and Teaching). On this 800-hectare (1,975-acre) research plantation, scientists are experimenting with the introduction of more than 5,000 varieties of 335 species of crops with economic potential. More than 2,500 varieties of coffee and 450 varieties of cacao, as well as numerous varieties of bananas and pejibaye palms, are part of the seed bank of CATIE.

Work is being done here on the critical problems of deforestation, overgrazing, and the sensitive ecology of the river basins. Guides demonstrate the cultivation, processing, and care of palms, coffee, cacao, and orchids, and there is also a guided tour of the Botanical Garden. If you are not visiting with a group, call ahead to arrange a tour (tel: 2256 2700).

Visitors to CATIE and the surrounding areas can stay at modest hotels in town or, about 5km (3 miles) out of town on the road toward Siquirres, the luxurious Casa Turire (tel: 2531 1111) is a lavish plantation-style hotel in the grounds of a sugar cane, coffee, and macadamia nut plantation. In the mountains above the valley, not far away, is the Turrialtico (tel: 2538 1111), which has handsome rooms with lovely views of Volcán Turrialba.

Guayabo National Monument

The site of a pre-Columbian city, the **Monumento Nacional Guayabo** ⓳ sits on the slope of Volcán Turrialba, 18km (11 miles) from Turrialba. Archeologists are still unclear as to whether this large site was purely ceremonial or a combination administrative and ceremonial center. The ancient stone ruins and the remains of imposing stone roads radiating out to surrounding areas date from 1000 BC to AD 1400, when the site was abandoned for some as yet unknown reason, prior to the arrival of the Spaniards. Speculation suggests disease or starvation.

Visitors can take an interesting guided tour along a forest trail to the excavated area, which contains a complex system of stone aqueducts, building foundations, and roadways amid a setting of guava trees, wild impatiens, and clusters of nests. Stone-lined graves, now empty, served as the first indication to archeologists that a cultural site was nearby. In addition, there are several large petrographs,

Around Guayabo grow the best pejibaye in the country. Every year at the end of October there is a Pejibaye Festival in Tucurrique where you can feast on pejibaye, in sweet or savory dishes, and even drink pejibaye chiche (moonshine).

BELOW: San José de Orosí, the oldest church still in use in Costa Rica.

BELOW:
Volcán Irazú.

the significance of which remains a mystery.

About 20km (12 miles) north of Guayabo, on the slope of Turrialba volcano, is Volcán Turrialba Lodge, with comfortable wooden cabins and wood-burning stoves to ward off the evening chill. Hikes and horseback rides to the volcano's extinct crater are exhilarating in the clear mountain air (tel: 2273 4335).

Irazú Volcano National Park

Easily accessible from Cartago is **Parque Nacional Volcán Irazú** , atop the massive volcano that dominates the landscape on the eastern side of the Central Valley. From the 3,800-meter (11,000ft) summit, it is possible on a clear day to see both the Caribbean and the Pacific. More often, you will climb above the clouds on your way to the top. Irazú, Costa Rica's highest volcano, also known as El Coloso, broke a 30-year period of silence with a single, noisy eruption on December 8, 1994. The previous eruption, on March 19, 1963, the day of the arrival of President John F. Kennedy in Costa Rica, was even more powerful.

For two years Irazú continued to shower ash over much of the Central Valley. People habitually carried umbrellas to protect themselves. Ash piled up on the Reventazón River, causing it to flood and destroy 300 homes. Roofs caved in from the weight of the ash and San José's air was temporarily turned black.

A visit to Irazú today is a relatively easy half-day tour from San José. Visitors can go to the top ridge, walk along the rim of the main crater, and look across an other-worldly landscape consisting of a brilliant green lake and black and gray slopes, punctuated with plumes of white steam jetting into the air, escaping from fissures in the rock. There are also wonderful hiking and birding trails in the Prusia sector of the park.

Braulio Carrillo National Park

Only 45 minutes from bustling downtown San José is **Parque Nacional Braulio Carrillo** ㉑, a true wilderness. Take the highway to Limón, passing through the Zurquí tunnel, the one and only tunnel in the country.

Occupying 445 sq km (170 sq miles) of mostly primary forest, Braulio Carrillo National Park was founded in 1978 thanks to pressure exerted by environmentalists who feared that the opening of a highway between San José and Guápiles would provide loggers and developers with access to rapidly vanishing virgin forest; deforestation had followed the opening of many other roads throughout the country. A compromise was reached: the road would go through, but the 32,000 hectares (80,000 acres) of virgin forest surrounding the highway would be preserved as a national park. The park thus embodies some ideals of enlightened progress.

Braulio Carrillo contains five distinctly separate forest habitats, dominated by the wet tropical forest. Hundreds of varieties of orchids and ferns, and the majority of the bird species native to Costa Rica, are found here. In order to understand the life cycles, to spot the camouflaged wild-life, and avoid missing hidden spectacular vistas, it is essential to arrange for a guide through the National Parks Service (www.costarica-nationalparks.com) or an ecotourism agency. Although the territory is vast, there are few through trails and many solo hikers get lost for days. The lingering impression of Braulio Carrillo is of vastness: huge canyons, misty mountains, and the ubiquitous broad-leaf plant, called the Poor Man's Umbrella, covering the hillsides.

The easiest way to experience the forest here is to walk the trails at the **Quebrada Gonzales** station, about 17km (11 miles) past the tunnel. The Las Palmas Trail, starting from the parking lot, gradually climbs up from the highway, quickly immersing you in the forest. This is a great birdwatching trail, but you have to get there early. The trails are often muddy, and snakes are sometimes basking on the trails, so be sure to wear sturdy boots, long pants, and mosquito repellent. If you don't have

all the right gear, all is not lost, as the birding from the parking lot can also be excellent.

Rainforests made easy

For a bird's-eye view of the forest canopy adjacent to Braulio Carrillo, you can take a ride on the **Rainforest Aerial Tram** ㉒ (tel: 2257 5961; www.rainforesttram.com; daily; charge includes tram ride, video, and a short hike; reservations recommended and can be made online). This is an 80-minute, 2.6km (1½-mile) trip through the forest's treetops, 35 meters (100ft) above the forest floor. The "tram" is an open, metal gondola, big enough for five passengers and a naturalist guide, equipped with a walkie-talkie to pass along information on wildlife sightings. Visitors can experience the forest canopy up close, breathe the steamy air, and catch the unforgettable tropical smell of damp, mossy tree trunks.

Although it is on every tour company's itinerary, this is not the most exciting experience and the chances of spotting wildlife from the tram are remote. You will have better luck down

Costa Rica's national orchid, the purple Guaria Morada.

BELOW LEFT: rainforest flora. **BELOW:** Red-eyed tree frogs are not endangered but their habitats are shrinking.

TIP

The San José suburb of San Pedro is one of the capital's liveliest areas thanks to the presence of the university. It features several good restaurants, bars, and nightspots, all of them noisy.

on the ground, during your short hike to the tram.

Amphibian lovers won't want to miss the **Butterfly and Frog Garden** here, where you can see the famous poison-dart frogs and Costa Rica's iconic red-eyed leaf frog (separate tour; charge). The Aerial Tram is about 5km (3 miles) north of Río Sucio on the road to Puerto Limón, about 50 minutes from San José.

San José suburbs

On the west side of San José lie the prosperous suburbs of Pavas, Rohrmoser, Escazú, and Santa Ana. The largely residential **Rohrmoser** and **Pavas** are chiefly of interest because of the presence of the United States Embassy and the embassies of other countries. Many diplomatic personnel live along the wide, nearly treeless streets of Rohrmoser, in modern houses protected by wrought-iron grille work.

Escazú ㉓ was originally a crossroads of trails between Amerindian villages. Because water was abundant there, the Amerindians found it a good place to

spend the night on their journeys, and gave it the name Escazú, which means "resting place."

Spanish settlers were also attracted to Escazú: they settled in the hills and began farming. It was during these early days that Escazú became known as La Ciudad de las Brujas (The City of the Witches). Today, the legends of witches remain, but the old adobe houses, painted blue and white to ward off *las brujas*, are being replaced by high-rise luxury condominiums and shopping centers.

Escazú is an interesting if sometimes chaotic blend of old Costa Rica and a modern, international community, with a large contingent of North Americans. It is often jokingly referred to as "Gringolandia." The town center has adobe buildings, an attractive, Ravenna-style church, and, of course, a soccer field. Just outside of town are enclaves of fancy homes owned by North Americans, Europeans, and wealthy local people, drawn to Escazú by the agreeable climate and the superlative views. Unfortunately, this has led to the town's main road being clogged

BELOW: farmer with his traditional ox-cart in the Central Valley. Farming revolves around the production of coffee, fruit, and dairy produce.

with traffic, and lined with fast-food chains, clothing stores, and tall condominium buildings.

In the hills to the east of the town, in an area called **Bello Horizonte**, are many fine old residences with lovely gardens. It is worth a drive through the hills of Bello Horizonte to visit **Biesanz Woodworks** (tel: 2289 4337; www.biesanz. com), the studio-workshop of Barry Biesanz, an accomplished artist who works with Costa Rican hardwoods. Wooden bowls and boxes, remarkable for their grace and fluidity, are on display in his *hacienda*-style showroom, which is surrounded by an interesting herb garden with an ornamental pond.

San Rafael de Escazú ㉔ is a newer section of town along the highway to Santa Ana. It has several shiny commercial centers where the town's glamorous inhabitants do their shopping, with international stores, supermarkets, a dazzling array of trendy restaurants, and glitzy interior-design stores.

On the old road between Escazú and Santa Ana, across from the new Los Laureles shopping center, there is a large walled compound with lights, guards, and surveillance paraphernalia. It isn't a high-security penitentiary: it's the residence of the United States Ambassador to Costa Rica.

Santa Ana

Although condominiums, luxury villas, and shopping centers are rapidly urbanizing the town, a rural atmosphere still survives in **Santa Ana** ㉕, a town once famous for its onions, which hang braided on the lintels and eaves of rustic restaurants along the road. On the west side of town there are still a few sprawling emporia selling pottery, baskets, and locally grown onions.

Lovely, rustic Santa Ana church, built in the 1870s, reverberates with the sound of chamber music at the Baroque Music Festival, usually held the second week of November. It's an intimate, evocative setting with excellent acoustics.

High in the hills above Santa Ana,

you can sit under the stars, overlooking the city lights, and enjoy the balmy breezes at **Rancho del Macho** (tel: 2282 9295). Or you could come on a weekend afternoon to listen to traditional marimba music. Another romantic spot is the **Mirador Valle Azul** (tel: 2254 6281), where you can drink in sparkling city views along with fine wines and Italian food, high above Escazú.

For a taste of modern luxury, the **Hotel Alta** (tel: 2282 4160), halfway between Escazú and Santa Ana on the old road, is hard to beat. It has an excellent restaurant and sometimes exhibits local artists' work.

If you are in search of more ordinary pursuits, look for **Multiplaza**, one of the largest shopping malls in all of Central America. It is just off the newly widened toll road on the way to Santa Ana, across the road from El Camino Real Hotel.

Ciudad Colón can be reached by back roads from Santa Ana, through rolling hills, or by way of the new toll road. It is best known for the **University for Peace**, which is on

An adobe house in the Central Valley.

BELOW: sample fresh, locally grown produce and support small-scale farms at farmers' markets.

a well-marked road not far out of town. The university, sponsored by the United Nations to study the ways of peace, and to offer a counter to the teachings of war colleges that predominate in many other countries, offers graduate courses to students from all over the world. There are hiking and birding trails throughout the property, as well as popular picnic areas beside a lake populated by geese and ducks.

Returning to Santa Ana via back roads, you will pass the **Hacienda El Rodeo** (tel: 2249 1013), a popular weekend restaurant where you can hire horses. The *comida tipica* food is nourishing but nothing special, but the gently rolling hills above the open-air restaurant are beautiful and perfect for horseback riding.

Sarchí and surrounding villages

For a half-day excursion of craft shopping and sightseeing around typical Central Valley coffee towns, head north through Alajuela toward Sarchí, stopping en route at **Grecia** ㉖. This little place is renowned for its tidi-

ness, claiming to be the cleanest town in Latin America. Compared to most towns in Costa Rica, it certainly is remarkably well kept. It is definitely worth taking a stroll around the Central Park and visiting the town's unusual, dark-red Church of Our Lady of Mercy, built in the 1890s with metal pieces imported from Belgium. The church is also famous for its restored organ, which plays a starring role in a music festival held each August.

Just a few minutes' walk away is the popular World of Snakes (tel: 2494 3700; daily 8am–4pm; guided tours; charge, free for children under 7), a serpentarium with 50 snakes from all over the world, plus some other interesting reptiles.

The approach to the mountain town of **Sarchí** ㉗ is unmistakable. Swirling, colorful decorative designs adorn practically every bus stop, bar, bakery, restaurant, and house. In the town's central park in front of the wedding-cake white church, there is a giant painted ox-cart, weighing in at 2 tons and delighting camera-toting tourists.

Sarchí is a crafts center heavily geared

Decorated Carts

Around 1910, as legend has it, a *campesino* (peasant) was crossing the Beneficio la Luisa when it occurred to him to decorate his ox-cart wheels with colorful mandala-like designs inspired by ancient Moorish decoration. Surprisingly, the art form caught on. Originally, each district in Costa Rica had its own special design and local people could tell just by looking at the cart where the driver was from. Each cart was also said to have its own "*chirrido*," or song of the wheels, by which people could identify who was passing by, without even glancing upward. As late as 1960, the ox-cart was still the most typical mode of transportation since it was the only vehicle that could handle the rugged Costa Rican terrain. Things have changed now, but you will still see ox-carts on the roads.

toward the tourist trade, where you can see artisans painting traditional ox-cart designs *(see opposite and pages 162–3)* and creating household furnishings out of tropical hardwoods.

There are pleasant little road-side stalls on the outskirts of Sarchí selling home-made candied fruits, honey, and fudge. In comparison to the large commercialized furniture shops that predominate in Sarchí, a visit to these small stands is extremely friendly and personal, like stepping into a Costa Rican home for a chat.

About 15km (9 miles) up the road is the town of **Zarcero** ㉘. Should you arrive on a day when the highland clouds are swirling through the town, famous for its cheese and fruit orchards, or when a drizzling fog is bathing everything in soft, diffused light, you might feel that you have just walked into a dreamland.

Topiary extravaganza

Unique in Costa Rica, and possibly the world, is the **Parque Francisco Alvarado** in Zarcero, a topiary extravaganza created by Evangelisto Blanco,

a local gardener, who clipped and pruned cypress bushes and hedges into a whimsical garden of amazing shapes and creatures: birds, rabbits, oxen, dinosaurs, a monkey riding a motorcycle, an elephant with light bulbs for eyes.

Evangelisto has been sculpting the hedges for more than four decades, and the energetic compulsion of his work has been compared to the creations of Modernist architect Antonio Gaudí, in Barcelona. Unable to afford marble or stone, Evangelisto works with the plants as his medium of self-expression, creating extraordinary sculpted shrubs.

About 8km (5 miles) after the turn-off for Sarchí, along the Pan-American Highway, is the exit for the 200-year-old colonial town of **Palmares**. This lovely area used to be a tobacco-growing center. Unaffected by the vicissitudes of modern tourism, it is a model town through which to stroll and view typical *Tico* life, except in mid-January when it hosts a huge, noisy music festival that attracts thousands of revelers. ❑

Butterflies are a common sight around the hedges of Parque Francisco Alvarado.

BELOW: Parque Francisco Alvarado, Zarcero.

POTTERS, SCULPTORS, AND GOLDSMITHS

The Amerindians of Costa Rica left behind gold, pottery, and stone artifacts. Sadly, most of their traditions were destroyed by the *conquistadores*

Because Costa Rica was a cultural and commercial meeting point for ancient American civilizations, native Costa Ricans absorbed and modified known techniques in ceramics, gold and jade work, weaving, and stone carving. Early inhabitants, especially in the pre-Columbian port of Nicoya (in the province of Guanacaste), traded with travelers from as far away as Ecuador and Mexico. They also developed their own style of decorating pottery: beasts that are half-bird, half-man; and people with exaggerated genitals, suggesting a fertility-rite culture. Examples of the pottery can be found throughout Central America. Visitors to the Gold Museum, the Jade Museum, and the National Museum in San José can see early pieces and learn more of their history.

While the Spanish never found the gold deposits that inspired the name "Rich Coast," early Costa Ricans worked with both gold and jade to make decorative pieces. Although these traditions have been all but lost, pottery and the more modern craft of ox-cart decoration have been revived by the tourist dollar. For pottery, visit Guatil and Nicoya; for other crafts, try Sarchí *(see panel, right)*. Other examples of Costa Rica's crafts are found in the south of the country: *molas* (hand-sewn appliqué) pieces are produced around Drake Bay, and both grotesque and beautiful balsawood masks are made by the Boruca people.

ABOVE AND LEFT: reproduction pre-Columbian jewelry and figures are popular souvenirs.

ABOVE: vestiges of Chorotega culture linger on in pottery produced in Guaitil, where the entire village is an open-air workshop and showroom.

BELOW: inexpensive vases and pots, decorated with whimsical animals and other pre-Columbian images, are for sale at road-side stands in Guanacaste.

ORNAMENTED OX-CARTS

Used exclusively to transport coffee and other agricultural products until well into the 20th century, wooden ox-carts are unmistakably Costa Rican, and symbolize the self-reliance of the small farmer. The father of two-time president Oscar Arias made his original fortune hauling coffee by ox-cart to Puntarenas.

Ideally suited for the country's mountainous conditions and rutted dirt roads, ox-carts are still common in many parts of the country. The carts, which come in all sizes (including a miniature about the size of a toy car), are made in Sarchí, the wooden crafts capital of the country. There, master carvers began painting the carts in the early part of the 20th century. Originally adorned with bright colors and geometric patterns, these days ox-carts are being decorated with jungle scenes, wild animals, flowers, and other non-traditional designs.

Visitors to Sarchí can have a go at painting the carts themselves with fine-tipped brushes, or alternatively they can leave it to the experts and order a custom-painted cart; these are often used as home bars or as decorations at hotels and the country estates of the wealthy.

ABOVE: a family tradition of whittling lives on in the charming, wooden "House of the Dreamer," carved by sculptor Macedonio Quesada in the Orosí Valley. His sons now create fascinating figures out of coffee-tree roots, for sale at very reasonable prices.

RIGHT ABOVE AND BELOW: in a Sarchí workshop, an array of paint cans stands ready to transform traditional ox-cart wheels into colorful kaleidoscopes. In the town's central park, you can snap a photo of the world's biggest painted ox cart.

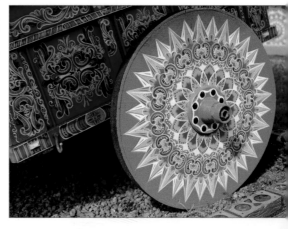

THE CENTRAL PACIFIC

The Central Pacific beaches are among the best in Costa Rica, and there is a host of natural wonders to see en route. Manuel Antonio National Park is the stuff of tropical dreams

W hen the chaos of San José becomes a bit too much, get away from it all and onto a Pacific beach. A new highway to the Pacific has put Playa Jacó, one of the country's most developed seaside destinations, within two hours' drive of the capital. If you prefer something a little less hectic, some of the country's finest beaches, in and around Manuel Antonio National Park, are just an hour's drive farther south of Jacó.

The road to the coast

If you go by car, and want to take the scenic route to the coast (as opposed to the new highway, *see page 170*), turn off the highway toward Atenas, past the Juan Santamaría International Airport, then head through La Garita de Alajuela. One of the first lowland towns that you will approach is Orotina, festooned with fresh fruit stands. The road to Orotina winds through coffee plantations built on precariously steep slopes. Driving along the ledges of these mountains, you will be treated to views of rich green farmland and undulating valleys.

As you approach the **Río Tárcoles bridge ❶**, you will notice tourists clustered at the railings, cameras and binoculars aimed downward. The fascination here is **crocodiles** – gray,

primordial behemoths, some as long as 7 meters (20ft), basking on the muddy banks or stealthily patrolling the brown river, with only snouts and crenellated spines showing above the water line. Most crocodilians in Costa Rica are the smaller cayman species. This is the easiest place to spot as many as 20 of these larger American crocodiles or *Crocodylus acutus* lurking here at the river's mouth.

The **Parque Nacional Carara ❷**, one of the country's smallest reserves but richest in wildlife, borders the highway

Main attractions
CROCODILES AT TÁRCOLES BRIDGE
PARQUE NACIONAL CARARA
LA CATARATA MANANTIAL WATERFALL
PLAYA JACÓ
RAINMAKER NATURE PRESERVE
QUEPOS
PARQUE NACIONAL MANUEL ANTONIO
PLAYA ESPADILLA
SURFING AT PLAYA HERMOSA

PRECEDING PAGES: Manuel Antonio National Park. **LEFT:** making a call at Playa Jacó. **RIGHT:** exotic plumage of the scarlet macaw.

TIP

Theft is on the increase all along the Central Pacific coast. Don't leave your belongings unattended on the beach or in a car; and keep valuables in your hotel's safe.

between Playa Jacó and Puntarenas just south of the bridge (daily 7am–4pm; charge). Because Carara lies in a transitional zone between humid and dry forest, it sustains wildlife from mountainous terrain, primary and secondary forests, lagoons, and marshlands of the Tárcoles River. The vegetation in Carara covers a similarly broad range: from shady evergreens to towering rainforest giants draped with epiphytes and strangling vines.

Among the birds most commonly spotted here are toucans and araçaris (similar to toucans, but smaller) and endangered scarlet macaws (*see box opposite*). Squirrel, howler, white-faced, and spider monkeys are often seen, and, very, very rarely, wildcats such as margays, jaguarundis, ocelots, and jaguars. There are also sloths, coatis, and agoutis, as well as a variety of reptiles, and lovely, blue morpho butterflies. Guides are invaluable in interpreting the ecological complexity of this reserve; they are available right at the park entrance, or by advance request (contact the National Parks Service; tel: 8383 9953).

In the evenings, when the lowlands cool, pairs of macaws fly down from their daytime feeding areas in the mountains. At sunset, park your car near the bridge over the Tárcoles River along the highway outside of the park entrance and listen for their raucous squawking as they fly to their roosting areas in the nearby coastal mangroves. Also watch for shorebirds and waders that frequent the estuary. Roseate spoonbills, with their startling pink plumage, are spectacular at sunset. Crocodiles bask on the river banks, apparently comatose, but they are waiting for a prize, such as a careless spoonbill.

Crocodile tours run along the Tárcoles River, but stay well away from irresponsible operators who encourage their clients to feed the crocs with pieces of meat. Once a crocodile associates a person with food, it is one dangerous animal.

Several kilometers from the Jacó–San José highway, 17km (10 miles) before Playa Jacó, you come to **La Catarata Manantial de Agua Viva Waterfall ❸** (daily 8am–3pm; charge),

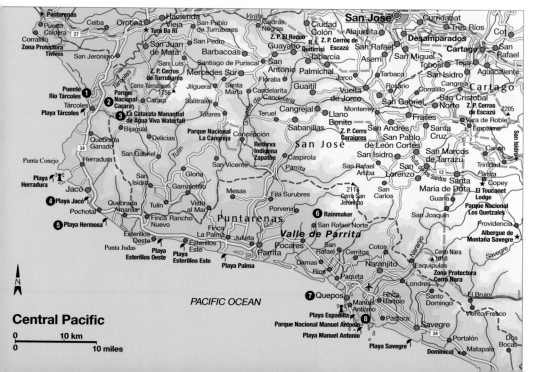

Central Pacific

a 200-meter (650ft) -high waterfall, one of the highest in the country. You can hike the 3km (2 miles) up to the falls if you are in good shape – take plenty of water with you – or you can drive up the dirt road 5km (3 miles) south of the entrance to **Hotel Villa Lapas**, which offers hikes along suspension bridges, a canopy tour and comfortable rooms in an all-inclusive resort hotel (*see page 268*).

The beaches

If you are anticipating the white-powder beaches washed by gentle, clear waters of tourist brochures, then the beaches of the Central Pacific could be something of a disappointment (Jacó sand is a dirty gray). The lure of these places is their proximity to San José, their big waves for surfers and their lively nightlife, not their picture-postcard perfection. Still, with a bit of exploration off the main road, away from the density and hustle of the central beach scene, you will find some clean and appealing beaches. **Playa Herradura** lies five minutes' drive north of Jacó, its waves are gen-

tle, and there are trees for shade and for stringing hammocks on the public end of the beach. The other end is dominated by the huge Marriott Los Sueños resort and marina. **Playa Esterillos** is a long 11km (7-mile) stretch of mostly deserted beach, about 10km (6 miles) south of Jacó, but beware of strong riptides. Best to avoid Playa Tárcoles, which is polluted.

Jacó Beach

Playa Jacó ❹, once famous for its year-round surfing waves and raucous, party-time ambience fueled by plenty of cold beer, has morphed into a concrete collection of high-rise hotel chains, condominiums, and outposts of trendy San José sportswear shops and restaurant chains. There are still a few inexpensive *cabinas* to rent near the beach, but most accommodations are in hotels, with swimming pools, bars, air conditioning, and tour packages to other points of interest in this coastal province. Perhaps the hotel pool is the best place to swim in Jacó since the water is not very clean and there are dangerous undercurrents. Jacó has no

A beach café's novel way of advertising its menu.

BELOW: a tranquil moment at Playa Jacó.

Conserving the Macaws

Scarlet macaws are the great glory of Carara National Park. These enormous red, yellow, and blue parrots mate for life and live for more than 30 years. They nest in December, and in January the young are still in their nests, easy prey for thieves who sell them on the black market. Public-education campaigns to discourage people from buying macaw chicks, along with checkpoints along the highways to search cars during peak vacation times, have had some effect in lowering the number of scarlet macaws in captivity. But it is impossible to estimate how many of the birds are still kept as pets by Costa Ricans. Thanks to conservation programs, there are more scarlet macaws in the wild than there were 10 years ago, but there are still fewer than 1,300 in the entire country.

Iced drinks for sale on Playa Espadilla, Manuel Antonio National Park.

BELOW: driving in Costa Rica is rarely without interest.

shortage of amusements: horses, bikes, scooters, and kayaks are available for rent. Chuck's WOW Surf Shop (tel: 2643 3844) rents and sells surfboards, gives lessons, and posts a daily surf report. For dancing, try Club Olé; for billiards, visit the Jungle Bar, above the Subway sandwich shop. Men should be aware that the companionship of a local girl may cost them more than the price of a few drinks, and thieves and drug-dealers add an unsavory note to the night scene.

A haven of elegance amid the honkytonk Jacó atmosphere is **Hotel Poseidon** (tel: 2643 1642), in the center of town on a quiet side street. The restaurant serves sophisticated fare with an Asian-infused take on fresh fish. At the far southern end of the beach, **Hotel Club del Mar Resort** (tel: 2643 3194) offers another enclave of sophistication, comfort, and tranquility (*see page 268*).

Along the coast some 3km (2 miles) from Playa Jacó is **Playa Hermosa ❺**, a world-class surfing spot with very strong beach breaks. It's the venue for many national and international surfing competitions. It is an easily accessible place where there is also a variety of wading birds to observe: great white herons and snowy egrets; and great blue, little blue, tricolor, and little green herons. You may also see jacanas, walking on lily pads on their huge yellow feet; and black-bellied whistling ducks.

Head east on the coastal highway for 40km (24 miles) to the small plantation town of **Parrita**, dominated by an enormous African oil-palm development, which was established in 1985. Oil palms do very well here. Palm-oil workers live next to the highway, in plantation villages of two-story, brightly painted homes, set in a "U" around what is the focal point of every *Tico* village: the soccer field.

Around 10km (6 miles) east of Parrita is the tiny village of Pocares from where you should turn inland and continue for around 6–7km (4 miles) to reach **Rainmaker ❻** (tel: 2777 3565), an exciting, 610-hectare (1,500-acre) private nature reserve and eco-project. Visitors can explore the rainforest canopy with the minimum of environmental disturbance, walking on boardwalks that link six suspension bridges;

A Faster Way to the Beach

After 35 years in the planning stages, the 77km (48-mile) Caldera Highway finally opened in January 2010. The new toll road was designed to reduce travel time to the Central Pacific beaches. Unfortunately, by the time it was finally built – with only two lanes most of the way and not enough passing lanes – the road couldn't handle the prevailing amount of traffic – which probably hadn't been anticipated when the planning began. What is more, long lines at toll booths added to the congestion. As a final blow, 11km (7 miles) of the highway was closed to traffic in June 2010 for repairs to prevent the road's steep sides from sliding down. If you do leave early enough on a weekday morning, though, you may just be lucky and sail through to Caldera in an hour.

one bridge spans 90 meters (300ft), and at the highest point of the trail you will be a dizzying 25 stories above the jungle floor. Visits must be booked in advance with operators in Quepos and Manuel Antonio (*see below*).

Manuel Antonio National Park

Once an important banana-shipping port, **Quepos** ❼ is now something of a dormitory town and business center for Manuel Antonio, 7km (4 miles) away. There are some good accommodations, restaurants, shops, banks, and nightlife, a regular bus service, and the flavor of an old-time fishing and banana town. The sport fishing here is excellent. Hotel reservations are essential during the vacation season at both Manuel Antonio and Quepos.

The **Parque Nacional Manuel Antonio** ❽ (tel: 2777 5185; Tue–Sun 7am–4pm) encompasses three long strands of magnificent white sand, fringed by jungle and the Pacific Ocean, along with 7 sq km (3 sq miles) of forest. The beaches are clean and wide. Above them are tall cliffs covered in thick jungle vegetation. This park is one of the few places in the country where the primary forest comes down to the water's edge in places, sometimes allowing bathers to swim in the shade. In order to protect the ecosystem of the park, rangers allow a maximum of 600 visitors on weekdays and 800 on weekends. It's best to avoid weekends when the beaches can be crowded; early morning is the best time to visit when tourist groups are fewer and animal sightings easiest. There are always licensed naturalist guides available at the entrance to the park; hiring one will greatly increase your chances of spotting wildlife.

Playa Espadilla is the very popular public beach just outside the north end of the park. It is beautiful but it has unpredictable riptides. From Playa Espadilla, you enter the park across an estuary, which at high tide often requires a boat ride. To get to **Playa Espadilla Sur**, the first beach in the park, follow the jungly path across a long sand spit called a *tombolo*. **Playa Manuel Antonio** and **Playa Puerto Escondido** require more hiking but

TIP

As tempting as it is to feed those cute monkeys begging on the beach, resist. It's unhealthy for visitors – they bite! – and it's unhealthy for the monkeys, which are starting to show high-cholesterol levels from eating junk food.

BELOW: white-faced capuchin monkeys in Manuel Antonio National Park.

Enjoying the beach at Manuel Antonio.

RIGHT: a three-toed sloth in Manuel Antonio Park.
BELOW: eco-hotel Sí Como No.

the latter, accessible only at low tide, is less crowded. All provide relatively safe swimming, but watch out for rocks hidden by high tides.

There are excellent trails for hiking and wildlife sighting. Keep an eye out for all four of Costa Rica's monkey species – the aggressive, white-faced (or capuchin) monkeys that may steal your picnic (or bite you, so don't feed them); the larger, acrobatic spider monkeys (*colorados*) that keep their distance; the sedentary leaf-eating howler monkeys (*mono congo*); and the tiny squirrel monkeys (*titís*) that tumble through the tree tops.

Birdlife encompasses more than 350 species, including boobies, frigate birds, pelicans, and terns. Snakes and iguanas abound, and if you are sharp-eyed, you may be able to distinguish a sloth from a heap of vegetation in a *cecropia* tree. You can sunbathe, body surf, swim and snorkel (if you bring your own gear), and picnic (if you bring your own food – there is no food service in the park). There are very rudimentary rest rooms and cold-water showers at playas Espadilla Sur and Manuel Antonio.

Activities outside the park

Outside the park, you can rent horses from **Equus Stables** (tel: 2777 0001) for a ride along the beach or to a waterfall; or you could go on a sunset sailing cruise, offered through **Iguana Tours** (tel: 2777 2052). Other options in areas outside the national park include mountain biking, white-water river rafting or sea kayaking tours, available from **Ríos Tropicales** (tel: 2777 4092). For excellent assistance and information on the area, as well as books and papers in English and local handicrafts, drop in at **La Buena Nota** shop at the north end of the village of Manuel Antonio, near the beach.

Just outside the park to the north, in the hills that rise up from the beach, there is a garish profusion of signs advertising an ever-growing number of hotels, restaurants, and *cabinas*. With rare exceptions, most accommodations on the ocean side of the road are built on the cliffs above the beach and offer views of the ocean rather than direct access to beaches. One of the best views is from **Hotel Sí Como No** (tel: 2777 0777; www.sicomono.com), a luxury eco-hotel that has won international prizes for its sustainability in both design and services (*see page 269*). For access to secluded beaches, the new eco-hotel **Arenas del Mar Beach and Nature Resort** is unbeatable (*see page 268*).

You can get to Manuel Antonio by car, bus, or plane. The road is paved all the way to Quepos, and new bridges have replaced the rickety old wooden ones. You will pass through some beautiful countryside, although the flat coastal section runs through endless green corridors of palm plantations, which can soon become monotonous. It's about a three-hour trip by car, some four hours by bus, and 20 minutes by plane. SANSA and NatureAir both fly daily to Quepos. Be sure to book your plane tickets well in advance, especially during the peak "dry season," January through April. ❏

The North

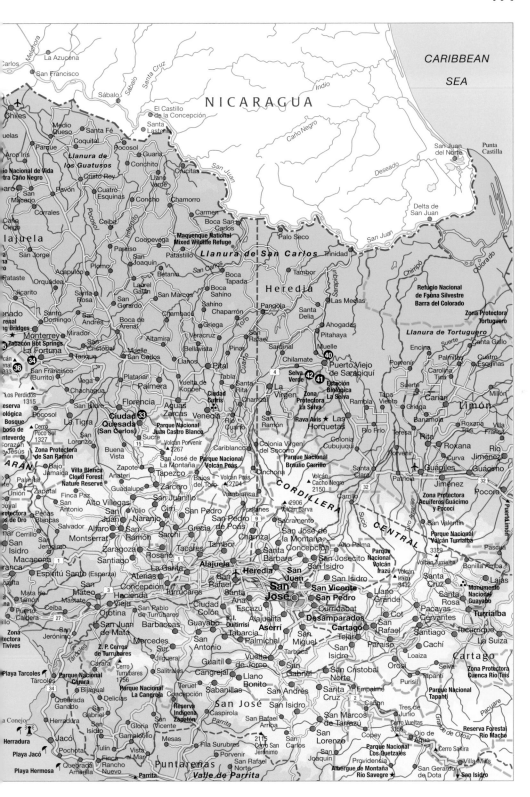

San José

THE NORTHWEST

Almost all of Costa Rica's natural attractions are represented in this large and rewarding region: miles of beaches and acres of tropical forests, interspersed with cattle ranges and cowboy towns

he northwest of the country spreads over two provinces, the largest of which is Guanacaste. This is Costa Rica's Big Country, where vast grasslands are punctuated by huge spreading guanacaste trees and bony, white Brahman cattle. During the rainy season, the landscape is a sea of green, but in the dry season, the savannahs become sun-baked tracts of gold. Though traditionally cattle country, Guanacaste is better known nowadays for its beaches, many of which have been developed as part of controversially large hotel resorts. Overdevelopment in some areas has even engendered a new word: Guanacastefición, signifying unsustainable tourist development. But with the promise of guaranteed sunny hot weather from December through April, sun-starved visitors from northern climes continue to arrive at the Daniel Oduber International Airport south of Liberia by the thousand, the majority of them on all-inclusive, package beach holidays.

The other province is Puntarenas, which straddles the Gulf of Nicoya and takes in the South Nicoya Peninsula. It is a vacation paradise of broad sandy beaches, turquoise waters, and shady palm trees. Also just within this region (though it actually belongs to Alajuela

province) is the extremely popular Monteverde Cloud Forest.

The Guanacastecos

The *Guanacastecos*, as the residents of this province are called, are self-reliant people. You may spot a bumper sticker on a local car, declaring (in Spanish, of course) "Thank God I was born in Guanacaste." Many are descended from the Chorotega Amerindians, with skin the color of tortoise shell, eyes a warm brown, black wavy hair, and an easy, friendly grace.

> **Main attractions**
> PUNTARENAS
> MONTEZUMA
> CABO BLANCO ABSOLUTE WILDLIFE RESERVE
> PARQUE NACIONAL PALO VERDE
> RINCÓN DE LA VIEJA NATIONAL PARK
> PARQUE NACIONAL SANTA ROSA
> PLAYA TAMARINDO AREA
> PLAYA NOSARA
> PLAYA SÁMARA
> PARQUE NACIONAL BARRA HONDA
> MONTEVERDE CLOUD FOREST
> RESERVA SANTA ELENA

PRECEDING PAGES: Playa Samara, in the Guanacaste province. **LEFT:** Montezuma inhabitants. **RIGHT:** the adobe Church of San Blas in Nicoya town.

Take a trip into the glorious waters of the Gulf of Nicoya aboard the luxurious, 21-meter (71ft) Manta Ray catamaran, which sails from the Calypso dock in Puntarenas.

Democratic decision

In 1787, the Captaincy General of Costa Rica, which then governed the country from Guatemala, decided that Guanacaste should be part of Nicaragua. There it stayed until 1821 when the Captaincy General was dissolved and the people of Guanacaste were asked to decide their own national identity. Opinions were divided: the Northerners around Liberia wanted to be a part of Nicaragua and the Southerners on the Nicoya Peninsula wanted to revert to Costa Rica. A vote was held and the majority elected to be a part of Costa Rica.

Puntarenas

Many people think **Puntarenas** ❶ (pop. 106,000) is simply a place to pass through to get somewhere else: namely, to the islands of the Gulf of Nicoya, or the southern part of the Nicoya Peninsula, via the car ferries that leave from Puntarenas to cross the Gulf of Nicoya.

Puntarenas used to be the country's main port, a mini-Marseilles, bustling with longshoremen, sailors on leave,

prostitutes, and merchants from San José who traveled by train to escape the city heat and conduct their import/export businesses. But the growth of the Caribbean port of Limón and the more recent opening of the deep-water port at nearby **Puerto Caldera** have made Puntarenas somewhat of a commercial anachronism.

Stretched along a narrow spit of sand – *punta de arenas*, or point of sand – Puntarenas is still worth exploring, though. You can even arrive here aboard a vintage diesel train, courtesy of the **Tico Train Tour**, which travels on weekends, leaving San José's old Pacific railroad station at 6am and arriving in Caldera at 11am (reserve ahead, tel: 2233 3300).

Today, fishing is the main industry of Puntarenas and a visit to the busy fish market is exciting. Go early in the morning and watch expert shellfish shuckers and fish gutters at work. Or perch on a stool at one of the food counters in the market and sample a *ceviche* (fish marinated in lime juice) or a filet of fish just off the boat, part of a catch that will soon be making its

BELOW: fisherman mending his net on Paseo de Turistas, Puntarenas.

way to the fish-packing plants at the entrance to Puntarenas or to Central Valley markets in refrigerated trucks. Tourism in the town is boosted by the arrival of huge cruise ships at the town's modern dock, and there are some comfortable beach-front hotels.

The **Puntarenas Marine Park** (tel: 2661 5275; Tue–Sun 8am–4.30pm; charge) at the east end of town has 28 large aquariums showcasing the marine life of the Gulf of Nicoya. With its views of the long, arching coastline, the beach along the gulf is beautiful, and the sunsets over Nicoya are quite spectacular. The downtown section of the beach is pleasant and clean, and flies the Bandera Azul (blue flag), denoting an eco-friendly, clean beach inspected by government officials. Swimming in the estuary and rivers, however, should be avoided.

Downtown

The crowded center of Puntarenas, three blocks back from the beach, bustles in the morning as the townsfolk, called *porteños*, conduct business, often getting around on bicycles.

Everyone seems in a hurry, perhaps to accomplish what they need to do before the onset of the afternoon heat. Though it is, like San José, an architectural victim of excessive concrete, Puntarenas still retains many of its older buildings: plank structures with latticework below the roof to permit the breeze, and "gingerbread" detailing reminiscent of Victorian mansions. The wooden buildings are painted in bright color combinations, and, together with the few remaining mansions of the merchants, a smattering of Art Deco buildings, and the magnificent stone church, they convey the flavor of Puntarenas in its prime.

Evening is perhaps the best time to catch Puntarenas. Enjoy a late afternoon *refresco* at one of the *sodas* (cafés) on the long, broad **Paseo de Turistas** fronting the beach and watch the sun sink below the mountains of Nicoya across the bay. The *sodas* offer a chance to try some native Costa Rican fruit drinks. This is perhaps the only place in the country to get *maté*, a type of milkshake with a lingering, nostalgic aftertaste. Or try a cold, creamy

When in Puntarenas, try a "Churchill" sundae, a sweet, icy fruit drink with condensed milk.

BELOW: selling kebabs on Paseo de Turistas.

TIP

If you like a game of golf or enjoy horseback riding, there are resorts on the Nicoya Peninsula that specialize in both activities.

"Churchill," a very sweet, icy fruit drink that includes condensed milk.

Seafood restaurants and hotels line the ocean front. Most are air-conditioned or are sited to catch the gulf breezes. On the estuary that runs parallel to the town, the professionaly managed Yacht Club is well protected, and is one of the very first stops a trans-oceanic yacht makes on the first leg of a trip from the West Coast of the US to more distant ports of call.

Just to the south, down the coast from Puntarenas, is **Playa Doña Ana**, on a cove well situated between two spectacular rocky headlands. Costa Rica's second-largest surfing wave is just offshore. A few kilometers along the road toward Caldera is a turn-off for Mata de Limón, where you can sit at a waterfront table and enjoy some of the tasty seafood and fish special-ties for which Puntarenas is famous, at the **Restaurante y Marisquería Leda** (tel: 2634 4087).

The Gulf of Nicoya

Car ferries, as well as a smaller, passen-ger-only *lancha* (launch), cross from Puntarenas to Paquera on the **Nicoya Peninsula**. The one-hour trip across the gulf passes by 40 or so islands, including **Isla San Lucas** ❷, Costa Rica's former prison island. The prison was closed in 1991 and the island deserted, except for the guards posted there to prevent vandalism. There are no restrictions prevent-ing visits to the island, however, and visitors who are so inclined can view disturbing reminders of the life pris-oners endured here.

Calypso Tours offers a cruise on its 21-meter (71ft) catamaran *Manta Ray*, outfitted with two on-deck pools, to the islands in the Gulf of Nicoya. It crosses the waters of the Gulf and visits **Isla Tortuga** ❸ (Turtle Island), where, in an idyllic setting of white sand and turquoise waters, you can enjoy a sea-food buffet, recently heralded in an article in *Gourmet Magazine*, served with white wine. There is also ade-quate time for swimming, snorkeling or optional kayaking and pedal boat rides, and, of course, for sunbathing.

Calypso, one of the oldest tour oper-ators in Costa Rica, also offers other

BELOW: tourists playing football on the beach at Puntarenas.

excellent tours, including fishing and diving trips (tel: 2256 2727).

The South Nicoya Peninsula

The ferry ride across the Gulf of Nicoya will bring you to a different world of seasonally dry grasslands, gigantic spreading trees, rolling cattle ranches, memorable bays, and some beautiful beaches.

From the ferry landing at Paquera, Tambor is just a short drive, and Montezuma is about an hour away. Buses wait to meet the Paquera ferry to head south to Montezuma, but there are no such direct services from the other ferry landing farther north at Playa Naranjo. If you are driving south from Paquera, the roads are largely unpaved, with few road signs, but the local people are used to giving visitors directions.

The drive along the peninsula, although rough, is rewarding. It traverses many kilometers of pasture land, through small towns and villages, past people on foot or on horseback, and dwellings of every description – and every now and again reveals views of the blue bays of the Pacific.

Some 7km (4 miles) south of the town of Paquera lies the **Refugio Nacional de Vida Silvestre Curú 4** (Curú National Wildlife Refuge; daily 7am–3pm; charge; tel: 2641 0100). Although small, the park encompasses five habitats and offers sanctuary to a surprisingly large and diverse number of plants, animals (including the white-faced monkey and a healthy group of reintroduced *mono colorado* (spider) monkeys), and more than 230 species of birds. It has three beautiful beaches, ideal for swimming and diving. There are very basic accommodations available, along with horseback tours and sea kayaking to nearby islands. The hiking is also excellent. The refuge is private property, owned by the eco-minded Schutt family; it's a good idea to call in advance to arrange accommodations and tours.

Bahía Ballena

Bahía Ballena 5, which means Whale Bay, is an expansive bay of surprising beauty and tranquility. The waters are gentle and warm, with large flocks of pelicans diving for fish. January is

Huge guanacaste trees punctuate the vast grasslands in the country's northwest.

BELOW: the pool and jacuzzi overlook the sea at Hotel Los Mangos in Montezuma.

Enjoy a romantic dinner under the trees at Playa de los Artistas, Montezuma.

an especially good time for sighting whales. The bay shelters two beaches, **Playa Pochote** and **Playa Tambor**, with shallow water ideal for wading. In the 1990s, however, its tranquil face was irrevocably and controversially transformed by the construction of the enormous, Spanish-owned resort, Hotel Barceló Playa Tambor. The project inspired a passionate debate about what kind of tourism is best for Costa Rica: mammoth projects such as this, which involved the removal of mangroves to create a beach, or small enterprises that reflect the character of their communities. In the end, big business won.

In the village of **Tambor**, inexpensive lodgings and good local-style meals can be found, and you might just get a sense of life as it was before the arrival of big-time tourism. Continuing southeast through the town of Cóbano, the road leads to Montezuma.

Montezuma

Montezuma ❻ in many ways feels like the end of the line. The partially paved road rolls down a steep hill (sometimes with actual gaps in the road) and ends abruptly in front of a row of funky hotels, trendy restaurants and bars, and *cantinas* (snack bars) on the beach front. Here, young North American and European travelers far outnumber the local people, who have accepted them with seeming good grace. Hotel rooms fill up quickly everywhere in Montezuma during the dry season and peak holiday times, so reserve well ahead.

Lodging and dining in Montezuma range from the basic to the luxurious, and the beach-going is exceptional. To the north of town there are wide, sandy beaches, with beautiful clear water. A scenic footpath leads north for 6km (4 miles) to a dramatic waterfall that spills into a pool right on the beach. To the south, the surf crashes against volcanic rock – and, just a short hike away up a river, there is another waterfall with a pool for swimming. Although it's tempting to dive in, don't; in recent years there have been some tragic accidents here when Tarzan-emulating young men have plunged head-first into the rocky pool. The first couple of

rocky bays north of Montezuma have strong currents, but Playa Grande is safe for swimming.

Sheer indulgence

You can rent bikes and boogie boards at agencies in town, and horses through the Finca Los Caballos, outside of town, as well as through in-town tour operators. But most visitors to Montezuma seem to spend their time swimming, sunning, or simply hanging out in this laid-back place that seems expressly designed for the youthful, low-budget traveler, as well as for more experienced travelers who appreciate its off-the-beaten-track casual atmosphere. Off in a world of its own, a 15-minute walk north along the beach, **Ylang Ylang Beach Resort** (tel: 2642 0636) caters to nature-lovers, with accommodations ranging from comfortable tents to charming bungalows in a lush garden setting complete with pool and spa services (*see page 271*).

Perhaps the most romantic restaurant in all of Costa Rica is tucked away on a rocky cove, a few minutes' walk south of town. Italian-owned **Playa de los Artistas** specializes in seafood served alfresco at driftwood tables illuminated at night by lanterns and starlight (tel: 2642 0920; Mon–Sat).

Cabo Blanco

It is almost 11km (7 miles) from Montezuma to the **Cabo Blanco Absolute Wildlife Reserve** ❼ (www.nicoya peninsula.com/caboblanco; Wed–Sun 8am–4pm) along a little-used, unpaved road that runs parallel to the beach. En route, there is a cluster of small *cabina*-hotels in the town of Cabuya. The reserve, established in 1963 through the inspiration and tireless efforts of Swedish immigrant and national parks pioneer Nils Olaf Wessberg (*see page 84*), is Costa Rica's oldest protected wildlife region.

Originally, Cabo Blanco meant what its name said (*blanco* in Spanish means blank as well as white), and there was no public access. All life there was to be protected, without any interference from humans. Today, however, visitors can see approximately one-third of the 1,200-hectare (3,000-acre) reserve, encompassing a wet, tropical forest on

Spiky agaves grow in Cabo Blanco.

BELOW: horseback riding on the beach at Montezuma.

Guanacaste Culture

Since the annexation of Guanacaste in 1824, its traditions have formed an important part of *Tico* culture. Annexation Day is celebrated as a national holiday on the Monday closest to July 25 throughout the country and particularly in the northwest. In honor of the latecomer province, the country's national tree is the wide-spreading Guanacaste tree that rises up out of many northwest cattle pastures. And whenever a national cultural event needs folk dancers, organizers call on Guanacaste dance troupes, the women dressed in colourful swinging skirts and the men in the traditional costume of white trousers and shirts, with red bandanas and straw hats. But Guanacaste's most pervasive contribution may be *gallo pinto*, the national dish of rice and beans which *Guanacastecans* claim to have invented.

Founded 20 years ago by a Swiss animal-lover, Las Pumas provides a haven for rescued wild cats and other animals. Since the death of its founder, it has been run by the non-profit Hagnauer Foundation; donations are welcome.

the tip of the peninsula. It is one of the most scenic spots along the whole Pacific coast. It is also one of the hottest, so bring plenty of drinking water. There is a large population of marine and shore birds here as well as mammals. In addition, there is a ranger station with rest rooms and picnic tables, well-maintained trails, and a lovely remote beach, where you can wade in to cool off.

To drive to the reserve you must cross two small streams – for which a four-wheel-drive vehicle is recommended. Remember that, as noted above, the reserve is closed on Monday and Tuesday to reduce the impact of tourism.

Beyond Cabo Blanco, the road heading up the Pacific coast is rough and unpaved. During the rainy season it is extremely muddy and some of the rivers and creeks without bridges are only passable in a four-wheel-drive vehicle. During the dry season things don't get any more comfortable either as vehicles churn up a fine, brown dust that coats travelers and plants along the roadway.

Surfers and nature-lovers gravitate to Malpais and Santa Teresa, two beaches about 6km (4 miles) north of Cabo Blanco. A cluster of hotels and restaurants has sprung up to cater to an international, young surfing crowd, along with a few luxury retreats aimed at well-heeled travelers who value creature comforts in a really remote setting *(see page 271).*

The Interamericana northbound

Past Puntarenas the Interamericana Highway, route C1, cuts northwest straight through the heart of Guanacaste, bisecting its capital, Liberia, and heading northward to Nicaragua.

At **Cañas** you first get the sense that immense Guanacaste is more like a separate country than it is a province of Costa Rica. Cañas, which was named for the fields of white-flowered wild cane that used to cover the countryside, is a cowboy town, with a frontier feeling, not unlike a village in Mexico.

Four kilometers (2½ miles) north of Cañas on the highway you reach **Las**

BELOW: father and son at a rodeo near Liberia.

Pumas ❽ (daily 8am–5pm; donations requested), a private wildlife refuge that provides shelter for some of Costa Rica's large cats that, for various reasons, are not able to live in the wild. For most visitors, this will be the only chance to see – and photograph – a jaguar or a puma, if not in the wild, at least rescued from the wild.

About 4km (2½ miles) north of Cañas, **Safaris Corobicí** (tel: 2669 6191) offers guided "floats" down the Corobicí River on its 6-meter (17ft) Avon rafts, a wonderful opportunity to observe the river habitat, especially the birds – laughing falcons, herons, trogons, wood storks, mot-mots, parrots, osprey, and, of course, egrets. Howler and white-faced monkeys all make their homes along the shores of the Corobicí. Plan for an early-morning trip to enjoy the best birding.

Palo Verde National Park

Parque Nacional Palo Verde ❾ (www. conozcacostarica.com/parques/paloverde. htm) is one of Central America's largest protected wildlife areas, occupying 198 sq km (76 sq miles) near the mouth

of the Tempisque River. To get there, take the road from Bagaces to the west, off the Interamericana highway. Four-wheel-drive is recommended, especially during the rainy season.

Palo Verde encompasses lakes, swamps, woodlands, grasslands, and forest, and is a major sanctuary for migrating waterfowl in Central America. Tidal fluctuations and seasonally overflowing rivers attract around 300 species of terrestrial and water birds, including herons, whistling ducks, ibises, and the immense Jabirú stork with its distinctive red neck band. Large mammals and reptiles are also abundant and can be seen especially well during the dry season when they gather at water holes. Coatimundis, armadillos, iguanas, and crocodiles measuring up to 5 meters (16ft) long are not uncommon here. You can stay in dormitory-style lodging in the park or in the slightly more comfortable lodge, with air conditioning, run by the Organization for Tropical Studies (tel: 2524 0607).

Only 25 years ago, currents and sediment run-off from Guanacaste

Sunday-best cowboy tack kept in mint condition.

BELOW: Costa Rican tack more closely resembles the Western gear used by North American cowboys than English-style equipment.

Back in the Saddle

Before tourism arrived with a bang in the 1990s, Guanacaste was cowboy country, and Liberia was literally a cow town, with dusty dirt roads. As late as 2000, you were as likely to see horses parked on the streets as cars.

There are still some working cowboys around – in Costa Rica they are called *sabaneros* or *vaccaros* – and the best way to see them in action is at a rodeo. Some towns hold rodeos as part of their annual saint's day fiestas: for example, Santa Cruz, which mounts the biggest rodeo during its early January festival.

Liberia also pays tribute to its cowboy past at the one-room Museo El Sabanero located in the Casa de Culture. Along with exhibits of old saddles, spurs, and harness, there is a fascinating collection of vintage photographs.

A statuesque white egret. These birds nest on Isla de Pájaros.

BELOW:
steaming volcanic mud pools at Rincón de la Vieja.

formed a sand bar, which then became stabilized as an island in the middle of the Tempisque River near the head of the Gulf of Nicoya. Today, it is known as **Isla de Pájaros**  (often confused with the Isla Pajáros Biological Reserve farther south in the gulf). From the park, you can charter a boat and guide to take you to this tiny sheltered islet. While the white ibis and a species of egret make up most of the birds that regularly nest here, roseate spoonbills, wood storks, and anhingas also make their homes on Isla de Pájaros. The noise during nesting season, when chicks are squawking for food, is deafening.

Directly across the river is **Rancho Humo** (tel: 2233 2233; www.rancho humo.com), a private wetlands preserve of more than 800 hectares (2,000 acres) that offers excellent day-long tours in quiet electric carts around a water wonderland teeming with wading birds and wildlife. Access is via the Friendship Bridge and backroads, starting from Honda Quebrada, on the Nicoya Peninsula; tours are by reservation only.

Liberia

The capital city of Guanacaste province, **Liberia** ⑪ was established more than 200 years ago. It is also known as Ciudad Blanca, the White City, owing to the traditional white adobe houses that were built using the white volcanic earth and gravel from the nearby slopes of Rincón de la Vieja and Miravalles volcanoes. In the *Puertas del Sol* – "Doorways of the Sun" – style, these houses were designed to let both morning and afternoon sunlight into north-facing corner houses. A few of these lovely old adobe homes can still be seen, along the city's narrow streets, just south of the park. Many of the houses have classical courtyards and grand rooms with high ceilings and 19th-century murals. The kitchens, to the rear of the house, open onto courtyards, where corn and other grains were once dried.

Early morning is an ideal time to take a walk through the center of Liberia. Visit **Agonía Church** (located at the end of the main street), an adobe structure built in 1852 and one of the oldest Catholic churches in the country. Stroll down Paseo Real, the last remaining colonial-era street, running east from the Central Park. Apart from these few colonial remnants, Liberia is starting to resemble a giant shopping mall, and even has a multiplex cinema on the outskirts of town.

Rincón de la Vieja National Park

About 5km (3 miles) north of Liberia along the Interamericana Highway, you will reach the turn-off for **Parque Nacional Rincón de la Vieja** ⑫ (www.conozcacostarica.com/parques/rincon. htm). This spectacular park contains four complete ecosystems within its 14,000 hectares (35,000 acres). The name, which applies to both the park and the volcano it protects, derives from the legend of an old woman who once lived on its slopes. Her house was referred to as "the old woman's corner" – hence Rincón de la Vieja.

Las Pailas

The road to the Las Pailas entrance, via the small community of Curubandé, is very rough, slow-going for 17km (10 miles). The road appears to be covered in snow but it's actually chalky limestone, the same rock that was used to build the early adobe houses in Liberia. Spectacular views along the way include the green slopes and towering cone of the volcano to the north and, to the west, a verdant valley with grassy coastal plains edging the Pacific Ocean, which you can see on a clear day glistening far below.

At the Las Pailas ranger station, you sign in and pick up a map of the park and the hiking trails. Just steps away is the park's most spectacular volcanic area, **Las Pailas**, Spanish for "the kitchen stoves." There is a well-marked, 3km (2-mile) self-guided loop tour of hot springs, boiling mud pots, sulfur streams, and vapor geysers that color the surrounding rocks red, green, and vivid yellow.

Researchers recently announced the discovery of a new organism that thrives here in the boiling mud and that may prove useful in helping plants adapt to higher temperatures with global warming. Your nose will also be tingling with the strong aroma of rotten eggs (sulfur) here. The warm mud from the so-called *sala de belleza* (beauty salon) makes an excellent facial mask. Visitors must exercise extreme caution, however, and stay on the trail. Breaking through the brittle surface of the area or getting a face full of steam can result in severe burns.

La Cangreja waterfall

From the Las Pailas entrance you can hike for about two hours to the **La Cangreja Waterfall**. The waterfall is 40 meters (132 ft) high and cascades down to form a blue pool. Take a dip in the refreshing swimming hole edged with pockets of contrasting thermal waters. If you tread softly, the wildlife viewing here can be very good. Listen and look for the park's famous resident, the long-tailed manakin, a red, blue, and black bird whose song sounds like "toledo" (the bird's name in Spanish).

The two closest lodges to the park are **Rincón de la Vieja Lodge** (tel: 2200

Testing the skin-nourishing benefits of warm mud at a hot spring.

BELOW: tumbling waters at La Cangreja Waterfall, one of the hiking destinations in Rincón de la Vieja.

TIP

In Parque Nacional Santa Rosa there are fine views from the lookout point at the Monumento a los Héroes – a large concrete arch that commemorates those who fell in battle at Santa Rosa in 1856.

0238), a collection of rustic cabins with good hiking trails to nearby hot springs and an excellent canopy tour; and **Haci-enda Guachipélin** (tel: 2666 8075), a more upscale lodge with comfortable rooms and good food. It is also a working ranch, with first-rate horses and many kilometers of hiking and birding trails and adventure activities, including canopy tours and river tubing.

To the Nicaraguan border

At the end of a day in this region, consider making a short trip east to the village of Santa Cecilia to watch the sun set over **Lake Nicaragua**, or, as the Nicaraguans have named it, "the Sweet Sea." You may be fortunate enough to see freshwater sharks. A rise in the bumpy road about 8km (5 miles) beyond the center of Santa Cecilia brings the vast inland sea that is Lake Nicaragua into view. The infamous William Walker (see page 51) planned to conquer Nicaragua and to use the Nicaraguans as a labor force to build canals from Lake Nicaragua to the Pacific. He envisioned a waterway to transport goods by boat across the isthmus from the Pacific to

the Atlantic. Although wealthy investors in the United States backed this plan, Walker's defeat first by Costa Rica, and later in Honduras, put an end to the venture.

A trip to **Puerto Soley**, on Salinas Bay, passes through the small town of La Cruz, a stopping place for those traveling north through Central America, and for migrant laborers from Nicaragua crossing back and forth, seeking work in Costa Rica.

From La Cruz, there are wonderful windswept views of the valley and Salinas Bay below. Winding down the hill, you will pass a ranch established by Anastasio Somoza, the ex-dictator of Nicaragua, before reaching Puerto Soley, a windy beach with a new villa complex. The wind is so strong here that the windsurfing conditions rival Lake Arenal.

Kite-surfing has also become popular here at **Playa Copal** where two schools offer lessons: the Kite Surfing School operates year-round (tel: 8826 5221); Cometa Copal Kite Surfing Centre (tel: 2676 1192) operates from November through April.

BELOW: kite-surfing lessons can be had at Playa Copal.

Guanacaste National Park

Parque Nacional Guanacaste ⓭ (www.conozcacostarica.com/parques/guanacaste.htm) was created in 1989 with foreign funds donated to Costa Rica's Neotropica and National Park foundations in order to protect the migratory paths of animals living in the adjacent protected area of Santa Rosa National Park *(see below)*.

Parque Nacional Guanacaste encompasses a wide band of largely deforested land that extends from the Orosí and Cacao volcanoes to the Pacific coast. Although it covers only 2 percent of Costa Rica, it contains an astonishing 65 percent of the country's biodiversity. Dry tropical forest dominates this vast land, but habitats ranging from mangrove swamps and beaches to rain- and cloud forest are also within the park's boundaries. Over the past several hundred years, complex patterns of cutting, grazing, burning, and farming have dissected Guanacaste's landscape into a complex mosaic of life zones. Recent forest fires have also taken their toll on huge tracts of regenerating forest.

Despite setbacks, the American visionary ecologist, naturalist, and conservationist, Dan Janzen, whose life work has been the preservation and reforestation of Guanacaste, feels that this park will ultimately be restored to its original state. "Dry forests have been destroyed," Janzen says, "but they are tough, able to withstand six months of drought a year and are very regenerable." In 200 or 300 years, full-grown tropical dry forests may again dominate Guanacaste. For the moment, most of the park is restricted to researchers, but you can arrange a stay by reserving in advance (tel: 2666 5051).

Santa Rosa National Park

Parque Nacional Santa Rosa ⓮ (www.conozcacostarica.com/parques/santarosa.htm; 8am–4.30pm) encompasses virtually all of the environmental habitats of the region. An almost infinite system of trails takes visitors through zones of deciduous tropical hardwoods to arid mountains with deserts of cactus and thorny shrubs, and along rivers lined with forests to mangrove swamp estuaries near the beach. Two of its

Strolling on one of Santa Rosa's remote beaches.

BELOW: Santa Rosa Park is home to white-faced capuchin monkeys.

Diving into Guanacaste

Some of the country's best diving spots are clustered along the Northwest Pacific coast. From north to south: Off Santa Rosa National Park, Murciélago Island is home to bull sharks, lurking in submerged rocks. This is fairly rough water, so only experienced divers should attempt it. Farther south, in the protected waters of the Papagayo Gulf, there is calmer water for beginning divers and good visibility for catching sight of manta rays, moray eels, and huge schools of fish. The Catalina Islands, off Playa Flamingo, are famous for sharks, including nurse, white-tipped, and bull sharks.

The best diving months are March through October, when winds are lighter. Excellent PADI-certified dive shops abound in Playa Hermosa, Playas del Coco, Playa Ocotal, Playa Flamingo, and Tamarindo.

A pestle and mortar at La Casona.

BELOW: surfing is popular along the Nicoya Peninsula.

remote beaches, Nancite and Naranjo, are important turtle nesting sites. Elsewhere, many mammals, including monkeys and peccaries (wild pigs), plus more than 20 species of bats, live in the national park.

During more than 20 years of scientific work at Santa Rosa, biologist Dan Janzen has taught two generations of local people an intelligent appreciation of the forest. Through his work, residents of Guanacaste now have experience and expertise in firefighting, maintaining horses, and managing cattle, identifying plants and dealing with "biotic challenges" like ticks, diseases, thirst, and wounds. Jobs as research assistants, guides, and reserve caretakers provide many with skills and a stable, long-term source of income.

Much of the park is quite difficult to access and requires strenuous hiking. An easy and very accessible trail is the short **Naked Indian Path**. As with many of the park's trails, you pass through forest that, during the dry season, loses many of its leaves, making wildlife viewing easier for the naturalist. Huge multicolored iguanas are commonly seen in the trees bordering the trail. Hiking toward Duende Creek and the bat cave, look for them sunning on tree branches.

Santa Rosa's historical significance as the location of the battle against William Walker *(see page 51)* was a primary factor in the government's decision to make it a national park. A decisive battle against Walker took place at the hacienda called **La Casona** (The Big House; daily 8am–4pm). By coincidence, on the three occasions that Costa Rica has been invaded, it has been here that the invaders were eventually turned back.

Today, a different kind of battle is fought in Santa Rosa: park rangers versus hunters. Though hunting is outlawed in the park, the law is virtually unenforceable due to the inadequate number of rangers. Armed hunters are frequently met by unarmed rangers who often must engage in fights with them to remove them from park boundaries. The low-paid rangers often risk their lives in these skirmishes.

The long-running battle between rangers and poachers reached a

terrible climax in May 2002, when a pair of disgruntled hunters set fire to La Casona, the historic farm estate *(see opposite)*, and burned it to the ground. The house, a landmark in Costa Rican history, has since been rebuilt and once again provides a window into the life of Costa Ricans during the colonial period.

A trail leads from the house to a memorial to the heroes and martyrs of the battle. President Juan Rafael Mora's famous speech, in which he exhorted his countrymen to defend Costa Rica against William Walker, is preserved on an historic plaque.

Expropriated land

Back in the 1970s, during the Nicaraguan Civil War, the Costa Rican government was interested in expanding Santa Rosa Park to help stabilize population levels for some of the park's species. Just to the north of the park, on the border with Nicaragua, former dictator Anastasio Somoza lived on his family ranch, conveniently located so he could move easily and clandestinely back and forth across the border.

Costa Rican leaders felt that the country's best interests were not served by the presence of an ousted military dictator near its border. So, in 1979, the Hacienda Murciélago, owned by the Somoza family, was expropriated and made part of the national parks system. The hacienda, which lies on Santa Elena Bay with access to Playa Blanca and its untouched white-sand beach, is now a part of Santa Rosa Park.

A more recent addition to the park includes land that was once occupied by the formerly secret Santa Elena Airstrip, used to bring in supplies to aid rebel efforts to overthrow the ruling Sandinistas. Built with the blessing of ex-president Alberto Monge, in violation of Costa Rica's neutrality law, the airstrip was torn up under the administration of Oscar Arias in 1986. The Reagan administration took great umbrage to this and drastically decreased US aid money for Costa Rica.

Santa Rosa beaches

A rugged 13km (8-mile) hiking trail, or a road accessible by four-wheel-drive during the dry season (impassable during the wet season), leads from the Santa Rosa ranger station to **Playa Naranjo**. White sand and clear water with excellent surf breaking near Roca de la Bruja (Witch's Rock; *see page 96*), a stone monolith 2km (1 mile) offshore, make Naranjo a popular but remote surfing destination. Boats can be chartered from Playas del Coco to Naranjo. Alternatively, there is camping at both playas Naranjo and Nancite (tel: 2666 5051).

Playa Nancite ⓯, one of Costa Rica's most pristine beaches, is northwest from Naranjo. Each month, usually on a waxing three-quarter moon, turtles come ashore here to nest. Tens of thousands may participate in the event, called an *arribada*, one of Costa Rica's grandest natural spectacles *(see pages 238–9)*. Exact times are unpredictable, as they are with most biological phenomena. Even though a full-scale *arribada* may not be taking place, solitary turtles can sometimes be seen nesting on Nancite and Naranjo beaches.

The Santa Elena Airstrip was financed by a bogus Panamanian company set up by Oliver North, then a member of the US National Security Council, to aid the Sandanistas' opponents, known as the Contras.

BELOW:
a sharp-eyed
Iguana.

Papagayo to Playa Ocotal

And now for something completely different... If you like a beach holiday with lots of action, the Pacific beaches to the southwest of Liberia are extremely popular. This coast is the hub of tourism in Guanacaste, largely owing to the expansion of the Daniel Oduber International Airport just 45 minutes away. Huge, all-inclusive resorts cater to masses of winter-weary tourists arriving in Liberia from the north, in search of sun, surf, and sand.

The Papagayo Peninsula project already has an 18-hole golf course and an ultra-expensive flagship hotel, the Four Seasons Costa Rica Resort, with more hotels and private villas planned. Around **Playa Panamá ⑯**, half a dozen all-inclusive resorts are packed in the high season with budget-minded package travelers who rarely leave the manicured hotel grounds.

To the south is **Playa Hermosa ⑰**, a sparkling half-moon cove with gentle surf. Despite some large-scale development at the northern end, this beach still has some charm and some excellent small restaurants and hotels. It is

also a major diving center, with the long-established Diving Safaris (tel: 2672 1259). Hotel Playa Hermosa Bosque del Mar (tel: 2672 0046), one of the only hotels right on the beach, sits in a lush garden, shaded by mature trees. It's small and as laid-back as a beach hotel can be.

Nearby **Playas del Coco ⑱** is a working beach town with a large fishing fleet. The beach is neither pretty nor great for swimming but it is the launching point for diving, surfing, and sport-fishing trips. The town itself has lots of character, albeit a little honky-tonk, with plenty of open-air bars, discos, and tacky souvenir stalls. But there are also some excellent seafood restaurants to suit every price range.

The north end of the beach caters to a more sophisticated crowd with small bed and breakfast establishments and the stylish, Italian-owned Hotel La Puerta del Sol (tel: 2670 0195).

Just a couple of kilometers south of Coco lies the dramatic **Playa Ocotal ⑲**, a black-sand beach fringed with cliffs. Dominating the highest point is upscale **Ocotal Beach Resort** (tel:

BELOW: the sandy crescent of Playa Flamingo.

2670 0321), overlooking the sandy coves, rocky capes, and islands off the Nicoya coast, and famous for its dive shop. You can take a boat trip to a nearby island to find great swimming and snorkeling, or arrange a diving expedition either in local waters or as far away as Isla del Caño.

Playa Flamingo

From Comunidad, head south on the highway toward Belén. From there it is a short distance to **Playa Brasilito** and the Playa Flamingo area, which includes **Playa Potrero**. In the dry season, if you are feeling adventurous and have a four-wheel-drive car, you can negotiate the bumpy Monkey Trail short cut that starts near Sardinal and emerges near **Playa Pan de Azúcar** (Sugar Loaf Beach). Ask local people for directions.

Playa Conchal, once a deserted slice of beach composed of bottomless drifts of pink, orange, mauve, and sunset-colored seashells, lies just south of Flamingo. It is an ideal place to snorkel. The huge **Paradisus Playa Conchal Beach & Golf Resort** looms over the beach, blocking access from the main road. But you can still reach the public beach by walking south for a kilometer (½ mile) along the shore from **Brasilito**, a bustling little town with a few interesting restaurants and the vintage **Hotel Brasilito** (tel: 2654 4237), which has modest rooms in an old wooden building close to the beach. Good seafood restaurants here include **El Camarón Dorado** (tel: 2654 4028), practically on the beach; and **The Happy Snapper** (tel: 2654 4413), a more casual bar/restaurant.

About 7km (4 miles) north of Brasilito you will find **Playa Flamingo** [20], one of Costa Rica's loveliest, longest, white-sand beaches. The natural harbor formed by Flamingo Bay is home to a huge charter-boat fleet. For more than six years the marina has been closed while local authorities make up their minds about granting a new concession, but the fishing boats and pleasure sailboats are moored in the bay.

The town itself climbs up a steep hill to the **Mar y Sol Restaurant and Bar** (tel: 2654 4151) with a terrace that has the best view in the area, as well as the

Pineapples – the taste of the tropics.

BELOW LEFT AND RIGHT: cigar salesman and swimmers at Playa Conchal.

A glorious sunset over the Nicoya peninsula.

best food, a blend of tropical and classic French *(see page 279)*. You will feel as though you have stumbled onto the Côte d'Azur (but at half the price).

To the north is **Playa Potrero**, a cove of coconut palms and calm water, which is an excellent place for a picnic and a dip in the ocean. A cluster of new hotels, from modestly comfortable to extravagantly luxurious, dots the beach. The views get better, although the roads get worse, as you continue north along this picturesque coastline toward **Playa Pan de Azúcar**, Sugar Loaf Beach. When you arrive at Pan de Azúcar, it is obviously the last resort. Stop in at the **Hotel Sugar Beach** (tel: 2654 4242), the only hotel on the beach, for incredible views and enjoy a drink, lunch, or a swim in the cove.

Playa Tamarindo area

Go through Brasilito to Huacas and continue for 13km (8 miles) south, where you will need to make a right turn for **Playa Grande** ㉑ and **Playa Tamarindo** ㉒. Tamarindo does have a national wildlife refuge, though you would scarcely realize it. The

BELOW: Playa Tamarindo featured in the cult surfer flick *Endless Summer*.

wildlife seems more concentrated in the town's many bars and clubs than it is in the nearby estuary. The lush and lovely **Hotel Capitán Suizo** (tel: 2653 0075), at the south end of Playa Tamarindo, is still the most luxurious hotel in town and has the best location, right on the beach *(see page 271)*. Some relatively inexpensive lodging is still available in the village of Tamarindo, but over the past five years, Tamarindo has experienced such a major growth spurt that it seems to resemble a construction site more than a tourist town. Commercial centers and condominium developments have popped up everywhere. On the plus side, there is a lot more to do in town, including dining at a plethora of international restaurants.

Tamarindo is a favorite surfers' haunt, so there is no shortage of surf shops, including the well-run **Iguana Surf** (tel: 2653 0148), where you can rent boards and snorkeling equipment. Iguana Surf also offers tours: one of its most popular is a two-hour guided paddle through the estuary – a great way to see birds and wildlife.

Wet and Wild in Tama

Along with its surfing renown, established in the classic 1960s surfer movie *Endless Summer*, Playa Tamarindo is famous as a party town, starring in its own episode of Entertainment Television's *Wild On* international party-scene series.

The hot clubs come and go, along with the transient surfers who arrive in town, stay long enough to get a nightspot hopping, and then depart in search of the next wave. Barbecues and dancing on the beach around a bonfire are highlights for the 20-somethings, along with dance clubs and atmospheric lounges; just ask around to find out where the latest action is. Older beach-goers may enjoy the Friday-night beach barbecues with folkloric music at the elegant Hotel Capitán Suizo at the south end of the beach.

Playa Grande is just a 5-minute boat ride across an estuary; by car it is a one-hour drive over dirt roads. Famous for its surfing waves by day, Playa Grande is also a major leatherback turtle nesting habitat by night, and the site of ongoing environmental conflicts between conservationists and developers. The developers appear to be getting the upper hand but the beach itself is still protected.

Parque Nacional Marino Las Baulas

Parque Nacional Marino Las Baulas, which incorporates Playa Grande, was created in 1991 to protect the world's most important leatherback hatching area, and was expanded in 1995. It was estimated at that time that there were only about 35,000 leatherbacks left in the world and approximately 900 of them came to Playa Grande to lay their eggs each year. Sadly, the population has subsequently fallen into a dramatic decline despite concerted efforts by the National Park Service and scientists to protect them.

During the long nesting season from August to February, if you are lucky, you may see one or two turtles struggling up the beach to dig a nest. Visitors must join a guided group since beach access is strictly limited, and flash photography of the wildlife is forbidden.

On the beach at Playa Grande is **Hotel Las Tortugas** (tel: 2653 0423), a congenial, turtle-friendly hotel, with low lighting at night to avoid disorienting nesting turtles *(see page 271)*. Catch the Guanacastecan breezes from a comfortable hammock near the turtle-shaped swimming pool, chat with the garrulous owner of the hotel, Lewis Wilson, who was instrumental in establishing the marine park, or take a guided tour of the mangrove estuary in a kayak, which ensures a quiet trip for riders and the birds they observe.

Idyllic spots

Playa Langosta, immediately south of Tamarindo beyond a rocky headland that is impassable at high tide, is also frequented by surfers who ride waves just in front of the estuary at the southern end. More sedate than its noisy neighbor, Playa Langosta is home to a

Lifeguards have been re-installed at Tamarindo after a period when funding dried up.

BELOW:
Tamarindo town.

The Vampire Bats of Guanacaste

Most bats are beneficial, pollinating plants and eating insects. But there is one that inspires fear and dread, along with spooky legends

There are 105 species of bat in Costa Rica. That number represents more than half of all the mammals found in the country. They are everywhere. Peek under a bent heliconia leaf in a forest and you may spot a sleeping bat dangling from the spine of the leaf. Look up, under the overhang of a lodge roof, and you may spy more bats. Hang around the entrance to the deep caves of Barra Honda in the early evening, and you may hear the shrill flutterings of millions of bats rising up. As night falls, wherever you are, you will spy winged shapes swooping through the air.

Bats are the only mammals that can fly. Most are benevolent, if curious looking, animals that feed on nectar, fruit, and insects. They are highly beneficial, even necessary, as significant pollinators and disseminators of seeds, especially in deforested areas in Costa Rica. Bats also do a lot

to control insect populations; it is estimated that a colony of 1 million bats can consume more than 4,500kg (10,000lbs) of insects a night.

Within Santa Rosa Park in Guanacaste, however, inside a cave near the Naked Indian Path, lives a group of *Desmodex rotundum*, the much-feared vampire bat. Only three bat species in the world drink blood, and all of them are native to the neotropics.

Victorian novelists, followed by Hollywood, have done their part in creating the myth of the vampire who lives on the blood of innocent human beings. The Irish author Bram Stoker (1847–1912), creator of Dracula, was the first to link Transylvanian vampire legends with the scientifically studied habits of neotropical vampire bats.

There are certain other factors that contribute to the legends that surround these creatures. They are not attractive: the vampire bat has large thumbs that protrude from the wings, appendages used for stealthy crawling toward its prey. It has a flat, red, pig-like nose, large eyes, prominent front teeth, and relatively small and pointed ears, making it one of the least appealing creatures of the night. Vampire bats are also the only mammals in the world that feed exclusively on blood.

Among the misinformation and myths, it is true that this species feeds mainly during the darkest hours, before the moon is out, quietly alighting upon a sleeping victim and making a painless incision with razor-sharp teeth. Contrary to the myth, though, bats don't suck out the blood of the victim; instead, they lap it up, much as a cat drinks milk.

A bat does not drink its victim dry. Instead, the real harm comes from rabies and other infections, introduced through the wounds. Sleeping humans are sometimes prey as well, but only rarely.

Cattle ranchers, in particular, strike back against the vampire bat by dynamiting, and gassing their caves with toxic substances. Such methods, often born of an irrational aversion to the bat, do not specifically target the vampire variety, and other misidentified, beneficial bats are also killed. Anything and everything in the area is also harmed or destroyed. Ironically, before forests were cleared and livestock introduced, vampire bats had far fewer animals to feed on.

On the positive side, recent research into bat saliva, which is so effective at preventing blood from clotting, may one day lead to advances in preventing heart attacks and strokes. ❑

LEFT: fruit-eating bat homing in on a papaw.

few lovely bed and breakfast establishments. Directly south from Tamarindo, along a bumpy road, **Playa Avellanas** and **Playa Negra** are popular surfers' turf. So far, they have escaped the overdevelopment of the Tamarindo area. At Playa Avellanas, there is an idyllic beach café called **Lola's on the Beach** (tel: 2652 9097) where you can lounge under palm trees. Or you can take a nature walk in the mangroves in front of **Cabinas Las Olas**, a favorite with surfers. Even if you're not a surfer, the Playa Negra Hotel (tel: 2652 9134) is a charming place to stay, with round, thatched-roof cabins overlooking the ocean and a circular pool.

Head inland from Tamarindo for some 18km (11 miles) and, at the junction of the village called 27 de Abril, turn toward the coast and proceed for approximately 12km (8 miles) to lovely **Playa Junquillal**, a paradisiacal, wide beach with high surf that gives you the sense of having found a secret place.

Inland to Santa Cruz

Heading inland from the coast at Paraíso, few populated areas disturb the unbroken beauty of the rolling hills and valleys. An occasional cluster of three or four houses indicates a village. Here chickens, ducks, and the occasional cyclist claim the road. The kilometers are marked by the infrequent passage of herds of noisy Brahman cows, turning traffic into a cattle drive, followed in their leisurely journey by *sabaneros* on horseback. These *Guanacasteco* cowboys don't direct the animals out of the road; they let the automobile wend its way through them. The cattle, with their sensitive faces, seem neither concerned nor particularly curious.

Santa Cruz ㉓ (pop. 18,000) is a bustling market town and administration center. In the central plaza, the modern church stands beside the original colonial clock tower of the old church that was destroyed by an earthquake in 1950. The central park is a quiet, shady place for sitting and viewing the life of a Guanacaste town.

Santa Cruz is most famous for its popular folklore festival held in mid-January, featuring bullfights (the Costa Rican kind where the bull is teased but

The best surfing along the Nicoya Peninsula can be experienced between December and April.

BELOW: small boats ply the estuary between Playa Grande and Playa Tamarindo.

A piece of Guaitil pottery, an ancient craft that has been revived.

not killed), rodeos, folk dancing, and traditional marimba music. At the entrance to town, the **Hotel Diriá** (tel: 2680 0080) provides air-conditioned rooms and a swimming pool.

One of the main visitor attractions in this part of Guanacaste is the village of **Guaitil** , which specializes in re-creating ceramic pots in the style of the pre-Columbian inhabitants of this part of Costa Rica. After the Conquest, pottery-making died out here, possibly because the images adorning pots were considered pagan by the Catholic Church. The craft has been revived in recent years and today the popularity of these giant ceramic pots is obvious from their presence in the lobbies and dining rooms of many hotels in Guanacaste. Almost every house in Guaitil has a kiln and pots for sale in the yard. The widest selection, however, is next to the soccer field in front of the church.

Nicoya

From Guaitil it is a scenic 20-minute drive on a smoothly paved highway to the town of **Nicoya** ㉕, the former colonial capital of Guanacaste. The pride of Nicoya is its central park and the **Church of San Blas**, a white, adobe colonial building dating from 1644, that is now a museum (irregular hours). Nicoya is a good place to stop and shop, eat at one of the town's many Chinese restaurants, and top up your gas tanks at one of its 24-hour service stations.

Playa Nosara

The beaches of Nosara and nearby Sámara are popular destinations for North American and European vacationers who prefer a calmer alternative to the high-octane tourist scene in northern Guanacaste. **Playa Nosara** ㉖ is the more remote beach. The actual town of Nosara is a small, nondescript inland place. The attractions here are idyllic Playa Pelada and Playa Guiones, two long white-sand beaches with excellent surfing waves and many kilometers of beach bordered by forest and tendrils of green sea grape edging the sand. The last 18km (11 miles) of the road from Nicoya are nearly impassable during the rainy season, and many visitors fly here from San José.

The Arribada

Created to protect the endangered Olive Ridley turtle, the Ostional National Wildlife Refuge is witness to the spectacular phenomenon known as the *arribada*, when tens of thousands of turtles come to the beach to lay their eggs. It is estimated that during these brief periods as many as 100,000 Olive Ridleys may come ashore to this isolated beach, and leave behind more than 10 million eggs. *Arribadas* generally occur at two- to four-week intervals between the third quarter and full moon from April to December, peaking during July through September.

Presently, there is a controversial program of egg collecting in operation at Ostional, which gives the people of the nearby village the legal right to gather as many of the turtle eggs as they can during the first 36 hours of every *arribada* in an attempt to prevent further poaching. One of the pro-collecting arguments is that the first eggs will be dug up by succeeding waves of nesting turtles anyway.

If you wish to see the amazing sight of thousands of these creatures laboriously coming ashore to thump the sand with their flippers and dig their incubation holes to lay their eggs, make a reservation with the local group at the guard station on the beach. You can only visit during an *arribada* as part of a guided group. Remember to watch the activities as unobtrusively as possible, and leave your flash attachment back at the hotel.

Despite the difficulty getting here by road, the Nosara area is in the midst of a building boom. Private villas, small hotels, and restaurants are being built by an international cast of characters, including a large contingent of nature-loving Swiss. Nosara is also a haven for New Agers; yoga, alternative therapies, and vegetarianism abound. A large part of Nosara is still protected as a reserve, and as a result it is more forested and richer in wildlife than other parts of the region. There is also excellent snorkeling, tide pool exploring, and camping in the area.

Endangered eggs

At the far northern edge of Nosara, **Lagarta Lodge Biological Reserve** (tel: 2682 0035) occupies an eagle's aerie, high above its own private nature reserve with hiking trails leading down to the Nosara River. About 7km (4½ miles) north of Nosara, the **Refugio Nacional de Vida Silvestre Ostional** is an important turtle-nesting site for Olive Ridley turtles, which arrive by the thousands to nest on the beach *(see*

box opposite). To witness an *arribada*, as it is called, you must join a guided tour organized by a village cooperative (tel: 2682 0428; charge).

Sadly, in season, you can still buy the eggs of endangered turtle species, considered by many men to be an aphrodisiac. Some of the eggs have been excavated by adventurers, but most are part of a cache of eggs taken legally by local villagers who are given permits by the government to take the eggs during the first 36 hours of an *arribada* *(see box opposite)*.

Playa Sámara and south

Playa Sámara ㉗, nearly an hour south of Nosara along dicey roads that are either muddy or dusty, depending on the season, has a beautiful white-sand beach and a good reef for snorkeling, which also protects the beach from direct waves. Swimming is safe in crystalline, shallow waters with minimal surf. Off season, there is a feeling of dramatic isolation. During the high season, Playa Sámara is popular with Costa Ricans, and many *Ticos* have summer homes here.

If you don't already find that Nosara is the sort of place where you can totally unwind, try seeking out the Nosara Yoga Institute, where you can join in a daily yoga class or make an appointment for a relaxing massage.

BELOW: ride along the beach at Playa Sámara.

TIP

Riptides are a danger in Costa Rica and kill several visitors every year. Ask around first whether a beach is safe for swimming. If you are caught by a riptide, don't panic and do not swim against it. Try to swim parallel to the shore, and eventually the breaking waves will carry you back in.

Diving, snorkeling, fishing, bicycle and horseback tours, and kayaking can be arranged by all the local hotels. The waves are small for surfing, but just right for beginners. To the north of the beach are some basic *cabinas*, small hotels, and some excellent restaurants. A block north of the beach, **Hotel Giada** (tel: 2656 0132) has a lot of Italian style, and the best food in town. If you drive south from Nicoya, the winding, scenic road is smoothly paved all the way. There are also regular flights from San José to Sámara.

Another 7km (4 miles) south of Sámara is **Playa Carrillo** ㉘, a near-flawless, white-sand beach protected by an offshore reef and populated only by coconut palms. Beyond Carrillo are other extraordinary beaches: isolated, lonely places, sometimes with fresh water available, sometimes not. **Playa Caletas**, just a little way south of Carrillo on unpaved, almost nonexistent roads, has large surf with offshore breezes. Farther south still is **Punta Islita**, home to one of Costa Rica's most luxurious hotels, **Hotel Punta Islita Luxury Beach Resort** (tel: 2656 2020).

With wonderful ocean views and a spectacular blue-tile infinity pool, this collection of private villas, with their own gardens and plunge pools and every conceivable comfort, is the *ne plus ultra* of sophistication (*see page 271*). Most guests arrive by small plane (or private helicopter), but you can drive in the dry season from Sámara.

Parque Nacional Barra Honda

About 21km (13 miles) east of the town of Nicoya is **Barra Honda National Park** ㉙, a rocky outcropping containing a vast network of caves. Look for national park signs pointing the way on the Nicoya side of the Friendship Bridge that spans the Río Tempisque. On the flat ridgeline, 300 meters (1,000ft) above the caves, a *mirador* (lookout point) can be reached via marked paths. Standing on the ridge, you can drink in the view across the vast Nicoya Peninsula, accompanied by the sounds of an enormous waterfall, screeching tropical birds, scary-sounding howler monkeys, and iguanas scuffling in the trees.

BELOW: a shady spot on Playa Carrillo.

You don't have to be a dedicated spelunker to enjoy Barra Honda, though some of the caves are quite deep and require steep vertical drops to enter. With names such as *La Trampa* (The Trap) and *Terciopelo* (Fer-de-Lance viper), they may not sound inviting, but the formations are dazzling, including one called The Organ, which produces melodic tones when gently touched.

Blind salamanders, vampire bats, and strange birds share the world of darkness in the Barra Honda caves, which have escaped vandalism and exploitation because they lack an easily accessible horizontal entrance. A community group has the exclusive right to lead cave tours. Basic lodging and good *campesina* food (try Las Delicias) are also available. In the dry season (Dec–Apr) it gets extremely hot, so be sure to bring a wide-brimmed hat and water.

Monteverde Cloud Forest

Atop the Continental Divide, some 170km (106 miles) northwest of San José, lies the **Reserva Biológica del Bosque Nuboso de Monteverde ③⓪** (tel: 2645 5122; daily 7am–4pm; charge). Despite some recent road improvements, it is still a difficult place to get to and you should allow three to four hours' driving time from San José. After the turn-off for Puntarenas on the Interamerican Highway, continue along the Interamericana to the Rancho Grande turning on the right at Km 133. Follow this partially paved road through Sardinal. Count on an hour to make the 37km (21-mile) ascent from the main highway to Monteverde.

Despite the ordeal to get here, every year tens of thousands of people visit the preserve. In order to protect the flora and fauna and the trails themselves, visitors are now limited to 220 at any given time – which means you may have to wait your turn. You should book at least one night's accommodation in advance; to get the best out of the area you need to stay three days.

More visitors are attracted to Monteverde Cloud Forest than to any other forest reserve in Costa Rica, and usually for one purpose only: to sight the resplendent quetzal, the most colorful and spectacular bird in the tropics. Be warned, however: it is a difficult bird to spot. With the exception of their almost luminous crimson breast, they are cloaked in radiant green plumage and easily disappear among the rich colors of the cloud forest. The best time to spot them is January through September and especially during the mating season, which runs from March through June *(see page 204)*.

Monteverde is much more than an opportunity to spot a quetzal, however. This misty, verdant, high-altitude cloud forest is home to a multitude of diverse creatures: 448 species of birds identified so far, about 700 species of butterflies, 3,000 species of plants, and 130 species of mammals, of which 70 are bats. Pick up a checklist and map at the Visitors' Center. Guided tours are available. Before leaving the forest, visit the **Hummingbird Gallery**, across the road from the entrance, to observe the hummingbirds that buzz around a group of feeders and to see an

See iridescent hummingbirds at the Hummingbird Gallery or when on a guided tour in Monteverde Cloud Forest.

BELOW: birdwatching in Monteverde Cloud Forest.

The Resplendent Quetzal

Costa Rica is a delight for bird-watchers, many of them in search of one of the most beautiful and sought-after birds in the world

The resplendent quetzal is rightly acclaimed as the most magnificent bird in the western hemisphere. Some 40 species of the trogon family, to which the quetzal belongs, inhabit the tropics worldwide, and 10 of those are found in Costa Rica. But the quetzal is the star, regarded as one of the country's greatest natural treasures.

The pigeon-sized male owes his elegance to the intensity and brilliant contrasts of his colors, the sheen and glitter of his plumage, the beauty of his adornments, and the great dignity of his posture. The rich crimson of his underparts contrasts with the shining, iridescent green of his head, chest, and upper parts. His head is crowned with a narrow crest of upstanding feathers that extends from his small yellow bill to his nape. The pointed tips of the long, loose-barbed coverts of his wings project over the crimson of his sides, creating a beautiful, contrasting scalloped edge. Most notable of all are his central tail coverts, which stretch far beyond his tail and, like two slender green pen-dants, undulate gracefully when he flies.

The quetzal is a fruit eater, its diet almost entirely reliant on wild avocados, but when these are not available, the birds will eat insects and even frogs.

As witnessed by many an ancient sculpture and painting, the long tail coverts were highly valued as personal adornments by the Aztec and Maya nobility. Mayan kings prized the iridescent green tail feathers of the quetzal more than gold itself. They also believed the bird could not live in captivity, and it was therefore the supreme symbol of freedom. This belief persisted for some time, but modern aviculturists have learned how to keep them alive in captivity – a hard negation of a beautiful myth.

The quetzal's song is eminently worthy of a bird so splendidly attired. Fuller and deeper than those of any other trogon, their songs are not distinctly separated but slurred and fused into a flow of soft, mellow, and unforgettably beautiful sound.

Monogamous pairs of quetzals nest in the holes of trees located in mountain forests or in nearby clearings. The hole, like that of a woodpecker, extends straight downwards from the opening at the top. Usually it is deep enough to conceal all of the sitting birds except the ends of the male's train. On the unlined bottom of the chamber, the female lays two light-blue eggs. She incubates through the night and the middle of the day. The male takes a turn on the eggs in the morning and again in the afternoon. His train arches over his back and projects through the doorway, fluttering in the breeze. On an epiphyte-burdened trunk, the ends might be mistaken for two green fern fronds.

Sometimes, when his partner arrives to relieve him of his spell in the nest, he soars straight upward, right above the tree tops, loudly shouting a phrase that sounds almost like "very-good very-good." At the summit of his ascent he circles, then dives into sheltering foliage. These "joy flights" seem to express the bird's great vitality.

Resplendent quetzals are still abundant in Costa Rican tracts of unspoilt mountain forests (as they are in Guatemala, where it is the national bird). So long as such forests are preserved, they are in no danger of becoming extinct, but if they are destroyed, then Central America will lose its most magnificent bird. ❏

LEFT: the resplendent quetzal is protected in four national parks and two cloud forest reserves.

exhibition of the remarkable photos of Michael and Patricia Fogden, biologists and pre-eminent nature photographers, who spent two decades recording the fauna of Monteverde.

Monteverde's Quaker community

The community of **Monteverde** ㉛ was established by a group of Quakers who moved here from Alabama in 1951. To support themselves, the Quakers began making cheese from milk brought to their primitive processing plant each morning by *Tico* dairy farmers. Today the Quakers produce tons of cheese daily: Monteverde cheese has become a proud Costa Rican specialty and can be found in markets throughout Central America. En route to the reserve, stop in at their cheese-processing plant, **La Fábrica de Queso** (The Cheese Factory), to watch the production through windows in the plant. Better still, order a milkshake made with their excellent ice cream. Don't expect to see too many Quakers elsewhere in Monteverde, however. They keep themselves to themselves on their farms and gen-

erally avoid the commercialized town that Monteverde has now become.

Just north of here look in at **CASEM** (Comité de Artesanías Santa Elena-Monteverde), an arts and crafts cooperative founded by eight women in 1982. Today, more than 140 artisans contribute their work, which is on sale at less-than-downtown prices at the CASEM shop (tel: 2645 5190). Across the road is the popular coffee shop, **Stella's Bakery**, and **Meg's Stables** (tel: 2645 5419), which offers horseback-riding tours.

Other Monteverde attractions

Adjacent to Monteverde Cloud Forest preserve are two much smaller private reserves. There is usually good wildlife viewing at the 81-hectare (200-acre) **Reserva Sendero Tranquilo** (Quiet Path Reserve), which is open for small-group guided tours, led by expert, bilingual nature guides. You must book ahead by contacting the Hotel El Sapo Dorado (tel: 2645 5010; charge).

Opposite the Hotel Heliconia, on the road to Santa Elena, follow the signs to **El Jardín de las Mariposas** (Butterfly

Vivid Monteverde flora.

BELOW: sunlight pierces the canopy of Monteverde Cloud Forest.

Garden; tel: 2645 5512; daily 7am–4pm; charge), which exhibits all the butterfly species of the region. Guided tours take you through the various stages of a butterfly's life and into a screened garden where hundreds of species flutter freely. The best time for a visit is a sunny morning. There is also a leaf-cutter ant colony exhibition. Reptile-lovers won't want to miss the **Serpentarium** (tel: 2645 6002; daily tours at 7.30am and 1pm; charge) where you can safely observe more than 40 species of reptiles and amphibians.

More frogs are on view at **The Frog Pond** of Monteverde (tel: 2645 6329; daily 9am–8.30pm), on the south side of Santa Elena. The best time to visit is toward evening when the frogs become more active. An alternative adventure is a visit to the **Bat Jungle** (tel: 2645 6566; daily 9.30am–8.30pm; tours available) across from CASEM, where you can learn all about these fascinating nocturnal mammals.

Skywalkers and artists

One of the most popular Monteverde attractions is **The Sky Walk** (tel: 2645 5238), a 2.5km (1½-mile) series of trails and five hanging bridges suspended Indiana Jones-style from platforms in the tree canopy. It's a wonderful way of getting a bird's-eye view of the forest, up to 41 meters (138ft) above the ground. For the truly adventurous the same company also offers **Sky Trek**, a high-speed, high-adrenaline canopy tour that involves donning mountain-climbing harnesses and zipping through the trees suspended on strong cables.

Monteverde is also famous for its artistic community, with many resident wildlife painters, sculptors, and textile artists. An international music festival is held every year, from February to March. Both local musicians and international guest artists perform programs ranging from jazz to classical to Latino. Concert proceeds benefit local school music programs.

Santa Elena Reserve and around

Around 5km (3 miles) northeast of Monteverde village is an outstanding local initiative, the **Reserva Santa**

Elena ❷ (Santa Elena Rainforest Reserve). Comprising some 310 hectares (766 acres) of mixed montane and elfin forest, the reserve was created in 1992 as a local high-school project and includes several kilometers of well-kept paths and a visitors' center. On clear days, you are treated to views of magnificent Arenal Volcano to the north. Tours are well organized and cheaper than Monteverde, yet the flora and fauna (including quetzals and howler monkeys) are every bit as impressive as those of its famous neighbor. There are four principal trails, all short enough to be done in a day. You also avoid the crowds here, plus you will feel good that a proportion of your admission charge will go toward the funding of Monteverde's schools.

The most exciting way of exploring the forests around the reserve is on a canopy zip-line tour. **Selvatura** (tel: 2645 5929), a private park just south of the Santa Elena Reserve, provides an 18-platform canopy tour within a cloud forest, as well as hanging bridges and wildlife exhibits.

East of Monteverde Cloud Forest, on the Atlantic slope, is the vast **El Bosque Eterno de los Niños** (Children's Eternal Forest; tel: 2645 5003). Back in 1987, a group of Swedish schoolchildren raised and donated enough money to purchase 6 hectares (15 acres) of forest. Now, with support from young people from all over the world, they have bought more than 22,000 hectares (54,000 acres), covering a range of cloud-, rain- and seasonal evergreen forest. The most easily accessible section of the forest, called the **Bajo del Tigre trail** (daily 8am–4.30pm; charge), is just south of CASEM. A self-guided tour takes you along a 1.5km (1-mile) trail dotted with information panels.

Just below the Monteverde Cloud Forest Reserve is the **Ecolodge San Luis** (tel: 2645 8049; www.uga.edu/costa rica), part of a 60-hectare (150-acre) farm and forest reserve operated as a satellite campus by the University of Georgia. Visitors can take part in plant and insect identification workshops, tour the botanical garden and sustainable farm, and take guided natural-history walks. ❑

A visitor and resident at Monteverde's Serpentarium.

BELOW: gaze on pristine forest from the Continental Divide viewpoint in Monteverde Cloud Forest.

Costa Rica's Wings of Wonder

With more than 850 species of birds, Costa Rica is one of the world's foremost destinations for professional ornithologists and amateur birders

Despite its small size, Costa Rica has almost the same number of bird species as the whole of North America, and significantly more than Europe or Australia. This tremendous diversity is explained, in part, by the country's tropical location, and partly by its position on one of the world's great bird migration routes, over the Central American land bridge linking North and South America.

For most birders Costa Rica's resident species – rather than its migrants – are the ones that hold the most interest. The most sought-after sightings are undoubtedly the resplendent quetzal, two species of toucans, and two endangered macaws, the scarlet and the green. Opportunities for birdwatching are everywhere in Costa Rica, with eco-lodges, reserves, and tours geared to it. A world-class cadre of resident birding guides also makes birdwatching here a pleasure, even for visitors who have never bothered to look at a bird before.

NECTAR FEEDERS

Costa Rica has 54 species of tiny but pugnacious hummingbirds, including the violet sabre-wing, the largest at 152mm (6ins); and the volcano hummingbird, one of the smallest at 76mm (3ins). Hummingbirds feed largely on a diet of sugary nectar and insects. They are often lured to artificial feeders filled with sugar water and placed around eco-lodge verandahs and in gardens. Station yourself and your camera nearby and you are in for an unbeatable spectacle of color and whirring wings.

ABOVE: The fairy-like green violet-ear, one of the country's 50-plus species of hummingbirds, harvests nectar from a flower. Only 4½ins (11.5cm) long, this hummer lives in the highlands.

BELOW: Thanks to conservation efforts, the scarlet macaw has been brought back from the brink of extinction. The most reliable location for spotting them in the wild is at the Osa Peninsula, near Carate.

LEFT: The keel-billed toucan with its colorful, hollow bill is called *Arco Iris* in Spanish, which means "rainbow." His cousin, the chestnut-mandibled toucan, has an equally impressive brown and yellow bill.

ENDANGERED SPECIES

Despite Costa Rica's efforts to protect its forests, habitat destruction has had a serious effect on some of its birds. The quetzal is particularly vulnerable because it largely depends for survival on one special *aguacatillo* tree, found only in cloud forest. The three-wattled bellbird shares this habitat, and is equally threatened when forests are converted to pasture. Great green macaws are the most threatened species of macaw. Conservation efforts on the Caribbean coast, where they exclusively live, include honoring farmers who maintain the *dipteryx* trees upon which the macaws feed. There are only 30 active nests recorded in the protected breeding area straddling Costa Rica and Nicaragua. National parks and private reserves, such as Maquenque National Wildlife Refuge, are a lifeline to survival.

Even higher on the critical list is Costa Rica's biggest raptor, the American harpy eagle. This giant monkey-eating bird is known to breed in the forests of the Osa Peninsula, but sightings of it have become extremely rare. A handful of species, such as the cattle egret and roadside hawk, have actually benefited from man-made changes to the environment, because they need open ground on which to feed.

ABOVE: Montezuma oropendolas inhabit colonies of hanging nests, built by females and patrolled by males. At sunset, you may spot flocks of oropendoloas flying back to their nests, making a gurgling sound.

ABOVE: A great green macaw. **RIGHT:** From his perch on a tree snag in a river, this green heron is concentrating on catching fish for his supper. While herons are plentiful, the great green macaw is on the endangered list, owing to deforestation of his natural habitat.

THE NORTHEAST

Volcán Arenal is the star of the region, though the Sarapiquí River and nearby rustic eco-lodges and wild nature reserves are hotspots for more adventurous travelers

T he region to the northeast of San José corresponds roughly to the area known as the Northern Zone. The landscape is lush and agricultural for the most part. The main attractions for visitors are the spectacular Arenal volcano with its surrounding hot springs and spas, and some remote rainforest reserves.

Around Ciudad Quesada (San Carlos)

At the foot of the Cordillera Central, **Ciudad Quesada ⬦**, often called by its former name San Carlos, is the gateway to the country's northern attractions. A bustling town of around 44,000 people, San Carlos is also the agricultural and commercial heart of the region.

Some 7km (4½ miles) east of San Carlos, **Termales del Bosque** (tel: 2460 4740) is a cozy, family-run hotel with its own *termales*, thermal hot springs, in a forest setting alongside a fast-running river. You can soak in a series of pools at different temperatures, and then cool off in the river. There are also trails through primary and secondary forest, and ponds filled with tilapia, destined for the hotel restaurant. Horseback riding, guided nature tours, and natural spa treatments are also on offer.

The **Tilajari Hotel Resort** (tel: 2462 1212), near Muelle, around 22km (14 miles) north of Ciudad Quesada, is a luxurious spread, set on several hectares of gardens, overlooking the wide San Carlos River. It makes a good base for exploring this region, and offers tennis, swimming, horseback riding, and hiking in 400 hectares (1,000 acres) of rainforest, as well as spa and beauty treatments. Farther afield you can take fishing trips, and jungle river tours to Caño Negro Wildlife Reserve *(see page 218)*.

Main attractions
ARENAL VOLCANO
CATARATAS DEL RÍO FORTUNA
TABACÓN HOT SPRINGS
LAGUNA DE ARENAL
MAQUENQUE NATIONAL WILDLIFE
   REFUGE
CAÑO NEGRO NATIONAL WILDLIFE
   RESERVE
PUERTO VIEJO DE SARAPIQUÍ
LA SELVA BIOLOGICAL RESERVE
RARA AVIS

PRECEDING PAGES: Tabacón hot springs.
LEFT: Cataratas del Río Fortuna waterfall.
RIGHT: riding near San Ramón.

TIP

Tabacón Springs is pricey and often crowded, especially on weekends, so try to choose an off-season weekday to visit.

The Tilajari is also the lift-off point for an enchanting hot-air balloon ride over the **San Carlos Valley** with Serendipity Adventures (tel: 2558 1000). Standing in a traditional wicker balloon basket under a multicolored balloon, you ascend just after dawn, over tree tops where howler monkeys and toucans are just waking up, then float over cattle pastures alternating with fields of sugar cane and pineapple. It's expensive – more than $300 per person – but it really is a once-in-a-lifetime experience.

La Fortuna

From Muelle it's around 25km (16 miles) west to **La Fortuna** ❸ (also known as Fortuna de San Carlos). This busy, sun-baked village near the base of Arenal Volcano is the center for tours, accommodations and eateries.

Some 5km (3 miles) east of La Fortuna is the turn-off to the **Cataratas del Río Fortuna**. These falls are accessible in an hour's easy horseback ride from La Fortuna through pastures and fields of corn, bananas, and peppers. If you are going to drive, the trip requires

a four-wheel-drive vehicle. Once at the falls, a muddy hike down a slippery slope to the swimming area at the base of the falls makes the clear, fresh water all the sweeter.

Tabacón Hot Springs

Closer to the volcano, between La Fortuna and Lake Arenal, **Tabacón Hot Springs Resort and Spa** ❺ is one of Costa Rica's most popular tourist destinations. From here you can look directly up the volcano slopes, glowing with hot boulders. The volcano appears dangerously close – and it is. Volcanologists have predicted that if Arenal erupts, Tabacón Springs will likely be in the path of the lava flow. Meanwhile, the volcano has a benign effect, heating Tabacón's therapeutic waters to a perfect temperature. Tiled slides, waterfalls, and pools of varying temperatures are surrounded by tumbling warm-water creeks and exquisitely landscaped gardens.

Although the springs are often crowded with day-trippers, hotel guests can watch the erupting volcano at night from a quiet pool under a starry

BELOW:
the active Volcán Arenal is an unforgettable sight.

sky. And should you be there when the full moon waxes over Arenal, that single experience may be worth the expense of staying here.

Just west of La Fortuna, you can luxuriate in the warm mineral waters of the more affordable **Baldi Hot Springs** (tel: 2479 9917). For US$27, you can enjoy a warm soak with a volcano view and children can play on three water slides.

Down the highway, past the Tabacón Hot Springs Resort, is a dirt road to the left leading 9km (5 miles) to **Arenal Observatory Lodge** (tel: 2479 1070), formerly a volcano research facility for the Smithsonian Institution. It is the only lodge in the national park and the closest accommodations to the volcano. From here Arenal is only 1km (½ mile) away, and if you come on a clear night, you can enjoy the natural fireworks from the privacy of your balcony. The lodge has comfortable rooms in bungalows, set in a huge estate with primary and secondary forest, waterfalls, and hiking and horseback trails. The birdwatching here is quite spectacular.

Arenal Volcano

Until early July 1968, Arenal was a heavily wooded low hill, similar to many others in the area, near the village of La Fortuna. One morning local people began feeling a few earth tremors. Suddenly, the forest started smoking and steaming. Women washing their clothes marveled at the sudden warm water that flowed in the creeks. Then, on July 29, **Volcán Arenal** ③⑥ exploded. Rolling clouds of gas and fountains of red-hot boulders and molten lava hit the countryside. Official estimates put the death toll at 62, but local people claim that more than 80 people were killed. More than 5 sq km (2 sq miles) of land near the volcano was abruptly changed from pastoral farmland to a landscape out of Dante's *Inferno*. Since then, Arenal has been continuously active.

It is everyone's preconception of a volcano: conical, rising abruptly out of flatland vegetation. But do not attempt to climb it. The molten lava running down the western slope has a temperature of 926°C (1,699°F), and an unpredictable spew of rocks, intense heat,

A sign at the base of Arenal Volcano reads "Volcano influence area. If you notice abnormal activity, run away from the area and report it to the nearest authority."

BELOW: beautifully landscaped grounds of the Tabacón Hot Springs Resort.

Misty Lake Arenal has a resident monster, reputedly seen by local fishermen who described a hairy serpent with horns. Today, the Monster of Lake Arenal is entrenched in local folklore.

and poison gases. Sadly, every couple of years there is a visitor who disregards the warning signs and the volcano claims another life.

The road west to **Nuevo Arenal** ❸ is perennially dreadful; although it is paved, it is often washed out, especially during the rainy season. This New Arenal is a town reborn from the old village of Arenal, in the valley that was flooded in 1973 to create the lake and the huge hydroelectric project here. Along the road to Nuevo Arenal there are some very pleasant small hotels and bed-and-breakfasts (*see page 273*).

Lake Arenal

Laguna de Arenal ❸ offers some of Costa Rica's most challenging freshwater fishing. Whether or not you choose to fish, do charter a boat and a guide to take you sightseeing on the lake. Better still, set off in a rented kayak. Go in the early morning, when, for much of the year, the lake's surface is like glass, and the volcano can be viewed as a crystalline reflection.

From December through March, usually in the afternoon, northeasterly

winds blow almost daily, and the lake is anything but calm and glassy. Between 40 and 50 knots of sustained breeze whips the west end of the lake into a sea of whitecaps, making it a favorite destination for experienced windsurfers. **Tico Wind** (tel: 2692 2002), 30km (18 miles) west of Nuevo Arenal, rents a full range of windsurfing equipment and offers lessons from December 1 through mid-April.

Hotel Tilawa (tel: 2695 5050), within walking distance of the best windsurfing, is an arresting replica of an ancient Cretan palace, 9km (5 miles) north of the town of Tilarán. It runs a well-equipped windsurfing school. Even if you are not a windsurfer, this is a good place to spend the night, refreshingly cool in a hilltop-garden setting above the lake.

To Arenal via San Ramón

An alternative route to Arenal from San José is via **San Ramón**, a bustling market town famous for its earthquake-proof concrete church and as the birthplace of Costa Rica's most famous poets – Lisimaco Chavarria

BELOW RIGHT: it is possible to take a boat across Lake Arenal to Monteverde.

A Celestial Experience

One of the most enchanting, and least visited, national parks is **Tenorio Volcano National Park**, about 55km (38 miles) north of Cañas on the road to Upala. The most beautiful river runs through it: the Río Celeste, which lives up to its name with heavenly blue water. The color is actually a chemical reaction of sulphur and calcium carbonates, but it's magical, nonetheless.

You can hike through primary cloud forest to a waterfall and swim in the cool blue water. Along the river there are also pockets of hot springs and volcanic mud, which you can smear on your face for a natural facial. Butterflies, birds and wildlife abound, including snakes that enjoy sunning themselves on sunlit paths, so be sure to wear hiking boots and look where you are treading. The park office (daily 8am–4pm) has restrooms and fresh water.

You can stay overnight nearby at **Las Heliconias Lodge** (tel: 2466 8483), an eco-lodge run by a local cooperative, near the village of Bijagua. Basic cabins and comfortable private bungalows overlook Lake Nicaragua in the distance and there are miles of birding trails running through the adjoining forest. This is one place in the country where you have a chance of spotting the tiny and rare tody motmot *(Hylomanes momotula)*, the smallest of the motmot bird family.

Palma and Felix Ángel Salas Cabezas. In keeping with its cultural heritage, the **José Figueres Cultural Center**, across from the north side of the church, offers art exhibits, concerts, and a small museum about "Don Pepe" Figueres, the president who abolished Costa Rica's army *(see pages 59–60)*. The cultural center occupies the house where he was born.

About 20km (12 miles) north of San Ramón, along a scenic, winding road, is **Villa Blanca Cloud Forest Nature Reserve** (tel: 2461 0300). The hotel is like a village of small *casitas*, perched in a cloud forest. Each bungalow is luxuriously furnished and equipped with a cozy fireplace. Some also have jacuzzi bathtubs, making this hotel a favorite with honeymooners. There are nature trails to explore, on your own or with resident naturalist guides, and there is a full-service spa for those who prefer indoor experiences.

Heading north

If you want to get off the beaten track, head northeast from San Carlos toward Aguas Zarcas, then take the gravel road past Pital to reach **Laguna del Lagarto Lodge** (tel: 2289 8163), a total of 135km (78 miles). This remote eco-lodge has rustic rooms and serves buffet-style meals *(see page 272)*. The main attraction is the setting, in 505 hectares (1,250 acres) of rainforest, home to almost 400 species of birds. As its name promises, there is also a reedy lagoon that shelters *lagartos* (caimans). There are 10km (6 miles) of hiking trails, plus horseback riding, canoeing, and opportunities for boat trips up the Río San Carlos to the Nicaraguan border.

The lodge is a member of the new **Ruta de Las Aves** conservation project *(see page 218)*, as is nearby **Maquenque Eco-Lodge** *(see page 271)* tel: 2479 7785; www.maquenqueecolodge.com), a newer, more luxurious lodge, with high-roofed cabins, a swimming pool, and an excellent restaurant set around lakes in the newly created 60,000-hectare (148,000-acre) **Maquenque National Wildlife Refuge.**

Both the above lodges are smack in the middle of the last remaining breeding grounds for great green macaws. You will need a four-wheel-drive

Heavy clouds often obscure Arenal Volcano. If your heart is set on seeing Arenal in action, plan to stay at least two nights in the area to increase your chances of getting a clear view.

BELOW: tranquil countryside around the town of La Tigra, near San Ramón.

The nectar of the hibiscus flower is highly prized by hummingbirds.

BELOW: paddling along the Río Frío in Caño Negro National Wildlife Reserve.

vehicle, and be sure to bring stout rubber boots for walking the trails.

Caño Negro

West of San Carlos, north of Arenal toward the Nicaraguan border, lies another natural treasure, the magnificent and still uncrowded **Refugio Nacional de Vida Silvestre Caño Negro ③9** (Caño Negro National Wildlife Reserve), part of the Unesco Agua y Paz International Biosphere. It provides excellent birdwatching opportunities, mostly from quiet boats navigating a huge, shallow lake that covers around 800 hectares (2,000 acres). The lake is created during the wet season when the nearby Río Frío overflows, but dries up almost completely during the dry season. Residents include large flocks of water birds: anhingas, roseate spoonbills, white ibis, and Jabirú storks, the largest bird of the region and in great danger of extinction. Caño Negro is also home to caimans and crocodiles, although their numbers are threatened by poachers, often from neighboring Nicaragua, who hunt the crocodilians for their valuable skins.

Access to Caño Negro is from La Fortuna, Los Chiles, or Upala, on good roads northwest of Cañas. Basic accommodations are available in Los Chiles, and the village of Caño Negro has two upscale hotels *(see page 212)*. Several tour agencies in La Fortuna, including **Sunset Tours** (tel: 2479 9800), offer day trips to Caño Negro.

The Sarapiquí region

The lush, tropical jungles of the **Río Sarapiquí** region, on the Caribbean side of the Cordillera Central, are less than 100km (60 miles) east of San José. Yet once you are there it seems as though it is another continent. La Selva Biological Station, Selva Verde Lodge and Rara Avis *(see page 219)*, private reserves with lodging, are all accessible via the Braulio Carrillo Highway east of San José, through the spectacular Parque Nacional Braulio Carrillo. An even more scenic route, via Heredia and Varablanca, suffered such heavy damage during the 2009 Poás earthquake *(see page 145)*, that it is indefinitely closed. Beware of driving the Braulio Carrillo highway after

Ruta de Las Aves

In an effort to promote ecotourism in the more remote areas of Sarapiquí-San Carlos, the Costa Rican Bird Route (Ruta de las Aves) was created to bring together a dozen eco-lodges and 15 nature reserves, which are home to more than 520 species of birds, including the endangered great green macaw. The first birding trail of its kind in Central America, the Bird Route's ultimate goal is to preserve habitat by making more visitors aware of the region's incredible biodiversity. The key to the route is a map guide of the entire San Juan-La Selva biological corridor. The waterproof map includes information and bird checklists for each lodge and reserve along the route. For more information on the route and where to buy the map, visit www.costaricanbirdroute.com.

sunset, however, as thick night fog blankets this steep, winding route.

Puerto Viejo de Sarapiquí and Rara Avis

Puerto Viejo de Sarapiquí ❹ is a small port town from which river boats used to depart for otherwise inaccessible settlements along these jungle waterways, before the coastal canal was built. Boats still depart from the dock, but most are loaded with tourists on a scenic river trip with a naturalist guide to point out the monkeys, birds, and other riverside animals along the way. You can also take a full-day trip up the Sarapiquí to the **Río San Juan**, on the Nicaraguan border; be sure to bring along your passport because the river crosses into Nicaraguan territory.

Oasis Nature Tours (tel: 2766 6108) organizes both kinds of river trips. If you are looking for more hands-on, exciting action, there are stretches of the Río Sarapiquí with various classes of whitewater for river rafting. **Hacienda Pozo Azul** (tel: 2438 2616) offers a range of whitewater rafting trips.

Rara Avis (tel: 2764 1111) is a pristine, 600-hectare (1,500-acre) rainforest reserve adjacent to Barulio Carrillo National Park. Established in 1983, it was Costa Rica's first eco-lodge. The main office and departure point for the reserve is in Las Horquetas, a village 17km (11 miles) south of Puerto Viejo de Sarapiquí. Whether you are continuing by horseback or tractor-drawn cart, travel to Rara Avis can be grueling, especially in wet conditions, which are the norm. It can only be recommended for those who are both physically and mentally fit. The bumpy three-hour journey encounters ruts, bogs, and rivers. On the road, the transition from cattle ranches to deep jungle illustrates the devastating effects of deforestation more dramatically than any textbook or film could possibly do.

Deforested land ends at El Plástico, named for a former prison colony where inmates slept under plastic sheets. It's another 6km (4 miles) along a trail through a cool, cathedral-like forest to Waterfall Lodge, high in the forest. The lodge, just a five-minute walk

No through road – even for a four-wheel-drive.

BELOW: Caño Negro has a protected caiman colony.

Sloths descend to the forest floor once a week to defecate – unusual behaviour that may be an attempt to move their scent away from their home.

from a spectacular waterfall, has eight rustic rooms, each with its own bathtub with hot water. There are also separate cabins, one along the river, and three cold-water cabins nearby. The main attractions here are birdwatching, forest hiking, swimming, and wildlife viewing. Because it is such a rarefied and isolated place, you must always book well in advance, and you should stay for at least two nights to make the journey worthwhile. Although access is difficult, most people feel that the experience is worth it.

La Selva Biological Reserve

About 7km (4 miles) south of Puerto Viejo you will see the sign for "OTS" (the Organization for Tropical Studies) and the gravel road to La Selva. The diversity and abundance of life in the lowland tropical forest of the Sarapiquí River region attracted tropical biologists here more than 40 years ago. They subsequently founded OTS and in 1968 established the **Estación Bió-logica La Selva ❹** (La Selva Biological Reserve and Research Station; www.ots. duke.edu/en/laselva).

BELOW: a stream in the lowland rainforest.

In 1986 the Costa Rican government also made a major commitment to rainforest conservation by extending the boundaries of Braulio Carrillo National Park to meet the outer reaches of the La Selva Reserve. As a result of this decision, a total of 21,000 hectares (52,000 acres) of virgin forest now preserves the migratory pathways and large territories required for the survival of several species of Costa Rica's rare and endangered birds and mammals.

La Selva has become one of the most important sites in the world for tropical rainforest research, and today virtually all of the world's tropical biologists have spent time at La Selva as students, teachers, or scientists – or at the very least they have been strongly influenced by the vast amount of scientific research that has been accomplished there over the past few decades And it's not just biologists who are taught here, either; many Sarapiquí residents who work at eco-tourist lodges were also trained as naturalist guides at La Selva.

The reserve is primarily a research

and educational facility, but it offers excellent, naturalist-led tours of the trails (tel: 2766 6565; daily; charge). There is a well-developed trail system and some of the trails have boardwalks in order to give access during the wet season. Comfortable new cabins for visitors have greatly improved the accommodations here, and overnight guests can enjoy the trails on their own. But visitors still share the cafeteria-style food with the students and researchers who live in dormitories.

Selva Verde

In 1986, Giovanna and Juan Holbrook, conservationists from Florida, bought **Selva Verde** ⓸ (tel: 2766 6800; from the US tel: 800 451 7111; www.selvaverde. com), 200 hectares (500 acres) of primary and secondary tropical lowland forest, along the banks of the Sarapiquí River, in order to save the land from deforestation. They designed their beautiful river lodge to have minimal impact on the environment, perching it on posts above the forest floor.

Guests stay in tropical hardwood rooms at the end of covered corridors, which radiate from a central conference room into the forest. The jungle and its denizens are never more than a few meters away. Selva Verde carries the Certification for Sustainable Tourism, a voluntary program that sets a standard for lodges in sustainability, including environmental and community impact.

Spectacular birds are commonplace at Selva Verde: keel-billed and chestnut-mandibled toucans feed on the fruit of the nutmeg trees near the front porch of the lodge. A stroll along the path to the main lodge building is likely to be rewarded with the iridescent colors of several species of hummingbirds. Nearby, Montezuma oropendolas utter gurgling mating calls, which harmonize with the songs of other birds and countless frogs and insects in a continual symphony. The lodge's other main wildlife attractions are incredibly slow-moving arboreal sloths.

Selva Verde lodge is very popular with tour groups, so be sure to book in advance. If you are not staying here, you can also come just for lunch and a trail walk. ❑

The attractive Heleconia latisphata, or Expanded Lobster Claw, grows wild in this region.

BELOW: keel-billed toucans are easily sighted at Selva Verde.

MOUNTAINS OF FIRE

Vulcanologists are always busy in Costa Rica, which has five active volcanoes and some 112 dormant and extinct ones on the mainland

Costa Rica is a land of earthquakes and volcanoes, where hikers and mountaineering enthusiasts can climb the Central Valley's four active cones in just two days. Visitors should remember, though, that an active volcano demands respect; proper equipment is essential. Taking a guided tour will ensure the greatest safety. Local people are proud of their explosive geology, and have made Poás and Irazú volcanoes the country's most visited parks.

The most dynamic and majestic of Costa Rica's active volcanoes is Arenal, a nearly perfect cone. The 1,633-meter (4,950ft) -high volcano rises above farmlands, adjacent to its own lake, and offers a spectacular show. Loud thunder-like explosions announce an eruption, and clouds of gas and steam spew out of the top. Dormant until the late 1960s, Arenal was thought to be an extinct volcano until July 29, 1968, when it erupted, causing widespread damage. More than 80 people died after being poisoned with volcanic gas and struck by rocks, and many homes were leveled. Since then, the volcano has continued to rumble and erupt on a more reduced scale, sometimes several times per day, spewing forth fiery cascades of lava, and rocks the size of small houses.

ABOVE: on its best daytime behavior, Arenal Volcano is picture-perfect with its cone-shaped profile etched against the sky. But the pointy tip often catches passing clouds, disappointing many a photographer.

BELOW: when Arenal spews out streams of red-hot rocks and lava at night, visitors are treated to spectacular pyrotechnic show.

BELOW: a short hike along a forest trail leads visitors to the placid crater lake in Poás Volcano National Park. Along the way, watch out for volcano juncos, chubby sparrow-like birds, hopping along the path.

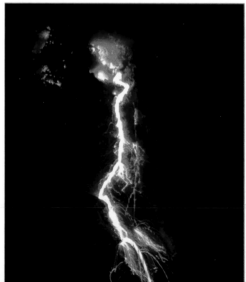

BELOW THE VOLCANOES

To observe Arenal in true luxury by day or night, pamper yourself at the Spanish colonial-style Tabacón Hot Springs Resort, built on the site of a 1975 hot avalanche deposit that provides the source of heat for the thermal waters.

Although vulcanologists feel there is a risk of future hot avalanches, this hasn't stopped the *Ticos* and tourists who flock here to exclaim excitedly over the activity of the volcano and soak their aching muscles. A dip in the waters is also supposedly beneficial for anyone suffering from skin problems and arthritis.

Twelve pools of varying depths and temperatures (the warmest is a sizzling 38°C/102°F), a jacuzzi, hot waterfall, slides, and an individual tub tucked deep in the beautifully landscaped tropical gardens mean fun for everyone from children to senior citizens.

A spa offers mud facials, and the resort has lockers, towel rental, and showers. The hotel here is elegant and expensive. Book well in advance.

If you are on a tight budget, try the Baldi Termae just west of La Fortuna or the low-key but lush Termales del Bosque near San Carlos.

ABOVE AND BELOW: hot springs, heated up by Arenal Volcano, create a water wonderland for visitors at upscale Tabacón and other nearby thermal resorts, including the lower-key Termales del Bosque, near San Carlos, where hot pools edge a cool, fast-running river.

ABOVE: the vast craters of Volcán Irazú look deceptively peaceful, but since 1723 this very active volcano has erupted more than 20 times.

BELOW: Poás Volcano has the world's largest active crater.

POÁS VOLCANO IS IN ACTIVITY
YOU ENTER UNDER YOUR OWN RISK
SPN – MIRENEM

THE CARIBBEAN COAST

Beautiful warm water glowing blue and turquoise, radiant sunshine, and coconut palms rustling in the gentle breeze welcome you to Costa Rica's Caribbean coastline

The three-hour drive from San José to the Caribbean coast is on a paved, slow-moving highway winding past the canyons, mountains, waterfalls, and virgin forests of Parque Nacional Braulio Carrillo. Descending from the cool cloudiness of Braulio Carrillo into the tropical lowland forests of the Caribbean, the temperature rises and the air becomes heavy.

Puerto Limón

Puerto Limón ❶ (pop. 105,000) is pure Caribbean. With its rich, ripe jumble of sights and sounds and smells, it is a hot, steamy, laid-back place. Most middle-class *Ticos* who live in the Central Valley consider it something of a disgrace, crime-ridden and poor. But multimillion-dollar plans are afoot to give Limón a face-lift and make it more visitor-friendly. The main tourist focus here is the huge cruise-ship dock that disgorges thousands of visitors every year.

In the center of Limón you won't find the usual cathedral or soccer field facing a plaza such as you see in all the towns of the Central Valley. Instead **Parque Vargas**, named after a local governor, is filled with huge banyan trees with buttress roots that the townspeople use for seats while they wait for a bus.

There are few decent hotels in Limón. Most travelers stay at the **Hotel Park** or more upscale hotels north or south of the city center. Beware, however, that theft (particularly from cars) and muggings are a problem in the city and it is worth paying a little more for accommodations.

Coffee, bananas, and the railroad

Commerce began in Limón in the 17th century, when cacao plantations were worked by slaves. It wasn't until

Main attractions
LIMÓN CARNAVAL
TORTUGUERO NATIONAL PARK
CAHUITA NATIONAL PARK
MISS EDITH'S CARIBBEAN RESTAURANT
PUERTO VIEJO
SURFING THE SALSA BRAVA
LA PECORA NERA RESTAURANT
SNORKELING AT PUNTA UVA
MANZANILLO
REFUGIO NACIONAL DE VIDA SILVESTRE GANDOCA-MANZANILLO

PRECEDING PAGES: Coco's Bar, Cahuita.
LEFT: Tortuguera Park. **RIGHT:** coconut trees painted in Rasta colors, Manzanillo.

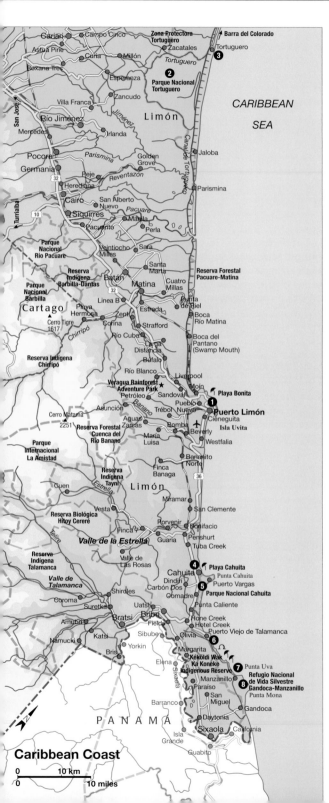

Caribbean Coast

0 ___ 10 km

0 ___ 10 miles

1871, however, when the growth of the coffee market demanded an Atlantic port, that "El Limón," a migrant black fishermen's village consisting of just five huts, was chosen.

That same year, the government contracted the construction of the Atlantic railroad from San José to the Caribbean Coast. Minor Keith, the North American responsible for building the railroad, had the bright idea of planting and cultivating bananas alongside the track in order to raise additional funds for the rising costs of construction of the Atlantic railroad.

Limón thus became a railroad and banana town, populated largely by Afro-Caribbean and Chinese immigrants who had come to Costa Rica looking for work. Since 1872, Limón and the banana industry have experienced great booms and busts: bumper banana crops (even exceeding the value of Costa Rica's coffee exports); labor troubles and violent strikes; and hard times of high unemployment when the United Fruit Company abandoned the Caribbean Coast.

Throughout all those hardships, Limón was effectively ignored by the national government of Costa Rica. The black workers and their families had no rights of citizenship; they were not permitted to work in the Pacific Zone nor in the Central Valley. After the Civil War of 1948, living conditions improved somewhat for the black residents of the city. Today, they are at last full-fledged citizens of Costa Rica, and can travel and work anywhere they wish.

Carnaval

For many people, Puerto Limón's annual *Carnaval* (Carnival) is the best reason to visit the place. This week-long jubilant event is held every October (rather than in February, the usual carnival month elsewhere). It is not an ancient Puerto Limón tradition: Carnival first began here in 1949, under the leadership of a barber called Alfred Henry King, who timed the festivities to coincide with the anniversary of Christopher Columbus's landing near Limón on October 18, 1502. *El Día de la Raza*, "The Day of the People," which falls during Carnival Week and traditionally includes the participation of the indigenous peoples who live in the region, has recently been renamed *Día de las Culturas* (Day of the Cultures) in recognition of the fact that not everyone remembers Columbus with equal affection. It is also a tribute to the contributions made to Costa Rica by people of various different cultures.

The highlight of Carnival Week is the parade, when local people joined by thousands of visitors take to the streets to revel in a glorious music and dance spectacle. The drums, the heat, the shining bodies of dancers and drummers in bright costumes, urge spectators to abandon their inhibitions and to surrender to the Caribbean beat. And so they do, *Limonenses* and tourists alike, filling the streets, shimmying, shaking, singing, and carousing, while the irresistible rhythms of steel drums fill the warm, humid air.

Tortuguero

Travel on the **Tortuguero canals**, up through the area north of Limón, has been likened to a trip on the *African Queen*, or to floating dreamily down the Amazon. It is certainly one of the most wonderfully lyrical trips to be taken anywhere in the world. As you drift lazily along, awash in the fragrance of white ginger blossoms, lavender water hyacinths and the ylang ylang flower, the tranquility here soothes all your cares away.

With the help of an expert naturalist guide, you may catch glimpses of sloths, crocodiles, and basking freshwater turtles. High up in the exuberant vegetation, multicolored parrots squawk noisily, while cranky howler monkeys shake the branches. Around 19,000 hectares (47,000 acres) of the coast and hinterland have been designated as the **Parque Nacional Tortu-**

guero ❷ (Tortuguero National Park). There are many ways to navigate its maze of waterways, including renting a dugout canoe or kayak. The best way to tour the canals is on a boat with an electric motor, guided by an expert naturalist. Or take a package tour that includes a room at one of the jungle lodges that range from modest to luxurious, plus meals, naturalist guides, and the trip through the canals. All of the Tortuguero hotels offer guided river trips and transportation either by bus and boat or by small plane from San José. Launches going up to Tortuguero also depart from Moín, just a few kilometers north of Limón. NatureAir and SANSA have short, scheduled flights from San José to Tortuguero, and NatureAir has charter flights to **Barra del Colorado**, which is north of Tortuguero, near the Nicaraguan border. From there you can hire a boat to travel south through the canals.

The green sea turtle

Tortuguero, from *tortuga*, which means turtle in Spanish, is the main nesting

A baby iguana in Tortuguero National Park.

BELOW: taking a boat along Tortuguero's canals is the best way to spot wildlife.

Veragua Rainforest Adventure Park (tel: 2296 5056), just west of Limón, combines hiking trails through pristine primary forest, accessed via an aerial tram, with wildlife exhibits and working research labs staffed by INBio biologists, plus a canopy tour.

area in the Caribbean for green sea turtles, which have been listed as endangered since the 1950s. The **Caribbean Conservation Corporation** (CCC) was established at Tortuguero for the purpose of studying and protecting these vulnerable creatures.

The CCC runs a **Natural History Center** (www.cccturtle.org) between the village and the more remote John H. Phipps Biological Field Station on the Tortuguero River. The center has a wildlife photo gallery and you can watch an informative video packed with information about the region's plant and animal life, including, of course, the green sea turtle. The area has been known for its turtle-hunting grounds since at least the mid-16th century, and turtles were exploited for their meat, shells, and eggs with impunity until as recently as 1970, when the area was established as a national park. Although poachers still exist, now at least the visiting green sea turtles and their leatherback cousins are afforded some degree of protection.

If possible, go to Tortuguero during the turtle-nesting season, in the

company of a knowledgeable naturalist guide to help you understand the habits and sensitivities of these magnificent creatures. Official turtle-watching season is from February through November, and you must go with a certified guide. If you are lucky enough to spot a nesting leatherback turtle, it is an experience that affects even the most world-weary traveler.

Another exciting option for turtle-watching is the beach at **Parismina** halfway between Tortuguero and Puerto Limón. Accessible only by boat from Siquirres, this remote Caribbean village has opened a turtle hatchery for leatherback and green turtles. Tourists are warmly welcomed in this small community to help with the **Save the Turtles of Parismina Project** (www.parisminaturtles.org), and there are a few *cabinas* and rooms to rent in the village, as well as an upscale fishing lodge *(see page 273)*.

Tortuguero village

Farther north, up the canals, the village of **Tortuguero** ❸ sits on a narrow spit of land bordered by the Caribbean Sea

BELOW: turtle tracks on the beach in Tortuguero Park.
RIGHT: Tortuguero village resident.

and the Tortuguero River. The best thing about this village is that there are no cars, just narrow paths winding through exuberant greenery, with palm trees rustling overhead. Wooden houses sit on stilts, amid a growing number of restaurants, shops, and *cabinas* catering to tourists. Even so, village life seems to continue in a timeless way.

Canadian naturalist Daryl Loth (tel: 8833 0827; www.casamarbella.tripod.com) can answer your questions about Tortuguero. And if you're hoping to sample Caribbean rice and beans cooked in coconut milk, make a reservation at **Miss Junie's**, one of the most popular restaurants in the village (tel: 2709 8102).

Talamanca

Most travelers who come to the Caribbean are heading to the beach, following the coastal drive south, with glimpses of rivers off to the right, and the Caribbean Sea to the left.

Somewhere near Tuba Creek begins the **Talamanca** region of Costa Rica, extending from the Caribbean coast and reaching into the mountains that run from the Central Valley southeast into Panamá. This area was the refuge of many indigenous people who fled the Spanish conquerors.

Until the 1970s, the Talamanca region was populated mainly by the Bribrí and Cabécar who lived in the mountains, and by the descendants of English-speaking black immigrants from the Caribbean islands who settled along the coast. The black settlers were farmers and fishermen following the old ways brought from Jamaica, most affectionately described in their own words in Paula Palmer's fascinating folk history, *What Happen*. They developed a local cuisine based on the foods they grew, and planted the coconut trees that still line the beaches. For the little money they needed, they sold coconut oil, hawksbill turtle shells, and cassava starch.

They spoke a creole English, played cricket, danced quadrilles, carved dugout canoes from local trees, and recited Shakespeare for amusement. Isolated by the sea and the mountains, no roads connected these people with the rest of Spanish-speaking Costa

Where am I? Canal signs help visitors get their bearings and put a name to the canal they're being guided along when taking a boat trip in Tortuguero Park.

BELOW: a well-camouflaged green snake in Tortuguero Park – don't reach for a branch without looking first.

Language Differences

Most of the older black residents on the Caribbean coast still speak both English and Spanish, while more and more young people speak Spanish only. If you overhear older folks talking, listen carefully to pick up the local Caribbean patois form of English.

A few of the more common expressions: "Wh'appen?" ("What's happening?") is the usual form of greeting, replacing the "Adiós" of the Central Valley. "How de morning?" is "Good morning" and "Go good" is "Take care." The polite form of address is to use someone's first name preceded by Mr or Miss.

With the influence of Jamaican reggae, accompanied by local people draped in dreadlocks, you will also hear a lot of "irie," meaning everything that is good, from nice to awesome.

TIP

Animal-lovers shouldn't miss the **Aviarios Sloth Sanctuary of Costa Rica** just north of Cahuita. The sanctuary conducts serious research, with the aim of returning orphaned and injured sloths to the wild. A visit here includes an informative video presentation, a visit with the resident sloths, and a canoe tour along canals to view birds and wildlife (tel: 2750 0775; charge).

Rica, and their life continued quite peacefully and independently. All that has changed now, with the opening of a slick new highway and other roads connecting the sleepy coastal towns of Talamanca with San José and the rest of the world.

Visiting the reserves

For the most part, the indigenous peoples of the region now speak Spanish in addition to their own native language (of which there are several), and take part in regional political and economic life, although many maintain ancient beliefs and customs. There are three indigenous reserves in Talamanca: the large Talamanca-Bribri Reserve, the Talamanca-Cabécar Reserve, and the smaller Keköldi Reserve. Access to the reserves by non-indigenous people is limited, and you usually need to obtain permission in advance. Tours in the **Keköldi Wak Ka Koneke** reserve, run by residents, focus on history and culture, medicinal plants, crafts, and traditional foods, as well as birdlife and mountain hikes (tel: 2750 0191 for tour information).

Cahuita

Local legend has it that in 1828 a turtle fisherman named William Smith (known as "Old Smith") sailed north from his home in Panamá to fish for turtles. Finding a beautiful calm bay protected by a coral reef near Cahuita Point, he decided to settle there with his family. In those early days, green and hawksbill turtles were plentiful and, as they had not yet learned to fear man, made an easy catch. Old Smith is said to have been the first English-speaking Afro-Caribbean settler to the area, which at that time was populated with Amerindians, and frequently visited by pirates.

Cahuita ❹ is a small scruffy town of faded but dignified-looking wooden houses, once painted bright colors that are now soft pastels, with a touch of Caribbean whimsy in the gingerbread details. Young travelers from Europe, Canada, and the US, oblivious to more modest local sensibilities, amble along the beaches and roadways in bright, scanty beachwear.

The main activities in Cahuita are snorkeling and eating. You can find

BELOW: the sandy beach in Cahuita National Park.

both, side by side, with **Tano's Snorkel Tour**, which departs from The Snorkeling House, right next door to **Miss Edith's** restaurant, famous for its spicy Afro-Caribbean cuisine and Sunday-only *rondon*, a hearty stew based on fish and root vegetables (*see page 281; tel: 2775 0248* for both Tano's and Miss Edith's). Sophisticated, international seafood dishes are also served at **Cha Cha Chá** (*see page 281; tel: 2755 0476*), the most upscale restaurant in town. For tours and excursions farther afield, **Cahuita Tours** (tel: 2755 0000) is the most reliable tour operator in Cahuita.

Be aware that Cahuita has drug problems, and that petty crime against – and amongst – tourists is also rife, even though the authorities crack down every so often in an attempt to keep a lid on the situation.

Cahuita National Park

To the immediate south of Cahuita is **Parque Nacional Cahuita ❺**, famous for its fine, sandy beach and coral reef. The reef extends 500 meters (1,500ft) out to sea from **Punta Cahuita** and offers great snorkeling, although the point of the reef was severely displaced during an earthquake. There are many species of tropical fish, crabs, lobsters, sea fans, anemones, sponges, seaweed, and innumerable other marine creatures to observe amidst the coral formations. You can admire it all and keep your feet dry aboard a glass-bottomed boat, or you can swim from the Puerto Vargas end of the beach. Diving equipment may be rented at **Reef Runner Divers** (tel: 2750 0480) in Puerto Viejo.

The main entrance to the park is at Puerto Vargas, 5km (3 miles) south of town (daily 7am–4pm; charge). Lifeguards patrol the beach and there is good snorkeling at Punta Cahuita. Camping is permitted in the Puerto Vargas sector, which has toilets, showers, and picnic tables. Coatis and raccoons frequent the campgrounds looking for fruit and other edibles, and are not above overturning a tent to get

them. From Puerto Vargas you can hike along a nature trail into the jungle.

North of Cahuita is a black-sand beach with gentle waters excellent for swimming. Accommodations, some with kitchens, are available throughout town and on the beach. Reservations are essential during Christmas and Easter periods and during Carnival, the second week in October. The best time to visit Cahuita is from February through April, and in October when the weather is driest.

Coconuts and cacao

Heading south toward Puerto Viejo, along a partially paved road that runs parallel to the beach, you pass houses of every style and class, but there is something magical about the Caribbean air that gives even the humblest shack a picturesque quality when it is set amidst tall coconut trees. You won't find the spruced-up charm of any developed Caribbean island here. The settlements along this coast are mostly ramshackle and, quite frankly, shabby. But the total lack of pretension seems to sit easily with footloose young

Traditional wooden architecture in Cahuita town.

BELOW: the faded colors of a home in Cahuita, built on stilts to avoid insects.

Along the roadside look out for stands advertising "Hay Pipas." They are selling green coconuts with refreshing juice inside. The vendor will slice one open for you with a wicked-looking machete.

people from all over the world, as well as older Europeans in search of an idyllic and affordable beach life.

Just before the turn-off to Puerto Viejo is **Hone Creek**, named after a short palm with large roots. When the Jamaicans came to the Talamanca coast to work on the railroad in the 1890s, they began calling it "Home Creek," and today there are road signs in the area announcing both "Hone Creek" and "Home Creek." There is usually a checkpoint with a guard at Hone Creek, seeking to stem the flow of contraband goods north from Panamá. From here, the road to Puerto Viejo is in various states of disrepair, so slow down.

Along the sides of the road, watch for cacao trees in the now-abandoned cacao plantations, destroyed by a country-wide fungus infestation. The fruit grows from the trunk of the tree and turns wonderful colors as it ripens: some becomes a soft turquoise color, others a brilliant coral. The seeds of the ripe fruit are slightly sweet and undeniably chocolatey, even in this raw state. To experience chocolate

from bean to chocolate bar, you can choose between two chocolate tours: **Cacao Trails** (tel: 2756 8186), 5km (3 miles) south of Cahuita, focuses on the history of cacao, as well as the processing of chocolate. The tour ends with a tasting and includes lunch. South of Puerto Viejo, **Chocoart** (tel: 2750 0075) is run by a Swiss owner, who knows how good chocolate should taste. The two-hour tour takes you through a healthy cacao plantation and ends with a tasting of the just-made, meltingly delicious product.

Puerto Viejo

Cahuita has a certain shabby dignity, but **Puerto Viejo de Talamanca** ❻ – to distinguish it from Puerto Viejo de Sarapiquí – is a tumbledown community. It is a hodgepodge of dilapidated wooden houses amidst tall grass. At the entrance to the town you pass a rusted-out barge anchored just off the black-sand beach.

It wasn't long ago that there were no roads to Puerto Viejo: no cars, no tourists, no money. But things have changed. Puerto Viejo's beautiful

BELOW: Puerto Viejo de Talamanca.

undeveloped beaches and easy-going ways have been discovered. New *cabinas*, hotels, and commercial developments throughout the area proclaim the arrival of tourism.

Puerto Viejo is famous in surfing circles for the **Salsa Brava**, a hot, fast, explosive wave that breaks over the reef from December through April and again in June and July. It attracts surfers from all over the world. At other times of the year the sea is quiet, particularly inside the reef, and good for snorkeling.

If you want to stay in town, where the action is, especially at night, try the **Casa Verde Lodge** (tel: 2750 0015), a tidy, Swiss-run collection of colorfully decorated *cabinas* set in a lush garden. It's cheap and cheerful and in great demand, so make a reservation well in advance *(see page 274)*. To catch the reggae beat, head to **Johnny's Place** on a Friday or Monday night. For salsa and merengue, **Stanford's**, practically on the beach, is the place to go on weekend nights. Or just wander through town at night, browse the souvenir stalls set up along the beach, and let your ears lead you to "wha'happen."

Soda Miss Sam's is one of the few restaurants left that offers Caribbean-style fish or chicken served with tasty beans and rice, and a good selection of fruit drinks. Vegetarian-friendly **Chile Rojo** on Main Street serves spicy Thai and Middle Eastern food. For casual breakfasts and baked goods, try **Pan Pay**, near the beach. Or treat yourself at the more upscale **Bread and Chocolate**, near the post office, which is famous for its oatmeal pancakes, muffins, French toast, and incredible brownies. This is notably one of the few restaurants in the entire country that serves excellent coffee made in individual French presses *(see page 281)*.

To the south of town there are *cabinas* and sophisticated hotels and restaurants lining the road across from beautiful stretches of white-sand beach edged by palm and beach almond trees. Award-winning **Bungalows Cariblue** at Playa Cocles is renowned for serv-

ice, style, and gourmet Italian food (tel: 2750 0035). Another Italian import is **La Pecora Nera** (tel: 2750 0490). Incongruously, this is perhaps the best restaurant in the whole country, hidden away off the main road south of Playa Cocles. Owner/chef Ilario Giannoni is always on hand to recite the day's specials – go for the tuna whenever it is offered *(see page 281)*.

If you haven't got a car, rent a bicycle and join the legions of cyclists meandering along the potholed road that is alternately muddy or dusty. Cycling is a great way to get around Puerto Viejo and to the nearby beaches.

If you would like to learn more about the Talamanca region, the non-profit **Talamanca Association for Ecotourism and Conservation** (ATEC; tel: 2750 0191) provides environmentally and culturally oriented tours led by local guides who speak Spanish and English. Choices for outings include snorkeling, fishing, birdwatching, adventure treks, visits to the Talamanca indigenous reserves and to the houses of local people for home-cooked meals.

A bike is a handy way of getting about on the coast.

BELOW:
Jammin' restaurant, Puerto Viejo.

TIP

Divers can rent
equipment and sign up
for dive trips at Aquamor
Talamanca Adventures
(tel: 2759 9012) in
Manzanillo, at the end
of the paved road. They
also offer scuba courses
and operate snorkeling
tours.

Punta Uva and Manzanillo

To the south of Puerto Viejo is heavenly **Punta Uva** ❼, probably the best, most easily accessible beach along Costa Rica's Caribbean coast. Crystalline, aquamarine water laps quietly on the palm-lined beach, and both the air and water temperatures seem fixed at a constant, perfect 27°C (80°F). This is the best snorkeling beach on the coast, with a healthy reef just meters offshore. It is also the only Caribbean beach where you can catch the sunset – it actually is sited in a westerly direction.

You can cycle here from Puerto Viejo and there are plenty of charming and affordable accommodations all the way down the road to Punta Uva. For people who like the idea of camping but don't want to rough it, there is **Almonds & Corals Tent Lodge Camp** (tel: 2759 9056), in the middle of a cool, shaded former cacao plantation. You will sleep in comfortable tents nested within larger tents set on platforms and complete with electricity, hot-water showers, and flush toilets.

Farther south, still on the beach, is **Manzanillo**, a tiny fishing village that can be reached by walking along the sand for about two hours from Punta Uva, or 20 minutes from Puerto Viejo by car along the paved road that terminates here. Coral reefs offshore create a natural harbor. The water can be as calm as a lake for swimming in the early morning and late afternoon. Surfers enjoy it, too, for its fast beach break. Local people have decorated the beach with colorful painted concrete garden tables and benches, and a clean-up crew arrives every morning to remove litter and spruce up the beach. Local children play in the waves or bathe in the river, young men play a game of pick-up soccer on the beach, and elderly people sit around and talk quietly in the shade. Except for the bus loads of day-trippers from Limón who arrive on Sunday, not much else goes on around here. This is Costa Rica at its most relaxed.

You will see small fishing boats pulled up onto the sand all along the beach. The supply of fresh fish is put to good use at **Restaurant Maxi's** (tel:

BELOW: Playa Uvita at Punta Uva.
BELOW RIGHT: playing in the surf at Manzanillo.

2759 9073), a two-story wooden estab-lishment, with a bar/disco downstairs and a breezy multi-roomed restaurant upstairs overlooking the beach. Gener-ous portions of fish, whole or filleted, are perfectly cooked here, or you can splurge on lobster *(see page 281)*. Café Oh-la-la has added a new French touch to town, serving breakfast and lunch.

There is a cluster of wooden houses back from the beach, a couple of *sodas* serving hearty breakfasts and *comida tipica*, a grocery store, and very inex-pensive *cabinas* at the entrance to the village *(see page 273)*.

A short walk along the beach, south of the village of Manzanillo, is the **Refugio Nacional de Vida Silvestre Gandoca-Manzanillo** ❽, which pro-tects swamplands, coral reefs, turtle nesting grounds, and the only man-grove forest on Costa Rica's Carib-bean coast. The hiking trail along the coast crosses streams, clambers over rocks, and then climbs uphill into for-est, where birds and wildlife are abun-dant. To get the most out of a hike, hire a local guide from the Associa-tion of Indigenous Naturalist Guides

of Manzanillo (tel: 2759 9064). Bring your own supply of drinking water since there are no facilities available in the refuge.

Banana country

Sixaola is a banana town on the Pan-amá border, 44km (26 miles) south of the turn-off to Puerto Viejo on the coastal highway. The road is paved until just outside of Bribrí: the rest of the way it is gravel, in fair condition. There are no tourist attractions or services, save for the border crossing. Panamá and Costa Rica have signed an agreement to build a new border cross-ing here to replace the present one-way rickety railway bridge.

The area stretching from just outside the village of Bribrí to the border at Sixaola is "Banana Land," with banana-processing plants all along the road. It's interesting to stop for a break at one of the open-air plants to watch the work-ers handling the large bunches, called *racimos*, cutting bunches of bananas off the stalks, sorting, washing, and putting them in boxes bound for the waiting cargo ships in Limón.   ❏

Bananas grow in abundance on this part of the coast.

BELOW: Manzanillo's idyllic setting is matched by its relaxed, unhurried pace of life.

Going Bananas

Banana cultivation began as a by-product of the Atlantic railroad, but quickly became one of the country's major exports. In 1889 Minor Keith, the Atlantic railroad pioneer, formed the United Fruit Company and turned Costa Rica into Central America's first banana republic. Unfortunately, United Fruit soon became a symbol of the evils of foreign domination and control over the local economy. The company's ruthless meth-ods and exploitation of labor were widely reviled, but it was also highly successful. By 1913 Costa Rica was the world's top banana exporter. In the 1930s, after dis-ease devastated the crop, United Fruit pulled out of Limón province for good, leaving behind a virtually destitute region. Nowadays, the area is once again pro-ducing bananas on a large scale.

Sea Turtles

"Save the turtles" has become a conservationists' rallying cry, and Costa Rica is on the front line in the battle to do just that

Sea turtles look more like their close but extinct relatives, the dinosaurs, than animals of today. Remarkable adaptations to life in the sea have enabled them to survive, largely unchanged, for more than 150 million years. They "fly" like birds through the water using front flippers as wings. Yet they retain terrestrial traits and must surface to breathe air and crawl ashore to nest and lay their eggs.

Costa Rica is home to five species of sea turtles: green, hawksbill, Olive Ridley, leatherback, and loggerhead. They are more easily viewed here than anywhere else in the world. They nest at several well-known beaches on both Caribbean and Pacific shores. During the nesting season, if you happen to be in the right place at the right time, you may see one of the most amazing spectacles in the animal kingdom: *the arribada*, when 100,000 or more Olive Ridley turtles come ashore to nest simultaneously *(see page 200)*. Or, equally spectacular, is the sight of a 680kg (1,500lb)

leatherback hauling her massive body out of the water and up the beach to bury her clutch of eggs in the sand.

Tortuguero Beach, a 35km (22-mile) stretch on Costa Rica's northern Caribbean coast, is the most important nesting area for green turtles in the Western Caribbean. Here, you can see green turtles, hawksbill turtles, and Ridleys.

Green turtles mate and nest several times from September through November. With the sharp hook on his front flippers, the male holds and mounts the female. If the sexually aggressive male can't locate a mate, he will eagerly clamber on top of anything that floats. Chunks of wood, other male turtles, even skin divers are not safe from a male's misguided passion.

An impregnated female waits offshore until dark before beginning her long struggle up the beach to the nesting site. During her crawl up the sand, disturbances such as noise and light will cause her to abort the nesting procedure, and to return to the safety of the sea. But once she has begun digging the nest, nothing will distract her.

Using her rear flippers, she scoops out a vase-shaped hole, approximately 1 meter (2–3ft) deep. One hundred or more leathery, golf-ball-sized eggs covered with a mucus "fungicide" drop into the nest one or two at a time until the entire clutch is deposited. She covers the nest, tamps

down the sand and begins her long crawl back to the sea, leaving her progeny at the mercy of coatimundis, dogs, raccoons, and human scavengers, known as *hueveros*, who steal the eggs and sell them to local bars.

In undisturbed nests, baby green turtles hatch in a couple of months. Using a temporary egg tooth, they tear open their shells. Soon the entire clutch is ready to rise to the surface. A critical mass of about 100 turtles all working together is needed to excavate the 1 meter (3ft) of sand that is covering them. Usually before dawn, they erupt onto the beach, look for the brightest part of the horizon over the sea, and scramble for the water running the gauntlet of ghost crabs and birds, perhaps then only to be met by sharks and predatory fish once they do reach the water. Hundreds of thousands race for the sea and probably less than 3 percent survive. Those that do make it go offshore to floating rafts of sargassum weed where they find shelter and food for their first and most difficult months at sea.

For several decades they live nomadic lives, migrating over vast distances of the open ocean to feed on turtle grass in the remote Miskito Keys off Nicaragua or at Cahuita on the Talamanca coast. Some navigate several thousand kilometers to the Windward Islands, using no apparent landmarks or visual cues. It is thought that crystals of magnetic iron located in the turtles' brains perhaps serve as internal compasses, guiding them across the seas. Or, more prosaically, they may just follow a certain smell or substance.

Although no one knows for certain, marine biologists estimate that it takes 15–30 years for these turtles to reach sexual maturity, at which point they reconvene on the beaches where they were born and proceed to mate, nest, and complete their incredible reproduction cycle.

To early explorers, fresh turtle meat was a welcome change from salt beef and sea biscuits, and, of course, this was before people became aware that species could be wiped out. Tropical peoples still relish meat from the sea turtle. But sadly, the species is being endangered more from frivolous use than for subsistence purposes: six or seven species of sea turtle are on the brink of extinction. In bars from the Caribbean to Sri Lanka, sea turtle eggs are sucked from the shells in the mistaken belief that they act as aphrodisiacs. Tortoiseshell has a high value when carved, polished, and made into jewelry, combs, and spectacle frames. Turtle skin is even being used as a substitute for alligator skin in shoes and purses.

Sea turtles remain on the endangered species list, although worldwide conservation programs are under way. Importation of turtle products into the US and other countries is strictly prohibited and carries stiff penalties. But more and more adult turtles are caught in shrimp trawls and longline fishing nets, and fishermen continue to hunt them, illegally.

Silt from unlawfully deforested land near Tortuguero washes onto the beaches, bringing weeds that take away valuable nesting space from the turtles. And floodlights from beach-side hotels and developments frighten off females who are ready to nest, and disorient hatchlings trying to reach the sea.

The future for many turtles is bleak, though in 1991 a new national park was created at Playa Grande on the Nicoya Peninsula and named Las Baulas, the Spanish word for leatherback turtle. And the National Park authorities now take a very strict line on poaching. Perhaps this, plus the efforts of the many volunteer programs and the commercial demands of ecotourism, will yet save the endangered turtles. ❑

LEFT: Olive Ridley *(Lepidochelys olivacea)* sea turtle returns to the sea after laying its eggs on the beach.
RIGHT: baby sea turtle making its way to the sea.

THE SOUTH

Even by local standards, the south is a wild region. It includes the highest peak in Central America and the largest, most inaccessible national park with the most pristine tropical wet forest

The Zona Sur, or Southern Zone, rises in the highlands around Cerro de la Muerte, the highest point in the country, then falls away into the agricultural lands of the Valle de El General and ends in the tropical lowlands at the Panamanian border. This is an area for hikers and nature-lovers with a sense of adventure, who like exploring off the beaten path.

Playa Dominical

A beautiful drive of 35km (22 miles) on a paved road from San Isidro de El General, west through misty mountains, brings you to the Pacific Ocean and **Playa Dominical ❶**. Dominical can also be reached by a two-hour drive along the newly paved *Costanera Sur* highway from Quepos, passing by beaches alternating with dense palm-oil plantations. Whichever way you choose, it's a scenic drive, with both ocean and forest vistas.

In Dominical stop off for the night at secluded **Pacific Edge** (tel: 2787 8010), a collection of comfortable wooden cabins perched high on a forested ridge with spectacular sea views. Or spend some time down at sea level at **Hacienda Barú** (tel: 2787 0003), in the middle of a private forest reserve, hiking through kilometers of forest and beach trails with excellent naturalist guides.

The beach at Dominical is a long stretch of brown sand offering excellent surfing waves, though beware of dangerous currents when swimming. Lifeguards, when they are on duty, mark off with flags the safer areas to swim. There are shady places on the sand for camping, but be sure to bring mosquito nets and repellent. The "town" is a funky conglomeration of trendy restaurants and bars, simple *sodas*, surf and souvenir shops, and some comfortable hotels along with basic *cabinas* and hostels catering to young surfers. Playa

Main attractions
PLAYA DOMINICAL
PARQUE NACIONAL MARINO BALLENA
BAHÍA DRAKE
ISLA DEL CAÑO
PARQUE NACIONAL CORCOVADO
GOLFO DULCE
TISKITA JUNGLE LODGE
WILSON BOTANICAL GARDEN
CERRO DE LA MUERTE
LA RUTA DE LOS SANTOS
SAN GERARDO DE DOTA
PARQUE NACIONAL CHIRRIPÓ

PRECEDING PAGES: ox-cart on the Pacific coast. **LEFT:** giant buttress roots of a tree near Hacienda Barú. **RIGHT:** Dominical beach.

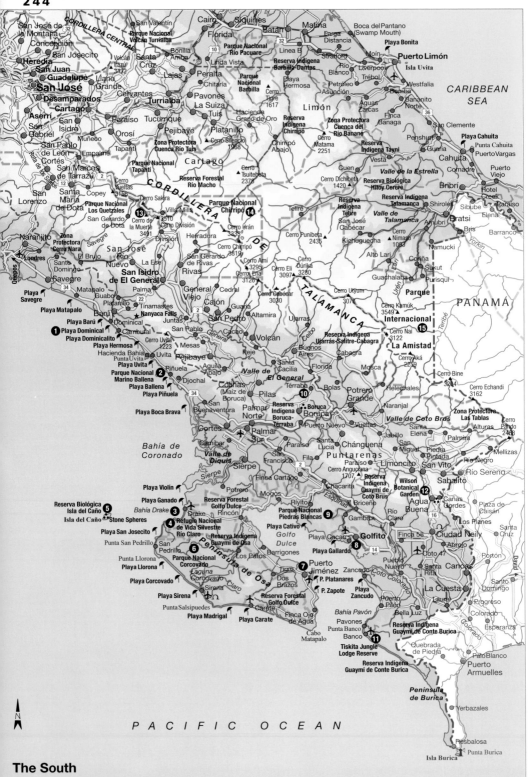

The South

N

0 ___ 15 km

0 ___ 15 miles

Dominical's weather can be hot and humid but there are cool spots above the beach on the coastal ridge.

A horseback trip to **Nauyaca Falls**, also known as Santo Cristo and Barú Falls, takes about two hours. The falls consist of two cascades a total of 65 meters (210ft) high, which tumble into a glorious warm-water swimming hole. **Don Lulo's Waterfall Tour** (tel: 2787 0541) arranges horseback trips to the falls; **Bella Vista Lodge** (tel: 2787 8069) offers sunset beach rides. Several operators in the area, including **Southern Expeditions** (tel: 2787 0100) on Dominical's main street, can book a wide choice of adventure tours.

Just south of Dominical is **Playa Dominicalito**, where there are good point-break waves for surfers. Swimming is best at low tide when beaches are exposed beyond coral rocks and there are beautiful views of the overlooking hills. This is also a great boogie-boarding spot and an ideal beach on which to stroll at sunset.

Up the hill from the community soccer field and across a shallow river, the **Pozo Azul** is a deep swimming hole at the base of a pretty waterfall, just a short hike in from the road. The local children have tied a Tarzan rope to a strong tree and you can swing out over the pool and plummet into it, making an impressive splash. There is no charge, but do tip the guard in the parking lot, if he's there, and don't leave any valuables in your car. If you are on foot, it's about a 20-minute walk up from Dominicalito beach.

Marino Ballena Park

Some 20km (12 miles) to the south of Dominical lies **Parque Nacional Marino Ballena ❷**, easily accessible via four bumpy access roads off the smoothly paved Costanera Sur. Marino Ballena offers beautiful swimming beaches, camping on some beaches, a coral reef for snorkeling, and mangroves where you can spot caimans and wading birds. Along with the dolphins that play year-round in the bay, humpback whales and their young visit the park from December through April.

Two sandy beaches within the park sweep to a meeting point at Punta

TIP

For a bird's-eye view of Marino Ballena Park, climb the hill to Cristal Ballena, a new luxury hotel with the best and biggest swimming pool on the coast, and a terrace restaurant with ocean view.

BELOW: playing in the surf, Dominical.

Ants in Your Plants

A hands-on guide to investigating the strange and mutually beneficial relationships between tropical ants and forest flora

Should someone point out a "bull's horn acacia" to you, stop and have a close look at this thorny shrub. It measures between 1.5 and 3 meters (4–10ft) in height, and you will see along the branches pairs of reddish spines that look like miniature replicas of a Texas steer's horns. Hence its common name (its official name is *Acacia cornigera*).

Of the numerous symbiotic relationships that have evolved between tropical ants and plants, that of the bull's horn acacia and its stinging ants is one of the most curious. It is also one of the most dramatic examples of tropical co-evolution between species.

With some caution, shake the end of a branch. Ants burrow into the end of the spines (notice the tiny hole), excavate the inside of the branch, and set up a colony where they rear their young and go about the day-to-day business of being ants. When the plant is disturbed, as in the case of your shaking the branch, the pugnacious ants charge aggressively from the spines, stingers armed and ready to defend their acacia host. It would only take one nasty sting to convince you that this unusual defense system works.

In addition to repelling would-be grazers, ranging in size from caterpillars to cattle, the ants manicure the ground around the acacia, keeping it clear of sprouts from other plants that might deprive their host of living space in a tropical forest containing 1,200 species of competing trees and countless other plants.

And the acacia is appreciative. Not only does it shelter its guardians, it also feeds them. Tiny, sausage-shaped pores hang from the ends of the leaflets. Loaded with sugar and protein, these are harvested gratefully by the ants.

On the forest floor you are almost sure to spot trails carved by leafcutter ants as they march through the jungle in search of tender leaves to attack. Their trails are veritable highways of activity. Imagine thousands of people walking home on the highway, each rushing along, carrying a 1.5 meter by 2.5 meter (4ft by 8ft) sheet of green plywood overhead, and you have the basic concept of these ants.

Leafcutters are amazingly industrious insects, much to the distress of many a garden owner in Costa Rica. They can completely denude a full-grown mango tree overnight, carving circular slabs of leaf about 1cm (½in) in diameter, hoisting them overhead and marching down the tree trunk back to the hive, which may be a kilometer away or more.

Several highways lead to the ants' hive – often around the buttress roots of a large tree. Hives of more than 100 sq meters (120 sq yds), 2 meters (7ft) deep in the forest floor, are not uncommon. In these hives, millions, perhaps billions, of ants chew the leaf fragments, mixing them with nutrient-rich saliva, into a kind of gruel. From this gruel the ants grow and harvest mushrooms that provide their chief food source.

Large ant colonies can cut and process almost 45kg (100lbs) of leaves a day. During the decades-long lifespan of an ant colony, tons of vegetation decomposes and is worked back into the forest floor. Constant rain and heat rapidly degrade tropical soils, and so the vast storehouse of nutrients and compost from the ant mounds create a rich oasis in the soil. ❑

LEFT: Leaf-cutting ant in Manuel Antonio National Park.

Uvita, creating a sand bar at low tide that looks remarkably like a whale's tail.

In the village of **Bahía Ballena**, the main entry point to the park, there's a wide choice of cheap *cabinas* and *sodas*. **Dolphin Tours of Bahía Ballena** (tel: 2743 8013), on the road to the park entrance, can get you out onto the water for snorkeling, fishing, or whale- and dolphin-spotting. **Mystic Dive Center** (tel: 2786 5217), near Playa Ventanas south of the park, can get you under the water. And **Skyline Ultra Flight** (tel: 2743 8037), in Bahía Ballena, can take you above the water for a bird's-eye view from aboard an ultra-light plane.

Just south of the park, on the east side of the Costanera, is a sign for Ojochal, a French-Canadian enclave that is home to a French bakery and two wonderful restaurants that serve Mediterranean food with a tropical twist *(see page 281)*. The scenic Costanera highway continues south, offering dramatic ocean and coastal mountain views with every twist and turn. **Playa Ventanas**, just south of Ballena National Park, has nearby rocky islands and a huge rock formation, popular with sea kayakers who paddle through a passage in the rock navigable at low tide.

The Osa Peninsula

Jutting out more than 50km (30 miles) into the Pacific, the Osa Peninsula shelters the Golfo Dulce from ocean swells and creates a magnificent natural harbor. It is sculpted with picturesque beaches and rocky headlands, and dissected by streams and rivers that cascade over volcanic cliffs on their way to the sea. The most majestic forests in all Costa Rica cover the hillsides and line the valleys of the Osa Peninsula and, in many cases, represent the last stronghold of nature and endangered animals and plants, endemic to the South Pacific. It is an imposing, impressive, and wild place. The most famous attraction is Corcovado National Park, the jewel in the crown of Costa Rica's national park system.

Drake Bay

On the northern coast of the Osa Peninsula, **Bahía Drake** ❸ is reputedly where Sir Francis Drake, the first English navigator to sail around the world, landed in 1579. Until recently, this outpost, surrounded by crystal-blue waters, pristine beaches, and jungle, was accessible only on foot, by water or by charter plane. Now there is a dirt road from Rincón, built by the national power company to finally bring electricity to the village. There are also direct flights from San José to the Drake airstrip, passing over Manuel Antonio Park and, on a clear day, providing aerial perspectives of the south Pacific coast en route to Corcovado. As you land on the grass airstrip, look out for scarlet macaws.

A trio of upscale lodges in Drake Bay tops the wide choice of accommodations *(see page 275)*. The most romantic is **La Paloma Lodge** (tel: 2293 7502), built on a breezy bluff with sweeping views of the ocean; its elegant and comfortable *cabinas*, with thatched roofs and private decks, blend unobtrusively into the jungle environs.

A queen aechmea bromeliad.

BELOW: tidal pools at Matapalo, on the Osa Peninsula.

From the lodge you can arrange expeditions to fish or dive, kayak along a dreamy river, and visit Corcovado and Isla del Caño.

Just south of Drake Bay village, the Coastal Footpath begins. This easy-to-walk scenic trail cuts between dense jungle on the land side, and crashing surf on the Pacific side. There are also calmer sandy coves along the way. The path leads south all the way to **Punta Marenco Ecolodge** (tel: 2294 8947), in the 500-hectare (1,200-acre) **Refugio Nacional de Vida Silvestre Río Claro ④**. Guests stay in rustic but comfortable grass huts perched over the Pacific, with cool breezes, hammocks on private verandahs, and views of Caño Island.

Isla del Caño

The **Isla del Caño ⑤** biological reserve sits low on the horizon, about 19km (12 miles) seaward of the Corcovado coastline, a pleasant one-hour boat ride from either Marenco or Bahía Drake. According to archeologists, the island was both a cemetery for indigenous peoples and a refuge for pirates. Spot-

ted dolphins ride the boat's bow wave, and flying fish sometimes escort boats to the island. Between December and April, 40-ton humpback whales come from their feeding grounds in Alaska. Males sing haunting songs to attract females, and often leap high in impressive breaches during their procreative sojourn in Costa Rican waters.

The island is ringed with turquoise water, tiny beaches, and acres of coral-covered rock reefs. Brilliantly colored tropical fish are easily seen by snorkelers and scuba divers within 15 meters (50ft) of the shore at the park headquarters. Steep, well-manicured trails lead through a rich forest drooping with epiphytes and enormous philodendrons to a clearing with ancient stone spheres.

Parque Nacional Corcovado

Covering 445 sq km (172 sq miles), **Parque Nacional Corcovado ⑥** is Central America's largest lowland Pacific rainforest. It's the most important sanctuary of biological diversity and endangered wildlife in the country, and one of the most important in

BELOW: a colored anteater in Corcovado. **RIGHT:** Corcovado National Park.

the world. Because Corcovado Park is inundated with nearly 6 meters (20ft) of rain a year, it is technically known as a "tropical wet forest." But the simplicity of that classification belies the ecological complexity of the park. Thirteen distinct habitats here are each characterized by unique assemblages of plants, animals, and topography. Five hundred species of trees – one quarter of all the species in Costa Rica – more than 6,000 kinds of insects, almost 375 species of birds, plus frogs, butterflies, and many of the world's most endangered and spectacular mammals, including tapirs and jaguars, live in this place.

Estimates of the number of jaguars in the whole country range from 300 on up, but the forests of Corcovado can support, at most, only 50 jaguars. An adult jaguar needs an enormous amount of land with abundant prey animals such as peccaries, deer, and agouti, to meet its food requirements. You are more likely to see jaguar tracks on many of the trails, however, than an actual jaguar. Poachers hunting peccaries have, unfortunately, cut seriously into the jaguar's food supply. But an internationally funded program to increase the number of park rangers is having some success at rooting out illegal hunters.

Although jaguars may be scarce, birds are everywhere. Scarlet macaws are perhaps the most spectacular birds in Corcovado. Also sought after are the red-breasted Baird's trogon and the melodious riverside wren, both of which are endemic to these forests.

Seeds or husks dropping through the canopy will often reveal the presence of troops of squirrel monkeys. White-faced monkeys also abound here, along with larger *monos colorados*, or reddish-brown spider monkeys, famous for their acrobatics as they swing from tree to tree. Other animals you are likely to see are long-snouted, ring-tailed coatimundis. The males travel solo, but if you're lucky you may come across a group of females with youngsters – it's like a nursery-school playtime, with the babies scampering in the undergrowth and tumbling off lower branches. Agoutis, plump rodents that look like squirrels

TIP

In Corcovado Park, you are largely on your own among such dangerous wildlife as coral snakes and fer-de-lance vipers. Although it is rare to come across these creatures, use common sense: wear sturdy boots, long floppy pants, and watch where you walk.

BELOW LEFT: Squirrel monkey in Corcovado.

Corcovado Without a Tent

A pleasant alternative to days of grueling hikes and sleeping in a tent in Corcovado National Park is to bed down at one of the nearby eco-lodges *(see page 275)*. At one end of the scale is **Lapa Ríos**, set in its own primary forest preserve, with super-comfortable thatched-roof bungalows perched on a hillside overlooking the ocean. It's as luxurious as it gets here, but like all lodges this far south, Lapa Ríos is off the electrical grid, so there is no TV, no air conditioning and few reliable cellular phones. Nearby **Bosque del Cabo** is just as luxurious, and a favorite hangout for monkeys and the odd puma. In Carate, within walking distance of the La Leona park entrance, cheery, laid-back **Lookout Inn** is right on the beach, with guaranteed sightings of scarlet macaws, while **Luna Lodge**, famous for its yoga retreats, contemplates Corcovado from a mountain perch. The closest you can stay to the park entrance, in some comfort, is at **La Leona Eco-Lodge** (www.laleonalodge.com), in a cabin-like tent pitched on a platform, with a private bathroom attached. Guests at upscale **Casa Corcovado Jungle Lodge** can hike directly into the bordering park. Near the new El Tigre park entrance, rustic **Bosque del Tigre Lodge** in Dos Brazos has some of the best birding and hiking in the Osa. Close to Los Patos, affordable **Danta Corcovado Lodge** has simple but comfortable rooms, as well as private cabins in the woods.

One of the region's mysterious stone spheres.

without tails, are also common, rooting for fallen seeds and fruits. To improve your chances of seeing these animals, hit the trail before dawn and walk very softly, and always stand very still when you see an animal.

One of Corcovado's blessings is its inaccessibility. It is a park only for those who are prepared to make a considerable commitment in time and energy. A continuing source of embarrassment to local conservationists is that despite its importance, La Sirena's lodging facilities are beyond rustic; in fact they are downright shabby. Camping with your own tent – make reservations well in advance – can be more comfortable than staying at the Sirena lodge. But there are other ways to sample the beauties of Corcovado and the Osa Peninsula, from day trips by boat or charter flights, to accommodations at nearby luxury eco-lodges *(see page 275)*.

BELOW RIGHT: a young, watchful puma (cougar), one of the big cats in Corcovado.

The ideal time to hike and camp in Corcovado is during the dry season, from December through April. A visit might include a night at each of the three park stations, with days spent hiking from one station to the next. (Stations are joined by trails, each of which requires from three to 10 hours of hiking time.) It is important to come well equipped: a tent, mosquito net, insect repellent, sunhat and sunscreen, good hiking shoes, and a couple of changes of socks are essential – plus your own food.

Make arrangements for visiting the park at the administration office, next to the airport in Puerto Jiménez *(see next page)*. Apart from the lodge at the **La Sirena station**, other stations offer only camping facilities and you will need to walk to them or arrive by boat.

The park stations

The main **La Sirena station** has wonderful trails into the forest and along the beach, although the station itself, sadly, has been neglected. At the north end of the park is the **Los Patos Station**, an 11km (7-mile) hike from Sirena on a wide trail that runs parallel to the El Tigre River. The trail allows relatively easy wildlife viewing. Even though it passes through thick forest,

Mystery of the Spheres

At the highest point on Isla del Caño, where the forest thickens and becomes silent, dried leaves crackle underfoot as you approach the pre-Columbian cemetery of the Boruca people.

Two stone spheres sit among the trees. Green with moss and highlighted by shafts of sunlight from the forest canopy, the enigmatic spheres seem impossibly symmetrical in this forest of twisted plants. Thousands of spheres like this have been found in numerous locations in the south of Costa Rica, and a few also in northern Panamá. They pose one of the country's great riddles. Though their exact origin and significance have defied explanation, it is speculated that they were made in villages on the Osa Peninsula near Palmar Norte, brought to Caño in canoes, and then possibly rolled to the cemetery at the highest point of the island.

The smaller stone spheres, which are the size of oranges, were possibly toys, but the huge spheres, over 2 meters (6ft) in diameter, may have indicated the political or social standing of the deceased. Graves with spheres as headstones, oriented to the east, had secret chambers for precious ornaments and were covered with layers of sand, coral, and pebbles. Many spheres found in groups have been placed to reflect the positions of the stars.

you stand a reasonably good chance of seeing at least tracks of jaguar, ocelot, and tapir. Hikers used to be able to hike along the beach to the **San Pedrillo station**, midway between Drake Bay and Sirena, but that route has been temporarily closed because it was deemed too dangerous. You can still enter the park at the station if you arrive by boat. The **La Leona station** is the southernmost park station, and it's the easiest to hike to, along the beach from Carate. There is camping at all the stations, except Los Patos, at the moment.

A guide is a very good idea. Irish naturalist/zoologist Mike Boston of **Osa Aventura** (tel: 2735 5758) specializes in multi-day hikes through the park; his website also has the most up-to-date information on hiking rules in the park: www.osa.adventura.com.

Puerto Jiménez and Sierpe

Just outside Parque Nacional Corcovado to the east is **Puerto Jiménez ❼**, the biggest town of the Osa Peninsula and the main gateway to the park. It's a friendly, funky frontier town with a burgeoning tourist infrastructure. Inexpensive meals and lodging are available in the town, and there are some excellent new restaurants. A number of eco-lodges and ecotourism projects in all price ranges are to be found in the surrounding area. **Playa Platanares**, about 6km (4 miles) south of the airfield, has calm water for swimming, and a bird refuge bordering a sandy beach. Among the handful of beach-front lodges here, **Iguana Lodge** (tel: 8848 0752) stands out for its lovely gardens, comfortable cabins, and knowledgeable, conservation-minded American owners.

Puerto Jiménez is accessible by car, bus, or small airplane. It's about a seven-hour road trip from San José and most lodges will arrange transportation for guests. Rugged four-wheel-drive vehicles can continue south from Puerto Jiménez to Carate, which is literally the end of a very bumpy road and a trip back through time. The drive can be harrowing, especially when rivers rise, but it is a memorable experience, driving along a road completely devoid of power lines.

TIP

Peccaries (wild pigs) have an exaggerated reputation as the forest's most ferocious animal. Nonetheless, if a group of them approaches, or worse, surrounds you, then you would do well to climb the nearest tree.

BELOW: local *Ticos* in Puerto Jiménez.

A more adventurous way to access the remote Pacific coast of the Osa Peninsula is from the little inland town of **Sierpe**, where you board motorboats to cruise along the Sierpe River. The shores of the river are lined with mangroves whose branches and maze of roots support a healthy ecosystem of fish, crabs, iguanas, and water birds. Blue herons and snowy egrets may fly from the trees as the boat passes. Beware, however, that the water at the mouth (the *boca*) of the river, where it empties into the Pacific Ocean, is often very choppy. Make sure your boat is equipped with life-jackets and make sure yours is on when you near the *boca*.

Golfito

On the eastern shore of the Golfo Dulce, the port of **Golfito** ❽ has a perfect, sheltered harbor. In 1938, the United Fruit Company *(see pages 57 and 58)* realized Golfito's potential, and built a major shipping port here. By 1955 more than 90 percent of the bananas shipped from Costa Rica departed on banana boats from Golf-ito. Boatloads of crewmen and 15,000 *Guanacasteco* immigrants came to work the plantations, and turned Golfito into a boom town of brothels, smugglers, and drunks. Following crippling strikes and labor conflicts, United Fruit abandoned its Golfito operations in 1985 and economic depression set in.

The population today is about 30,000 and Golfito is making a slow comeback, based on tourism, sport fishing, and a new role as a base for the country's Coast Guard Academy and a port for US naval ships bent on intercepting drug traffic.

The old town, referred to as the **Pueblo Civil**, is regaining a touch of its boom-town atmosphere, with bars and restaurants overlooking the harbor and busy marinas. A duty-free shopping zone at the north end of town, known as *El Depósito*, sells consumer durables and liquor a little cheaper than in San José, and many Costa Ricans make weekend excursions to shop here. (Shoppers must stay in Golfito at least 24 hours in order to shop in the *depósito*.) The **American Zone** of Golfito was home to United Fruit

BELOW: the forest meets the sea at El Remanso Lodge, south of Puerto Jiménez on the Osa Peninsula.

Company executives, and many of the handsome wooden plantation-style homes on stilts, with screened porches and hipped roofs, have been restored. It's worth a drive or a wander, to see the lovely old houses shaded by stately old specimen trees that were imported from all over the world.

The main attractions here are sport fishing and boats to nearby eco-lodges that are only accessible by water. There is also a regular boat service between Golfito and Puerto Jiménez, across the Golfo Dulce; as well as boat taxis to Playa Zancudo, to the south. **Parque Nacional Piedras Blancas** and the **Refugio Nacional de Vida Silvestre Golfito**, important wildlife corridors, lie just north of town. There are regular domestic flights to Golfito; for the more patient traveler, the very scenic seven-hour bus ride from San José to Golfito is a memorable experience.

North of Golfito

Facing the Golfo Dulce, accessible only by boat, are beautiful pebbled beaches, and dense jungle that starts almost at the water's edge. A 20-minute speedboat ride from Golfito brings you to lovely **Playa Nicuesa Rainforest Lodge** (tel: 8824 6571), which offers kayaking, snorkeling, fishing, and dolphin-watching out the front door of the lodge; and hiking, birdwatching, and waterfalls in the mountain forest just steps behind the back door. The main lodge is hand-crafted with more than eight kinds of tropical wood, and secluded cabins are scattered around a lush tropical garden. In the next cove over is **Casa Orquideas** (tel: 8829 1247; Thur and Sun one-hour tours at 8.30am; charge), a beautifully landscaped garden of ginger, cacao, papaya, orchids, and tropical plants.

Parque Nacional Piedras Blancas ❾ partly owes its existence to the generosity of Austrians who contributed the money to pay landowners, whose land was expropriated by a cash-strapped government, to create

the park in 1991. Now incorporated into Parque Nacional Corcovado, this area has also been given the nickname "Rainforest of the Austrians." There's a biological station that houses students and scientists from around the world. More comfortable accommodation is available at **Esquinas Rainforest Lodge** (tel: 2741 8001). Hiring a local guide here is strongly recommended since the park trails are sometimes hard to follow.

Continuing north on the Interamericana Highway past Palmar Norte, the road heads east, following the Río Grand de Térraba. Just past Paso Real, watch for a steep, dirt road that leads to the village of **Térraba ❿**, a small village within the Boruca Indigenous Reserve. There is a small museum here showcasing Boruca culture, including exhibits of carved and painted wooden masks and colorful woven cottons. Over New Year's, the annual *Fiesta de los Diablitos* (Festival of the Little Devils) attracts many visitors to watch a re-enactment dance/fight between the Spanish and indigenous population – only this time the Amerindians win.

Butterflies are everywhere in Costa Rica and often found resting under leaves.

BELOW: El Remanso Lodge's private reserve is just around the corner from Golfo Dulce.

South of Golfito

Between the mouth of the Río Coto Colorado (just south of Golfito) and Punta Banco, the last major point of land before the Panamanian border, lie some of Costa Rica's most inaccessible and remote beaches. An old cable ferry is still the only way across the river, although a bridge is in the works. In Pueblo Nuevo, turn right for **Playa Zancudo**, an 8km (5-mile) -long, sandy crescent with excellent swimming and surfing, and several nice places to stay. Cabinas & Restaurant Sol y Mar (tel: 2776 0014) is very friendly and serves good food; Cabinas Los Cocos (tel: 2776 0012) has beach-front, self-catering cottages and offers kayaking and river tours.

Or continue on the road parallel to the coast to **Pavones**, just before Río Claro. This rocky beach is not suitable for swimming, but it is a renowned surfing spot. Basic lodging is available, along with more comfortable rooms at Cabinas La Ponderosa (tel: 8824 4145), which has a swimming pool set in a lush garden. Some funky new restaurants have been set up by surfers who

settled here, notably Café de la Suerte (tel: 2776 2388), a delightful vegetarian restaurant with free Wi-fi.

After the seemingly endless pot-holes, bogs, and washboard bumps in the road, continue on for another 30 minutes to **Punta Banco**. Wide inter-tidal flats of volcanic and sedimentary rock, riddled with tide pools full of marine life and battered by continual surf, characterize Punta Banco.

At the end of the point, a gate on the left marks the entrance to **Tiskita Jungle Lodge** ⓫ (tel: 2296 8125), a private rainforest reserve, experimental tropical fruit farm, and eco-lodge. The tortuous drive (a four-wheel-drive vehicle is essential) can be avoided by chartering a small airplane from Golf-ito that sets down on a grass airstrip near the lodge. Comfortably rustic cabins, some with ocean views, are sprinkled along trails, a short walk from the main lodge. Well-designed trails lead to waterfalls, idyllic swim-ming holes, and various points of natural history interest in Tiskita's 320-hectare (800-acre) primary and secondary forests. More than 100 spe-cies of fruit trees from around the tropical world are under cultivation here, attracting legions of monkeys and flocks of birds.

Wilson Botanical Garden

For the ultimate experience in tropi-cal botany, visit the **Wilson Botanical Garden** ⓬ (daily 8am–4pm; charge), 6km (4 miles) south of San Vito in the Coto Brus region high above Golf-ito. The gardens are part of the Las Cruces Biological Station, operated by the Organization for Tropical Studies (OTS). Trails wind through extensive, beautifully arranged collections of "lobster claw" heliconias, bromeliads, tree ferns, orchids, and palms. Birds abound and there are early-morning birding walks, as well as garden tours. Overnight guests can also hike into Wilson's wild forest reserve, following the Río Jaba into primary forest full of birds and wildlife. Comfortable guest

BELOW: handsome tropical plants grow along the roadside in some parts of Costa Rica.

cabins have private verandahs, perfect for birdwatching. At family-style meals, you can talk with visiting scientists and researchers (tel: 2773 4004).

The nearby town of **San Vito** was founded by immigrants from post-war Italy, who were encouraged by the Costa Rican government to settle there. It's a clean, modern town of 16,000 inhabitants, high in a mountain valley, at a refreshingly cool 960 meters (3,150ft) above sea level. Nearby indigenous reserves are home to Guaymí, who work mostly in the surrounding coffee *fincas*. When the women come to town, they bring a splash of color with their intricately embroidered long dresses. You can get a good Italian meal here at popular **Pizzería Liliana**, in the center of town (tel: 2773 3080).

The winding, paved road north from **Ciudad Neilly** rises precipitously, offering spectacular views along the climb up to San Vito. The other approach to San Vito, traveling east from **Paso Real**, follows an equally scenic high ridge, with panoramic views of valleys on either side, and the vast Talamanca range rising in the distance.

Valle de El General

Since colonial times, people had attempted to find a pass through the Talamanca Mountains to join the Central Valley with the unknown lands on the other side of the Dota Mountains. But it was not until the end of the 1860s that Don Pedro Calderón found a way through. The opening of the road led to the colonization of the **Valle de El General**, and later, to the building of the Interamericana Highway, which connects San José and the Central Valley with the southern Pacific zone of Costa Rica. If you are traveling south to the Valle de El General, start early to avoid the fog and rain that often appear later in the day. From San José take the Interamericana Highway toward Cartago, veering right to take the road to San Isidro.

The route to the Valle de El General passes over the spectacular **Cerro de la Muerte** ⑬ (Death Mountain), which rises to 3,491 meters (11,520ft). Named for early travelers who died here from exposure while trying to cross on foot, the mountain is not as inhospitable as its name suggests. Still, it is not difficult

A Heliconia rostrata, also known as "lobster claw," at Wilson Botanical Garden.

BELOW:
Valle de El General.

The country estate of former president Don Pepe (José) Figueres lies just off the highway as you start to climb Cerro de la Muerte. The house is called La Lucha Sin Fin (The Endless Struggle) since it was here that he formulated many of the political views that led to the Civil War.

to imagine the hardships the early pioneers endured on the week-long journey. Rain, cold, and fog can make the first half of the drive miserable, but the road quickly rises above the clouds to cool, crisp sunshine, fields of flowers, and hillside farms. Blue hydrangeas and white cala lilies grow wild, and clouds swirl through the valleys and over peaks.

For almost-guaranteed quetzal sightings, visit the affordable **Paraíso del Quetzal Mountain Lodge** (tel: 2771 4582), just off the main highway at Km 70. Lodging here is in simple, wooden cottages with spectacular mountain views. Hot-water showers and hot-water bottles to warm beds help get you through the chilly nights. Many kilometers of trails are great for both hikers and birdwatchers. The lodge dining room, serving fresh trout, is kept cozy by a wood-burning stove.

Villages of the Valley

Down the road to the right from Empalme, at Km 51 on the Interamericana Highway, is **Santa María de Dota**, a traditional coffee town with a beautiful park and church. The paved road,

which continues toward San Marcos de Tarrazú, San Pablo de Léon Cortes, and San Cristóbal Sur, is called **La Ruta de Los Santos** (The Route of the Saints), since all the picturesque coffee towns here are named after saints. In **Copey**, a village in the mountains above Santa María, you can fish for trout at one of the many local trout farms, take a tour of an organic coffee farm, or lodge comfortably at **El Toucanet Lodge** (tel: 2541 3131), a comfortable mountain lodge with verdant vistas and reliable quetzal sightings.

Continuing south on the Interamericana Highway, there is a sign at Km 80 for San Gerardo. This is the turn-off for **San Gerardo de Dota**, 9km (5 miles) down a phenomenally steep, partially paved road that runs parallel to the Río Savegre. In the midst of the valley, Don Efráin Chacón and his family offer comfortable *cabinas*, some with fireplaces and bathtubs, at the **Savegre Hotel, Natural Reserve & Spa** (tel: 2740 1028).

The area is renowned for its cloud forests and offers one of the best opportunities in the world to see the resplendent quetzal, which feeds on the fruit of the *aquacatillo* trees scattered along this mountain valley. There are many kilometers of challenging trails here, including a hike to a magnificent waterfall. Resident bird guides can help you find some of the rarer highland species that live here, and you can gaze for hours at the hummingbirds buzzing around the hotel's gardens and bird feeders. Bring plenty of warm clothing as it becomes surprisingly chilly at night.

The winding drive down the mountain to **San Isidro de El General** is beautiful once the fog clears from Cerro de la Muerte. San Isidro, also known as Pérez Zeledón, is the commercial center for this agricultural area, a busy town with a large central park, crowded shopping streets, and lots of noisy traffic. The open-air market every Thursday is a visual and gustatory experience, laden with local produce and colorful photo opportunities.

BELOW: see hummingbirds, quetzals, and woodpeckers at Paraíso del Quetzal Mountain Lodge.

Parque Nacional Chirripó

Parque Nacional Chirripó ⑭, lying some 150km (94 miles) south of San José, covers 49,000 hectares (121,000 acres). Its main attraction, apart from the challenge of climbing the highest peak in southern Central America (at 3,819 meters/12,530ft), is its diversity of landscapes, including *páramos* – alpine moors – tall oak forests, fern groves, cloud forests, and crystal-clear glacial lakes.

Only really fit walkers willing to brave a long day of hiking, starting before dawn, in the cold, and quite possibly rain, make the ascent to the top of **Mount Chirripó**. A lodge and several trails, which are regularly maintained, make the ascent at least possible. Daytime temperatures reach 27°C (80°F) but at night-time they can drop to almost freezing. The best months to attempt Chirripó are February and March, the driest time of year, but during the rainy months the flora is splendid. Visits to Chirripó require reservations, many months in advance during popular times.

If you arrive without reservations, you can try your luck at the ranger station in **San Gerardo de Rivas** (tel: 2742 5083). The best way to reserve is online at reservacioneschirripo@gmail. com. The hike to the top of Chirripó, including a day on the summit, takes at least four days. It costs $15 to enter the park and $10 for each day you are there. At the time of writing, the rules are about to change, with the aim of making access easier, and the accommodations when you reach the top more comfortable.

It's a good idea to arrive a couple of days in advance of your climb in order to acclimatize to the altitude. To get an early enough start, you should spend the night before your climb at one of the inexpensive hotels clustered in and around San Gerardo de Rivas *(see above)*. Before entering the park, check in at park headquarters in San Gerardo and pick up a park map. Good, large-scale topographical maps are available in San José. Rangers can put you in touch with guides and local people with horses who will be able to haul your pack to the hut ahead of you.

BELOW: feeding hummingbirds at Paraíso del Quetzal Mountain Lodge.

Accommodations that are close to nature but equipped with creature comforts.

The area around San Gerardo is well worth visiting, even if you do not attempt to climb Chirripó. Bird-watching is excellent all along La Valle del General, and shorter hikes are very satisfying, with beautiful lush scenery, waterfalls, and natural hot springs where you can relax your sore muscles. At Chimirol, you can soak up the stunning scenery in total comfort at **Monte Azul** (www. monteazulcr.com), a chic, new hotel that doubles as a contemporary artists' community, with studios and walking trails, set in a private nature reserve bordered by the rushing El General River.

A few kilometers beyond Chimirol, watch for a faded, wooden sign on the left advertising Queso Suizo/Swiss Cheese. A local family, in the small community of Canaán, learned to make Swiss cheese from a visiting cheesemaker, and now they sell their excellent produce from their house.

Parque Internacional La Amistad

Adjacent to Chirripó, **Parque Internacional La Amistad ⓑ** is part of the international Reserva de la Biosfera La Amistad, which straddles Costa Rica and Panamá. Most of the park's vast territory of more than 1,900 sq km (765 sq miles) is inaccessible. Unesco declared La Amistad (which means Friendship) a Biosphere Reserve and a World Patrimony site because of the diversity of its flora and fauna, and because of its great scientific value. More than half of La Amistad has yet to be explored. Hiking near **Reserva Forestal Las Tablas** is safe and rewarding, but only experienced tropical trekkers should venture into the interior.

There is a ranger station with camping facilities at the Altamira park entrance (tel: 2200 5355), and ASO-PROLA, a local rural tourism association, offers accommodations in a rustic lodge and arranges hiking tours (www. actuarcostarica.com). Day trips are possible from either San Isidro or San Vito, or you can stay at the eco-friendly, comfortable **Hacienda La Amistad Lodge** (tel: 2289 7667), above San Vito, with the option of camping out in the forest.   ❑

Island of Wonders

Scientists value this remote island's biogeographic uniqueness. But for Costa Ricans it is simply the country's No. 1 natural wonder

Isla del Coco is the most remote part of Costa Rica, adrift in the Pacific Ocean nearly 600km (over 360 miles) southwest of the mainland, on the same latitude as Colombia. Because of this isolation it only counts its visitors in the hundreds, yet millions have seen it on film, in the opening moments of *Jurassic Park*. In all senses, this is a place of high drama.

At its crown is a thick coniferous forest full of springs and rivers. The cliffs around the entire island that tower more than 100 meters (300ft) are covered with incredibly thick tropical vegetation with magnificent waterfalls plummeting straight down to the sea. In all, there are 200 waterfalls on the island. Lionel Wafer, a pirate physician who visited more than 300 years ago, wrote "what most contributes to the loveliness of the place is the number of clear, freshwater springs that fill the entire lower part of the island." And there are rocky crags and wondrously formed islets that have been shaped by the wind and water. No wonder then that it inspired Steven Spielberg, to whom it was the "Isla Nebular."

With a coastline of about 23km (14 miles), roughly 12km by 5km (8 miles by 3 miles), Isla del Coco is the largest uninhabited island in the world. In 1978 it was designated a protected National Park and is one of the richest in endemic species, with about 60 species, some of them endangered, that live only in or around this island.

As if these facts were not sufficiently alluring, the island's history is also full of pirate stories. Many insist that there is treasure hidden here still, although in the course of more than 500 expeditions none has ever been found.

Two bays, Wafer Bay and Chatham Bay, offer a way to tie up and gain entry to explore the island. Chatham Bay is small, with a rocky beach. Here, the ghosts of past explorers, and of pirates, are almost tangible. Today's visitors are mostly treasure hunters, divers and environmentalists.

Most visitors consider Wafer Bay to be the best access route to the island. From here, ancient natural paths follow steep cliffs all the way to the highest part of the humid forest. There are bountiful bromeliads, giant ferns, orchids, unnamed flowering plants, mosses, and ferns covering almost everything. And from a high peak there are views of an unbelievably blue sea above an impossibly green landscape, with white, angellike doves moving gently, hovering and fluttering in the air.

Every natural path, every river, every waterfall, every beach has some rare treasure. The peace is astounding and deafening. And the views of the coral reef, the crisp clarity of the water, the lushness of the landscape, all somehow contribute to an atmosphere where the mysterious legends of the past come alive.

Camping is not permitted on the island: you have to sleep on your boat. There is drinkable water, however; and good opportunities for hiking, although the trails are not marked. Contact the National Parks Service for information and permission to enter.

A number of specialist tour companies operate out of Puntarenas, and offer the easiest way to visit the island, but be warned: the price of a trip is very high. For the majority of people, Isla del Coco remains just a dream – and perhaps that is no bad thing.   ❑

RIGHT: the dense, deep, little-known jungle interior of Isla del Coco.

INSIGHT GUIDES TRAVEL TIPS
COSTA RICA

T RANSPORTATION

Getting There
and Getting Around

Getting There

By Air

Most international flights arrive in Costa Rica at Juan Santamaría Airport, about 16km (10 miles) from San José, the capital city. See www.alterra.co.cr for flight arrival and departure information for Juan Santamaría. (In Spanish only, click on *Información de Vuelos* for flight status: *estimado de salida* (estimated departure time), *demorado* (delayed), *salió* (departed).)

From the airport: It is a 20-minute ride (about US$25 by taxi) between downtown San José and the airport. Prices are standardized from the airport; pay at a designated kiosk, not the taxi driver. A bus ride into town costs less than US$1.

Five commercial airlines also fly to Daniel Oduber International Airport in Liberia, the main terminal for North Pacific destinations: American Airlines, Continental, Delta, United, and US Airways. Air Canada runs direct charter flights from Toronto.

From the US: Miami has the most direct flights, but you can also get to Costa Rica from the US in one hop from Atlanta, Charlotte, Chicago, Dallas, Denver, Fort Lauderdale, Houston, Los Angeles, New York, Newark, Orlando, Phoenix, and Washington DC. TACA and Air Canada offer direct flights from Toronto; Vancouver trips generally go through Houston or Dallas; flights from Montreal stop in eastern points of the US. Flights from Australia or New Zealand connect via Los Angeles and Dallas or Miami.

From Europe: Iberia offers direct flights from Madrid and Air France operates a direct service from Paris. Travelers from the UK may also connect in the US via Newark (the fastest route), New York, or Miami.

On departure: line-ups to check in can be horrendous, so observe the recommended two-hours-before-departure arrival at the airport on your way home. Confirm flights the day before in case there are changes, but most airlines do not require it.

Baggage allowance: weight limits per checked bag are usually 23kg (50lbs), maximum two bags. If necessary, determine how the airline is equipped to handle surfboards, bicycles, etc. Have your luggage well tagged and identified. Be prepared in case your luggage is lost.

Limited amounts of liquids and gels are allowed in carry-on baggage (containers 100ml or less, all items must fit in a quart-size zip lock bag). However, to get the most up-to-date policies, see www.catsa.com (Canada), www.tsa.gov (US), or www.baa.co.uk (UK).

Ticket deals: while it still pays to check with travel agents for good deals, most cheap tickets are now found on a variety of budget-travel websites. Tried-and-true www.expedia.com and www.travelocity.com are good resources for global travelers coming from destinations all over the world. Look for www.cheapestflights.co.uk in the UK and www.travel.com.au in Australia.

Make reservations as far ahead as possible, especially from December to February, as these flights are usually booked well in advance.

Tax: there is a departure tax for foreign visitors of around US$26, payable in US dollars, or colones (not traveler's checks).

Airlines

Air Canada, tel: 888-247 2262 (US and Canada), 0871 220 1111 (UK), 2243 1860 (Costa Rica); www.aircanada.ca.

American, tel: 800-433 7300 (US and Canada), 0844 499 7300 (UK); 2257 1266 (Costa Rica); www.aa.com.

Condor Airlines, tel: 866-960 7915 (US and Canada), +49 (0) 180 570 7202 (Europe), 2243 1818 (Costa Rica); www.condor.com.

Continental Airlines, tel: 800-231 0856 (US and Canada), 0845 607 6760 (UK), 0800-044 0005 (Costa Rica); www.continental.com.

Delta, tel: 800-221 1212 (US and Canada), 0845 600 0950 (UK), 0800-056 2002 (Costa Rica); www.delta.com.

Iberia, tel: 800-772 4642 (Canada and the US), 0870 609 0500 (UK) 2431 5633 (Costa Rica); www.iberia.com.

JetBlue, tel: 800-538 2583 (US and Canada); www.jetblue.com.

Spirit Airlines, tel: 800-772 7117 (US and Canada), 0-800 011 1103 (Costa Rica); www.spiritair.com.

TACA, tel: 800-400 8222 (US), 800-722 8222 (Canada), +44-8702 410 340 (UK), 2299-8222 (Costa Rica); www.taca.com.

United Airlines, tel: 800-538 2929 (US and Canada), 0845 844 4777 (UK); www.united.com.

US Airways, tel: 800-428 4322 (US and Canada), 0845 600 3300 (UK), 0-800-011 0793 (Costa Rica); www.usairways.com.

By Bus

There are bus services to Costa Rica from Panama or Nicaragua.

Tica Bus, Paseo Colón, 200 meters N/100 meters W of Torre Mercedes, tel: 2221 0006; www.ticabus.

com, provides a comfortable, reliable service throughout Central America. Daily buses to and from Nicaragua and Panamá.

Trans Nica, Ca. 22, Av. 3, tel: 2223 4242; www.transnica.com.

Nicaragua, tel: 505-277 2104; El Salvador, tel: 503-2240 1212.

By Car

The most common car route from the US to Costa Rica runs along the Pacific coast of Mexico, Guatemala, El Salvador, Honduras, and Nicaragua. Along the Nicaraguan border, the only vehicle crossing is at Peñas Blancas, on the Pacific side. From the south, the main overland vehicle crossing is also on the Pacific side, at Paso Canoas, although a small post at Sixaola on the Caribbean side allows vehicles to pass over the bridge that joins the countries.

Driving license: Drivers will have to show their license, an original copy of certified ownership (or a notarized authorization from the owner if the car is someone else's), and a *hoja de salida* (exit permit) from either Nicaragua or Panamá (whichever country you are arriving from).

Customs will mark in your passport that you have entered with a car, and the car is given a three-month permit. You can exit the country once to renew the permit; after six months the vehicle is subject to heavy import taxes. Rental car companies do not allow their cars to be taken across the border.

There are two recommended books with reliable information to help you navigate the roads and border crossings: *Americas Overland – The Driving Handbook*, by Donald Greene (Lulu.com, US, 2008), and *99 Days to Panamá*, by John and Harriet Halkyard (Brindle Press, US, 2005). The website www.drivemeloco.com is also helpful.

It is advisable to confirm border information before travel because it can change without notice. For information on major driving regulations, see *Car Rental page 265*.

Car insurance: Costa Rica requires motorists to pay for insurance upon entry, which varies according to the value of the vehicle and the year, but starts around $18. The car is also fumigated (approximately $5).

Sanborn's Insurance (tel: 800-222 0158; www.sanbornsinsurance.com) in McAllen, Texas, is an excellent resource for insurance and information you'll need for the trip, including travel tips and an itinerary.

By Sea

Cruise ships come into Puerto Limón on the Caribbean coast and Puerto Caldera and Golfito on the Pacific. Check with a travel agent about which companies currently sail to Costa Rica. Private yachts are also popular. The main point of entry is Playas del Coco, although immigration and customs services are also available at Caldera and Golfito, all on the Pacific side. It is possible to go through these procedures on the Caribbean side at Limón, but impractical, as there are no yacht facilities. You will need the original and one copy each of crew members' and passengers' passports, the crew list, the boat's documents, and the departure document from the last port you visited. All other international shipping protocols apply (quarantine flag, etc). Wait until you are boarded and cleared by both immigration and customs before going ashore.

GETTING AROUND

Finding Your Way

San José uses a grid system for its streets. North–south-running streets are *calles*, east–west-running streets are *avenidas*. Avenida Central (Av Ctl) divides the city north and south; it becomes Paseo Colón west of Hospital San Juan de Díos. Calle Central (Ca Ctl) divides San José east and west. The southern avenues and western streets are numbered evenly. The northern avenues and eastern streets have odd numbers.

Avenida Central passes through the downtown core as a wide pedestrian walkway, passing by many of the major attractions and shopping, making walking a viable way of getting around. On most other streets, you'll often have to squeeze through the narrow patches of sidewalk left by *chinamos* (streetside stands), and even with the streetlight in your favor, crossing can be a challenge. Taking common-sense safety precautions, a walking tour of San José can be a pleasant way of seeing the sights.

Abbreviations used for addresses: Av = avenida, Ca = Calle, Ctl = central, Apto or Apdo = apartado (post office box, for mailing addresses). When an address is given using the street and avenues, the first part is the street or avenue on which the building is located, and the second part of the address indicates the streets or

avenues the building is between. For example: the Metropolitan Cathedral location is Ca. Ctl, Av. 2–4. That is, the Cathedral is on Calle Central between Avenidas 2 and 4. *(See San José city map, pages 128–9.)*

For the most part, there are no addresses or street names in Costa Rica. Although downtown San José has numbered avenues and streets, Costa Ricans do not refer to them. Homes and buildings are not numbered. Usually an address is given as the distance in meters *(metros)* north, east, south, or west from a known landmark. When it comes to walking, remember that cars have the right of way, not pedestrians, so always look twice before crossing the street.

By Air

Domestic flights *(vuelos locales)* are reasonably priced and are a comfortable alternative to many hours on bad roads. Nature Air allows one checked bag, up to 13kg (30lbs), per passenger; a heavier bag, up to 32kg (70lbs), costs $50–75. On SANSA, any bag weighing more than 12kg (27lbs) is charged $1 for each additional 450 grams (1lb). Passengers are weighed as well, so if the plane is too heavy, your luggage may have to follow you on a later flight. Pack as light as you can.

If you're crisscrossing the country and are short on time, consider an air pass that covers travel to the commercial destinations of the country's main domestic airlines. Nature Air offers a 15-day pass for $499 and a 30-day pass for $799.

SANSA
Tel: 2290 4100
Fax: 2290 3543
www.flysansa.com
Services to Coto 47, Golfito, Puerto Jimenéz, Palmar Sur, Nosara, Sámara, Tamarindo, Punta Islita, Quepos, Tambor, Liberia, and Drake Bay, with additional destinations available for chartered flights.

Nature Air
Tel: 2299 6000, 800-235 9272 (US and Canada)
Fax: 2549 7599
www.natureair.com
Flies to Liberia, Tamarindo, Nosara, Tambor, Quepos, Palmar Sur, Puerto Jiménez, Drake Bay, Punta Islita, Tortuguero, Bocas del Toro, Panamá, and Granada, Nicaragua, with additional destinations available for chartered flights. Surfboards accepted if there is space available, with an extra charge. Also offers a number of

inter-destination flights.

Aerotaxi Alfa Romeo
Tel: 2735 5353
Fax: 2735 5178
www.alfaromeoair.com
Air taxi from Puerto Jiménez into
Serena Ranger Station in Corcovado
National Park. Also offers charter
services to 40 Costa Rican
destinations, including San José,
Carate, La Fortuna, among others.

Paradise Air
Tel: 2231 0938
Fax: 2296 1429
www.flywithparadise.com
Pavas Airport. Charter flights and
flights to other Central American
destinations.

By Bus

You can go virtually anywhere by bus
in Costa Rica, just as most Ticos do.
Around San José: the Sabana
Cementerio bus cuts across town in
both directions, just north and south
of the center; ask for the stop closest
to you (¿Dónde está la parada para
el Sabana Cementerio?). All other
buses leave for the suburbs from their
respective quadrants; for example,
those heading west (Rohrmoser,
Escazú, Santa Ana) leave from the
Coca-Cola area; ones heading east
(Los Yoses, San Pedro, Curridabat)
leave from near the east end of the
pedestrian walkway.
Farther afield: San José has no
central terminal for long-distance
buses, each bus hub handles travel
to a certain region. Major ones
include the "Coca-Cola," near a
former bottling plant at Ca. 16, Av.
1–3, the departure point for the
Central Pacific; the Caribbean bus
terminal, Ca. Ctrl, Av. 11 (just east of
the Children's Museum); and MUSOC,
Ca. Ctrl, Av. 30, to San Isidro (the hub
for buses to the Southern Zone). Pick
up a schedule at the Costa Rican
Tourist Institute (ICT) office in the Gold
Museum (www.visitcostarica.com).
   Buy tickets a day in advance for
popular routes and several days
in advance for Easter week travel.
Companies often only sell one way
at a time; buy your return ticket upon

Airports

Juan Santamaría (international
flights), tel: 2437 2626
Daniel Oduber, Liberia
(international flights), tel: 2668
1010
Tobias Bolaños, Pavas (domestic
flights), tel: 2232 2820

arrival to ensure a seat. Watch your
belongings closely.
   Gray Line and **Interbus** provide
reasonably priced (between $25 and
$55) shuttle transportation in air-
conditioned, comfortable vans. Hotel-
to-hotel service makes this a good
option. There are week-long passes
for unlimited travel.

Gray Line
Tel: 2220 2126
www.graylinecostarica.com.

Interbus
Tel: 2283 5573
www.interbusonline.com.
The Costa Rican Tourist Institute (ICT)
office below the Plaza de la Cultura
has a list of bus companies' names
and phone numbers, tel: 2222 1090.

By Taxi

Taxis are by far the easiest way of
getting around San José; they are
widely used and inexpensive. You'll
rarely have to wait long, although it is
sometimes difficult to catch a cab in a
rainy rush hour. All taxis should have
operational meters (marías); be sure
the drivers use them. If not, negotiate
before getting in. If you are greatly
overcharged, write down the driver's
name and license number, and call
the taxi company number marked on
the outside of the cab.
   Arrangements can be made to take
trips by taxi to places outside San
José. Beware – taxi drivers who are
parked in front of major hotels will
always charge more, and most will
charge fixed rates. Taxis are red and
have a "Taxi" sign on the roof of the
car. If they are not red and have no
numbered yellow triangle on the door,
then they are pirate taxis, or piratas,
and are unlicensed.

Taxi Companies

Alfaro, tel: 2221 8466
Coopetaxi, tel: 2235 9966
Coopetico, tel: 2224 7979
Coopeirazu, tel: 2254 3211
Coopeguaria, tel: 2226 1366
San José Taxis, tel: 2221 3434
Taxis Unidos, tel: 2221 6865

By Train

San José's recently revived train
service across town takes you within
a hair's breadth of some buildings,
but isn't particularly convenient. The
central station is near the Clínica
Bíblica on the south side of town,
with a commuter-oriented schedule
sending trains west from Estación
Pacífico to Pavas at 5.08am, 6.18am,
7.28am, 4.23pm, and 5.37pm

and east to San Pedro at 6.20am
and 7.26am, 4.23pm and 5.39pm,
returning from both sides of town
approximately 40 minutes later,
weekdays only. A full cross-town trip
takes 60 minutes, much longer than a
taxi unless it's rush hour. Tickets cost
approximately $0.60.
   Newly restored train service
between San José and Heredia has
trains leaving from San José's Atlantic
Station, northeast corner of Parque
Nacional, every half-hour, 6–8.30am;
3.30–8pm; from Heredia, near the
Central Market, on roughly the same
schedule.

By Ferry

Most travelers to the southern Nicoya
coast will arrive via the Puntarenas-
Paquera ferry route (approximately 90
minutes), served by two companies.
There is not much difference between
the two services; the Tambor option
is owned by the Hotel Barceló and is
slightly snazzier, but at certain times
can be packed with hotel guests.
Avoid Friday and Sunday afternoons
and evenings; you could be stuck
waiting for hours.
   Most travelers won't need to use
the Puntarenas–Naranjo ferry, but
it is an option if you are heading
further north on the peninsula.
Generally though, those sites are
better served by bus or car via the
Tempisque bridge. Drivers must
leave the car to purchase tickets; any
vehicle passengers must purchase
tickets separately, and embark and
disembark on foot.

Peninsula de Nicoya
Coonatramar R.L.
Tel: 2661 1069
www.coonatramar.com.

Puntarenas to Playa Naranjo
Departs 6.30am, 10am, 2.30pm, and
7.30pm.

Playa Naranjo to Puntarenas
Departs 8am, 12.30pm, 5.30pm,
and 9pm.

Tambor
Tel: 2661 2084.

Paquera to Puntarenas
Tel: 2641 0118
Departs 6am, 9am, 11am, 1pm, 3pm,
5pm, and 7pm.

Puntarenas to Paquera
Departs 5am, 9am, 11am, 1pm, 3pm,
5pm, 9pm.

By Bicycle

Mountain bikers can see Costa Rica's
back country, especially on the lightly
traveled dirt roads crisscrossing rural
areas. But cycling is very dangerous

on paved roads since they have no shoulders. Consider installing KEVLAR inner tube protectors (such as Mr Tuffy). Bring a good lock. Check with your airline about shipping. While it is possible to go on your own, armed with decent Spanish skills and maps, your best bet is to book with a good biking company that knows the safest routes and can take care of logistics.

By Car

Pothole-filled, unlit roads, careless (to put it mildly) drivers, and poor signage and road markings conspire to make driving in Costa Rica a definite challenge. But it can be done – extremely defensively.

Seat belts are compulsory, and drunk-driving laws are enforced. Drunk driving is defined as blood-alcohol levels of higher than 0.075 percent (in which case the driver is fined and loses his or her license and the car is confiscated). However, blood-alcohol levels between 0.049 percent and 0.075 percent qualify as "pre-drunk" and earn a fine. Current monetary penalties are very high under a new traffic law, approximately $400 for driving without a seat belt, $370 for driving tipsy.

Car Rental

Renting a car makes sense for off-the-beaten-path trips outside San José. Reserve a car well in advance and get written confirmation. Prepayment is advised, especially during high season. Rates generally start around US$60 per day, including insurance. Four-wheel-drive vehicles start around US$80 per day. Most insurance is deductible for the first US$750–1,000, although for an extra fee many companies offer a non-deductible policy. The following agencies all accept American Express,

MasterCard, and Visa. Most agencies insist that the driver is over 21 years of age, holds a valid passport and driver's license, and has a valid credit card for a deposit (not cash).
Alamo Rent a Car, Paseo Colón, tel: 2233 7733/2242-7733; US toll-free: 877-222 9075; www.alamocostarica.com.
Avis, Cruce San Antonio de Belén, tel: 2293 2222; www.avis.co.cr.
Budget, Paseo Colón, tel: 2436 2000; www.budget.co.cr.
Economy: Sabana Norte, tel: 2299 2000, toll-free 877-326 7368 (US); www.economyrentacar.com.
Hertz Paseo Colón, Ca. 38, tel: 786-955 8224 (Canada, US), 2221 1818 (Costa Rica); www.costaricarentacar.com.
National, La Uruca, shares a building with Alamo head office, tel: 2242 7878; reservations: 877-8NATCAR; www.natcar.com.

Private Tour Drivers

An alternative is to hire a knowledgeable bilingual driver, experienced with Costa Rican roads. Ask at your hotel or consult classified ads in the *Tico Times*.

Driving: A Survival Guide

Four-wheel-drive (doble tracción) is recommended for many areas as the roads outside the Central Valley, especially during the rainy season, are muddy and rutted. Chains work well in the mud; try letting some air out of your tires to increase traction if the car is stuck.
Licenses: operating a motor vehicle without a license is a serious violation and invalidates any insurance. A valid driver's license from another country can be used for three months. Always carry your passport (photocopies, including that of your entry stamp, usually suffice).

Import: foreign vehicles brought into Costa Rica for a period over 6 months must pay a large import tax. If you enter with a vehicle, you will have to leave with it or show papers proving you have sold it.
Driving habits: drivers weave all over the road to avoid the many ruts and holes. Two headlight blinks usually indicate the other driver is giving you the right of way (especially when you are making a left turn); on the highway two headlight blinks may mean that the police are ahead. Radar is often used. If waved over by the police, don't try to get away. They will radio ahead to have you stopped.
Accidents: Costa Rica has a high accident and death rate. Always drive defensively. The law requires motorists to carry a set of reflecting triangles, a reflective vest, a fire extinguisher, and a first aid kit. If you are in an accident, do not move your car – not even to the side of the road – until the police and INS, the government insurance agency, arrive. Give no statements, but take witnesses' names.
Parking: be careful not to park illegally. A yellow curb means no stopping. Even if you are in the car, police may prevent you from leaving and call a tow truck (grúa). You can ride in the car to the yard, where you will have to pay towing charges. Better to park in inexpensive parking lots (parqueos). This will reduce the chance of theft. Do not leave any valuables in cars. Thieves are known to have master keys to rentals and even "watchmen," people who offer to watch your car for a few coins, can work against you.
Flat tires or mechanical problems: If you are experiencing car trouble, drive to a well-lit area or gas station if possible. If not, keep an eye on your belongings and decline help from passers-by. There have been incidents where thieves pop your tire, distract you as they help fix it, as another person takes off with your belongings.
Corruption: unfortunately, there are corrupt police who target foreign drivers. You may be stopped for no apparent reason. Have all necessary automobile documents in the car and be polite. It is illegal for the police to demand payment on the spot. If you are badly treated, or if the policeman solicits a bribe or asks that you pay the fine immediately, ask for the ticket (Deme el parte), then ask for the officer's identification. Write it down, and report to the Dirección de Tránsito as soon as possible.

BELOW: vintage Toyota Landcruiser in the town of San Marcos.

ACCOMMODATIONS

HOTELS, YOUTH HOSTELS, BED & BREAKFAST

Where to Stay

The most popular places to stay in San José are in *el puro centro*, right downtown near the Plaza de la Cultura and in historic Barrio Amón, which has some boutique hotels with character. Other parts of downtown San José can be very noisy and polluted, so you may prefer to stay outside the center, in Escazú, Santa Ana, Alajuela, Heredia, and other Central Valley towns, which also give a good taste of Costa Rican life.

Note that high season in Costa Rica is from November 1 to April 30, and low season is from May 1 to October 31, excluding July and August, when greater demand means higher prices. During the low season, room prices may be discounted by as much as 40 percent. The price categories on the following pages indicate high-season rates.

Reservations made, but not paid for, may not be held, especially during

BELOW: jungle accommodations.

high season, near the beaches and in Monteverde. Discounts may be given for stays of more than one night. Ask at your hotel about green (wet) season discounts.

Hotels in categories $$ and up *(see price guide box)* include breakfast, unless otherwise indicated. Note that rates for remote lodges in areas such as Tortuguero or the Osa Peninsula may appear high but they usually include meals, and often transport and a tour or two.

Tourist office: the Instituto Costarricense de Turismo (ICT) is based in central San José, beneath the Plaza de la Cultura (tel: 2222 1090, www.visitcostarica.com), open 9am–5pm Mon–Sat. Closed during the lunch hour.

ICT has a system of classifications for lodging based on size and facility; however, there is a wide range of popular names used unofficially:
Apartotel Apartments with cooking facilities and living area in a hotel-style complex. Weekly and monthly rates.
Cabina Usually a one-room cabin with a shower and bath, often close to the beach in coastal resorts. *Cabinas* vary widely in quality and price.
Bed & Breakfast Price and quality vary widely, from a modest room in someone's own house to elegant guesthouses all to yourself with pools and tennis courts.
Lodge Popular in more remote areas, usually near parks or natural attractions. Price usually includes meals. Stays at lodges are almost always linked with some outdoor activity: birdwatching, guided hikes, or horseback tours.
Villa or Chalet Often indistinguishable from a hotel.
Inn Often a Bed & Breakfast, but with

more extensive amenities.
Resort Usually a luxurious, self-contained hotel complex.
Hotel Anything with more than 10 rooms.
Hostel There is a small youth hostel system. Prices vary.
Albergue/Pensión Modest, small hotels.

Homestays

To get a better understanding of the people and culture of Costa Rica, try a homestay. Visitors stay in the guest room of a host family and participate in as much of the family activities as they wish. Your options for finding a good homestay are best through one of the many language schools, which can help make homestay arrangements *(see page 297)*. Local families sometimes rent rooms at a price that includes meals and laundry. Check around the university and the bulletin board at the Costa Rican/North American Cultural Center, see the *Tico Times* or the local newspapers. For shared-lodging with *Ticos* or other foreigners, visit Craigslist Costa Rica. at www.costarica.en.craigslist.org.

Useful Websites

Costa Rican Hotel Association
Tel: 2220 0575
www.costaricanhotels.com
A good resource for hotel information.
Costa Rican Vacations
Tel: 2296 7715 (Costa Rica),
800-606 1860 (US and Canada)
www.vacationscostarica.com
A company that specializes in apartment, condo, and villa rentals.

ACCOMMODATIONS LISTINGS

SAN JOSÉ

Hotel Aranjuez
Ca. 19, Av. 11–13
San José
Tel: 2256 1825
Fax: 2223 3528
www.hotelaranjuez.com
A labyrinth-like historic building, with a new, modern annex, in the older part of town. The balance of economy, comfort, and character is among the best you will find in the capital. **$**

B & B Cinco Hormigas Rojas
Ca. 15 Av. 9–11bis
San José
Tel: 2255 3412
Fax: 2257 8581
www.cincohormigasrojas.com
Funky, verdant hideaway owned by artist. **$–$$**

Casa Ridgeway
Av. 6 bis, Ca. 15,
San José
Tel: 2222 1400
Fax: 2233 6168
www.amigosparalapaz.org
Small *pensión* managed by the Society of Friends (Quakers). A pleasant, welcoming place, with comfy lounge and cable TV. Use of kitchen and laundry. **$–$$**

Hotel Don Carlos
Barrio Amón

Ca. 9, Av. 9
Tel: 2221 6707
Fax: 2258 1152
www.doncarloshotel.com
This heritage building was once home to two presidential families. Art-adorned corridors, quiet gardens, and classic rooms provide an elegant environment in a central location. The gift shop is one of the city's best. Good value. **$$$**

Gran Hotel Costa Rica
Plaza de la Cultura
Tel: 2221 4000
Fax: 2221 3501
www.granhotelcostarica.com
An architectural landmark, right across the plaza from the National Theater. A plethora of amenities makes it a good option for those who want everything at their fingertips. Has the city's best sidewalk café. **$$$–$$$$**

Hotel Grano de Oro
Ca. 30, Av. 2–4
San José
Tel: 2255 3322
Fax: 2221 2782
www.hotelgranodeoro.com
There's nothing cookie-cutter about this blend of two heritage houses with a

dazzling new Victorian-style addition, housing the restaurant and private party rooms. Sophisticated and elegant; excellent restaurant. **$$$–$$$$**

Hotel 1492 – Jade y Oro
Barrio Escalante
Av. 1, Ca. 31/33
Tel: 2256 5913
Fax: 2280 6206
www.hotel1492.com
Pre-Columbian-style murals brighten the walls of this nine-room boutique hotel. A lush garden courtyard is the setting for tropical breakfasts. Complimentary evening glass of wine and cheese is a nice touch. **$$$**

Le Bergerac
Barrio Los Yoses
Ca. 35, Av. Ctrl
Tel: 2234 7850
Fax: 2225 9103
www.bergerachotel.com
Upscale elegance with minimal pretension in a quiet neighborhood, this French inn is cozy and convenient. The restaurant is a draw in its own right, serving gourmet Gallic delicacies. **$$$**

Hotel La Amistad
Barrio Otoya
Av. 11, Ca. 15

Tel: 2258 0021
Fax: 2258 4900
www.hotelamistad.com
Inside this sprawling corner building, all 34 rooms have direct-dial phones with voice mail; de luxe rooms and studio apartments have air conditioning. Wireless connections and in-house internet café, bar, and restaurant. **$$$**

Posada del Museo
Av. 2, Ca. 17
Tel: 2258 1027
Fax: 2257 9414
www.hotelposadadelmuseo.com
A range of colonial-style rooms fills this Victorian house near the National Museum, on a pedestrian boulevard. Ground-floor café is a good spot to get cultural information and Argentine pastries. **$$–$$$**

THE CENTRAL VALLEY

Alajuela

Hotel La Guaria Inn
Tel/fax: 2440 2948
Email: laguariahotel@netscape.net
Downtown Alajuela hotel has 22 standard rooms, four suites and five junior suites. Prices include taxes

if you pay in cash. All have cable TV. Close to airport. **$$**

Hotel II Millenium
Tel: 2430 5050
Fax: 2441 2365
www.bbmilleniumcr.com
Bed and breakfast, 1km (½ mile) from Juan Santamaría International Airport, close to bus stop. English-speaking owner, well-run and friendly. Monthly rates available. **$$**

Orquídeas Inn
Tel: 2433 7128
Fax: 2433 9740
www.orquideasinn.com

This Spanish hacienda-style hotel offers spacious rooms, suites, and a two-bedroom geodesic dome for groups, all awash in tropical colors. Restaurant serves inventive international and vegetarian cuisine; and there's the renowned Marilyn Monroe bar. **$$–$$$**

Xandari Resort and Spa
Alajuela
Tel: 2443 2020; (US) 866-363 3212
Fax: 2442 4847
www.xandari.com
An exclusive oasis with fantastic Central Valley

views, designed with an artist's eye. Spacious villas and intimate *jalapas* for the full-service spa are perfect for romance. Excellent restaurant serves gourmet dishes with healthy focus.

Also runs Xandari by the Pacific (tel: 2778 7070) in Esterillos Este on the Central Pacific. **$$$$**

Heredia

Hotel Bougainvillea
Santo Domingo de Heredia
Tel: 2244 1414
Fax: 2244 1313
www.hb.co.cr
Tranquil, tropical-garden setting, with reading area, heated pool, sauna, and lit tennis courts. Eighty-one tastefully decorated rooms. Close to INBio Park. **$$$**

Hotel Chalet Tirol
Tel: 2267 6222
Fax: 2267 6373
www.hotelchaleteltirol.com
A-frame cottages in the cloud forest above Heredia, set in a mini-Swiss village, bordering Braulio Carrillo National Park. **$$$**

Finca Rosa Blanca Country Inn
West of Heredia
Tel: 2269 9392
Fax: 2269 9555
www.fincarosablanca.com
Lovely and luxurious boutique hotel in the foothills of Heredia, awarded top sustainability rating. Bright, decadent tower suite with rainforest-themed bathroom generally causes a sensation. And

there's an excellent restaurant. **$$$$**

Hotel & Villas La Condesa
San Rafael de Heredia
Tel: 2267 6000
Fax: 2267 6200
www.hotellacondesa.com
Mountain hotel with luxury rooms, conference center, pool, good restaurants; hiking and nearby horseback riding trails. **$$$–$$$$**

Naranjo

Vista del Valle Plantation Inn
Naranjo, near Grecia
Tel: 2450 4493
Fax: 2451 1165
www.vistadelvalle.com
Simple Japanese architectural lines juxtaposed with the chaotic exuberance of surrounding forest. Some rooms have outdoor showers and private sunbathing patios. A short hike to a 91-meter (300ft) waterfall. **$$$–$$$$**

Orosí

Orosí Lodge
Tel/fax: 2533 3578
www.orosilodge.com
On the eastern edge of town, surrounded by fields of coffee. The second-floor rooms have valley and

volcano views. Funky coffee shop/art gallery serves tasty European pastries. **$$–$$$**

Santa Ana/Escazú

Hotel Alta
Santa Ana
Tel: 2282 4160
Fax: 2282 4162
www.thealtahotel.com
For style and views, this modern, Spanish-inspired hotel overlooking the Central Valley is one of the area's best. The gourmet restaurant also has one of the most varied menus. **$$$$**

Casa de las Tías
Escazú
Tel: 2289 5517
Fax: 2289 7353
www.hotels.co.cr/casatias.html
Peaceful, homey Victorian-style bed and breakfast in a lovely garden. All four rooms and the suite are airy; gourmet breakfasts. Extremely knowledgeable and helpful owners. **$$$**

Turrialba

Casa Turire
Tel: 2531 1111
Fax: 2531 1075
www.hotelcasaturire.com
Luxurious plantation-style hotel surrounded by sugar

cane, coffee, and macadamia fields, close to some of the country's best whitewater rafting. The Turrialba Mountains form a dramatic backdrop. Pool. **$$$–$$$$**

Turrialtico
Turrialba
Tel: 2538 1111
Fax: 2538 1575
www.turrialtico.com
Top-of-the-line location, with a budget price tag. Rooms in the wood structure are simple but comfortable. The restaurant serves traditional food with spectacular views of the Turrialba valley. **$$–$$$**

Volcán Turrialba Lodge
20km (12 miles) above Turrialba
Tel: 2273 4335
Fax: 2273 0703
www.volcanturrialbalodge.com
Cabins with wood stoves; lofty setting with excellent birding; close-up views of active Turrialba volcano. An additional $12 covers three meals. **$$**

Hotel Wagelia
Tel: 2556 1566
Fax: 2556 1596
www.hotelwagelia.com
Pleasant, affordable hotel in center of town. Eighteen rooms, some with air conditioning, face a courtyard garden. Terrace restaurant. **$$**

THE CENTRAL PACIFIC

Jacó and Area

AparHotel Vista Pacífico
Jacó
Tel: 2643 3261
Fax: 2643 2046
www.vistapacifico.com
Ocean views from most of the studios; apartments and pool. Two rooms adapted for visitors with disabilities; 2km (1 mile) from beach. Excellent choice for families. Canadian-owned. **$$–$$$**

Cabinas Las Olas
Playa Hermosa (near Jacó)
Tel: 2643 7021
www.lasolashotel.com
Rooms have private baths, heated water, ceiling fans, and kitchens. Swimming

pool. Friendly surfers' hang-out. **$$–$$$**

Hotel Club del Mar Resort
South end of beach
Tel: 2643 3194; (US) 866-978 5669
Fax: 2643 3550
www.clubdelmarcostarica.com
Jacó's most upscale lodging keeps itself at arm's length from the downtown hoopla. A range of options; condos are best value. Good restaurant. **$$$$**

Encantada Hotel (formerly Bacara Beach Resort)
Esterillos
Tel: 2778 7048
www.encantadacostarica.com
Two basic rooms, four larger cabins and oceanfront apartment, air conditioned,

a few hundred meters from the beach. Pool; surfboard and bike rentals. **$$$**

Villa Caletas
North of Jacó
Tel: 2637 0505
Fax: 2637 0404
www.villacaletas.com
A luxurious, Victorian tropical fantasy on a mountain top overlooking the Pacific. Lovely pool. Amphitheater with concerts; spectacular sunsets. **$$$$**

Hotel Villa Lapas
Near Carara National Park
Tel/fax: 2203 3553
www.villalapas.com
Secluded hotel in a lush rainforest setting will wow nature-lovers. Activities

include a suspension-bridge hike and canopy tour. **$$$**

Manuel Antonio

Arenas del Mar Beach and Nature Resort
Tel: 2777 2777
Fax: 2777 6281
www.arenasdelmar.com

New luxury eco-hotel with access to two secluded beaches, two pools, a spa and good restaurant. Excellent wildlife in surrounding forest. Rooms are spacious and stylish, with private terraces, and some with hot tubs. Built and run by the same owners as Finca Rosa Blanca. **$$$$**

Cabinas Pedro Miguel
Tel: 2777 0035
Fax: 2777 2200
www.cabinaspedromiguel.com
Comfortable rooms, some with air conditioning and TV, "eco-cabins" for four (no air conditioning or TV); rooms higher on the hill have an ocean view. Excellent value for the area and run by friendly, helpful *Tico* owners. **$$–$$$**

Cabinas Piscis
Tel/fax: 2777 0046
www.cabinaspiscicscr.com
Simple rooms with private or shared bathrooms on large property just 600 meters/yds from the

national park and 150 meters/yds from the beach; one equipped house with air conditioning. **$–$$**

Costa Verde
Tel: 2777 0584
Fax: 2777 0560
www.costaverde.com
On the forested bluffs above the area's crescent beach, this hotel advertises "More monkeys than people." Good range of equipped studios, efficient apartments and houses with great views. Two hillside pools. Breakfast not included. **$$$–$$$$**

Gaia Hotel y Reserva
Tel: 2777 9797; (US) 800-226 2515
Fax: 2777 9196
www.gaiahr.com
Belongs to "Small Luxury Hotels of the World." Accommodations, on a 5.7-hectare (14-acre) reserve, range from spacious studios to a huge villa; rates include personal valet service. Gourmet La Luna restaurant. **$$$$**

Hotel Karahé
Tel: 2777 0170
Fax: 2777 1075
www.karahe.com
Thirty-four rooms, including nine air-conditioned bungalows, surrounded by 600 hectares (1,500 acres) of grounds. Swimming pool and restaurant. Outdoor activities. **$$$**

La Mariposa Manuel Antonio
Tel: 2777 0355
Fax: 2777 0050
www.lamariposa.com
A view to beat all, spacious accommodations and an excellent staff make this an area favorite. Free transportation provided to the beach. **$$$$**

El Mono Azul
Near Manuel Antonio
Tel: 2777 2572; (US) 800-381 3578
Fax: 2777 1954
www.monoazul.com
Funky, family-friendly hotel with rooms and well-equipped villas. The gift shop was inspired by the owner's conservation-minded young daughter. **$$–$$$**

Sí Como No
Tel: 2777 0777
Fax: 2777 1093
www.sicomono.com
A favorite venue for weddings. Luxury rooms with rainforest and ocean views, and a renowned eco-consciousness; attractions range from nearby howler monkeys and a jungle spa

to a private movie theater. **$$$$**

Hotel Vela Bar
Tel: 2777 0413
Fax: 2777 1071
www.velabar.com
The jungle almost creeps into the rooms here. Rooms and kitchenette-equipped apartments have air conditioning and private baths. There's a popular restaurant. **$$**

Quepos

Cabinas Doña Alicia
Quepos
Tel: 2777 3279
Clean and friendly. The larger rooms have air conditioning, two have hot water; all rooms have private baths. **$$**

Hotel Ceciliano
Quepos
Tel/Fax: 2777 0192
Well kept and pleasant. Rooms with shared/private bathrooms, ceiling fans, and air conditioning. **$**

Rafiki Safari Lodge
Quepos (30km/18 miles south)
Tel: 2777 2250
Fax: 2777 5327
www.rafikisafari.com
Ten luxury safari tents (complete with bathrooms) on hardwood decks. Rafting, kayaking, and floats on the Savegre River, hikes in 283 hectares (700 acres) of private rainforest, horseback riding, and birding. **$$$$**

BELOW: the pool at Sí Como No hotel.

THE NORTHWEST

Flamingo Area

Bahía Esmeralda
Potrero
Tel: 2654 4480
Fax: 2654 4479
www.hotelbahiaesmeralda.com
Quiet, Italian-run garden

PRICE CATEGORIES

Price categories are for a double room; breakfast included from **$$** to **$$$$**:
$$$$ = $150 and up
$$$ = $70–150
$$ = $40–70
$ = up to $40

hotel offers comfortable rooms, with and without kitchenettes, equipped villas and suites close to a selection of uncrowded beaches. **$$$**

Hotel Brasilito
Playa Brasilito
Tel: 2654 4237
Fax: 2654 4247
www.brasilito.com
Vintage, wooden hotel on the beach with great views. Largely no frills, with the exception of stand-out Outback Jack's restaurant, which occupies the

downstairs lobby. **$–$$**

Hotel Flamingo Beach Resort
Tel: 2283 8063
Fax: 2654 4444
www.resortflamingobeach.com
Large, renovated hotel with huge swimming pool, steps from white-sand beach, with lots of water sports; family-friendly; all-inclusive packages available. **$$$$**

Flamingo Marina Resort Playa Flamingo
Tel: 2654 4141
Fax: 2654 4035

www.flamingomarina.com
Upscale, pretty hotel overlooking beach and bay; four pools; rooms and suites have private terraces. **$$$–$$$$**

Inland

Casa Vieja
Liberia
Tel: 2665 5826
Friendly staff, tiled floors, well-kept rooms, and a small kitchen area make this an excellent budget option just off the historic Calle Real. **$**

Hotel Hacienda Guachipelín
Rincón de la Vieja
Tel: 2666 8075; (US) 888-730 3840
Fax: 2665 2178
www.guachipelin.com
A working cattle ranch and adventure center bordering the national park, with comfortable, spacious rooms. Buffet restaurant serves good food and lots of it. All-inclusive packages offer the best value for canopy, tubing, and volcano tours; hikes and horseback rides to waterfalls. **$$$**

La Ensenada Lodge
Palo Verde
Tel: 2289 6655
Fax: 2289 5281
www.laensenada.net
Breezy *cabinas* overlooking the Gulf of Nicoya. Meals, horseback rides, birding, and boat tours available. **$–$$**

Rancho Curubandé
Rincón de la Vieja
Tel: 2665 0375
Fax: 2665 6331
www.rancho-curubande.com
A 134-hectare (330-acre) working ranch, with a back-to-the-land feel (including horse-and-buggy tour to an old-fashioned swimming hole). **$$–$$$**

Rincón de la Vieja Mountain Lodge
Tel: 2200 0238
Fax: 2666 2441
www.hotelrincondelavieja.com
Next door to national park, affordable dorm-style rooms in older cabins; newer, more spacious wooden cabins spread along a small lake. Excellent hiking, birding, canopy tour, and horseback tours to waterfalls. **$$–$$$**

Monteverde

Arco Iris Lodge
Santa Elena
Tel: 2645 5067
Fax: 2645 5022
www.arcoirislodge.com
Small lodge near Monteverde cloud forest. Rooms with hot water and private bathrooms. Great breakfast buffet. Laundry. A favorite with birdwatching groups. **$$–$$$**

Belmar
Monteverde
Tel: 2645 5201
Fax: 2645 5135
www.hotelbelmar.com
Chalet-style and homey with good views from its hilltop location. **$$$**

Hotel & Restaurante El Atardecer
Santa Elena
Tel: 2645 5685
Fax: 2645 5462
Budget rooms, most with views of the cloud forest and the Gulf of Nicoya. Restaurant serves Costa Rican fare. Breakfast included. **$$**

El Sol
4km (2½ miles) south of Santa Elena
Tel: 2645 5838
www.elsolnuestro.com
Three cozy log cabins equipped with kitchens and tubs. Reserve a massage with owner Elizabeth, and savor Ignacio's Mediterranean, German, and Central American gourmet dishes. Breakfast not included. **$$$**

Heliconia Hotel Monteverde
Tel: 2240 7311
Fax: 2240 7331
www.hotelheliconia.com
Rustic luxury in wooden lodge; relaxing spa and excellent restaurant. **$$$–$$$$**

Manakin Lodge
Santa Elena
Tel: 2645 5080
Fax: 2645 5517
www.manakinlodge.com
Basic rooms with mountain views – ask for one with a balcony. Common room on the second floor has a nice view. Breakfast included. **$–$$**

Monteverde Lodge
8km (5 miles) north of Santa Elena
Tel: 2645 5057
Fax: 2645 5126
Comfortable woodsy lodge is the area's highest-end option. Earth-toned, ample rooms complement the nature outside the picture windows. Relax in the jacuzzi, set in a stone floor facing a floor-to-vaulted-ceiling glass wall, or in the renowned gardens. **$$$–$$$$**

Pensión Santa Elena
Santa Elena
Tel: 2645 5051
Fax: 2645 6240
www.pensionsantaelena.com
Best budget digs in the area, ranging from camping (bring your own equipment) to rooms with shared baths and cabins. A favorite of backpackers and groups. **$**

Nosara-Sámara

Hotel Belvedere
Sámara
Tel/fax: 2656 0213
www.belvederesamara.net
Well-kept rooms and equipped apartments with air conditioning and a European touch; second-floor digs have small balconies. The shady gardens and sizeable pool are refreshing. Jacuzzi. Breakfast on the ocean-view terrace is included. **$–$$**

Casa del Mar
Sámara
Tel: 2656 0264
Fax: 2656 0129
www.casadelmarsamara.net
Comfy rooms with air conditioning in the center of town, close to the beach. Shared and private baths. Cool-water backyard jacuzzi. **$–$$$**

Hotel Giada
Playa Sámara
Tel: 2656 0132
Fax: 2656 0131
www.hotelgiada.net
Easily the pick of Sámara's boutique hotels. The design and creativity of the Italian owners infuse the space with a Mediterranean feel; the Pizza & Pasta a Go Go restaurant is worth a visit. **$$–$$$**

Harbor Reef Lodge
Playa Guiones, Nosara
Tel: 2682 1000
Fax: 2682 0060
www.harborreef.com
Comfortable rooms in garden property, perfect for surfers, with good breaks nearby; two pools, restaurant. **$$$–$$$$**

Lagarta Lodge Biological Reserve
Nosara
Tel: 2682 0035
Fax: 2682 0135
www.lagarta.com
This is the place to go for birdwatching, with excellent views of Ostional National Wildlife Refuge and private nature preserve. Just 10 minutes from Playa Guiones (along a steep trail). Exceptional breakfast buffet. **$$$**

Luna Azul
Ostional
Tel: 2682 1400 or 8821 0075
www.hotellunaazul.com
Excellent base for experiencing the *arribadas* (nesting of thousands of sea turtles). Swiss-run, stylish boutique hotel with brightly colored and private cabins, air conditioning, and open-air showers. Ocean-view restaurant, infinity pool, and natural health center. **$$$–$$$$**

Papagayo to Ocotal

El Ocotal Beach Resort
Playa Ocotal
Tel: 2670 0321
Fax: 2670 0083
www.ocotalresort.com
Elegant and secluded hotel overlooking the beach; two restaurants, tennis, pools, snorkeling, sport fishing, and excellent dive shop. **$$$–$$$$**

Hotel El Velero
Playa Hermosa
Tel: 2672 1017
Fax: 2672 0016
www.costaricahotel.net
Breezy beach-front hotel and hub for expats; pool, good restaurant; great base for sunset cruises and fishing. **$$$**

Four Seasons Resort Costa Rica
Papagayo Peninsula
Tel: 2696 0000
Fax: 2696 0010
www.fourseasons.com/costarica
Often referred to as the first hotel of its class in Costa

Rica, this ultra-high-end chain hotel welcomes guests with its trademark luxury and pomp. **$$$$**

Hotel Playa Hermosa Bosque de Mar
Playa Hermosa (Guanacaste)
Tel: 2672 0046
Fax: 2672 0019
www.hotelplayahermosa.com
On the beach, with a good seafood restaurant, shaded pool. *Cabinas* have private bathrooms, heated water, and ceiling fans or air conditioning. **$$$$**

La Puerta del Sol
Playas del Coco
Tel: 2670 0195
Fax: 2670 0650
www.lapuertadelsolcostarica.com
Coco's best luxury option, the hotel is a cluster of air-conditioned private rooms and one suite in precisely landscaped gardens with an inviting pool. Rooms have an airy Mediterranean feel. **$$$**

Villa Huetares
Playa Hermosa
Tel: 2672 0052
Fax: 2672 0051
www.villahuetares.com
You won't get a better deal in town than these family-oriented two-bedroom equipped bungalows and 16 spacious rooms. Newer rooms have air conditioning and cable TV. Restaurant serves local food. **$$–$$$**

Villa Casa Blanca
Playa Ocotal
Tel: 2670 0448
Fax: 2670 0518
www.hotelvillacasablanca.com
Ultra-romantic Victorian-style suites embedded in thick tropical gardens. Hillside location, just past gates for El Ocotal Beach Resort. The breakfasts at this B&B also rank among the best in the region. **$$$**

Southern Nicoya

Hotel Amor de Mar
Montezuma
Tel/fax: 2642 0262
www.amordemar.com
Just south of town, on a rocky point overlooking the Pacific, with a natural seawater pool; great breakfasts. Rooms small but affordable. **$$–$$$**

Hotel Ancla de Oro
Cabuya de Cobano
Tel: 2642 0369
www.caboblancopark.com/ancla
Secluded "jungalows" (A-frame cabins on stilts) near Cabo Blanco Reserve with a variety of beaches nearby. **$–$$**

Blue Jay Eco-Lodge
Mal País
Tel: 2640 0089
www.bluejaylodgecostarica.com
Ten hillside cabins set in the jungle just 200 meters/yds from the beach; ask for a higher one to get an ocean view. The greenery virtually spills into the rooms, restaurant and pool area. **$$$**

Cabinas Playa El Carmen
Santa Teresa
Tel: 2640 0179
Twelve budget rooms, two with private toilets, all shared cold-water showers, just 50 meters/yds from the beach. Shared kitchen and fridge. **$**

Hotel El Jardín
Montezuma
Tel/fax: 2642 0074
www.hoteleljardin.com
The ambience of a resort in a boutique-hotel setting near the beach. Fifteen rooms and two villas, some with simple but beautiful stone and wood architectural details. Breakfast not included. **$$$**

Hotel & Restaurante La Cascada
Montezuma
Tel/fax: 2642 0057
www.playamontezuma.net/cascada.php
Budget lodgings, three nicer rooms with air conditioning, all have private baths. Rooms on both floors have ocean views, 400 meters/yds from downtown Montezuma. Pleasant second-floor balcony. **$$**

Hotel Lucy
Montezuma
Tel: 2642 0273
This two-story converted house is the best of the budget options in this area. Accommodations are basic but comfortable, some shared baths, and a restaurant serves local food – the big draw is the location, just south of town

and close to the beach. **$**

Hotel Milarepa
Santa Teresa
Tel: 2640 0023
Fax: 2640 0663
www.milarepahotel.com
A craggy coastline setting and antique four-poster beds draped with gauzy mosquito nets evoke a tropical dream. The Indonesian-style hotel is designed to blend into the environment, with partly open bungalows with bamboo-striped walls; two are right on the beach. **$$$$**

Peninsula
Hotel Flor BlanCa. Resort
Santa Teresa
Tel: 2640 0232
Fax: 2640 0226
www.florblanca.com
Gorgeous, ultra-luxurious, and romantic villas. Private outdoor tub and shower; yoga; and poolside gourmet restaurant. **$$$$**

Punta Islita Hotel
Punta Islita
Tel: 2656 3036
Fax: 2232 2183
www.hotelpuntaislita.com
Truly secluded luxury hotel with gorgeous Pacific views; most guests arrive by plane. Lodgings, amenities, and spa services provide the ultimate indulgence. The hotel is also renowned for extensive community involvement. **$$$$**

Ylang Ylang Beach Resort
Montezuma
Tel: 2642 0636
Fax: 2642 0068
www.ylangylangresort.com
Ten-minute beach walk north of town, romantic bungalows and suites, beautiful gardens and pool. **$$$–$$$$**

Tamarindo to Junquillal

Cabinas Las Olas
Playa Avellanas
Tel: 2652 9315
Fax: 2652 9331
www.cabinaslasolas.co.cr
Popular surfers' hotel, with beach access but also a quiet, secluded spot with lots of wildlife in bordering mangroves. Spacious

private cabins. **$$$**

Capitán Suizo
Tamarindo
Tel: 2653 0075
Fax: 2653 0292
www.hotelcapitansuizo.com
The height of small-scale luxury. Beach-front hotel with two-level rooms and bungalows and elegant equipped apartment. Shaded pool and recommended restaurant. **$$$$**

Guacamaya Lodge
Playa Junquillal
Tel: 2658 8431
Fax: 2658 8164
www.guacamayalodge.com
Poolside rooms, studio apartments with ocean view and equipped villa, all with air conditioning, close to one of the country's best beaches. Golf course just 20 minutes away. **$$–$$$**

Iguanazul
Playa Junquillal
Tel: 2658 8123
Fax: 2658 8124
www.hoteliguanazul.com
Cliffside complex with 24 cabins (12 with air conditioning); also condos and a beach house. Popular gathering place for "Happy Hour." International restaurant and entertainment room. **$$–$$$**

Hotel Las Tortugas
Playa Grande
Tel: 2653 0423
Fax: 2653 0458
www.lastortugashotel.com
Turtle-friendly hotel on a long, wide, beautiful beach. Conservationist management. Good restaurant. Pool. Excellent surfing directly in front of hotel. **$$–$$$**

Hotel Pasatiempo
Tamarindo
Tel: 2653 0096
Fax: 2653 0278
www.hotelpasatiempo.com
Popular Tamarindo

PRICE CATEGORIES

Price categories are for a double room; breakfast included from **$$** to **$$$$**:
$$$$ = $150 and up
$$$ = $70–150
$$ = $40–70
$ = up to $40

institution and hang-out. Each air-conditioned room has its own hand-painted mural. At night, the bar and restaurant fill up and the place comes alive with music. **$$–$$$**
Hotel Playa Negra
Playa Negra
Tel: 2658 9134
Fax: 2658 9035
www.playanegra.com
Across from the hotel is the

surf break made famous in the *Endless Summer II* movie. Non-surfers can sunbathe on the white-sand beach 100 meters/yds to the south. The round, thatched-roof bungalows are bright and breezy. Breakfast is not included. **$$$**
Villa Alegre
Playa Langosta
Tel: 2653 0270

Fax: 2653 0287
www.villaalegrecostarica.com
Popular for beach-front weddings, this homey, upscale B&B has five rooms and two villas, each decorated with a different travel theme. Friendly and knowledgeable owners; great breakfasts. Pleasant pool and steps to beach. **$$$$**
Sueño del Mar

Playa Langosta
Tel: 2653 0284
Fax: 2653 0558
www.sueno-del-mar.com
You'll never tire of looking around this arty beach-front B&B. Richly decorated double rooms with showers open to the sky, well-equipped *casitas* and a honeymoon suite. Excellent breakfasts served in the garden patio. **$$$$**

THE NORTHEAST

Arenal Area

Cabinas Oriuma
La Fortuna
Tel/Fax: 2479 9111
Email: oriuma@ice.co.cr
Central budget option popular with backpackers. Almost all rooms have air conditioning and balcony; communal balcony with volcano view. **$–$$**
Arenal Observatory Lodge
La Fortuna area
Tel: 2290 7011
Fax: 2290 8427
www.arenalobservatorylodge.com
Best site for volcano viewing. The more expensive rooms have views of the volcano. Lots of observation decks. Pool, jacuzzi, trails, excellent birdwatching. Includes breakfast.
$$$–$$$$
La Catarata Lodge
La Fortuna area
Tel: 2479 9522
Fax: 2479 9168
www.cataratalodge.com
Excellent volcano views, butterfly garden, and internet access. **$$–$$$**
Hotel/Restaurante La Pradera del Arenal
La Fortuna (2km/1 mile west)
Tel: 2479 9597
Fax: 2479 9167
www.lapraderadelarenal.com
For a few dollars more, it's worth choosing the individual wood cabins, but the concrete rooms are comfortable too. All have air conditioning and volcano views. Pool, jacuzzi. **$$$**
Las Cabanitas
La Fortuna
Tel: 2479 9400

Fax: 2479 9408
www.hotelcabanita.com
One of La Fortuna's more pleasant places to stay. Comfortable, traditional tile-roofed *cabinas*. **$$$**
Hotel Las Colinas
La Fortuna
Tel: 2479 9305
Fax: 2479 9160
www.lascolinasarenal.com
While not much to look at from the outside, this central hotel offers a step above what you would expect in this price range, particularly with the spectacular volcano views from rooms 33 and 27. Breakfast included. **$$**
Montaña de Fuego Hotel & Spa
La Fortuna
Tel: 2479 1220
Fax: 2479 1240
www.montanadefuego.com
All 66 air-conditioned rooms and 18 suites have picture-window views of the volcano. Pool, spa, jacuzzi, and sauna. An excellent luxury base for exploring the Arenal area. **$$$–$$$$**
Tabacón Grand Spa & Thermal Resort
Lake Arenal
Tel: 2519 1999, US: 877-277 8291
Fax: 2519 1940
www.tabacon.com
Luxury resort famous for hot springs in landscaped gardens with views of Arenal Volcano. **$$$$**
Hotel Tilawa
Lake Arenal
Tel: 2695 5050
Fax: 2695 5766
www.tilawa.com
Columned hotel modeled

after a Cretan palace overlooks Lake Arenal, favorite base for kite- and windsurfing aficionados. Hot springs, jungle trails, and animals delight the whole family; child-friendly skate park is also a hit. Rooms, suites, and apartments available with lake or garden views. Breakfast not included. **$$–$$$**

Central Plains

Caño Negro Natural Lodge
Tel: 2471 1000
www.canonegrolodge.com
Italian-run, upscale hotel with 42 comfortable rooms, pleasant grounds, pool, and a decent restaurant. Fishing and birdwatching tours. **$$$**
Hotel de Campo
Tel: 2471 1490
www.hoteldecampo.com
Fisherman's delight: lakeside location, with tackle and boats on hand to catch tarpon. Lodging in comfortable, wooden bungalows. **$$$**
La Laguna del Lagarto
San Carlos area
Tel: 2289 8163
Fax: 2289 5295
www.lagarto-lodge-costa-rica.com
Remote lodge on a hill with views, with comfortable rooms. Hiking, horseback riding, boat trips on the Río San Carlos. **$$**
Las Heliconias Lodge
3km/2 miles north of Bijagua
Tel/Fax: 2466 8483
Rural tourism at its best; new bungalows with jacuzzis and balconies in forest; also budget rooms, on the skirts of Tenorio

Volcano. Excellent base for tours to the national park and Río Celeste. **$$–$$$**
Maquenque Eco-Lodge
BoCa. Tapada
Tel: 2479 7785
www.maquenqueecolodge.com
High-ceilinged, ultracomfortable, modern cabins with lagoon and forest views, in vast wildlife refuge, part of Ruta de Las Aves. Hiking, birdwatching, canoeing. Chances to see great green macaw. Swimming pool and excellent restaurant. **$$$**
Termales del Bosque
Aguas Zarcas
Tel/Fax: 2460 1356
www.termalesdelbosque.com
Enjoy natural rainforest hot springs, accommodations and breakfast for less than the price to visit better-known hot springs elsewhere in the country. New spa and excellent restaurant, specializing in tilapia. Eco-hikes through private reserve and nearby Juan Castro Blanco national park.
$$$–$$$$
Hotel Tilajari Resort
Near Muelle
Tel: 2462 1212
Fax: 2462 1414
www.tilajari.com

Spacious rooms and acres of rolling lawns on the San Carlos River. Tennis, spa, swimming, horses, pool. **$$$**

Nuevo Arenal

Chalet Nicholas
Tel: 2694 4041
www.chaletnicholas.com
Three immaculate rooms in a large house with lake and volcano views. More than 100 orchid species flourish in the tropical gardens. The three resident Great Danes are gentle giants. No credit cards. **$$**

La Ceiba Tree Lodge
Nuevo Arenal area
Tel/fax: 2692 8050
www.ceibatree-lodge.com
Lovely B&B on a hilltop, with an organic garden. Named for majestic, 500-year-old ceiba tree on property. Views of Lake Arenal, five homey rooms. **$$–$$$**

San Ramón

Villa Blanca
Near San Ramón
Tel: 2401 3800; (US) 877-256 8399
Fax: 2461 0302
www.villablancacr.com
Updated, luxuriously appointed, separate *casitas* with fireplaces, generous bathtubs. Movie theater,

guided hikes into adjoining Los Angeles Cloud Forest Reserve. **$$$$**

Sarapiquí

Hotel Ara Ambigua
Puerto Viejo de Sarapiquí
Tel: 2766 7101
Fax: 2766 6401
www.hotelaraambigua.com
The nicest cabins have teak walls, rough-hewn wooden furniture, and stone-slab floors. Concrete options are acceptable. Large pool forms a blue clearing amid lush jungle gardens. Breakfast included. **$$–$$$**

La Quinta de Sarapiquí Country Inn
North of La Vírgen
Tel: 2761 1300
Fax: 2761 1395
www.laquintasarapiqui.com
Classy rooms with patios. Several in-house attractions: butterfly garden and frog garden, lush heliconia, ornamental and organic gardens, pool. **$$$**

La Selva Biological Station
Puerto Viejo de Sarapiquí (4km/2½ miles south)
Tel: 2524 0607
Fax: 2524 0608
www.threepaths.co.cr
A birding delight, with sightings of more than 400

resident and migratory birds. Dorms are no-frills but eight new private cabins are very comfortable. More than 50km (30 miles) of trails take you deep into the rainforest. Rates include three meals and half-day tour. **$$$**

Hotel Mi Lindo Sarapiquí
Tel/fax: 2766 6281
Small hotel in the town center. Clean rooms, TV, and hot water. Student discount available. **$**

Rara Avis
Near Las Horquetas
Tel: 2764 1111
Fax: 2764 1114
www.rara-avis.com
For the most intrepid birders and nature-lovers only. Three-hour trip by tractor-pulled wagon to rustic lodge in spectacular forest setting. Rates include all meals, some tours. **$$$**

Selva Verde Lodge
Near Puerto Viejo de Sarapiquí
Tel: 2766 6800; (US) 800-451 7111
www.selvaverde.com
Beautiful river lodge. Spectacular birdwatching, nature walks, horseback riding. Breakfast is included. **$$$–$$$$**

Varablanca

Peace Lodge
3km (1½ miles) north of Vara

Blanca
Tel: 2482 2720
Fax: 2482 1092
www.waterfallgardens.com
Sensuous luxury mountain resort set on the grounds of La Paz Waterfall Gardens. Decadent stone waterfall showers and balcony jacuzzi tubs help make these rooms some of the country's most romantic. **$$$$**

Poás Volcano Lodge
Varablanca, Heredia
Tel: 2482 2194
Fax: 2482 2513
www.poasvolcanolodge.com
Almost entirely rebuilt after the 2009 earthquake. The new rooms have fireplaces and bathtubs, terraces with mountain views or private plunge pools in garden; the original rooms are still cozy. Birdwatching, horseback riding, or hiking in clear mountain air are all available. **$$$–$$$$**

Villa Decary
Nuevo Arenal area
Tel: 8383 3012
Tel/fax: 2694 4330
www.villadecary.com
Large rooms and bungalows in a lovely country inn with a lake view. Great birding, hearty breakfasts, and excellent service. **$$$–$$$$**

THE CARIBBEAN COAST

Cahuita Area

Alby Lodge
Cahuita
Tel/fax: 2755 0031
www.albylodge.com
Four rustic thatched-roof cabins in natural materials, with fans, mosquito nets, verandah hammocks, and hot-water showers. Communal kitchen/dining room available. Surrounded

by lush vegetation. No credit cards. **$$**

Cabinas Arrecife
Cahuita
Tel/fax: 2755 0081
www.cabinasarrecife.com
Diagonal to Restaurant Edith, with clean rooms and shared verandah with hammocks. **$**

Cabinas Iguana
Cahuita
Tel: 755 0005
Fax: 2755 0054
www.cabinas-iguana.com
Pleasant *cabinas* and two equipped houses; three rooms with shared bathroom. Organic fruit garden, pool with waterfall; bookshop. Good value. **$–$$$**

Chimuri Beach Cottage
Playa Negra
Tel/fax: 2750 0119
www.greencoast.com/chimuribeach.htm
Three pretty Caribbean cottages on a black-sand beach, well-equipped, and with hammocks on the porch. Two-night minimum stay. It's a good option for those looking for privacy. **$–$$**

Casas Wal-Aba
Punta Uva
Tel: 2750 0147
Friendly budget lodging. Two cabins, sleeping two and four people, and two houses, which sleep six and 12. Communal kitchen. Low per-person price. **$**

San José

Manzanillo

Almonds and Corals
Manzanillo
Tel: 2271 3000
Fax: 2272 2220
www.almondsandcorals.com
Furnished luxury tents on raised platforms in the heart of a dense jungle; magically tropical atmosphere. Rates

---

include breakfast and dinner. **$$$$**

B & B El Encanto
Cahuita
Tel: 2755 0113
Fax: 2755 0432
www.elencantobedandbreakfast.com
Affordable bungalows, one equipped apartment, and a house (sleeps six); beautiful Zen garden. Breakfast included. **$$–$$$**

Bungalows Cariblue
Cocles
Tel: 2750 0035
Tel/fax: 2750 0057
www.cariblue.com
Hardwood bungalows, thatched-roof rooms, and an equipped house are comfortable, cool options for the Caribbean heat. Close to beach, upscale-funky vibe. **$$$**

Cabinas Casa Verde
Puerto Viejo
Tel: 2750 0015
Fax: 2750 0047
www.cabinascasaverde.com
Bright mosaics highlight the laid-back structure. Cabins have private baths, rooms don't. Enjoy the frog garden, beautiful pool with waterfall, and therapeutic hut for massage, Reiki, and other alternative therapies. Discounts for cash. **$–$$$**

Cabinas Manzanillo.
Tel: 2759 9033
Budget option at village

entrance, short walk to beach. Simple, clean cabins; ceiling fans, hot-water; no breakfast. **$**

La Costa de Papito
Playa Cocles
Tel: 2750 0704
Fax: 2750 0080
www.lacostadepapito.com
Private, airy bungalows, one with wheelchair access and open-air bathroom, jungle gardens, child-friendly, just across from beach. Pure Jungle Spa provides reasonably priced, natural pampering. Breakfast included. **$$–$$$**

Escape Caribeño
Puerto Viejo area
Tel/fax: 2750 0103
www.escapecaribeno.com
Cabinas near Salsa Brava. Porches, private bath. **$$$**

Magellan Inn
Cahuita
Tel/fax: 2755 0035
www.magellaninn.com
Simple, elegant rooms, two with air conditioning have a covered outdoor sitting area. Sunken reef pool, restaurant serves spicy French Creole dishes (dinner only). **$$$**

Puerto Viejo de Talamanca
Samasati
Puerto Viejo
Tel: 2756 8015;
(US) 800-563 9643

Fax: 2224 5032
www.samasati.com
Luxury holistic retreat on 100-hectare (250-acre) private reserve. Natural spa treatments, yoga, and meditation; tours include a visit to a native shaman. Transport to beaches (7 km/4 miles away) available for nominal cost. Vegetarian meals included. **$$–$$$**

Shawandha
Puerto Viejo
Tel: 2750 0018
Fax: 2750 0037
www.shawandhalodge.com
Thatched wooden bungalows with style (one of the French owners is a decorator). The chef creates Gallic and local fusion cuisine in recommended restaurant. **$$$**

North

Casa Marbella
Tortuguero
Tel: 2709 8011
Fax: 2709 8094
http://casamarbella.tripod.com
Comfortable rooms in B&B on canal, kitchenette, porch, Canadian owner provides excellent tours. Best option for independent travelers. **$**

Mawamba Lodge
Tortuguero
Tel: 2293 8181

Fax: 2239 8082
www.grupomawamba.com
A specialty in incentive travel means you risk sharing the place with large groups, but the advantage is top-notch facilities at a reasonable price. **$$$$**

Pachira
Tortuguero
Tel: 2256 7080
Fax: 2223 1119
www.pachiralodge.com
Fresh rooms with wicker furniture and turtle-shaped pool at a modern wooden lodge. Enjoy the 5.6-hectare (14-acre) property, kayaks and trails, and, in season, the turtles. **$$$–$$$$**

Tortuga Lodge
Tortuguero
Tel: 2257 0766
Fax: 2257 1765
www.costaricaexpeditions.com
Pleasant lodge 2km (1 mile) from village. Package available including meals and transportation from San José. **$$$$**

Puerto Limón

Hotel Park
Av. 3, Ca. 2–3, Limón
Tel: 2798 0555
Fax: 2758 4364
Email: parkhotellimon@ice.co.cr
Best option in town; ocean views, air conditioning, and safe parking. **$$**

THE SOUTH

Cerro de la Muerte

Albergue de Montaña Paraíso del Quetzal
Tel: 2771 4582/2200 0241
www.paraisodelquetzal.com
High-altitude, rustic cabins with fabulous mountain views; hot-water showers; great hiking trails and birdwatching for resplendent quetzal; dinner and breakfast included. **$$–$$$**

Cabinas San Clemente
Dominical
Tel: 2787 0055
Fax: 2787 0191
Email: sanclemente@dominical.com
Lively surfer and backpacker hang-out with

three houses right on the beach. Dorms with shared bath, or private rooms. **$**

DantiCa. Lodge and Gallery
4km (2½ miles) off Interamerican Highway to San Gerardo de Dota.
Tel: 2740 1067
www.dantica.com
Ultra-stylish, ultra-comfortable cabins with jacuzzis, electric heaters, kitchenettes, satellite TV, and picture-window views of mountain valley. Perfect for birdwatching, and browsing in tasteful Latin American artisan gallery. **$$$$**

El Toucanet Lodge
Copey
Tel/fax: 2541 3045

www.eltoucanet.com
Tranquil mountain lodge near Ruta de Los Santos, bordering new Los Quetzales Nacional Park. Comfortable wooden cabins and luxury suites with jacuzzis. Excellent bird-watching and hiking. Friendly hosts. **$$–$$$**

Savegre Hotel de Montaña
San Gerardo de Dota
Tel: 2740 1028
Fax: 2740 1027
www.savegre.co.cr
Remodeled, cozy rooms and newer cabins with fireplaces and bathtubs, in the cool mountains near Cerro de la Muerte. Spot quetzals, watch hummingbirds at

feeders, and enjoy fresh trout. Best hiking trails and naturalist guides in area. Meals included. **$$$$**

Corcovado (Drake Bay)

Casa Corcovado Jungle Lodge

Corcovado
Tel: 2256 3181
Fax: 2256 7409
www.casacorcovado.com
Sumptuous luxury bordering the country's most remote and vibrant national park. First-class food and guides, spectacular views, and a plethora of activities. Minimum two-night stay, but it's a better deal to stay three. Exciting boat ride from Sierpe to hotel. **$$$$**

Drake Bay Wilderness Resort
Drake Bay
Tel: 2775 1715
Fax: 2775 1741
www.drakebay.com
Slightly more rustic than other options. Choose between spacious, airy cabins with hot-water showers and ceiling fans; or adventurous platform tents at water's edge. Sea-water swimming pool; beautiful views; ocean breezes; all meals included. **$$$**

La Paloma Lodge
Drake Bay
Tel: 2293 7502
Fax: 2239 0954
www.lapalomalodge.com
On an ocean bluff with sweeping views and breezes, this romantic eco-lodge in lush landscaping has upscale, two-story cabins with sea views, and spacious rooms with jungle views. Excellent guides and restaurant. **$$$$**

Poor Man's Paradise
San Josecito
Tel: 2771 4582
Fax: 2771 8841
www.mypoormansparadise.com
Book through Selva Mar. Equipped tents, including meals. The best deal near Drake; also more expensive cabins. Camping (depending on weather); restaurant; helpful owner. **$$–$$$**

Punta Marenco Lodge
Río Claro National Wildlife Refuge
Tel: 2294 8947
Fax: 2292 1828
www.corcovadozone.com
Thatched-roof huts overlooking the Pacific have great breezes and views of Caño Island. Hiking and wildlife tours in adjoining forest. Rates include family-style meals and exciting boat ride to lodge. **$$$**

Corcovado (Puerto Jiménez)

Bosque del Cabo
Cabo Matapalo
Tel/fax: 2735 5206
www.bosquedelcabo.com
Luxurious, very private bungalows with garden showers, ocean or garden views, plus three equipped houses; small pool and excellent restaurant. Great birding, myriad monkeys and wildlife, nature trails, and excellent resident guides. **$$$$**

Bosque del Río Tigre Lodge
Dos Brazos del Tigre, west of Puerto Jiménez
Tel: 8383 390; (US) 888-875 9543
Fax: 2735 5045
www.osaadventures.com
Rustic lodge set in a remote birdwatching paradise on a 12-hectare (31-acre) private reserve. Four comfortable open-air rooms (with shared bathroom) and one cabin. The energetic hosts are fountains of hospitality and knowledge about nature. Rates include three gourmet meals. Great value. **$$$**

Danta Corcovado Lodge
La Palma, near Los Patos
Tel: 2735 1111
www.dantalodge.com
Rustic but comfortable rooms and forest cabins, within walking distance of Los Patos entrance to Corcovado Nacional Park. **$$**

Iguana Lodge
4km (2½ miles) from Puerto Jiménez
Tel: 8829 5865
www.iguanalodge.com
Suites in beach-front, two-story cabins with verandahs, elegant furnishings. Candlelit dining brings guests together at dinner for sophisticated, international cuisine. Good buffet breakfasts. Also runs nearby Pearl de Osa, with slightly cheaper but still upscale rooms; and fully equipped beach-front Villa Kula Kula. **$$$$**

Lapa Ríos
Puerto Jiménez/Corcovado
Tel: 2735 5130
Fax: 2735 5179
www.laparios.com
Luxurious, thatched-roof bungalows in hilltop eco-lodge on a large private reserve, each with private garden and terrace, where monkeys come to visit. Resident nature guides. Highest environmental sustainability rating. Excellent service and all meals in first-rate restaurant included. **$$$$**

Lookout Inn
Carate
Tel: 2644 5967
www.lookout-inn.com
Choose from tent-like cabins on 3-meter (10ft) platforms, screened-in cabins, or luxurious rooms at this funky, friendly hillside hotel high above the beach (steep stairs). Excellent seafood and international cuisine served on breezy terraces with gorgeous ocean views. Killer margaritas accompany spectacular sunsets. **$$$–$$$$**

Below: ocean views from the Lapa Ríos bungalows.

Luna Lodge
Carate
Tel: 8380 5036
www.lunalodge.com
Round, thatched cabins with garden showers, verandahs, high on a hill with mountain and sunset views. More traditional rooms and comfortable tent options. A favorite with yoga groups. Lovely pool, full spa, waterfall hike; creative, healthy meals included. **$$$–$$$$**

Cabinas Marcelina
Puerto Jiménez
Tel: 2735 5007
Email: cabmarce@hotmail.com
Eight safe, basic rooms, four with air conditioning, all private baths. Buffet breakfast is included in high season. Prices lower in green season. **$$**

Dominical Area

Hacienda Barú
North of Dominical
Tel: 2787 0003
Fax: 2787 0057
www.haciendabaru.com
Renowned eco-lodge on 330 hectares (815 acres) of nature reserve. Simple, equipped, two-bedroom wood cabins, great for families, plus spacious new rooms facing pool. Best naturalist guides in area for birdwatching and tours, plus tree-climbing and canopy tour adventures. **$$–$$$**

Pacific Edge
South of Dominical
Tel/Fax: 2787 8010
www.pacificedge.info
Mountain-top, beautifully crafted wood cabins with bird's-eye view of Pacific. Small pool, lookout towers, hammocks on verandahs; friendly hosts. Steep access requires four-wheel-drive. **$$–$$$**

Golfito

Las Esquinas Rainforest Lodge
Golfito area

Tel/fax: 2741 8001
www.esquinaslodge.com
Rainforest jungle lodge with
cabinas, natural pool, and
large, comfortable common
areas. Excellent trails and
local guides. **$$$**
Hotel Las Gaviotas
Golfito
Tel: 2775 0062
www.lasgaviotasmarinaresort.com
This is a solid choice if you
find yourself in Golfito for the
night. Pool, restaurant.
Arranges sport fishing tours.
$$$
**Playa Nicuesa Rainforest
Lodge**
Golfo Dulce
Tel: 2258 8250
www.nicuesalodge.com
New, palatial tree-house
lodge; secluded cabins.
Accessible only by boat.
Trails, tours, water sports.
All-inclusive, with excellent
meals and guides. **$$$$**

Inland

Wilson Botanical Garden
San Vito

Tel: 2524 0607
Fax: 2524 0608
www.esintro.co.cr
On Las Cruces Biological
Station, spacious private
rooms with birdwatching
balconies and views over
extensive botanical
gardens, plus hiking trail
in primary forest. Family-
style meals. A favorite
with birders and botanists.
$$$

Pavones

Cabinas La Ponderosa
Pavones
Tel: 2776 2076
www.laponderosapavones.com
Just steps from the best
surfing break, comfortable
rooms in cabins set in 5
hectares (14 acres) of lush
gardens with swimming
pool. Meal package
available. **$$**
Tiskita Jungle Lodge
Near Pavones
Tel: 2296 8125
Fax: 2296 8133
www.tiskita.com

Rustic and comfortable
cabinas with great ocean
views. More than 100
varieties of tropical fruit
trees attract birds and
monkeys. Trails and
waterfalls. Cabins, made
from mahogany and
rosewood, have screened
windows and hammocks on
porches. Meals included.
$$$$

San Gerardo de Rivas

El Pelícano Mountain Hotel
South of San Gerardo de Rivas
Tel: 2742 5050
www.hotelpelicano.net
An excellent staging area
for climbing Chirripó;
affordable cabins, plus
budget rooms. There's a
pool, restaurant, and
sculpture gallery.
Experienced guides and
rides to the trailhead. **$**
Hotel Uran
San Gerardo de Rivas
Tel: 2742 5004
Fax: 2742 5482

www.hoteluran.com
Located near the trailhead,
this simple but clean and
comfortable hotel offers
budget dormitory rooms
with shared bath, as well as
eight rooms with private
bath. **$**

Zancudo

Cabinas Los Cocos
Playa Zancudo
Tel/fax: 2776 0012
www.loscocos.com
Four charming cottages on
beach, equipped for self-
catering and swinging in
hammocks on breezy
verandahs. The friendly,
knowledgeable hosts
organize boat tours, water
taxi and river kayak
expeditions. **$$**
Cabinas Sol y Mar
Playa Zancudo
Tel: 2776 0014
www.zancudo.com
Tranquil *cabinas* facing
breezy beach. Private
bathrooms with fans, and
bright, airy bathrooms. **$$**

CAMPSITES AND HOSTELS

CAMPING

There are few established
campsites with facilities.
Property owners in rural
areas will often permit
visitors to camp on their
land. Sometimes rural
hotels, for a small fee, will
permit campers to stay on
their grounds. While
campers face little risk of
prosecution if they bunk
down on the beach,
conflicts between campers
and resorts have thrust
beach camping into the
public spotlight.
    The best camping is in
the national parks (www.
costarica-nationalparks.com).
Prices range from $3 to $6
per person, plus any
national park entry fee.
Antorchas
Dominical (South)
Tel: 2787 0307 (Spanish) or 2771
0459 (English)

www.campingantorchas.net
Just 25 meters/yds from the
beach, includes tent rental if
required. Shared bathrooms
(cold water) and kitchen. Also
rooms with private baths.
Active surfer vibe; lots of
mosquitoes, so be sure you
have a mosquito net.
Camping Arrecife
Punta Uva (Caribbean)
Tel: 2759 9200
www.arrecifepuntauva.net
Sandy sites facing the
beach, near nature refuge
and great snorkeling reef.
Shared bathrooms,
communal kitchen.

HOSTELS

Cheap cabins are fairly easy
to come by, so hostelling is
not as developed as in more
expensive destinations. A
few places are affiliated with
Hostelling International
(www.hihostels.com).

Bekuo Hostel
325 meters/yds west of the Spoon
in Los Yoses
Tel: 2234 1091; (US) 602-773 6910
www.hostelbekuo.com
Slightly cramped dorms in a
large house, but this is one
of the more homely hostels.
Private rooms available.
Kitchen, internet, breakfast
included. Free long-term
storage. **$–$$**
Hostel El Museo
Downtown San José
Tel: 2221 7515
www.hostelmuseo.com
New, well-run hostel with
bright, cheery dorm and
private rooms, right across
from National Museum.
Kitchen open to guests. **$**
Hotel Costa Linda
Manuel Antonio
Tel: 2777 0304
www.costalinda-backpackers.com
Closest backpacker
lodgings to beach; dorm,
private rooms with shared
baths, and one apartment.
Restaurant serves breakfast

and dinner. **$–$$**
Gaudy's Backpackers
Av. 5, between Ca. 36–38, San José
Tel/fax: 2248 0086
Fax: 2258 2937
www.backpacker.co.cr
Spacious rooms, with kitchen
facilities and common areas,
close to downtown. Free tea,
coffee, and internet. **$**

PRICE CATEGORIES

Price categories are for a
double room; breakfast
included from **$$** to **$$$$**:
$$$$ = $150 and up
$$$ = $70–150
$$ = $40–70
$ = up to $40

E ATING OUT

RECOMMENDED RESTAURANTS, CAFÉS, & BARS

What and Where to Eat

Thanks to the influx of international tourists and restaurateurs, Costa Rica's culinary offerings are very cosmopolitan, along with traditional local fare, *comida tipica (see Tico Cooking, pages 106–9)*. San José and Escazú have the best dining, but Tamarindo, on the Pacific coast, and the Puerto Viejo area, on the Caribbean coast, have a cluster of tasty options.

Reservations are a good idea at upscale eateries, but usually not necessary elsewhere. Menus should show prices with tax and tip included (totaling 23 percent), although some do not – ask if it is not clear. Unless the service is truly excellent, an extra tip is not necessary, since there is a 10 percent service charge.

Vegetarians beware – *sin carne* means "without meat," but is often understood as "without beef." Specify *sólo vegetales* if you want to be sure.

Weekly markets are a bonanza of tropical fruits and vegetables at farm prices. They're also good for quick breakfasts, as vendors of *gallo pinto*, corn pancakes, and fresh juices set up around the action. Most areas have a market on Saturday or Sunday; try the Zapote market by the old bullring, southeast of San José (Sunday); the Coronado market near the Gothic church (Sunday); and Heredia's Saturday market, which stretches a kilometer (½ mile) along the old railroad tracks. Get there before 9am for the best choices.

Drinking Notes

Local beers include Imperial, Pilsen, Rock Ice, and Bavaria. All are good, but none is exceptional. Wine is not common with meals, but there are some good-value South American wines available.

Guaro, the local sugar cane-based firewater, is cheap and can strip paint.

Opening Times

Monday to Saturday, most bar/ restaurants open any time from 8.30am to 11am, and stay open until around midnight or 2am. On Sunday, some may close earlier, others do not bother to open at all. Friday and Saturday nights are busy, but earlier in the week you may find happy hours and other attractive offers.

Legalities

You must be 18 years of age to drink alcohol in Costa Rica. Some bars require you to show identification.

R ESTAURANT L ISTINGS

SAN JOSÉ AND ENVIRONS

Delicias del Perú
(Peruvian)
Ca. 3 between Av. 7–9, across from Hotel Santo Tomás.
Tel: 2222 9249
Tasty Peruvian fare at bargain prices. Signature *chicharrón de calamar* dish is a generous serving of the juiciest fried squid you will ever eat. Lunch only 11am– 4pm, closed Sun. **$**
Grano de Oro (international)
Ca. 30, Av. 2–4, Paseo Colón

Tel: 2255 3322
The most elegant dining room in town, with haute Costa Rican cuisine to match, set in a Victorian mansion; romantic courtyard tables, too. Famous for velvety cream of *pejibaye* soup and decadent desserts. Polished, friendly service. **$$$**
La Criollita (Costa Rican)
Across from INS, Barrio Amón

Tel: 2256 6511
The best breakfast in town and hearty local fare; garden tables beside a large, chirpy aviary. Closed Sun. **$**
L'Ile de France (French)
Hotel Le Bergerac, Ca. 35, Los Yoses
Tel: 2283 5812
Intimate and consistent, this is the city's best traditional French restaurant. Excellent wine

list and authentic rabbit pâté. Reservations advised. Closed Sun; dinner only.
$$$
Lubnán (Lebanese)
Paseo Colón, Ca. 22–24
Tel: 2257 6071
Excellent Middle Eastern

PRICE CATEGORIES

Prices are for dinner for two:
$$$ = US$50 plus
$$ = US$25–50
$ = US$25 or less

food, and a hopping tapestried bar in the back. Thursday-night belly dancing show is great, but arrive early to order. Closed Mon, lunch only Sun. **$$**
Manolo's (Costa Rican)
Av. Central, 2
Tel: 2221 2041
Good place to grab a cup of espresso or sandwich; outdoor tables are the best for prime people-watching, or sit on upstairs balcony. Try the famed *churro* (fried dough) with chocolate sauce. Open 24 hours. **$$**
Café Mundo (international)
Ca. 15, Av. 9, Barrio Otoya
Tel: 2222 6190
Trendy, cosmopolitan cuisine in an attractive old

house and garden in this historic district. Popular with tourists and local people, so there is always a buzz. Closed Sun. **$$**
Park Café (French-inspired Fusion)
100 meters/yds north of RostiPollos, Sabana Norte
Tel: 2290 6324
www.parkcafecostarica
Innovative, sophisticated cuisine by Michelin-starred British chef, in exquisite, romantic garden setting, surrounded by Balinese antiques. Duck confit in chocolate sauce is not to be missed. Dessert sampler is pure delight. Closed Sun and Mon. **$$$**
Shakti (vegetarian)

Av. 8, Ca. 13
Tel: 2222 4475
Healthy burgers and soups in a bright and cheery room, very busy at lunch time. Platters offer a chance to try unusual local root vegetables. Closed Sun. **$**
Café del Teatro Nacional
Teatro Nacional
Av. 2, Ca. 3
Tel: 2221 3262
Cultured, central spot for light lunches, specialty coffees, excellent fruit shakes and scrumptious desserts, next to the Beaux-Arts lavish lobby of the National Theater. **$**
Tin Jo (Asian)
Ca. 11, Av. 6–8

Tel: 2221 7605
Covers all the pan-Asian culinary stops – Indian, Thai, Chinese and Japanese – and adds creative touches. Elegant, themed rooms; good service. A favorite with vegetarians, too. **$$–$$$**
Whapin' (Caribbean)
200 meters/yds east of El Farolito, Barrio Escalante
Tel: 2283 1480
Authentic Afro-Caribbean dishes served in a funky, island-style room, with a bar that opens onto the street. Try the fried breadfruit if it's in season. Occasional live music. Closed Sun. **$–$$**

THE CENTRAL VALLEY

Alajuela

La Fiesta del Maíz (Costa Rican)
La Garita, Alajuela
Tel: 2487 5757
More corn-based dishes than you've ever seen in one place. Family restaurant, always packed. Good stop on the way back from the Central Pacific or after a visit to Zoo Ave. **$**
Xandari (international)
Tel: 2443 2020
Excellent open-air restaurant with valley view serves upscale fare, with an emphasis on organic, low-fat and vegetarian options. Excellent salads. **$$$**

Cartago

La Casona del Cafetal (Costa Rican/international)
Cachí, Cartago
Tel: 2577 1414
Popular stop on the Orosí loop, with panoramic view of the reservoir from terrace tables. Huge buffet with fish, pork, barbecue, salads, with notable array of coffee-flavored desserts. **$**
Restaurante 1910 (Costa Rican)
Irazú, Cartago
Tel: 2536 6063
Brimming with historical

memorabilia on the name-sake earthquake, a good stop for a hearty lunch after exploring Irazú Volcano. Lunch only Sun. **$$**
Sanchirí Mirador (Costa Rican/international)
Paraíso, Cartago
Tel: 2574 5454
The big draw here is the magnificent Orosí Valley view through huge glass windows. Simple local dishes, lots of meat. **$**

Escazú

Chez Christophe (French)
Across from Centro Comercial Paco
Tel: 2228 2512
The best French bakery in Costa Rica, now a café serving light lunches and dinners, creative salads, all accompanied by authentic French bread, on a terrace or in a cozy café. The *pains au chocolat* here transport you to France. **$–$$**
Di Bartolo (Italian)
Guachipelín road, Escazú
Tel: 2288 6787
Superb northern Italian dishes served in a Tuscan-inspired, elegant dining room; casual bar area, lined with wine racks, great for thin-crust pizza and authentic antipasti. The best veal Marsala in the

country. Expensive but worth it. **$$$**
Inka Grill (Peruvian)
Centro Comercial Paco, Escazú
Tel: 2289 5117
Perfectly prepared Peruvian dishes in an upscale, modern room. Try the chunky *ceviches* or the *causa limeña*, mashed potatoes filled with shrimp or chicken. **$$$**
Mirador Valle Azul (international)
San Antonio de Escazú
Tel: 2254 6281
One of the best views of the Central Valley. Decent, albeit pricey, fare and good service. Reservations recommended. **$$–$$$**

Heredia

Barco de Mariscos (Costa Rican/seafood)
San Rafael de Heredia, south of church
Tel: 2263 3909
Excellent *ceviche* – try one with avocado – and fish dishes in a rustically elegant 100-year-old wooden hacienda set in a rose garden, with both indoor and verandah tables. **$**
L'Antica Roma (Italian)
Ca. 7, Av. 7, Heredia
Tel: 2262 9073
Great thin-crust pizza baked

in wood-fired oven, served in candlelit, classic trattoria. **$**

Santa Ana

Bacchus (Mediterranean)
300 meters/yds east of Musmanni Bakery
Tel: 2282 5441
Excellent Mediterranean fare in a chic, restored historical house with a garden patio in downtown Santa Ana. Excellent desserts, including a winning Nutella crêpe. Reservations recommended. Closed Mon. **$$–$$$**
Taj Mahal (Indian)
1km (½ mile) west of Centro Comercial Paco, old road to Santa Ana
Tel: 2228 0980
The first exclusively Indian restaurant in the country, in an old mansion sumptuously decorated Indian-style, with indoor and garden tables. Authentic curries, biryanis, and tandoor. Will spice up dishes to your taste. Closed Mon. **$$–$$$**

Turrialba

Restaurante & Marisquería Don Porfí (Seafood)
5km (3 miles) north of Turrialba on volcano road

Tel: 2556 9797
Excellent seafood served in an elegant restaurant; try the casserole of corvina (sea bass) in a shrimp

béchamel sauce. **$–$$**
Restaurante Rancho del Sapito
12km (7 miles) west of Santa Cruz
Tel: 2534 1818

This typical mountain rancho roadside restaurant serves local cheese specialties, delicious fresh trout, and huge platters of

meat. There's lots of fun for children in the attached playground. Gets very busy on weekends. Closes 6.30pm. **$**

THE CENTRAL PACIFIC

Jacó Area

El Pelícano (Costa Rican/seafood)
Playa Herradura
Tel: 2637 8910
Open-air, beach-front restaurant with excellent fresh seafood and ocean breezes. **$$**
Jungle Surf Café (Tex-Mex/Costa Rican)
Playa Hermosa
Tel: 2643 1495
Tex-Mex, sandwiches, and burgers, hefty portions of fresh fish; lively surfer crowd. Bring your own wine in the evening. Closed Wed. **$**

Poseidon (seafood grill)
Hotel Poseidon
Downtown Jacó
Tel: 2643 1642
Noted for creative, trendy fish and seafood dishes. You can watch the chef at work in the open kitchen. **$$–$$$**

Manuel Antonio

Barba Roja (international)
Tel: 2777 0331
Popular gathering place for local people, especially in the late-night bar. Huge portions of good fresh fish. **$$**
Claro Que Sí (Costa Rican/seafood)
Sí Como No Hotel
Tel: 2777 0777
Outdoor, elegant dining with ocean view and live music. Caribbean-focused cuisine, with excellent fish and seafood. **$$$**
El Gran Escape (seafood)
Past bridge, entering Quepos
Tel: 2777 0395
Close to the fishing fleet, popular place serving generous portions of fresh fish. Sashimi makes a great appetizer. Closed Tue. **$$–$$$**
El Patio Bistro Latino (international)
Quepos

Tel: 2777 4982
Inventive fusion cuisine. Owners also run popular Café Milagro next door. **$$**
Sunspot Grill (international)
Hotel Makanda by the Sea
Tel: 2777 0442
Elegant open-air restaurant in adults-only hotel. Top-notch dishes, but the real draw is the romantic, poolside atmosphere. **$$$**
Vela Bar (seafood/vegetarian)
Vela Bar/Hotel
Tel: 2777 0413
Romantic, thatched-roof restaurant; seafood and Costa Rican dishes with vegetarian options. **$**

THE NORTHWEST

Flamingo Area

Marie's Restaurant (Costa Rican/seafood)
Playa Flamingo
Tel: 2654 4136
Traditional *casados*, hearty fish and seafood platters; shrimp-stuffed avocado for a light lunch. Save room for famous banana-chocolate bread pudding. **$–$$**
Mar y Sol Restaurant and Bar (French/Mediterranean)
Playa Flamingo
Tel: 2654 5222
Sophisticated, southwest French fare with innovative tropical twists, served on romantic, breezy terrace with unbeatable view of sky, sea, and sunsets. Excellent wine list and polished service. **$$–$$$**

Inland

Restaurante y Marisquería Paso Real (seafood)
South side of Central Park, Liberia
Tel: 2666 3455
A happy buzz here, on

second-floor balcony. Excellent *ceviche, sopa de mariscos* (seafood soup), and shrimp-topped fish fillet. **$$–$$$**
Tres Hermanas BBQ (barbecue)
Interamerican Hwy at Tempisque Bridge turn-off, Abangares
Tel: 2662 8583
Look for a giant bull by the road side and come hungry for spicy, slow-cooked barbecued beef, pork, and chicken. Some fish, too, but this is carnivore country. Unusual sides of stewed lentils, spiced carrots. **$–$$**

Monteverde

El Márquez (seafood)
Main street, Santa Elena
Tel: 2645 5918
Best place for fresh seafood. Casual atmosphere, excellent value. Try to get a table with a view of the bird-filled garden. **$**
Johnny's Pizzería (Italian)
Road to Monteverde Reserve
Tel: 2645 5066

Reliably good, thin-crust pizza baked in wood-fired oven, and a killer baked-pasta casserole for really hungry customers. Lovely patio tables looking onto a lush, tranquil garden. **$$**
Restaurante de Lucía (surf and turf)
Tel: 2645 6659
Hearty meals with a Chilean accent amid South American decor. Choose your own cut of meat or fresh fish to be cooked to order, and save room for the creamy *tres leches* cake. **$$**
Sofia (new Latino)
Tel: 2645 7017
Innovative fare served in a stylish restaurant with two dining rooms. Ask for a table with a jungle view. Tasty squash and plantain soup. **$$**

Nosara to Sámara

Giardino Tropicale (Italian)
Playa Guiones
Tel: 2682 4000
Best brick-oven pizzas in

town plus delicious carpaccio of marlin. Dollops of the chef's own hot-pepper sauce spice up pizzas. Very popular and busy, but worth the wait. **$–$$**
Café de Paris (international)
Guiones Beach, Nosara
Tel: 2682 0087
French bread and pastries, and killer chocolate tarts. Famous nachos, excellent salads, plus more sophisticated meats and fish with sauces, served in airy rancho. **$$**
Pizza & Pasta a Go Go
Hotel Giada, Sámara
Tel: 2656 0132
Authentically Italian pizzas and pastas, and an extensive wine list to match, in a casual terrace restaurant. Exceptional tiramisú. **$$**

PRICE CATEGORIES

Prices are for dinner for two:
$$$ = US$50 plus
$$ = US$25–50
$ = US$25 or less

Papagayo to Ocotal

Ginger (tapas/fusion)
Playa Hermosa
Tel: 2672 0041
Tasty and trendy tapas in chic, modern dining room. Asian-fusion with some Mediterranean flavors. Very popular, so be sure to reserve. Closed Mon. **$$**

Villa del Sueño
(Mediterranean)
Playa Hermosa
Tel: 2672 0026
Elegant French-leaning restaurant, most formal in the area, with gourmet-level meat and seafood. Shrimp-topped *mahi-mahi* is tops. Cool jazz and easy rock on weekends, plus occasional concerts. **$$–$$$**

Puntarenas

Restaurante y Marisquería La Leda
(seafood)
Mata Limón (near Caldera)
Tel: 2634 4087
Fresh, flavorful *ceviches* and garlicky *chuchecas* – black clams only found around Puntarenas, served on a terrace overlooking a tidal lagoon. **$–$$**

Restaurante La Yunta
(seafood)
Paseo de los Turistas
Tel: 2661 3216
Old-fashioned, breezy veran-dah, facing gulf. Classic surf and turf, with some interest-ing tropical-fruit sauces for fish and chicken. **$–$$**

Southern Nicoya

El Sano Banano Restaurant (café/international)
Main street, Montezuma
Tel: 2642 0638
Popular hang-out with deli-cious vegetarian, fish, and chicken dishes; emphasis on natural, healthy ingredi-ents. Delicious ice-cream concoctions. Nightly movie screening. **$–$$**

Peninsula
Néctar (international)
Florblanca Resort, Santa Teresa
Tel: 2640 0232
Romantic, poolside spot with sophisticated Mediter-ranean/Pacific Rim cuisine. Sushi menu and daily fresh fish specials. Reservations recommended. **$$$**

Playa de los Artistas
(Mediterranean)
South side of Montezuma
Tel: 2642 0920
Arguably the country's most romantic dining spot, perched on surf-swept rocks. Excellent fish and seafood platters, served Italian style. Closed Sun, and mid-May to mid-June; mid-Sept to mid-Nov. **$$$**

Tamarindo to Junquilla

Dragonfly Bar & Grill
(international)
Tamarindo
Tel: 653 1506
Creative seafood and meat dishes with Asian influen-ces, in stylish, garden setting. Vegetarian options. Reservations recommended on weekends. **$$**

El Coconut
Tamarindo
Tel: 2653 0086
Seafood and fish with un-usual tropical sauces, plus surf and turf in an elegant, open-air restaurant; more formal than most other beach restaurants and pricier, but worth it. **$$–$$$**

Lola's (international)
Playa Avellanas
Tel: 2652 9097
Funky, beach restaurant with lots of vegetarian options. Lunch only, and excellent fruit drinks and cocktails until sunset. Closed Mon, and Oct to mid-Nov. **$–$$**

Seasons by Shlomy
(Mediterranean)
Arco Iris Hotel, Tamarindo
Tel: 8368 6983
Cordon Bleu-trained chef serves excellent fresh Mediterranean-fusion creations and spicy sashimi, sautéed calamari. Will also cook your own catch. Deli-cious desserts. **$$–$$$**

THE NORTHEAST

Alajuela

El Mirador (Costa Rican)
On road to Poás Volcano
Tel: 2441 9347
Good meats and seafood and a magnificent view of Central Valley below. **$–$$**

Arenal Lake

Gingerbread (continental)
Nuevo Arenal
Tel: 2694 0039
Sophisticated restaurant serving continental-style beef and pork with selection of whatever fish is freshest. Home-made desserts. **$$**

Mystica (Italian)
Nuevo Arenal
Tel: 2692 1001
Excellent thin-crust pizzas and home-made pasta in a hilltop restaurant overlooking windy west end of Lake Arenal. **$$**

Willy's Caballo Negro
(German/vegetarian)
3km (2 miles) west of Nuevo Arenal
Tel: 694 4515
Hearty Teutonic fare – pork schnitzels, sausages – side by side with vegetarian food. First-rate arts and crafts gallery attached. **$**

La Fortuna

Don Rufino
(international)
Across from gas station
Tel: 2479 9997
Relaxed atmosphere in town's most elegant restaurant; good steaks and decent salads; bar area is popular tourist hang-out. **$$**

La Choza de Laurel
(Costa Rican)
100 meters/yds northwest of church
Tel: 2479 7063
Ideal for breakfast. Chickens roasting on a huge rotisserie are irresistible. **$–$$**

Lava Rocks Café (Costa Rican/international)
Tel: 2479 8039
A cut above the usual *soda*; fruit smoothies and plates of rice, beans, and meat. Good budget option. **$**

Varablanca

Restaurant Francés Colbert
(French)
Tel: 2482 2776
Fantastic French food, deca-dent pastries, in elegant auberge with wood stove and close-up views of hummingbirds at feeders. Perfect stop after visiting Volcán Poás or La Paz Waterfall Gardens. Lunch and early supper. Closed Thur. **$$**

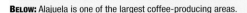

BELOW: Alajuela is one of the largest coffee-producing areas.

PRICE CATEGORIES

Prices are for dinner for two:
$$$ = US$50 plus
$$ = US$25–50
$ = US$25 or less

THE CARIBBEAN COAST

Cahuita

Cha Cha Chá (eclectic)
Main street
Tel: 2755 0476
Mediterranean/Thai mix,
prepared by Québécois chef
in town's most sophisti-
cated restaurant. Laid-back
vibe, excellent service.
Closed Mon. **$$–$$$**
Miss Edith (Caribbean/
Costa Rican)
Near Police Station
Tel: 2755 0248
Local institution with spicy
curries and, on Sundays,
rondón, Caribbean-style
root-vegetable stew with
fish. Sit on beach while you
wait for your order. **$–$$**

Playa Cocles

La Pecora Nera (Italian)
Playa Cocles

Tel: 2750 0490
Top Italian restaurant on
Caribbean coast, featuring
delicate Tuscan pasta dishes,
savory tuna carpaccio, and
perfectly cooked fish.
Attentive service, including
table visits by the chef.
Dinner only. Closed Mon.
Also owns nearby Gatta Ci
Cova, open for lunch. **$$$**

Manzanillo

Maxi's
On beach
Tel: 2759 9073
Worth the drive to the end
of the road to feast on
locally caught fish and
lobster, served on platters
with salad and *patacones*
(plantain fritters). Breezy
upstairs dining rooms, atop
bar vibrating at night with
reggae. **$$**

Puerto Viejo

Amimodo (Italian)
South Main Street,
Puerto Viejo
Tel: 2750 0257
Delicious Italian-by-the-sea
cuisine; lobster ravioli is a
standout. Romantic tables
under thatched roof, right
on beach. **$$–$$$**
Bread and Chocolate
(café)
South of Post Office
Tel: 2750 0723
Chocolate-lover's delight;
brownies and Queen of
Sheba chocolate cake.
Open for breakfast and
lunch till 6pm, with
scrumptious oatmeal-
banana pancakes, hearty
jerk-chicken sandwiches,
and coffee in individual
French presses. Closed Mon
and Tue. **$**

Chile Rojo
(Thai/Middle Eastern)
Main Street
Tel: 2750 0319
Exotic flavors, including
hummus, samosas, Thai-
grilled tuna, and tasty
vegetarian options. **$$**
Soda Miss Sam
(Costa Rican/Caribbean)
Tel: 2750 0108
Simple Caribbean staples –
fish with coconut rice –
served on rickety wooden
verandah. **$**

Tortuguero

Miss Junie's
(Caribbean)
Tel: 709 8102
An institution in Tortuguero,
Miss Junie serves
inexpensive, stick-to-your-
ribs fare in her simple
open-air restaurant. **$**

THE SOUTH

Dominical

Coconut Spice (Thai)
Downtown Dominical
Tel: 2787 0073
Spicy South Asian fare:
curries, butter shrimp, and
tom yan goong soup, served
on wooden deck with river
views. **$$**
ConFusione (Italian)
Hotel Domilocos, south end of
Dominical beach
Tel: 2787 0244
Sophisticated restaurant,
authentic wood-fired pizzas,
creative pastas, fresh
seafood. Good wine list. **$$**
La Parcela (international)
4km/2½ miles south of Dominical
Tel: 2787 0016
Dramatic setting on breezy,
rocky point. Excellent
seafood, delicious desserts,
great fruit shakes. **$$$**

Ojochal

Citrus (eclectic)
Entrance to town
Tel: 2786 5175
Stylish, Moroccan-inspired
setting; riverside garden
tables. New-world cuisine,

Mediterranean to Thai, plus
classic French *escargots*
and duck. Great cake and
desserts. Branch in San
Isidro de El General. Closed
Sun and Mon. **$$–$$$**
Restaurant Exótica
(French/international)
Tel: 2786 5050
Acclaimed French cuisine
with tropical accents served
on airy patio. Breakfast,
lunch, and dinner. Free Wi-fi
at breakfast and lunch.
Closed Sun. **$$–$$$**

Pavones

Café de la Suerte
(vegetarian)
Tel: 2776 2388
An oasis of hearty, inventive
vegetarian cuisine in the
outback. Delicious home-
made yogurt and hummus
and frothy fruit *naturales*.
Free Wi-fi. **$**

Puerto Jiménez

Corcovado Marisquería
(seafood)
Waterfront near city dock
Tel: 2735 5659

Huge selection of appetizers
such as *ceviche* and fried
shrimp, plus plates of
seafood rice, at tables
scattered around garden.
Open till 11pm daily. **$**
Pizza Mail.it (Italian)
Beside post office
Tel: 2735 5483
Terrific pizza plus home-
made pastas cooked by
Trieste couple, on cheerful
terrace overlooking soccer
field. Open 4–10pm only.
Closed Tue. **$**

San Vito

Pizzería Liliana (Italian)
West of Central Park
Tel: 2773 3080
Family-run, serving great
pizza and home-made pasta
dishes. Tables on plant-filled
terrace are best. **$**

Santa María de Dota

Café de los Santos
San Marcos de Tarrazú
(Ruta de los Santos)
Tel: 2546 7881
Lovely spot to take a break.
Choose from dozens of

coffee specialties and light
pastries, both savory and
sweet. Closed Sun. **$**

Stopovers on the Mountain of Death

There are plenty of road-
side stops along the winding
mountain road, with
24-hour buffets and
capacious toilet facilities.
The most famous trio of
rest stops is the friendly **Los
Chespiritos** chain, with
outposts at Km 51, 61, and
78, which serve inexpensive
local fare. The most historic
stop is the white wooden
Restaurant La Georgina,
Km 95. Along with typical
Tico buffet fare you get wild
hummingbirds coming for a
sip of sugar water at the
feeders outside the window.
For a more substantial
lunch, stop at **Mirador
Vista del General** (tel:
2200 5465) at Km 119,
famous for fried rainbow
trout, and bird feeders that
attract exquisite birds to the
restaurant's garden.

A CTIVITIES

FESTIVALS, THE ARTS, NIGHTLIFE, SHOPPING, SPORTS, AND HIKING

FESTIVALS

(PH = public holiday)
January 1 Culmination of week-long festivities in San José and other locations *(Fiestas del Fin del Año)*. Celebrations continue on the following day. PH
Mid-January Fiestas in Santa Cruz (Nicoya Peninsula) with rodeos, bullfights, music, and dancing; giant music festival in Palmares (Alajuela).
February/March Annual Orchid Show; also the best time to see orchids in bloom at Lankester Gardens, Cartago. San José National Theater Symphony season begins in March. Rodeos in San José. The Caribbean and Monteverde hold music festivals in March.
Mid-March National Handicraft Fair, downtown San José. Feast of San José (St Joseph), patron saint of San José. *Día del Boyero* (Day of the Ox-Cart Driver) parade and blessing of the ox-carts *(carretas)*, San Antonio de Escazú.
March/April *Semana Santa*, Holy Week: banks, post offices, and government offices, as well as most shops and restaurants, are closed Thursday and Friday. *Jueves Santo*, Holy Thursday. PH; start of Holy Week ceremonies. *Viernes Santo*, Good Friday: religious processions at 1am and 4pm. PH. "Roman soldiers," biblical personages, and black-clad mourners; San Joaquín de Flores, Heredia, has one of the most impressive processions.
April 11 Juan Santamaría Day; hero of Costa Rica, died in the Battle of Rivas in action against William Walker in 1856; celebrated

especially in Alajuela. PH
May 1 Labor Day: Workers' March in San José. Election of the president of Congress. PH
May/June Feast of Corpus Christi on the Thursday after Trinity Sunday.
June 29 Feast of Sts Peter and Paul.
July 25 *Anexión de Guanacaste*. The president commemorates the annexation of Guanacaste province; horseback parades and concerts. PH
August 2 *Nuestra Señora de los Angeles*, Feast of Patron Saint of Costa Rica, at the Basilica in Cartago. Thousands of pilgrims converge on Cartago in the preceding days. PH
August 15 Feast of the Assumption, and Mother's Day. PH
September 15 Independence Day. Independence from Spain (since 1821) is celebrated nationwide. At 6pm on the 14th, everyone sings the national anthem. PH
October 12 Columbus Day, *El Día de la Raza* (also called *El Día de las Culturas*). Week-long Carnival in Puerto Limón with floats, dance contests, and an elaborate parade. PH

What's On

The *Tico Times* newspaper (in English) publishes a calendar of activities and shows in its weekly edition (Friday), as well as a daily brief with selected events on its Daily News Page (www.ticotimes.net/daily.htm). The Spanish-language daily *La Nación* publishes an extensive events calendar in its Friday *Tiempo Libre* section, as well as daily theater and music ads.
  AM Costa Rica (www.amcostarica.com/calendar.htm) has fairly comprehensive online listings.

Mid-December: Festival of Lights: gigantic Christmas parade, fireworks throughout the month.
December 25/last week of year: Christmas Day. PH. *Festejos Populares*, with fireworks and activities in Zapote, December 25 to January 3. Parade of horses *(tope)* December 26 noon, downtown San José.

THE ARTS

Art & Galleries

An active artists' community in the city keeps the art scene alive.
  More than 30 galleries showcase creativity that runs the gamut from an in-depth survey of Costa Rican art from colonial through modern periods (the Museo de Arte Costarricense) and indigenous masks from the country's southern Boruca region (Galería Namú) to local and traveling experimental and multimedia installations (Jakob Karpio, TEORética).
  The **Costa Rica Art Tour** (tel: 8359 5571, www.costaricaarttour.com) showcases several artist-run studios; reservations are recommended for this day tour of five studios/galleries.

Music

The Costa Rican music scene is dominated by Editus, the jazzy fusion trio that has won two Grammies for its work with Panamanian singer-songwriter Rubén Blades, and by Manuel Obregón, an internationally renowned pianist, now the culture minister. Vibrant music festivals in Monteverde and the Caribbean, as well as the Credomatic International Music

Festival, showcase musicians in venues ranging from the rainforest to the National Theater.

Local *mariachis* serenade diners in some traditional restaurants, and the mellow sounds of the *marimba* (a large, wooden xylophone) can be enjoyed in city squares and at many hotels. While best known for its reggae, the jewel of the Caribbean music scene is Walter Ferguson, a calypso legend.

The National Orchestra season runs March–November. Costa Rica-based Papaya Music captures many local sounds in its wide selection of recordings *(see Shopping, page 284)*.

Dance

Costa Rica's modern dance scene is one of the best in Central America. The **National Dance Company** performs both classical and modern works, some by Central American choreographers. The **Teatro Melico Salazar** on Av. 2, Ca. Ctrl in San José stages productions several times a month; another regular dance venue is the **Teatro Nacional** on the Plaza de la Cultura. Tickets can be bought at very reasonable prices.

Theater

Spanish-language offerings at several small-scale venues lean towards bawdy humor, peppered with thoughtful dramas and political pieces. Most recently, the long-running *El Nica* (The Nicaraguan) by César Meléndez, a one-man portrait of a Nicaraguan immigrant in Costa Rica, became a runaway hit, making a splash as far away as the United States. The expatriate-driven **Little Theatre Group** is Costa Rica's oldest theatrical troupe and puts on at least four English-language productions a year. Ticket prices are very cheap, tel: 8858 1446; www.littletheatregroup.org.

The **National Theater** and **Melico Salazar Theater** publish their schedules online in Spanish *(see Getting Tickets in box)*.

Movies

San José, Escazú, San Pedro, and Curridabat have multiple cinemas, most in malls, showing movies that are usually several months behind releases in North America. Tickets are $5 or less; Wednesday shows at most theaters are half-price. Animated features or other movies for children are usually dubbed in Spanish, with subtitled screenings at larger cinemas.

Getting Tickets

Major international headliners are often sponsored by the credit-card company Credomatic, and sometimes early sales are restricted to Credomatic card holders. There is no major central ticket agency in Costa Rica; points of sale, usually stores, vary according to sponsors; *La Nación* ads generally list the ticket outlets. Tickets for local theater and musical presentations can be purchased by phone at major theaters, in person at the box office, or, in the case of the National Theater, online.

Mundo Ticket, tel: 2206 7770, www.mundoticket.com
Limited listings of sports, theater, music, and other events for online purchase (in Spanish).
National Theater, tel: 2221 5341, www.teatronacional.go.cr (in Spanish)
Melico Salazar Theater, tel: 2233 5172 or 2257 4483, www.teatro melico.go.cr (in Spanish)

Venues are popping up around the country: in Heredia, Liberia, San Ramón, San Carlos, and San Isidro de El General. Check the *Tico Times* for English descriptions of movies and theater information; *La Nación* provides a more detailed grid of times and locations, along with ads (which are useful if you don't recognize the Spanish titles).

Bookstores

7th Street Books, Ca. 7, Av. Central 1, tel: 2256 8251.
Best-known English-language bookstore in San José has a large selection of travel guides, maps, Latin American studies, reference books, and posters. Run by helpful owners.
Librería Internacional, Multiplaza, Escazú; Barrio Dent; Mall Internacional, Alajuela; Heredia and Rohrmoser, tel: 2253 9553; www. libreriainternacional.com. English and Spanish books.

Latin Dance Classes

Learning a few salsa, *merengue*, or energetic *cumbia* steps adds a kinetic joy to your trip, and will come in handy if you plan on hitting the town at night. Your best bet is well-established Merecumbé, which offers group and private classes at several studios around the country. Most language

schools offer an optional dance component.
Centro Merecumbé, tel/fax: 2224 3531; www.merecumbe.net. Studios in San Pedro, Guadalupe, Rohrmoser, Heredia, Alajuela, Escazú, and Cartago. The most popular classes are from 7–9pm, and it's a great way to meet people.

NIGHTLIFE

Nightclubs & Dancing

San José's nightlife offers up a decent variety for the slim offerings. Karaoke, Latin dance clubs, techno, reggae, US-style classic rock, jazz, and gay-friendly establishments can all be sniffed out.

The **Centro Commercial El Pueblo**, near Villa Tournón in northeast San José, is a complex of boutiques, galleries, restaurants, nightclubs, and bars; some stay open until 4am.

Calle de la Amargura (Street of Bitterness) a boisterous street of restaurants and bars near the University of Costa Rica in San Pedro, is popular with a younger crowd. Both places have been the sites of violence (not involving tourists), but are generally safe – for partiers alert enough to keep an eye on their drinks and belongings, and to take cabs.

Outside of the capital, options are generally limited to bar/restaurants, but Tamarindo, Manuel Antonio (Quepos), Jacó, and Puerto Viejo offer up a handful of hopping nightspots.

San José

Castro's
Av. 13, Ca. 22
Tel: 2256 8789.
Crowded. Good place to practice Latin dance moves. While the bar is safe, the area is not so hot – take a taxi.
Club Oh!
Ca. 2, Av. 14–16
Tel: 2221 9341
Formerly Dejá Vu, still gay-friendly but caters to a more varied crowd now. Electronic music.
El Cuartel de la Boca del Monte
Av. 1, Ca. 21–3
Tel: 221 0327.
Situated downtown, close to Cine Magaly, this is a popular singles bar. Live music, packed on Monday.

Jacó

Ganesha Lounge
Tel: 2643 3916, www.ganeshaloungejaco.com

Next to the Hotel Balcón del Mar, this is a hotspot for dancing. Buy two get one free on Tuesday and Thursday.
Murphy's Monkey Bar
Tel: 2643 2357
Roots, hip-hop and more.

Puerto Viejo
Baba Yaga
Tel: 2750 0587
This disco features reggae nights, ladies' nights, and happy hours.
Johnny's Place
Perched on the beach in the heart of Puerto Viejo, Johnny's Place plays a mix of reggae and hip-hop. It fills on the weekend with locals and tourists.

Quepos
Bambu Jam
Tel: 2777 3369, www.bambujam.com
Live music Tuesday and Friday.
Hotel Byblos
Tel: 2777 0411,
www.bybloshotelcostarica.com
With a casino, late-night restaurant and sports bar, there is definitely variety when it comes to spending a night at Hotel Byblos.
Liquid Lounge
Tel: 2777 5158
A new gay-friendly bar located in Manuel Antonio. Closed Monday.

Tamarindo
AQUA Discoteque
Tel: 2653 1782, www.aquadiscoteque.com
A 600 sq meter (720 sq yd) club featuring VIP areas, lounge spaces, and dance floor.

Monkey Bar
The Monkey Bar is one of the busiest places on Friday nights. Located in the Best Western, it features two dance floors, one with live music.

Escazú
Trejos Montealegre shopping center
Several bars, most popular with young, upscale crowd.

Bars

In San José try the following:
Henry's Beach Café and Grill, San Rafael de Escazú, tel: 2289 6250, www.henrysbeachcafe.com. Good mix of local people and expatriates; sophisticated crowd, and a popular venue.
Jazz Café, next to the Banco Popular, San Pedro, tel: 2253 8933. Best live music venue, varied menu. Also has a location in Escazú.
Calle de la Amargura, near the University of Costa Rica, is lined with

a variety of spots, from cheap college drinking holes to outdoor bar/restaurants. Extremely popular.

Gay Venues

La Avispa
Ca. 1, Av. 8–10, tel: 2223 5343.
Salsa/merengue. Three dance floors and pool tables. Women only one Friday a month.
El Bochinche
Ca. 11, Av. 10–12, tel: 2221 0500.
Pop music.

Casinos

Hotel Fiesta
Puntarenas
Tel: 2663 0808
7pm–11am.
Hotel Irazú
San José
General Cañas Highway
Tel: 2232 4811
11am–5am.
Hotel San José Palacio
San José
Tel: 2220 2034
5pm–3am.
Hotel Corobicí Crowne Plaza
Sabana Norte
Tel: 2232 8122
3pm–2am.
Club Colonial
Downtown San José
Tel: 2258 2807
11am–5am.

SHOPPING

What to Buy

Costa Rica's selection of souvenirs has been increasing slowly but steadily over the past few years. The traditional classics – ox-carts, wood products, indigenous masks, and coffee – are now sold alongside locally produced CDs that rival any world-music offering. It is also worth checking out conservation organizations, such as ANAI *(see Conservation page 289)*, which raise money by selling beautiful souvenirs. Bartering is low-key, but even in malls you can usually get a discount off the ticket price for paying cash.
The following products can be found just about everywhere.

Ceramics

Be skeptical of many of the "indigenous" ceramics you see for sale. The best are made in the northern Pacific area – Guaitil and

What to Avoid

Visitors **should not** purchase any of the following:
• Coral
• Tortoiseshell items
• Furs (such as ocelot or jaguar)
• Items made from tropical hardwoods (such as mahogany, laurel, and purple heart – if in doubt, ask the seller what kind of wood has been used)
• Anything made from crocodile, caiman, or lizard skins

Santa Cruz – where artisans still use pre-Columbian pottery techniques.

Coffee

Costa Rican coffee is excellent and relatively inexpensive. Café Britt stands out for its wide variety of top-quality coffee in flashy packages – great for gifts, and available in grocery stores and gift shops. Top-quality Coopedota coffee from the Tarrazú region is available in some supermarkets. If it is just what's inside that counts, rather than the packaging, Café Rey and Café Volio are good, inexpensive alternatives.

Woodwork

Wooden items, including bowls, plates, cutting boards, and boxes, are widely available in most gift shops. The mountain town of Sarchí is known for its woodwork. The finest quality wooden boxes and bowls are made by Barry Biesanz of Biesanz Woodworks. He welcomes visitors to his beautiful, light-filled studio in Bello Horizonte, near Escazú: www.biesanz.com.

Leatherwork

Leather bags, wallets, and briefcases are good quality and available in many stores throughout the Central Valley. While they are a bit bulkier, fold-up leather rocking chairs, packed for shipping, are a great deal.

Woven Bags

Look for interesting woven-cotton bags and hats colored with natural dyes by indigenous artisans, available at many locations.

Jewelry

Inexpensive handmade earrings and jewelry are sold everywhere, including street artisans' stalls in San José.

Music

Papaya Music releases are available at 7th Street Books, Universal,

Lehman's, and many other stores, featuring local legends and traditional tunes. The great sounds, funky art, and English liner notes for tourists make the CDs a great souvenir.

Paper
Beautiful handmade papers, made from recycled plant materials – bananas, coffee, mangoes – and using natural dyes, are sold in many gift stores.

Camping Equipment
Alumicamping, Moravia, tel: 2225 1532. Purchase, rental, and repair of tents and other equipment.
Centro de Aventura, North side of the former Guadalupe rotunda, tel: 2257 0253, www.centrodeaventura.net. One of the best-equipped stores.

Other Items
There is the usual array of tourist souvenir goods: T-shirts, painted feathers, and watercolors of country life in every tourist destination.

Where to Shop

After weaving through shelf after shelf of decorative miniature ox-carts and polished wooden place mats you may decide it's worth a trip further afield. In Sarchí, famed for the aforementioned carts (carretas) and wood products, there are other craft products that will catch your eye and you can watch the artisans at work.

Shops outside San José are more likely to have unique offerings from local craftspeople. But if you're looking for convenience, the following are some of the best places to find the above items in the Central Valley.

San José
There are craft stalls in the **Plaza de la Democracia**, next to the national museum, at **La Casona**, Ca. Central, Av. Central – 1, and at the **central market**.
Galería Namú, Av. 7, Ca. 5 – 7, tel: 2256 3412, has an excellent selection of local art and indigenous crafts.
Annemarie Boutique, in Hotel Don Carlos, Av. 9, Ca. 9, tel: 2233 5343, sells ceramics, wooden souvenirs, and jewelry.
Jagua Arts & Crafts, beside the airfield in Puerto Jiménez, has individual original jewelry and the best selection of local arts and crafts.

Moravia
About 100 meters/yds south of the Red Cross (Cruz Roja). Souvenir shops

and arts and crafts galleries line two city blocks in the center of town. Look out for hand-painted wall mirrors.

SPORT

Birdwatching

Costa Rica has more than 850 species of birds, including macaws, hummingbirds, kingfishers, toucans, trogons, and the rather shy resplendent quetzal. For an entertaining overall view of what's happening, birding-wise, in the country, visit expert guide Patrick O'Donnell's birding blog: www.birding craft.com/wordpress.
The following lodges and tour companies offer excellent birding:
Paraíso del Quetzal Mountain Lodge
Km 70 Interamerican Highway
Tel: 2771 4582
www.paraisodelquetzal.com
One of the most reliable places to spot a quetzal.
Costa Rica Birding Journeys
Tel: 8889 8815 (Costa Rica), 970-315 4023 (international)
www.costaricabirdingjourneys.org
Experienced guide, focusing on trips in Carara National Park. Tours for beginners as well.
Costa Rica Expeditions
Tel: 2257 076
www.costaricaexpeditions.com.
Birding trips with well-trained local guides.
Horizontes
Tel: 2222 2022
www.horizontes.com.
Customized birding trips, including bird photography tours.
Keköldi Wak Ka Koneke
Tel: 2756 8033

Indigenous group gives migratory bird tours in the southern Caribbean (best from Feb to Apr).
Organization for Tropical Studies
Tel: 2524 0607
www.ots.ac.cr
OTS arranges bilingual group trips and runs La Selva Biological Station.
Savegre Hotel de Montaña
Tel: 2740 1029
www.savegre.co.cr
Excellent birding trails and guides; highland species and quetzals.

Bungee Jumping

The 80-meter (265ft) gorge below the Río Colorado bridge will pass before your eyes (if you can keep them open) on these plunges. Both companies listed below are based approximately one hour northwest of San José, in Grecia.
Costa Rica Bungee and Rappel Adventures, tel/fax: 2494 5102
www.bungeecostarica.com.
Tropical Bungee, tel: 2248 2212
www.bungee.co.cr

Cycling

You can rent a bicycle from bike shops around the country. Road biking tours are available, but this is more mountain-bike territory. Favorite routes include the trails around Lake Arenal in the Northern Zone, the rolling hills of Orosí or, for the hard-core, a Caribbean-to-Pacific trek. Most companies specializing in cycling tours provide excellent equipment, but you are welcome to bring your own (check with airlines on their bicycle policy). For Sunday-style riders, most towns and many hotels have bike rentals, although the equipment quality tends to be a bit more wobbly.

BELOW: avid birdwatchers at La Tigra, in the south.

Bi.Costa Rica, tel/fax: 2446 7585; www.bruncas.com/bicostarica.html. Knowledgeable owner; variety of tours around the country.
Coast to Coast Adventures
Tel: 2280 8054
www.ctocadventures.com
Combination adventure trips (biking, trekking, rafting, kayaking). Known for two-week coast-to-coast trip. No motor vehicles.
Lava Tours
Tel: 2278 2558 or 888-862 2424 (US and Canada)
www.lava-tours.com
Mountain biking and adventure tours.

Diving

Underwater visibility is best during the dry season (Nov–Apr). October is usually the best month on the Caribbean coast. Northern Guanacaste, the west side of the Osa Peninsula, and the Southern Caribbean have the best diving.
Costa Rica Adventure Divers
In Hotel Jinetes de Osa, Drake Bay
Tel: 2231 5806 or (US) 303-339-0221
www.costaricadiving.com
Also offers underwater cameras.
Diving Safaris, Playa Hermosa, Guanacaste, tel: 2672 1259, fax: 2672 0231, www.costaricadiving.net.
Costa Rica's largest and oldest operation. Diving expeditions, equipment rental, and diver certification classes.
Ocotal Beach Resort
Playa Ocotal
Tel: 2670 0321
www.ocotalresort.com
Has a full-service diving operation.
Reef Runner Divers
Puerto Viejo
Tel: 2750 0480 or 8337 2033
www.reefrunnerdivers.com
South Caribbean coast diving.
Aguamor Talamanca Adventures
Manzanillo
Tel: 2759 0612
Diving trips, courses, and equipment rental at entrance to Gandoca-Manzanillo Wildlife Refuge.

Fishing

Fishing permits are required and are usually taken care of by fishing guides. On the Pacific, permits are paid for just before boarding the boat. On the Caribbean, they are bought at lodges; some lodges provide all-inclusive deals. Costa Rica now has a combination fishing license for freshwater and saltwater. If you encounter rangers while fishing, they

will ask you to present your permit and your passport (a copy of which may suffice).
Good sources of information on fishing in Costa Rica are:
Carlos Barrantes, La Casa del Pescador, a tackle shop at Ca. 2, Av. 16–18, tel: 2222 1470.
Costa Rica Outdoors, a fountain of fishing information (tel: 2231 0306/800-308 3394, www.costaricaoutdoors.com), publishes fishing columns bimonthly in *Costa Rica Outdoors* and arranges fishing expeditions around the country.

Golf

If you're looking to tee off between ecotours, your options outside of the Central Valley are concentrated in major hotels along the Pacific. Most are open to the public, and equipment is available for rent.
Costa Rica Golf Adventures, tel: 239 5176 or 877-258 2688, www.golfcr.com, is a good information source for golfing in Costa Rica.
Los Delfines Golf and Country Club, tel: 2683 0333, Tambor. 9-hole course.
Cariari Country Club, tel: 2293 3211, Cariari, northwest of San José. 18-hole course. Open to members and guests of the Ramada Inn.
Four Seasons Resort, tel: 2696 0000, Papagayo, on the Northern Pacific coast. 18-hole Arnold Palmer-designed course; hotel guests only.
Hacienda Pinilla, tel: 2680 7000, outside of Tamarindo. 18-hole course, wide fairways.
Los Reyes Country Club, tel: 2438 0004, Guácima, Alajuela. 9-hole course, open to the public Sun–Fri.
Marriott Los Sueños Golf Resort, tel: 2630 9000, Playa Herradura on the Central Pacific. 18-hole Ted Robinson-designed golf course.
Paradisus Playa Conchal, tel: 2654 4123, Playa Conchal. 18-hole course. Guests only.
Parque Valle del Sol, tel: 2282 9222, Santa Ana. 18-hole course.
Tango Mar Resort, tel: 2683 0001, Nicoya Peninsula near Tambor. 9-hole course.

Hiking

Hiking is an inherent part of most visits to Costa Rica, whether it's wandering through a national park spotting sloths or getting to the next hanging bridge to admire the canopy.
Chirripó (3,820 meters/12,533ft) is Costa Rica's highest peak. While 10 walk-ins per day are accepted, traffic for the two-day trip is capped at 35

people per day, so make a reservation at least a month ahead of time. Fit and experienced hikers can also ranger-station hop across Corcovado National Park, a three-day trip. In addition to the following resources, most adventure tour operators can arrange hiking and trekking trips according to your ability.
Corcovado National Park
Tel: 2735 5580
www.acosa-cr.org
In charge of reservations to hike Corcovado; the website has lots of information, but only in Spanish.
Chirripó Nacional Park
Tel: 2742 5083
www.aguastierras.com; www.chirriporural.org
The above websites offer good information on how to hike Chirripó. For reservations, call the park office or email: reservacioneschirripo@gmail.com

Horseback Riding

Horseback riding is widely available in Costa Rica, from hour-long rides on the beach to a riding break on a working cattle ranch. The following offer interesting options:
Caballeriza El Rodeo, book with Desafío Adventures, tel: 2479 9464, www.desafiocostarica.com. Horse-friendly option for Monteverde–La Fortuna ride.
Centro Ecuestre Valle de Yos-Oy
Tel: 2282 3222
Horseback tours around Santa Ana, in the western Central Valley.
Finca Los Caballos, Montezuma, tel/fax: 2642 0124, www.naturelodge.net. Four-hour trail rides through beautiful scenery.
La Garza, Planatar, tel: 2475 5222, fax: 2475 5015, www.hotellagarza.com. Ranch with *cabinas* and horses.

Hot-Air Ballooning

Available through **Serendipity Adventures**, tel: 2558 1000, fax: 2558 1010, www.serendipityadventures.com. Balloon trips start from Talajari Hotel near Ciudad Quesada.

Kite-Surfing

New to Costa Rica, kite-surfing is really only found on the North Pacific.
Kitesurfing Center and School
Playa Papaturo, near Playa Copal
Tel: 8826 5221
www.bluedreamhotel.com
Instructor Nicola Bertoldi gets you up in the air with lessons and equipment. Associated Blue Dream Hotel and Spa has 14 cabins and a restaurant.

Mountaineering

Costa Rica is not known for climbing, since the most challenging spots are excessively difficult to get to. If you're looking for a little bouldering and some climbing, Cachí, near Cartago, is the place to go. **Mundo Aventura**, Paseo Colón, tel: 2221 6934, www.maventura.com. Has a climbing wall and a fledgling climbing culture, and is able to arrange tours.

Rafting & Kayaking

Plentiful rainfall and steep topography provide ideal conditions for rafting, with the Pacuare, Reventazón, Savegre, and Sarapiquí rivers among the top draws. If you are traveling as a family, check age limits – some trips are for 12 years and older only. **Aventuras Naturales**, tel: 2256 3222, www.crica.com/tours/aventura.html **Costa Rica Expeditions**, tel: 2257 0766, www.costaricaexpeditions.com. **Costa Sol Rafting**, tel: 2431 1183, fax: 2431 1185, www.costasolrafting.com. **Desafío Adventures**, tel: 2479 9464, www.desafiocostarica.com. Focus on Northern Zone waters. **Ríos Tropicales**, tel: 2233 6455, www. riostropicales.com. Rafting and sea kayaking. An ideal river for beginners is the Corobocí (Guanacaste).

Sailing

Sailing tours tend to be focused on sunset dinner cruises and, not surprisingly, are mostly offered on the Pacific coast, concentrated in Guanacaste – where you might catch the famed green flash as the sun dips below the horizon. The Central Pacific also has operators. **Hotel El Velero**, Playa Hermosa Tel: 2672 1017, www.costarica hotel.net. Beach-front hotel with sailing tours. **Sunset Sails** Tel: 2777 1304 www.sunsetsailstours.com The name speaks for itself; in Manuel Antonio. **Varso Travel** Tel: 8395 6090 www.papagayovargastours.com Pacific sunset cruises.

Island Cruises

Calypso Tours, tel: 2256 2727; US 800-887 1969; fax: 2256 6767, www. calypsocruises.com. Catamaran cruises from Puntarenas to Isla Tortuga, or the private reserve of Punta Coral. **Bay Island Cruises**, tel: 2258 3536; www.bayislandcruises.com. One-day tour to Isla Tortuga. Departs from San José by bus.

Swimming & Surfing

There is good swimming and surfing on both the Caribbean and Pacific coasts, although some beaches may not be suitable all year round. Dangers include riptides (see below) and large waves, caused by heavy swells that may hit you when leaving the water. Always ask local people before entering the sea. The following are good surfing beaches: **Pacific coast**: Boca Barranca near Puntarenas, Tamarindo, Jacó, Hermosa, Dominical, and Pavones. **Caribbean coast**: Puerto Viejo, Punta Uva, Salsa Brava, Black Beach.

For up-to-date information on surfing conditions, see www.crsurf.com or www.alacransurf.com.

Riptides: several beaches throughout Costa Rica are known for their strong rip tides. Riptides or ripcurrents are forceful ocean currents that travel 5–10km (3–6 miles) an hour, faster than even very strong swimmers. If you are unfortunate enough to get caught in a strong ocean current, relax and don't fight it. Let it carry you. Its strength will eventually diminish. Once it does, swim parallel to the beach, toward the incoming waves, and let them carry you ashore. The following beaches are infamous for their riptides:

On the **Pacific** coast: Jacó, Esterillos, Junquillal, Barú, Dominical, Manuel Antonio's North Espadilla. On the **Caribbean** coast: Cahuita, Playa Bonita.

BELOW: Playa Tamarindo is another popular place to surf.

Tennis

The big tennis sporting event, the Copa del Café (junior pro), is held at the Costa Rica Country Club in Escazú in January. Many upscale resorts have a court or two for guests, but public spaces are scarce. San José and Tamarindo are your best bets. **Academia de Tennis Valle del Sol**, Near Santa Ana, tel: 2282 9222, ext. 4, www.vallesol.com. The 10 exceptionally good courts are open to the public. **Parque La Sabana**. Four courts open to the public.

CHILDREN'S ACTIVITIES

From active volcanoes and white-water rapids to clouds of butterflies and prankster monkeys, just about every corner of Costa Rica has something to capture young imaginations. While it's a safe country for any age, many tour operators suggest children be aged five and up. The San José area has any number of child-focused activities, but two of the best are the interactive exhibits at the **Museo de Niños**, housed in a former prison; and at **INBioParque** (tel: 2507 8107, www.inbioparque.com), with snakes, butterflies, bullet-ant colonies.

Children usually enjoy **La Paz Waterfall Gardens** (tel: 2482 2720, www.waterfallgardens.com) in Varablanca, about an hour north of San José, with its chain of impressive waterfalls, snake exhibit, and butterfly gardens.

The rumbling, steam-belching **Arenal Volcano** is always a hit – especially when conditions are right and you can see the glowing red lava.

It's not hard to convince anyone to spend a day immersed in a world of chocolate. On the Caribbean coast, try the Chocoart **Chocolate Tour** near Puerto Viejo (tel: 2750 0075), or in the Southern Zone, near Puerto Jiménez, **Finca Köbö** (tel: 8398 7604) gives tours of its organic chocolate process.

For beach fun, **Tamarindo** on the North Pacific is a good beginner's beach for fledgling surfers. **Punta Uva** on the southern Caribbean coast and sheltered **Playa Manuel Antonio** on the central Pacific coast provide child-friendly snorkeling and swimming.

Night insect tours with **The Bug Lady** (tel: 8867 6134, www.thenighttour. com) add a touch of eerie fun. Older children may want to stay up for the mystical, nocturnal spectacle of giant **sea turtles laying eggs** at Tamarindo, Tortuguero, or Ostional.

A – Z

A HANDY SUMMARY OF PRACTICAL INFORMATION, ARRANGED ALPHABETICALLY

A dmission Charges

As in many developing countries, attractions in Costa Rica sometimes charge two prices: one for tourists, and a lower one for Costa Ricans. Many of the smaller museums are free; the rest range from less than $1 to $9 (for the Gold Museum), usually with student and child rates. Most art galleries don't charge admission; an exception is the Museum of Costa Rican Art ($5), but Sundays are free. National park admission fees vary, but are usually around $10.

Airport Taxes

Tourists must pay a $26 exit tax upon leaving Costa Rica by air. This can be paid upon arrival, or at the airport prior to leaving (in US$ or colones, not traveler's checks). Leave extra time at the airport, as line-ups at the counter can be long. Guests at some luxury hotels can pay the tax along with their bill. Avoid paying with a credit card if possible as airport personnel will swipe it as a debit card and you may be faced with credit card fees when you return home.

B udgeting for your Trip

Many visitors find Costa Rica more expensive than they expected. It still can be an economic destination, and much of Costa Rica can be enjoyed independently, allowing you to keep costs down – although an itinerary organized by a tour operator may be worth the extra cost in efficient time savings. Costs for guided tours may be high for independent travelers, too (from $30 to $80, generally), but it is worth splurging on at least one or two such tours – particularly if you want to get the most out of a nature hike.

Shoestring travelers can get away with $50 or less a day, for just sun, sea, and self-guided hikes. An extensive public bus system gets you almost anywhere in the country from San José for less than $6 a time. Cheap cabins (usually cold or shared showers and less privacy) for under $25 per night (double occupancy) abound, especially at the beach – but they fill up fast in the high season and on weekends. If you stick to the local *sodas* (small eateries), full plates of rice, meat,

and beans that stick to your ribs are rarely more than $5. And you should still have enough for a few sunset beers (about $2).

To upgrade the comfort level, expect to pay $50 to $70 a night (double occupancy) for moderate lodging (private baths, hot water, some views, parking, extra amenities). Air-conditioned, minivan door-to-door hotel transport to the beach costs between $30 and $55 per person one way from San José. A dinner for two with a glass of wine can be easily had for $25 or less.

No matter what your budget, you'll take cabs somewhere along the line. Taxis charge $0.96 for the first kilometer and $0.02 cents every four seconds afterwards, but outside of San José taxi drivers tend to use their own flat rates, although it is illegal. Try to settle on a price before you set off.

Business Hours

Business hours are generally 9am–5pm, often with a lunch break from noon–1pm. State banks usually open from 8.30am–4.30pm Mon–Fri and some also open on Saturday.

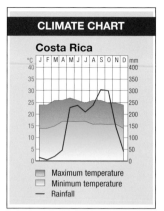

CLIMATE CHART

Costa Rica

- ▢ Maximum temperature
- ▢ Minimum temperature
- — Rainfall

C limate

Costa Rica has two seasons; the rainy or green season, which Costa Ricans call winter *(invierno)*, and the dry season or summer *(verano)*. In the Central Valley, the rainy season lasts from May through November and the dry season from December through April. Even during the rainy season, most mornings are bright and sunny.

During the rainy season there are fewer tourists and you can take advantage of green-season discounts in hotels.

Rain can fall at any time on the Caribbean coast; October is the driest month. It is generally more humid on the Caribbean coast.

The average temperature in San José is 24°C (75°F). In the highlands, temperatures drop approximately 0.6°C for each 100 meters (500ft) of elevation. The temperature on the coasts varies from the mid 20s°C (70s°F) to the 30s°C (low 90s°F).

Conservation

Costa Rica is heralded worldwide for its progressive conservationist policies and biodiversity, making it a hotspot for ecotourism, a term that started out closely linked to conservation, but now is used to describe just about any activity or lodging in a nature setting.

Costa Rica tries very hard to do a great deal with few resources. The following are some of the more popular environmental organizations that are actively involved in saving and protecting Costa Rica's natural resources.

APREFLOFAS (Association for the Preservation of Wild Flora and Fauna) is a private, non-profit, non-governmental organization for nature conservation. Tel: 2574 6861, fax:

2574 6010; www.preserveplanet.org.
Caribbean Conservation Corporation: runs the green turtle tagging project at Tortuguero Beach on the Caribbean coast. Tel: 352 373 6441 (Florida); www.cccturtle.org, or tel: 2297 5510 (Costa Rica).
CEDARENA (Environmental and Natural Resource Legal Center): educates the public and government officials on the use of the law to protect the environment. Tel: 2283 7080; www.cedarena.org.
Corcovado Foundation: Created by concerned neighbors of Corcovado National Park to protect the wild heritage and future of the area through education and fundraising. Tel: 2297 3013; wwwcorcovadofoundation.org.
Friends of the Osa: Dedicated to preserving the Osa Peninsula's globally significant biodiversity through habitat conservation, science and research, and education. Tel: 2735 5756; www.osaconservation.org.
Fundación Neotrópica (Neotropic Foundation): works to foster "sustainable development" in communities near wildlife preserves, parks, forest reserves, and other protected areas. Tel: 2253 2130, fax: 2253 4210; www.neotropica.org.
INBio (National Biodiversity Institute): this private non-profit research organization is amassing a catalogue of the country's flora and fauna and runs the 5.5-hectare (14-acre) INBioparque in Santo Domingo de Heredia. Tel: 2507 8107, fax: 2507 8271; www.inbio.ac.cr.
Kids Saving The Rainforest: based in Manuel Antonio, runs child-oriented conservation projects including an adopt-a-tree program ($20 to sponsor a planting), and Titi monkey bridges. Tel: 2777 2592, fax: 2777 1954; www.kidssavingtherainforest.org.
Rainforest Alliance: promotes sustainability by transforming land-use practices, business practices, and consumer behaviour. Tel: 212-677 1900 (US); www.rainforest-alliance.org.
Rainforest Concern: buys and protects virgin forest, and helps locals develop responsible ecotourism. Partnering with The Endangered Wildlife Trust, the organization runs a turtle research and protection program just north of Limón. Tel: 020-7229 2093 (UK), fax: 020-7221 4094; www.rainforestconcern.org.
The National Conservancy: US-based organization committed to land protection, focusing on two tracts of land in the Osa Peninsula and the Talamanca region. Tel: 2220 2552, (US) 703-841 5300, fax: 2220 2551, www.nature.org.

World Society for the Protection of Animals: Provides local mobilization and support for international campaigns, including whale conservation and Farm Watch. Tel: 617-896 9214 (US), 2562 1200 (Costa Rica); www.wspa-international.org.

Crime and Safety

Theft is a growing problem in Costa Rica. Pickpocketing, chain and watch snatching, backpack grabbing, and other thefts are becoming more common, especially in downtown San José and popular beach towns. It is, for the most part, non-violent, snatch-and-run thievery. Do not be paranoid and frightened, but do be vigilant.

• Do not take valuables with you when you walk on the streets of San José. Carry only as much cash as you will need. Leave your backpack, passport, and jewelry in the hotel, preferably in a locked office. Keep an eye on wallets and shoulder bags. If you buy valuable items, make your return trip by taxi.

• While walking on the street, be aware of who is around you, and act confidently.

• When driving through the city by car, keep your windows rolled up high enough so no one can reach inside.

• Avoid deserted streets at night and walking in isolated areas.

• Be especially watchful in these areas: the pedestrian walkway near the Coca-Cola bus terminal; the Plaza de la Cultura; Parque Central; Av. 4 and Av. Central; and Ca. 12 from Av. 10 to Av. 5.

• Thefts from rental cars are common everywhere in the country. Do not leave anything unattended in your car, especially when you are unloading in a hotel parking lot. Do not assume items in a locked trunk are safe: they are not. Whenever possible, park in a guarded area.

• Do not leave anything unattended on the beach, including towels, clothing, tents, and camping gear.

Most importantly, if you are mugged, don't resist.

Ask for the Fuerza Pública if you need a street police officer. For emergencies, call 911. English-speaking officers are few and far between but a new contingent of Tourism Police patrol high-tourist areas, usually on bicycles, and are specially trained to help tourists; they also man a post at the arrivals hall of the main airport, to offer safety advice. Report theft immediately to the Judicial

TRANSPORTATION

ACCOMMODATIONS

EATING OUT

ACTIVITIES

A – Z

LANGUAGE

Investigative Police (OIJ, pronounced oh-ee-ho-ta) if your passport is stolen or you require a police report for insurance purposes. Otherwise, this is a time-consuming process that will likely result in no more than a file collecting dust.

Customs and Entry

Personal effects may be taken into the country and up to six rolls of film, 500g (18oz) of tobacco, 2kg (4lbs) of candy, and 3 liters (170fl oz) of wine or liquor (if over 21). Carry prescription drugs in original containers. Anyone caught with illegal drugs can face 8–20 years in jail and no bail.

Visas & Passports

Citizens of the US, Canada, UK, Ireland, Australia, New Zealand, and South Africa need only a passport valid for at least six months beyond the date of entry to Costa Rica. Travelers may remain for 90 days. If you leave the country for 72 hours, when you return you will be allowed another 90 days. But immigration is cracking down on "perpetual tourists" so multiple exits and entries are not advisable.

More and more often, airlines are requiring that *before* they board their flight to Costa Rica travelers present a ticket showing they are leaving within 90 days.

Identification: Leave your passport in a safe place in your hotel, but always carry a photocopy including the page that contains your entry stamp in case of immigration authorities' spot checks. Report lost ID to the police immediately.
Travelers from other nations Contact the nearest Costa Rican consulate or embassy, or try the website: www.rree.go.cr.

Exit Regulations

Costa Rica, like many Latin American countries, does not permit minors (up to and including those of 17 years of age) born in Costa Rica or living there

Useful Numbers

Local collect calls: **110**
Information: **113**
International information: **124**
Airport information: **2437 2626**
Tourist information: **2222 1090**
Rate of exchange: **2243 4143**
Time: **112**
Fire, police, ambulance: **911**
National Parks: **192**

for extended periods to leave the country unaccompanied without the permission of Immigration.

D isabled Travelers

Much of Costa Rica's claim to fame is based around rugged nature, and the country's buckled and potholed roads and sidewalks (where they exist) can be difficult to navigate at the best of times. By no means, however, should people with mobility difficulties write off the idea of a rainforest vacation. Tourism establishments have made efforts to open up the country's treasures, although definitions of "accessible" vary widely – call ahead with specific questions to avoid disappointment.

A variety of attractions, including Poás volcano, is set up to facilitate travelers in wheelchairs, and a handful of local companies organize excursions or arrange transport.
Accessible Journeys
Tel: 800-846 4537 or 610-521 0339 (US); www.disabilitytravel.com.
Organizes tours September through May.
RoadMap
Tel: 2771 7482; www.moniquechabot.com.
Personalized itineraries for accessible vacations.
Vaya con Silla de Ruedas
Tel: 2454 2810 or 8391 5045; www.gowithwheelchairs.com.
Arranges tours and transport for people with disabilities.

E lectricity

110 volts, 60-cycle current. Two- and three-prong flat plugs. Australian and European appliances need a two-prong adapter. Most accommodations have equipment to convert power.

Embassies and Consulates

Embassies Abroad

Australia: Honorary Consulate, PO Box 205, Sydney, tel: 006-129 969 4050; costa-rica.visahq.com.
Canada: 325 Dalhousie Street Suite 407, Ottawa, Ontario, K1N 7G2, tel: 1-613-562 2855; www.costarica embassy.com.
South Africa: Honorary Consulate, 56 Dennis Road, Blandford Ridge, Johannesburg, tel: 0027 11 705 3434; http://costa-rica.visahq.com.
UK: 14 Lancaster Gate, London W2 3LH, tel: +44 207 706 8844; http://costarica.embassyhomepage.com.
US: 2112-S. Street, NW, Washington DC 20008, tel: 202-234 2945; www.costarica-embassy.org.

Consulates in San José

The Canadian Consulate has an agreement to assist **Australian** nationals.
Canada
Oficentro La Sábana, Building 5, tel: 2242 4400, fax: 2242 4410; www.sanjose.gc.ca.
South Africa (Honorary Consulate): 150 meters/yds west of entrance to Pacific Rail Terminal, Downtown, tel: 2222 1470 or 2221 9262.
UK
Edificio Centro Colón, 11th Floor, tel: 2258 2025, fax: 2233 9938; www.ukincostarica.fco.gov.uk.
US
Ca. 120, Av. 0, Pavas, tel: 2519 2000, fax: 2519 2305; www.usembassy.or.cr.

Emergencies

Dial **911** anywhere in Costa Rica for emergency assistance.
Car Accidents: tel: 800-872 6748 (Transit Police in San José) and 800-

BELOW: find English-language reading material at bookstores and newsstands.

800 8000 (National Insurance Institute in San José).
Reporting a crime: tel: 2295 3272 (OIJ in San José, 24 hours).
24-hour Pharmacy: Farmacia Clínica Bíblica (tel: 2257 5252, downtown San José), Farmacia CIMA (tel: 2208 1080, Escazú).
Stolen Visa Card: tel: 0-800-011 0030.
Stolen MasterCard: tel: 0-800 011 0184.

Etiquette

Ticos are infinitely hospitable – so always accept a bite to eat and a drink if invited to a private home.

Preceding any request with *Me puede hacer el favor de...* (Could you do me the favor of...) will go a long way to ensuring the best service. While you'll see Costa Ricans snapping their fingers at wait staff and calling out *muchacha* or *muchacho* (girl or boy), foreigners should stick to the more respectful *Disculpe, señor/a* (Excuse me sir/ma'am).

Greeting: people shake hands when first introduced. Women usually greet each other with a kiss on the cheek and say goodbye in the same fashion; this also applies when a friendly relationship exists, and men and women often greet in the same way. Children are very affectionate and usually greet their elders with a kiss. However, among adults, excessive displays of affection in public are not well received, as attested to by the occasional *No se permite escenas amorosas* (No public displays of affection) sign in some establishments. Having said that, such displays are quite common.

Elderly Costa Ricans are commonly addressed as Don (men) or Doña (women) followed by their first name, an honorific considered an archaism in most Spanish-speaking countries.
Nude bathing: there are no nudist beaches in Costa Rica and topless bathing is not acceptable; nor is wearing bathing suits on the streets.
Prostitution: the sex trade is legal in Costa Rica, but pimping is not. With no official medical records kept for prostitutes, however, the health risks are high. Some beautiful "women" are in fact transvestites. Aids is a formidable reality in Costa Rica, so practice safe sex. Sex with a minor is illegal and punishable by imprisonment. The government has cracked down on pedophiles, with some success.

G ay and Lesbian Travelers

Relatively free of active oppression and intolerance, Costa Rica has become a favorite spot for gay and lesbian travelers from around the region. It now even has its own Gay Pride Parade (in June). The atmosphere is distinctly "don't ask, don't tell," and the general public tends to be uncomfortable with same-sex displays of affection.

San José and Manuel Antonio both have clusters of gay-only and gay-friendly hotels, restaurants, and bars.
Gaytours Costa Rica (tel: 2294 0606 (Spanish) or 8305 8044 (English); www.gaytourscr.com) specializes in gay and lesbian travel around Costa Rica and operates the Gaybus from San José to Manuel Antonio during the high season.
Gay-Costa Rica (tel: 860-633 1872 (US) or 877-852 2230, www.gay-costarica.com) offers three package tours at different prices to hotels that are gay-owned or very gay-friendly.

The free bimonthly magazine *Playita Circuit* (Manuel Antonio) can be picked up at gay-friendly outlets, or checked out on a link on the Gaytours site *(see above)*.

Guides and Tour Operators

Thanks to high levels of English spoken in a well-established tourism circuit, and extensive, inexpensive transport, visitors to Costa Rica will find the country fairly easy to navigate as independent travelers.

However, booking with a local tour company can save transport time – and hair-raising driving experiences – and most are valuable resources if a wrench is thrown into your plans. In some remote areas, such as Tortuguero, options are largely, but not completely, restricted to a two- or three-day package, including meals, tours, and often transport.

Drive-yourself tours, such as those offered by Costa Rican Trails (www.costa

Specialist Tour Operators

Diving Safaris
Playa Hermosa
Tel: 2672 1259
Fax: 2672 1260
www.costaricadiving.net.
Long-established dive and adventure operator.
Costa Rica Expeditions
Tel: 2257 0766
Fax: 2257 1665
www.costaricaexpeditions.com.
The original whitewater rafting company. Offers nature tours to Tortuguero, Corcovado, and Monteverde, with knowledgeable, bilingual guides.
Coast to Coast Adventures
Tel: 2280 8054
Fax: 2225 6055
www.coasttocoastadventures.com.
Adventure tourism and races; cycling tours.
Costa Rica Sun Tours
Tel: 2296 7757
Fax: 2296 4307
www.crsuntours.com.
Off-the-beaten-track tours with a naturalist focus. Volcanoes, national parks, cloud forests, rainforests, beaches. Turtle-watching tours. Whitewater rafting, hiking, biking, and horseback riding tours.
Costa Rican Trails
Tel: 2280 6705
Fax: 2225 8842
From US: 888-803 3344
From Canada: 866-865 7013
www.costaricantrails.com.

Friendly company that offers a variety of nature, family, and adventure tours including motorcycling.
Discovery Costa Rica
Tel: 2215 1490
Fax: 2215 1774
www.discoverycostarica.com.
Design your own package from a large range of tours.
Horizontes
Tel: 2222 2022
Fax: 2255 4513
www.horizontes.com.
Customized nature tours of all types throughout Costa Rica, including tours for families, photographers, birdwatchers. Day trips in the Central Valley.
Ríos Tropicales
Tel: 2233 6455
Fax: 2255 4354
www.riostropicales.com.
Leading tour company for rafting and kayaking.
Serendipity Adventures
Tel: 2558 1000
Fax: 2558 1010.
From US: 877-507 1358
www.serendipityadventures.com.
Specialists in hot-air ballooning.
Swiss Travel
Tel: 2282 4898
Fax: 2282 4890
www.swisstravelcr.com.
Organizes upscale ecotourism and adventure vacations.

TRANSPORTATION

ACCOMMODATIONS

EATING OUT

ACTIVITIES

A – Z

LANGUAGE

ricantrails.com), balance well-planned itineraries and in-country support with independence. Agro-tourism tours are among the best ways to immerse yourself in Costa Rica and its culture while directly benefitting local communities.

Regardless of how independent you would like to be, hiring a good guide is essential for spotting wildlife. The National Apprentice Institute has an excellent program that trains and licenses naturalist guides. Another good yardstick is a recommendation from your hotel or established tour agency.

The **National Chamber of Tourism** (CANATUR) lists tourism agencies on its website (www.canatur.org/afiliados_agencias.aspx). The page is in Spanish, but you can generally reach an English speaker at any of the listed phone numbers. A few good agencies are:

Costa Rica Temptations
Tel: 2508 5000
www.crtinfo.com.
Known for tours of a coffee farm, Poás Volcano, Sarapiquí River, and La Paz Waterfall, as well as a variety of one-day and multi-day tours.

Desafío Adventure Center
Tel: 2479 9464
www.desafiocostarica.com.
Solid operator specializing in Northern Zone activities: rafting, caving, extreme hiking, and more.

Selva Mar
Tel: 2771 4582
www.exploringcostarica.com.
Southern Zone experts.

Ecotourism

Ecotourism is still the buzz word in Costa Rica and hotels can provide or recommend excellent guides. A fledgling organized rural tourism network is the latest way of guaranteeing a vacation that minimizes impact on the environment and maximizes benefits to those working in tourism. The new bilingual (English/Spanish) Rural Community Tourism Guide put out by COOPRENA (tel: 2290 8646, www.turismoruralcr.com), a national ecotourism network, lists several of these rural tourism projects. The following are some options:

Active and Progressive Women's Association of Costa de Pájaros
Gulf of Nicoya
Tel/fax: 2678 8054
Women's group that has developed alternatives to the fishing economy. Butterfly garden, tours of mangroves and the Gulf of Nicoya, medicinal gardens, traditional fishing tours.

Adventura Naturales Yorkin
Talamanca

Tel: 2200 5211 or 2290 8646
Offers one-day or overnight visits to an indigenous tribe with opportunities to converse with the people and learn medical practices.

Rural El Encanto de Piedra Blanca
Tel: 2228 7922. A good day-tour option from San José. Traditional sugar mill, dances, and food in the hills of San Antonio Escazú.

Rural Tourism Association (ACTUAR)
Tel: 2248 9470, www.actuarcostarica.com. Well-established community tourism with extensive network of rural lodges.

Simbiosis Tours, tel: 2290 8646, www.turismoruralcr.com
The tourism branch of COOPRENA, an environmental organization. Works with cooperative lodges.

H ealth and Medical Care

Costa Rica ranks near the United States, Canada, and other Western nations in health-care standards. **Inoculations:** no inoculations are required for visiting Costa Rica. **Water:** in San José and the Central Valley, water is treated. It is, with some exceptions, potable throughout the country. If you have persistent intestinal problems, take a stool sample to the Clínica Bíblica (tel: 2522 1000, results in minutes) to be analyzed (about US$20).
Illness: malaria is not generally a problem in Costa Rica, except in the remote regions of Talamanca. Cholera is not usually a problem, either, due to Costa Rica's strong public health efforts. There has been a marked increase in the incidence of dengue fever, however. Dengue symptoms include the sudden onset of fever, headache, severe joint and muscle pains followed in most cases by a rash which starts on the trunk and spreads to the limbs and face. The fever subsides in a few days but a bout can last three weeks or more, from start to finish. Dengue is spread by the *Aedes aegypti* mosquito, which bites principally at dusk. There is presently no prophylactic treatment available for dengue, but medical attention can significantly reduce the effects. Prevention is the best medicine: use repellent and wear long-sleeved shirts and long pants.
Snake bites: although rare, it is worth wearing closed high-top shoes or boots and floppy long pants and walking with a stick. If you are bitten, apply a compress (not a tourniquet). Try to remember what the snake looked like so the doctor can locate the correct antivenin. Then get to a hospital.

Medical Services

Costa Rica has an excellent health-care system, much less expensive than in the US. Many doctors are trained in the US or Europe and speak English, especially those at private clinics. In some remote communities, you can get help through the public clinic system, called EBAIS.

Public Medical Centers

Hospital Dr Calderón Guardia
Tel: 2212 1000
Hospital de los Niños
Tel: 2523 3600 (for children).
Hospital México
Tel: 2242 6700
Hospital San Juan de Díos
Tel: 2257 6282.

Private Medical Centers

Clínica Bíblica
Central San José
Tel: 2522 1000.
Clínica Católica
Guadalupe
Tel: 2246 3000.
Hospital San José CIMA
Escazú
Tel: 2208 1000
Fax: 2208 1273.
Hospital Cristiano Jerusalem
Guadalupe
Tel: 2216 9191.

Dentists

Costa Rican dentists provide competent and affordable cosmetic as well as general dentistry. The *Tico Times* contains ads placed by English-speaking dentists, who can also be found on the US Embassy website at sanjose.usembassy.gov/medical.html.

I nsurance

It is essential to have comprehensive insurance when traveling to Costa Rica. Some bank cards and credit cards may include insurance, but this may not be adequate. You need enough coverage for both medical expenses and repatriation.

Insure yourself against theft of personal items and loss of passport and money.

Certain sporting activities may necessitate paying an additional insurance premium – always read the small print to make sure that you are adequately covered for any accidents.

Internet

Internet cafés with high-speed connections abound in San José, making it easy and cheap (less than $1 per hour) to stay dialed in. With the latest in internet technology, the quality of computer-based calls has improved dramatically and internet cafés have essentially replaced public international call centers.

Once you leave the capital, you will be able to find public internet access in just about any town of any size, but service becomes slower and more expensive – up to $5 per hour in beach towns. If you really need to keep in touch in the most remote places, expect to pay astronomical amounts for satellite internet.

Most upscale hotels offer a computer with internet service, Wi-fi, or both. Eateries such as Bagelmen's outlets in San José and Denny's at the Hotel Irazú are popular wireless hotspots, but be extra careful when taking advantage of the service; reports of laptop theft near these centers have increased.

L eft Luggage

Neither international airport has an area for left luggage. However, most hotels and some tour companies will allow you to store extra gear and luggage for a few days for free or for a small charge.

BELOW: looking for an attraction, accommodation, bike hire, or internet?

M aps

The ICT tourist information centers at the airport and under the Gold Museum in downtown San José hand out decent, free road maps, but often run out of copies. A better bet is 7th Street Books (see Bookstores, Activities section, page 283).

If you are renting a car, it is useful to buy a road map; otherwise, the maps in this guide book and/or the free ICT map should be quite adequate.

For comprehensiveness, you can't beat Insight Map Costa Rica. The Rough Guide Map to Costa Rica and Panama is waterproof – a worthwhile investment. Check your local travel store or the web; the regional Amazon.com sites have a wide selection. Travelers from New Zealand and Australia can try Fishpond (www. fishpond.co.nz or www.fishpond.co.au). Check Maptak (www.maptak.com) for detailed topographic and political maps of Costa Rica's provinces, national parks, and more. For simple maps, directions, and driving distances, www.costaricamap-online.com is a good pre-trip reference.

Media
Radio

Radio stations in English include 107.5 FM, which plays classic rock and has news and other information in English, and Radio Dos (99.5 FM), a Spanish-language station that plays pop and rock classics, has a morning show in English, and news in English, every other hour.

Television

There are more than 70 cable TV channels listed in the local TV guide; more are available. Programming includes approximately 30 channels in English, one in German, one in French, and one in Chinese.

Newspapers & Magazines

Available in English, Spanish, and other languages, at bookstores, supermarkets, newsstands, and hotel outlets. Weekly English-language publications include:

The Tico Times (tel: 2258 1558 www. ticotimes.net), published weekly on Friday. Widely available at most newsstands in central San José, Cartago, Heredia, and Alajuela. Gives the week's news in Costa Rica, up-to-date listings of what's happening, and where. Also provides online daily news and publishes a Restaurant Guide.

Costa Rica Outdoors (tel: 2231 0306, www.costaricaoutdoors.com). Bimonthly magazine featuring fishing, birding, and Tico culture. Daily Spanish-language newspapers include: La Nación, La Prensa Libre, La República, and Al Día.

Money Matters

The currency unit is the colón. The current rate of exchange can be found in the English-language Tico Times business pages; the daily La Nación publishes a daily list of the rates offered at each bank. The Central Bank posts a page with the daily rates of the country's institutions at www. bccr.fi.cr/flat/bccrflat.htm.

State Banks: the main ones are Banco Nacional (tel: 2212 2000) and Banco de Costa Rica (tel: 2287 9000), with offices throughout the country. If you need an early bank stop, the latter has a branch that opens at 7.30am on the east side of town in Curridabat.

Private banks: the main ones are HSBC (tel: 2287 1000) and BAC San José (tel: 2295 9595). Other private banks include Scotiabank, Banco Promerica, and Banco CMB. Many of these have branches that are open until 7pm. BAC San José's Rápido Bancos in most Central Valley malls are even open Sunday for basic transactions, including exchange.

Traveler's checks: while the tourism industry has become more familiar with traveler's checks, high fraud rates have led some businesses to ax this method of payment. For safety, it's a good idea to bring some money in this form, which can always be changed in banks, but check with stores or hotels before trying to pay this way. You must have your passport with you to cash traveler's checks or to get cash advances on credit cards.

Cash: you may not be able to break 10,000 colón notes when paying for taxis and such. US dollars in small denominations are often accepted in taxis and shops, particularly in towns and cities. Counterfeiting has made many businesses highly suspicious of US$100 bills – better to bring smaller denominations.

Credit cards: American Express, Visa, and MasterCard are widely accepted in the Central Valley area. Their telephone calls are handled by local credit card firm **Credomatic**, tel: 2295 9000.

Access numbers for international credit card calls are:
AT&T: 0-8000-114 114
MCI: 0-8000-122 222
Sprint: 0-8000-130 123
Canada Direct: 0-8000-151 161
British Telecom: 0-800-044 1044
Bank Machines: ATMs have multiplied dramatically in the past few years. Machines marked ATH are the best bets for foreign cards. For machine locations, visit www.ath.fi.cr; it's in Spanish, but if you click on Cajeros Automáticos, then Búsqueda de Cajeros, you can easily find out if and where your destination has a

TRANSPORTATION
ACCOMMODATIONS
EATING OUT
ACTIVITIES
A – Z
LANGUAGE

machine. Those marked *local* dispense only colones, those marked *ambas* (both) also give dollars. Some banks accept either Visa or MasterCard but not both; check www.mastercard.com/us/personal and click ATM locator; or http://lac.visa.com/home.jsp, to see where you can get cash advances in machines. Look for machines during the day, especially ones with nearby guards.

Changing money: exchange rates vary slightly between banks, and day-to-day rates go up and down. The fluctuation is generally no more than a cent per dollar, and most banks are within a cent of each other in rates. Private banks (particularly BAC San José) are the best places to exchange money if you want to avoid long line-ups. Your hotel may also change money for you. Some banks now handle euros as well as dollars.

Money can be exchanged at the airport (BAC San José) from 5am to 10pm – if you have colones, it's best to change them to euros or dollars before you get on the plane. Avoid the Casa de Cambio Global Exchange; as of this writing, its rates were consistently 10 percent less than the average.

Taxes and Tipping: restaurants add 13 percent tax to the bill plus a 10 percent service charge. Hotels add 16.4 percent tax and service. Bellboys should be tipped. In restaurants tipping is not expected, unless service is outstanding. Do tip barmen and taxi drivers who are helpful.

P hotography

Whether you've gone digital or are still using film, you won't regret packing along a telephoto lens to capture wildlife sightings. Water damage and theft are two very real threats to your photo equipment. Consider a dry bag, or at the least a waterproof case or plastic bag, and, depending on the value of your camera, you may want to insure it separately.

It is possible to upload and burn photos from your camera onto a CD or hard-drive key in most internet cafés; some even have a universal cable lying around if you forget yours.

Tours catering to the traveling photographer are directed at beginners, amateurs, and semi-professionals and often provide a stress-free way to find the best images.

Foto Verde Tours
Tel: 2463 0053
www.fotoverdetours.com.
Arranges one-day seminars and multiday excursions in many locations in the country.

Costa Rica Photo Tour
Tel: 2786 5018
www.crphototours.com.
Specializing in tours in the Osa Peninsula, this company offers year-round experiences and a handful of pre-planned itineraries that take visitors throughout the country.

Postal Services

Airmail between the US or Europe and Costa Rica should take about five days, but a wait of two or more weeks is not uncommon. The central post office is at Calle 2, Av. 1–3, tel: 2223 9766. Mail can be received there in the general delivery section (*Lista de Correos*). Outgoing mail should be posted at either a hotel desk or a post office. It is usually difficult, time-consuming, and expensive to receive

packages in the mail. Outrageous duties are sometimes applied and you can spend days trying to deal with numerous officials. A receipt showing a low value may help if it is included with the package. There are agents (*agencias de aduana*) listed in the phone book who will handle the customs clearances for a fee.

Couriers: there are many international courier services. The most popular are: FedEx and DHL. Consult the *Yellow Pages* for numbers.

Public Holidays

Costa Rica moves certain public holidays to the following Monday if a date falls on a weekend. When holidays fall within the week, government offices and some businesses will push the holiday to the following Monday, while other businesses will close on the day itself.

For a list of Public Holidays, see festivals marked with PH (there are 11) on page 282.

Public Toilets

There are very few public toilets in towns, but in the capital it is easy to slip into a fast-food restaurant; outside of the Central Valley many restaurants and road stops allow you to use the facilities, sometimes for a 100-colón fee. Always carry a small supply of toilet tissue.

R eligious Services

Costa Rica's official religion is visibly Catholic, but there is full freedom of religion. Visitors are welcome to sit in on Spanish-speaking services in the cathedrals, of course showing common-sense courtesy and dressing appropriately.

The Central Valley has active Anglican, Baha'i, Jewish, Baptist, Jehovah's Witness, and Quaker communities and many evangelical Protestant churches, among others, and approximately 25 houses of worship offer services in English. Check the *Tico Times* weekly newspaper's calendar section for an extensive list.

S tudent Travelers

An international student ID card will get discounts on some attractions, air fares to Costa Rica, and most museums. It never hurts to ask if a discount is available. But it's the proliferation of cheap *cabinas*, dirt-cheap transport, and affordable plates

Below: the Maria Inmaculada religion revolves around children.

of rice and beans that make Costa Rica a student-friendly destination.

Many conservation organizations charge low rates to take on student volunteers for a true immersion experience *(see Conservation)*. The Association of Volunteers Working in Protected Areas (ASVO, tel: 2258 4430, www.asvocr.org) is a good bet for short-term volunteering stints maintaining trails, monitoring marine turtle conservation, or teaching English, requiring only basic Spanish.

Youth-oriented hostels are springing up around the country – *see hostels in Accommodation section.*

T elecommunications

At present Costa Rica's telecommunications industry is still in the hands of the state-owned Costa Rica Institute of Technology (ICE). While the service is decent and relatively inexpensive, the system has been slow to embrace new technology and tends to make any transaction slow and complicated. The state monopoly also makes it very difficult for a foreigner to obtain a cell phone. A 2009 free trade agreement is poised to break up the telecommunications monopoly and offer *Ticos* a choice in their cell phone or landline provider.

Making Telephone Calls

Most telephones work with phone cards, which can be bought at many small shops, pharmacies, or supermarkets.

Fifty or 100 colón coins, and the public phones that use them, are being phased out but can still be found. Place the coin(s) in the slot on top of the phone, then dial the number; the coin will drop down when the connection has been made. Extra coins placed in the slot will fall automatically, only as needed.

International Calls

Dial 124 for country codes. International phone cards are available at various locations. If you do not have access to a phone, international calls can be made from any internet café.

Time Zone

Costa Rica is on North America's Central Standard Time which means it is six hours behind GMT. It does not observe Daylight Savings, so this time difference increases one hour during the northern summer months. Since Costa Rica is close to the equator, the number of daylight hours does not vary much from season to season; the sun sets year-round more or less around 6pm.

Tourist Offices

The **Costa Rican Tourism Institute's** (**ICT**) most useful office – and it is very useful – is at the entrance to the Gold Museum, but private agencies around the country provide just about everything you need to know. The following offices are particularly good:
ICT, open 8am–4pm, staffed by bilingual operators, tel: 1-800 343 6332 (from the US) or 506-2299 5800 (outside US), fax: 2291 5648, www.visitcostarica.com. **ICT** Gold Museum on the pedestrian walkway (tel: 2222 1090) open Mon–Sat 9am–5pm, closed during lunch hour; good information and maps.
Café Net El Sol, tel: 2735 5719, www. soldeosa.com. Southern Zone information, bulletin board, gathering place in Puerto Jiménez.
National Parks Information, tel: 2257 2239 or 192, fax: 2257 2239, www.fpn-cr.org. Fundación de Parques Nacionales; extensive information on all national parks.
Talamanca Ecotourism & Conservation Association (ATEC), tel: 2750 0398, www.greencoast.com/atec. htm. A good option for community and tourism information around Puerto Viejo.
Tamarindo Tourist Info Center, tel: 2653 2251, www.crparadise.com. A friendly resource with tourism and transport info.

W ebsites

AM Costa Rica: daily online tabloid www.amcostarica.com.
Chamber of Tourism (CANATUR): www.canatur.org
Costa Rican Foreign Relations Ministry: information on consulates and embassies; official translators. In Spanish. www.rree.go.cr.
Costa Rica General Guide: blogs, Costa Rican recipes, culture, real estate information www.costarica.com or www.costarica.net.
Costa Rican Tourist Board (ICT): comprehensive tourism information and news www.visitcostarica.com.
Info Costa Rica: online forums, articles on a wide variety of topics www.infocostarica.com.
Inside Costa Rica: daily summary of news in English www.insidecostarica.com.

La Nación Newspaper: summarizes news of the week in English on Friday www.nacion.co.cr.
Residents' Association of Costa Rica: helpful tourism and community information www.arcr.net.
Sustainable Tourism Certification: overview of program and detailed list of certified establishments www.turismo-sostenible.co.cr.
The Tico Times: weekly and daily news and general information www.ticotimes.net.

Weights and Measures

Costa Rica uses the metric system. When asking for directions, remember that 100 meters usually means one block, regardless of how long the block is. While most real-estate information speaks of square meters and hectares, the *manzana* (7,000 sq meters, or about 1.75 acres) is still widely used as a unit of measurement.

What to Bring

Clothing and footwear: pack to dress in layers. Sweaters and jackets are needed for the mountains and cool evenings, particularly in the Central Valley in December. Shorts are worn for athletic activities or at the beaches, not normally in the cities. Bring weatherproof gear and boots if you plan to do much hiking. Have a comfortable pair of walking shoes that are already broken in. Sidewalks are non-existent in many areas, and uneven at best. Costa Rican women are always well groomed and men like to wear cologne, lots of it. Bring dressy clothes for up-market San José restaurants and nightlife.

Personal items: a folding umbrella is essential. Bring what medications and specialty film you need, as well as sunscreen, and contraceptives: they are often expensive and difficult to find outside San José.

Insect repellent, natural brands included, is easily available in San José, if a little expensive.

Women Travelers

Costa Rica is considered to be a very safe destination for women, and rarely will women face persistent or physical harassment, but it is best to take precautions. Travelers of both sexes are advised to walk in pairs or groups, and take cabs at night. Always sit in the back seat, and make a note of the driver's ID.

TRANSPORTATION
ACCOMMODATIONS
EATING OUT
ACTIVITIES
A – Z
LANGUAGE

L ANGUAGE

UNDERSTANDING THE LANGUAGE

Survival Spanish

Spanish is Costa Rica's principal language, so learn some phrases before you arrive, if only the simple courtesies: "Good morning." "How are you?" "I'm well, thanks." These seemingly inconsequential phrases are an important part of daily life in Costa Rica. English is spoken by many people in San José and in the larger hotels, and one can always get by without Spanish; but if your idea of a good trip includes some contact with local people, then speaking a bit of Spanish is important.

If you are going on an extended trip, consider spending the first week enrolled in one of the many language schools, which offer tailored programs and schedules of all kinds, many with excursions and cultural programs.

A pocket-sized English-Spanish dictionary is a good idea, or a small electronic dictionary.

Numbers

1 *uno*
2 *dos*
3 *tres*
4 *cuatro*
5 *cinco*
6 *seis*
7 *siete*
8 *ocho*
9 *nueve*
10 *diez*
11 *once*
12 *doce*
13 *trece*
14 *catorce*
15 *quince*
16 *dieciseis*
17 *diecisiete*
18 *dieciocho*
19 *diecinueve*
20 *veinte*
21 *veinte y uno*
30 *treinta*
40 *cuarenta*
50 *cincuenta*
60 *sesenta*
70 *setenta*
80 *ochenta*
90 *noventa*
100 *cien*
101 *ciento uno*
200 *doscientos*
300 *trescientos*
400 *cuatrocientos*
500 *quinientos*
600 *seiscientos*
700 *setecientos*
800 *ochocientos*
900 *novecientos*
1,000 *mil*
2,000 *dos mil*
10,000 *diez mil*
100,000 *cien mil*
1,000,000 *un millón*

Common Expressions

Good morning *Buenos días*
Good afternoon *Buenas tardes*
Good evening *Buenas noches*
Goodbye *Hasta luego/Adiós*
How are you? *¿Cómo está Usted?*
I'm well, thanks *Muy bien, gracias*
And you? *¿Y Usted?*
Please *Por favor*
Thank you *Gracias*
No, thank you *No, gracias*
You're welcome *Con mucho gusto*
How kind of you *Usted es muy amable*
I am sorry *Lo siento*
Excuse me *Disculpe* (when apologizing). *Con permiso* (when leaving the table or passing in front of someone)
Yes *Sí*
No *No*
Do you speak English? *¿Habla Usted inglés?*
Do you understand me? *¿Me entiende?*
Does anyone here speak English? *¿Hay alguien aquí que hable inglés?*
Just a moment, please *Un momentito, por favor*
This is good *Está bueno*
This is bad *Está malo*

Shopping and Eating

What is the price? *¿Cuánto cuesta?* or *¿Cuánto es?*
It's too expensive *Es muy caro*
Can you give me a discount? *¿Puede darme un descuento?*
Do you have …? *¿Tiene Usted …?*
I will buy this *Voy a comprar esto*
Please show me another *Muéstreme otro, por favor*
Please bring me … *Tráigame por favor …*
coffee with milk *café con leche*
black coffee *café negro*
tea *té*
a beer *una cerveza*
cold water *agua fría*
a soft drink *una gaseosa*
the menu *el menú*
the daily special *el plato del día*
May I have another beer? *Puede darme una cerveza más, por favor*
May I have the bill? *La cuenta, por favor*
[To get the attention of the waiter/ waitress] *Disculpe Señor/ Señora/ Señorita*
Where is the dining room? *¿Dónde está el comedor?*
the pharmacy *la farmacia*
the gas station *la bomba* (the pump)

key *la llave*
manager *el gerente* (male)/*la gerente* (female)
owner, proprietor *el dueño* (male)/*la dueña* (female)
Can you cash a travelers' check? *¿Se puede cambiar un cheque de viajero?*
money *dinero* or *plata*
credit card *tarjeta de crédito*
tax *impuesto*
letter *carta*
postcard *tarjeta postal*
envelope *sobre*
stamp *estampilla/sello*

Getting Around

Please call a taxi for me *Pídame un taxi, por favor*
How many kilometers is … from here? *¿Cuántos kilómetros hay de aquí a …?*
How long does it take to go there? *¿Cuánto se tarda en llegar?*
What will you charge to take me to …? *¿Cuánto cobra para llevarme a …?*
How much is a ticket to …? *¿Cuánto cuesta un billete a …?*
I want a ticket to … *Quiero un billete a …, por favor*
Where does this bus go? *¿Adónde va este bus?*
Stop (on a bus) *¡Parada!*
Please stop here *Pare aquí, por favor*
Please go straight ahead *Vaya recto, por favor*
right *a la derecha*
left *a la izquierda*
What is this place called? *¿Cómo se llama este lugar?*
I'm going to … *Me voy a …*
bus stop *parada del bus*
reserved seat *asiento reservado*
reservation *reservación*
airplane *avión*
train *tren*
bus *bus*
Where is there an inexpensive hotel? *¿Dónde hay un hotel económico?*
Do you have a room with… *¿Hay un cuarto con …?*
bath *baño*
fan *abanico/ventilador*
air conditioning *aire-climatización*
Where is …? *¿Dónde está …?*
the exit *la salida*
the entrance *la entrada*
the airport *el aeropuerto*
a taxi *un taxi*
the police station *la delegación de policía*
the embassy *la embajada*
the post office *la oficina de correos*
a public telephone *un teléfono público*

a bank *un banco*
a hotel *un hotel*
a restaurant *un restaurante*
a restroom *un servicio*
a private bathroom *el baño*
the ticket office *la oficina de billetes*
a department store *una tienda*
the market *el mercado*

Driving

Fill it up, please *Lleno, por favor*
Please check the oil *Vea el aceite, por favor*
Please fill the radiator *Favor de llenar el radiador*
the battery *la batería*
I need … *Necesito …*
a jack *un gato*
a towtruck *una grúa*
a mechanic *un mecánico*
a tire *una llanta*
Help me, please *Ayúdeme, por favor*
Call a doctor quickly! *¡Llame a un médico de prisa!*

Speaking *Tico: Tiquismos*

If you already speak some Spanish, learn a few *Tiquismos*, uniquely Costa Rican expressions. *Tico* (Costa Rican) Spanish is rich with them.

The familiar "*tú*" (you) is not used in Costa Rica, even with children. They often use an archaic form, "*vos*." The rules regarding the use of "*vos*" are tricky and elude even advanced students of Spanish: best to stick with "*Usted*," which is always correct.

When walking in areas outside of San José, people passing on the street greet one another with "*Adiós*," or "*'dios*." "*Hasta luego*" is used to say "goodbye."

Costa Ricans love to use *sobrenombres*, nicknames. More often than not, the nicknames have to do with a person's physical appearance: *Macho/Macha* if he or she is ever-so-slightly fair-skinned or fair-haired (not to be confused with *machismo*, an attribute of Latin males, used in Mexico); *China* if she has a slight slant to the eyes, or is actually Asian; *Negro* if his skin is dark; *Gordito* for someone even slightly overweight; *Moreno* if the person is slightly dark-complexioned, and so on.

If someone asks, "*¿Cómo está Usted?*" it's always correct to reply, "*Muy bien, gracias a Dios*" ("Very well, thanks to God") or "*Muy bien, por dicho*" (Very well, fortunately") but you might want to try something a little more zippy and informal, such as:

"*Pura vida*" ("Great") or "*Con toda la pata*" ("Terrific" – literally, "with all the paw") or "*Tranquilo*" ("Relaxed, or cool").

Spanish Language Schools

Whatever a student's language needs, whether merely conversational, for business, or to master the structure of Spanish, an appropriate language school exists in Costa Rica. Listed below are some of the better-known schools. Consult the *Tico Times* for others.

COSI
Tel: 2234 1001
Fax: 2253 2117
www.cosi.co.cr
Intensive classes for groups and individuals. Programs from 1–16 weeks. Classes start every Monday in San José and Manuel Antonio. Arranges homestays.

CPI
Tel. 2265 6306
Fax: 2265 6866
www.cpi-edu.com
Classes, group and private, in Heredia, Monteverde, and Flamingo. Academic credit offered. Arranges homestays.

Instituto de Español Costa Rica
Tel: 2280 6622
Fax: 2283 4733
www.professionalspanish.com
Role playing, discussions, listening exercises, and videos are part of the classes. Courses at all levels for individuals or in groups. Also cultural programs such as Costa Rican cooking or Latin-American dance workshops.

ILISA
San José
Tel: 2280 0700
Toll-free from US: 1-800 ILISA-4-U (454 7248)
Fax: 2225 4665
www.ilisa.com
Courses with a maximum of four students. Also one-to-one programs. Spanish for professionals available. ILISA uses a communicative approach rather than a method. Arranges homestays and hotels. Free email and computer access.

Mesoamerica Language Institute
San Pedro
Tel: 2253 3195
www.mesoamericaonline.net
A department of the Institute for Central America Studies, dedicated to peace, justice, and the wellbeing of the people and land of Central America. Offers one and four-week programs.

FURTHER READING

Books

Because reference books are often unavailable or expensive in Costa Rica, buy books before leaving home. The ones listed below give a good insight into Costa Rican life.

A Bird Finding Guide to Costa Rica, by Barrett Lawson. New York: Cornell University Press, 2009. Highlighting 53 of the best birding destinations with itineraries and techniques for spotting birds in rainforest canopies.

The Birds of Costa Rica: A Field Guide, by Richard Garrigues, ill. by Robert Dean. New York: Cornell University Press, 2007. Extraordinary, up-to-date reference; 116 color plates.

Butterfly in the City: A Good Life in Costa Rica, by Jo Stuart. San José, Costa Rica: Litografia y Imprente LIL SA, 2006. Musings by long-term resident.

Costa Rica: National Parks, by Mario Boza. Madrid: Incafo SA, 2006. Lavish bilingual coffee-table book by one of the founders of the national park system.

The Costa Rican Indigenous People, by Rodrigo Salazar. San José: Editorial Tecnológico de Costa Rica, 2006. Bilingual overview of the country's indigenous history.

Costa Rica: A Traveler's Literary Companion, Barbara Ras (ed.). San Francisco: Whereabouts Press, 1993. English translation of 26 short stories by Costa Rican writers.

Costa Rica: Wildlife of the National Parks and Reserves, by Michael and Patricia Fogden. Fundación Neotrópica, 1997. Gorgeous coffee-table book with fascinating text.

Gallito Pinto: Traditional Recipes from Costa Rica, by Andrea Corrales. Costa Rica: Zona Tropical Publications, 2009. Recipes from Costa Rican homes with illustrations and cultural notes.

A Guide to the Birds of Costa Rica, by Gary F. Stiles and A.F. Skutch. Cornell University Press, 1990. The bible for birders in Costa Rica.

A Guide to Tropical Plants of Costa Rica, by Willow Zuchowski. San José, Costa Rica: Zona Tropical Publications, 2006. Highly recommended guide by a botanist.

The Green Republic: A Conservation History of Costa Rica, by Sterling Evans. University of Texas Press, 1999. History of conservation ethics in Costa Rica.

A Guide to Amphibians and Reptiles of Costa Rica, by Twan Leenders. Distribuidores Zona Tropical, SA, 2001.

The History of Costa Rica, by Iván Molina and Steven Palmer. University of Costa Rica, 2001. Complete overview of the country's history.

Hostile Acts: US Policy in Costa Rica in the 1980s, by Martha Honey. Gainesville, Florida: University of Florida Press, 1994.

INBio Pocket Guides: Various easy-to-carry and complete guides on plants, mammals, insects, butterflies, and fungi. INBio (www.inbio.co.cr).

Monkeys are Made of Chocolate, by Jack Ewing. Colorado: Pixy Jack Press, 2005. A collection of stories from a long-time conservationist on the southern Pacific coast of Costa Rica.

Osa: Where the Rainforest Meets the Sea, by Roy Toft. Costa Rica: Zona Tropical Publications, 2009. The Osa Peninsula seen through the eyes of a BBC photographer. Beautiful rainforest images.

The New Key to Costa Rica, by Beatrice Blake and Anne Becher. Berkeley, CA: Ulysses Press, 2009. Detailed information on bus travel, hotels, restaurants, and bars.

Potholes to Paradise, by Tessa Borner. Silvio Mattachione, 2001. Personal account and advice about moving to Costa Rica.

The Surfer's Guide to Costa Rica, by Mike Parise. Los Angeles: SurfPress Publishing, 2010. Low-budget but comprehensive surfing guide.

The Ticos: Culture and Social Change in Costa Rica, by M. Biesanz, R. Biesanz, and K. Biesanz. Colorado: Lynne Rienner Publishers, 1998. Fluent analysis of Costa Rican culture.

The Tico Times Restaurant Guide to Costa Rica, by Eliot Greenspan. San José, Costa Rica: The Tico Times, 2008. Comprehensive bilingual guide to the country's culinary hotspots.

What Happen, by Paula Palmer. San José, Costa Rica: Zona Tropical Publications, 2005. A history of the Talamanca Coast.

Send Us Your Thoughts

We do our best to ensure the information in our books is as accurate and up to date as possible. The books are updated on a regular basis using local contacts, who painstakingly add, amend, and correct as required. However, some details (such as telephone numbers and opening times) are liable to change, and we are ultimately reliant on our readers to put us in the picture.

We welcome your feedback, especially your experience of using the book "on the road." Maybe we recommended a hotel that you liked (or another that you didn't), or you came across a great bar or new attraction we missed.

We will acknowledge all contributions, and we'll offer an Insight Guide to the best letters received.

Please write to us at:
**Insight Guides
PO Box 7910
London SE1 1WE**
Or email us at:
insight@apaguide.co.uk

Other Insight Guides

Other guides that highlight destinations in this region include:
Insight Guide: Belize offers a full portrait of one of the world's leading ecotourism destinations, including its rainforests and coral reefs.

Insight Guide: Guatemala, Belize & the Yucatán provides in-depth coverage of this beautiful area, with revealing features and stunning photography.

Insight Guide: Mexico. In-depth coverage of the entire country with stunning photography and maps and revealing analysis.

Smart Guide: Cancún & the Yucatán for independent travelers looking for comprehensive listings presented in a snappy, easy-to-find way.

Insight Fleximap: Costa Rica is a fully laminated pocket-size map (scale 1:730 000), with handy practical data and illustrated highlights of top tourist attractions.

ART AND PHOTO CREDITS

AKG London 37, 43, 50, 60
Alamy 9T, 101
Corbis 42, 57
APA Glyn Genin 9M, 19, 21, 51, 151, 154T, 157T, 159T, 164/165, 170, 172T, 185T, 186, 187T, 189, 192T, 196T, 200T, 205T, 107T, 214, 219T, 237T, 240/241, 247T, 250T, 258
Henry C Genthe 38L/R, 49, 56/57, 80, 115
Genthe/Haber 38, 41, 48, 58, 59
Getty Images 61
Harvey Haber Collection 24/25, 45, 46/47, 52/53, 54
iStockphoto 90/91, 94, 97, 98, 99, 100, 146, 156, 157R, 161, 190, 221, 246, 248L
Mary Evans 40, 44, 55, 79
Still Pictures 7BR, 77, 198
Pictures Colour Library 134
Superstock 118/119, 188/T, 189T, 204, 218T, 238, 239
TIPS Images 7M
APA Corrie Wingate 1, 2/3, 4B/C/T, 5, 6B/TL/TR, 7BL/MR/TL/TM, 8L/R, 9B, 10/11, 12/13, 14/15, 16, 17B/M/T, 18, 20, 22, 23, 26B/L/R, 27/T, 28/29, 30, 31, 32, 33, 34, 35,

62/63, 64/65, 66, 67, 68, 69, 70, 71, 72, 73, 74, 75L/R, 76, 78, 81, 82/83, 84, 85, 86, 87, 92, 93, 95, 96, 104/105, 106, 107, 108, 109, 110, 111, 112, 113, 114, 116/117, 120/121, 122, 123B/T, 126/127, 130, 131, 132, 133, 135/T, 136, 137/T, 138/T, 139, 140/141, 142, 143, 145/T, 147L/R/T, 148, 150, 151/T, 152, 153/T, 154, 155, 157L, 158, 159, 160, 161T, 166, 167, 169/T, 170T, 171, 172, 173, 174/175, 178, 180, 181/T, 182, 183/T, 184/T, 185, 187, 191T, 192, 193, 914, 195BL/BR, 196, 197/T, 199/T, 200, 201, 202, 203/T, 205, 206L/R, 207, 210/211, 212, 213, 215, 216, 217, 218, 219, 221T, 224/225, 226, 227, 229/T, 203L/R, 231/T, 232, 233/T, 234, 235/T, 236L/R, 237, 243, 245, 247R, 248BR, 249, 251, 252, 253/T, 254, 255/T, 256, 257, 257, 258T, 260, 262, 265, 266/T, 269, 277, 280, 282, 285, 287, 288, 290, 293, 294, 296

PHOTO FEATURES

88–89: All Pictures APA/Corrie Wingate except: Photolibrary 89T
102–103: APA/Corrie Wingate 102/103, 102BL/BR, Courtesy Flyultralight.com 103M, iStockphoto 103BR, Daniel Beltra 103TR
162–163: APA Glyn Genin 162/163, 162BL/BR/TL, 163M, APA Corrie Wingate 163BR/TR
208–209: Still pictures 208/209, 209BL, iStockphoto 208BL/BR, 209TR, APA Corrie Wingate 209BR
222–223: APA Corrie Wingate 222/223, 222TL, 223BR/T, iStockphoto 222BR, APA Glyn Genin 222BR, 223BL/M

Map Production:
Original production Colourmap Scanning Ltd, updated by Apa Cartography Department
© 2011 Apa Publications GmbH & Co. Verlag KG (Singapore branch)

Production: Tynan Dean, Linton Donaldson, and Rebeka Ellam

INDEX